CHALLENGING THE CENTRE

●

TWO DECADES OF POLITICAL THEATRE

●

The work of The Popular Theatre Troupe
Order By Numbers
and
Street Arts Community Theatre Company

●

Edited by Steve Capelin

PLAYLAB PRESS
BRISBANE
1995

Enquiries should be made to the publishers:
The Editor,
Playlab Press,
PO Box 185, Ashgrove, Q. 4060
Australia.

Typeset in Bookman 10 point by Playlab Press.
Printed and bound by Merino Lithographics, 18 Baldock Street, Moorooka 4105

National Library of Australia
Card Number and ISBN 0 908156 52 9

ACKNOWLEDGEMENTS

This book would not have been possible without the support of many people. In particular I am indebted to Peter Stewart whose work, funded by the CCDB of the Australia Council, in compiling much of the information in the chapter on Street Arts made that task possible. The initial research grant from the Queensland University of Technology was instrumental in allowing me time to begin to develop and collect material for this book. David Watt must be credited with providing part of the inspiration for the beginnings of this project and for providing ongoing support.

Others who have assisted in various ways include Dean Tuttle, Clare Apelt, Pauline and Denis Peel, Gavan Fenelon, Lynne Samson, Katrina Devery, Trevor and Teresa Jordan, Helen Wallace, Diane Wallace, Brent McGregor, Ainsley Burdell and Ron Finney; the QCAN and Fryer Libraries; Richard Fotheringham, for his comments and assistance with the Popular Theatre Troupe material; Rod Lumer for his valued comments and keen eye for detail and Pam McElhinney for assistance with proof reading. Thanks also to the many students who passed through the Academy of the Arts, QUT, who helped to identify the need for such a book.

Finally, thanks to Andrea Lynch and our two children, Jessica and Nicholas, for their support throughout my Street Arts years and through the development of this book. While all of these people and the many others associated with the companies represented in these pages are part of this project, in the final analysis any errors of fact or misjudgements which occur in the text are mine. Every effort has been made to ensure these have been kept to a minimum.

STEVE CAPELIN
Editor

ARTS QUEENSLAND

This project sponsored by
Queensland Office of Arts and Cultural Development

CONTENTS

ILLUSTRATIONS

POPULAR THEATRE TROUPE

STREET ARTS COMMUNITY THEATRE COMPANY

INTRODUCTION

This book began its life in 1991 while I was lecturing in the Drama Program at the Queensland University of Technology in Brisbane. In the midst of a predominately mainstream theatre culture, I was concerned to open the eyes of students to the possibilities of other ways of viewing the place of the Arts in the community and other ways of utilising their skills to engage in a meaningful dialogue with their audiences. I attempted to keep this possibility before the students at almost every turn.

I was astounded to find among the students a general acceptance of the status quo and the lack of awareness of not only local Brisbane and Queensland theatre history, but a general ignorance of major events artistic or otherwise of national or international significance.

In a movement class, for example, I was introducing a routine which I had always known as Chairman Mao exercises. This was a set of stretches which reputedly had its origins in the daily ritual of post-Cultural Revolution Chinese village life. As I progressively introduced these, I was interrupted by a student enquiring about the origin of the strange rhythmic **chairmanmou** (as she pronounced them) activities. Something in her use of the term as one word alerted me to some confusion. At that point I stopped the class and proceeded to conduct a survey as to the meaning and origin of this *chairmanmou* reference. The answers were amazing. The guesses ranged from a variety of Vietnamese vegetable, the name of an eastern movement guru and the host of a multicultural program on SBS television. The closest we got to China was the mention of "some revolution or other". I continued this survey over a number of classes with much the same result, even those who were able to identify it as the name of the revolutionary Chinese leader were unable to elaborate any further on Chairman Mao's historic significance. Stunned by this lack of awareness of something that I felt was basic to a knowledge of recent history, I proceeded to enquire further as to their awareness of Martin Luther King, J.F.Kennedy, even Robert Menzies, with largely similar results. I began to feel very old and to wonder if I wasn't trapped in some sixties time warp.

I then became aware that, in speaking to other classes about the sixties era as a time of western cultural upheaval, I was speaking about ancient history in much the same way as the Second World War was ancient to me, even though my father had been enlisted and I had been born within a few years of its end. Further to that, in discussing the local theatre scene, there was no recognition of any companies beyond the State company and to a lesser degree La Boîte Theatre. The names Popular Theatre Troupe and Street Arts (who were still creating exciting work on their doorstep) — in fact any mention of theatre outside the mainstream — were met with blank faces and in most cases glazed eyes. I realised I was working in a vacuum. What I lacked was written accounts of work done in this State which could begin to counter the powerful legitimising influence of real histories written in real books about work done elsewhere.

There were articles available, many written by David Watt who has been diligent in documenting and critiquing community theatre in Australia over the past ten or more years. And there were one or two other accounts of the place of and philosophical underpinnings of Community Arts in this country, but nothing which addressed the local situation. *(See the Bibliography at the end of the book for a selection of these articles and books)*

It was as if the work had never been done. This was further exacerbated by the untimely publication of Leonard Radic's book *The State of Play (The Revolution in the Australian Theatre since the 1960's)* in which, out of two hundred and forty pages, one chapter is devoted to community and alternative theatre. In this chapter Radic manages to mention the Popular Theatre Troupe once in passing, fails to mention Street Arts at all and even gives only a line or two to La Boîte Theatre which has in a significant way supported and nurtured new Australian writing over a long period. This further perpetuated the myth that very little of significance happens outside Sydney or Melbourne. Students who read this, understandably looked to the southern states as centres of energy and innovation.

One of the things that Community Theatre has taught me is that you have to actively own your own history if you are to have any hope of retaining any sense of identity or of controlling your own destiny. The feminist movement has shown us that a version of history which is owned by a particular group of people or gender by its very existence automatically tends to exclude other possibilities. This book is an attempt to take possession of some of that history and put in place some foundations upon which future generations can build.

The "Political Theatre in Queensland" encompassed in this book does not pretend that there has been no other work of this type done in this state over the past twenty years. In fact I am acutely aware of the work which has not been alluded to in these pages. The work of companies such as Icy Tea, Feral Arts, La Boîte Theatre, Contact Youth Theatre, Brisbane Theatre Company, Access Arts, S'NOT Arts — all Brisbane based companies who use theatre at least as an element of their work — and many others statewide also deserve to be documented in an accessible form for future generations. In this book I have consciously chosen to trace a line which begins with the Popular Theatre Troupe in 1974 and flows through twenty years of political and community activism to Order By Numbers and the Street Arts Community Theatre Company of 1994. Many of the artists and organizers who worked in Queensland in this period became involved with these companies. Importantly the companies represent distinctly different approaches to the role of a theatre company with a social conscience. The book allows us to trace the pathways of key Queensland artists over this extended period. It also allows the reader to observe the development of a more sophisticated understanding of community, of culture and of cultural activism which was occurring throughout the nation but which is clearly represented in these pages. The other element which becomes clear is the international factor. Though the work represented is very much the product of local artists, the cross fertilization of ideas between British arts workers (in particular) and Australians is fascinating and significant.

A number of scripts have been included in this book in an attempt to give flesh to the bones of the histories which are presented. While some of these scripts were written for specific situations and in particular periods of political activity, they nevertheless provide some real insights into the issues and the artistry of the writers from whom they were born. Sadly most scripts from small companies such as these are never published and yet they represent the bulk of new work produced in Australia over the period covered. Hopefully they will be useful to readers, teachers, students and theatre companies as both research material and as scripts which will find life in future productions.

My hope is that this book is not seen as the closing of a chapter but as a meaningful addition to the ongoing work of community, political and youth theatre companies and artists throughout the country. It is dedicated to that generation of artists who stayed in Brisbane and lived and worked through the worst excesses of the Bjelke-Petersen years.

STEVE CAPELIN

PART ONE

●

POPULAR THEATRE TROUPE and STREET ARTS

THE POPULAR THEATRE TROUPE AND STREET ARTS: TWO PARADIGMS OF POLITICAL ACTIVISM

by David Watt

The Popular Theatre Troupe and Street Arts Community Theatre Company were pioneers in the development of a radical theatre scene in Australia. Based in Brisbane, both exerted an influence on emerging companies all over the country through the continuing example of their work and through the exportation of techniques to other companies by former members. And both acted as influences on the development of Australia Council funding policy through the 1970s and 1980s, all of which gave their work a secondary influence far beyond Brisbane.

Although one follows the other chronologically, both are products of the radicalism of the 1960s and 1970s which accompanied the international growth of what came to be called the "counter culture" or, more sensibly, given the diversity of this loosely organised movement, the "counter cultures". Although it has become unfashionable to regard it with much seriousness, this counter-cultural movement marks one of the most widespread expressions of political opposition to the capitalist status quo in the developed west in the twentieth century. The Popular Theatre Troupe and Street Arts represent two of the major strands of political theatre activity which emerged, not just in Australia but internationally, from the maelstrom of cultural activism the counter cultures gave rise to.

Unlike the previous great surge of political activism in the developed world during the Depression of the 1930s, the radicalism of the 1960s and 1970s was not produced by a general class-based response to economic hardship, but emerged in a period of apparent affluence. This made it a middle-class rather than a working-class movement, operating on the periphery of the conventional oppositional politics associated with the labour movement, and gave issues of culture a more central position than had been the case in the Depression. While some of the ventures which emerged from the movement developed connections with the organised labour movement, particularly the trades unions, they were almost invariably not born from it.

The Counter Cultures

The counter cultures were the product of an economic boom in post-war capitalism, which saw high levels of employment and a steady rise in the production and consumption of manufactured goods after the austerities of the post-war period. As can so often happen in a capitalist economy, when production of manufactured goods begins to outstrip the rate at which they can be consumed, "boom" can very quickly turn into "bust", as indeed it did in the mid-1970s. In an attempt to stave off the inevitable, western capitalist economies found themselves not only in the position of quarrying the Third World for raw materials and cheap labour to feed spiralling production, but also in the position of desperately seeking out new market areas, new areas of consumption. One clear manifestation of this "crisis" was a drive for consumption, partially represented by the development of "youth culture" as a market area, with more spending power than ever before in history. Another was in the sort of imperialising venture from the centres of economic power represented by the American intervention into Vietnam, with the enthusiastic and, as we have recently discovered, unrequested assistance of Australia.

For the generation which grew up in the 1960s and the early to mid-1970s, the verities of post-war middle-class life (thrift, hard work and caution) were replaced by a sense of economic confidence, engendered by increasing requests to consume, which to their parents looked like a feckless disregard for the realities of adult life. As well, the comparative ease of access to tertiary education, across a broader class base than ever before offered thousands the opportunity to occupy that "liminal" time between childhood and adulthood, formal education and full participation in the work-force, with its attendant entrapments of mortgages and the like. The "liminality" of tertiary education also offered a critical distance from the bourgeois world of one's parents, and the time to gain a theoretical understanding which made it easier to see the likes of the Vietnam war for what they really were. The cynical scrutiny this position made possible began to reveal an ugly, uncaring side of consumer capitalism, which led to sporadic acts of dissent. State responses quickly escalated from disapproval to violent repression to something like open warfare, represented most notoriously by the killing of four students by the American National Guard at Kent State University in 1970.

What this produced was a young, disaffected bourgeois intelligentsia with time on its hands, a privileged position from which to examine capitalist economies moving into crisis, and a consequent sense that all was far from well. The characteristic geographic movement of this new generation was from a green but boring suburbia back to the inner city slums their parents' generation had often battled to escape from not so many years before. Many of them were thus introduced, although superficially and temporarily, to the hardships of working-class life which had not been experienced by their parents, and also to an inner-city bohemianism with the same romantic charm as it had held for those rebel artists of the European metropolises thrown up by a similar economic boom in the early years of this century. We were acerbic critics of the class that bred us, and thus either political and cultural rebels, increasingly modelling ourselves on iconic figures like the intellectual-turned-guerrilla fighter in the jungles of Bolivia, Che Guevara, or, in the phrase coined by the Scottish avant-garde writer and self-confessed heroin addict Alexander Trocchi in 1962, "cosmonauts of inner space". What we lacked was any actual power to effect the social change we seemed to agree was needed.

The characteristic means by which the counter cultures managed to make their presence felt were always performative. The explosion in popular music of the 1960s and 1970s led to a proliferation of bands with at least an emotive sense of politics, manifested in the countless white versions of black American music or folk music as a means of declaring a class affiliation one mostly could not lay claim to. Elvis Presley had unnerved mums and dads in the 1950s, but the Rolling Stones, the Doors *et al.* set out to offend in a much more spectacular and calculated way and quickly learnt how to theatricalise their live perform-ances for huge crowds. Their performances became theatrical displays of an often incoherent hatred of the bourgeois respectability of their parents' genera-tion. The mere display of the fact that, for them, sometimes highly profitable "work" meant "playing" was a substantial affront to those brought up to believe that "work" was serious business. Modes of dress and behaviour themselves became the highly theatricalised display of an alternative lifestyle. Never before, or perhaps since, had so many middle-class children so proudly worn the second-hand clothes of the working class, to the point that the calculated rejection of the fashion industry became a fashion in itself as the industry adapted. And perhaps most significantly, the old standbys of those locked out of political decision-making, the sit-in and the street demonstration, were given a new theatrical edge for a mass audience on television by astute political agitators and purveyors of what came to be known as guerrilla street theatre. And theatre itself was embraced, though not that encompassed by the emerging subsidised theatre industry in Australia.

THE COUNTER CULTURE AND PERFORMANCE

Theatre, broadly defined, became a natural mode of expression for a generation, in ways which may now seem hard to understand. Largely via the American journal *TDR* (the *Tulane Drama Review* — now *The Drama Review*), and its British equivalent *Theatre Quarterly* in the 1970s, an emergent group of disaffected, predominantly middle-class university students in Australia dis-covered the possibilities of performance. This was not performance within the framework and methodologies of the "real" theatre, or even in the local amateur dramatic society, but "poor" theatre, portable, cheap and capable of reaching audiences other than those who patronised the "real" theatre, with self-gener-ated, group-written and group-directed "amateur" performances in non-theatre spaces, including outdoor public places. In doing so they discovered a medium which allowed the possibility of circumventing the major institutional means of conveying information.

TDR and TQ supplied plenty of models, from the performances of the San Francisco Mime Troupe, Teatro Campesino, Bread and Puppet Theatre and the guerrilla theatres associated with Students for a Democratic Society (SDS) in the USA; to Welfare State and the emerging agit-prop troupes like Red Ladder and 7:84 in Britain; to the often more esoteric performer-centred work of the Open Theatre and the Living Theatre in the USA; and to Portable Theatre, the People Show, the Pip Simmons Group and Freehold in Britain.[1] Here were apparently endlessly proliferating examples of theatre which required little in terms of material resources, and more enthusiasm than conservatory-honed skills at a time when enthusiasm was available in abundance.

These apparently new theatre forms, initially "alternative" but in most cases fairly quickly "oppositional" to the mainstream, varied widely, but they all had some common features. They all assumed a paucity of material requirements, which made it possible to ignore the institutional structures of the "real" theatre, so that "product" was very much in the hands of those who made it. They were easy to make accessible to what had conventionally been non-theatregoing audiences, which gave them a potential social reach the "real" theatre had probably surrendered at least a half-century earlier. And they all re-interrogated the nature of the relationship between performers and audiences, and thus escaped the comfortable protectiveness of the darkened auditorium in favour of more confrontational modes or, more often, the exploration of the social and communal nature of performance. Armed with the flexibility of these various modes of performance, the counter cultures turned "theatre" into what a major documenter of the period in Britain, Robert Hewison, has called 'the most visible and coherent product of 1968,' in which

> . . . the mixture of culture and politics which had seemed so confusing in the latter sixties had genuinely creative issue, where cultural and political practice achieved an uncompromised harmony of interests.[2]

THE POLITICS OF THE COUNTER CULTURE

Out of this social/cultural perspective and with these simple tools, the loose alliances which constituted the counter cultural movement managed to contrive some potentially genuinely insurrectionary moments, most famously in Paris in May 1968 but also throughout Europe and America. They at least ruffled some feathers in Australia through a series of huge rallies against the Vietnam disaster and the tour of the South African Springboks in the late 1960s and early 1970s, and contributed to the overthrow of twenty-three years of Federal conservative rule via the election of the Whitlam Labor government in 1972. English playwright David Edgar, a self-proclaimed member of what he calls "the class of '68", has written extensively on what he refers to as "the demonisation of the sixties", orchestrated by the Reaganite/Thatcherite Right on either side of the Atlantic in the 1980s, and points out that even the left has succumbed to the consequent denigration of the movement and all its works in recent years. He claims that, in Britain at least, the period has come to be characterised as that of "tower blocks, Charles Manson, herpes simplex and *nothing else*", and offers, by way of redress, what he describes as 'the longest single sentence ever printed in a British democratic socialist journal' — which I cannot resist citing, at least in part:

> So it's worth reminding both boomers and non-boomers alike that, for all its undoubted silliness and grandiosity, and despite the sourness of many aspects of its many ends, that confluence of movements and experiments and campaigns and indeed trends that have been collectively dubbed "the 1960s" added up to the most concentrated upsurge of political inventiveness within the progressive and socialist movements, certainly since the 1940s and arguably since the immediate aftermath of the Russian Revolution . . . that, culturally, it was one of only two periods this century (the other being the early 1920s) in which the political and artistic avant-garde walked hand in hand, and in which (and partly thereby) radical art was able to gain a significant purchase on a mass audience (from Ken Loach's television films to progressive rock); that it saw as a consequence the cultural enfranchisement of vast layers of the working class, particularly but not exclusively the young, as they bought (or made) clothes, books, artifacts and, of course, music in their own accents and on their own terms; that in addition to all the unquantifiable changes in social, sexual, familial, economic, political and racial relationships that resulted from the incalculable changes in lifestyle, behaviour, social forms, modes of living and political perception, it is possible to point to a list of solid, specific and irreversible victories, from the desegregation of the southern American states to the up-ending of French society post-May 1968 and, pre-eminently, to the most significant international left-wing mobilisation since the Spanish Civil War, the world-wide movement in support of the Vietnamese Revolution which, *en route* to forcing American withdrawal, brought down one President and provoked another into the actions that would bring him down too . . .[3]

Australia, and even Brisbane, did not remain untouched by all this.

As Edgar suggests, the counter cultures were never monolithic, but were characterised by "a diffuse counter-culture milieu" which Stuart Hall *et al.* in their 1976 account of youth subcultures in Britain, *Resistance Through Rituals*, describe as characteristic of its middle class "parent". They offer an account which indicates the range of perspectives and positions which emerged in the early 1970s:

> The Hippies of the later 1960s were the most distinctive of the middle-class sub-cultures. Their cultural influence on this sector of youth was

immense, and many counter-culture values must still be traced back to their Hippie roots. Hippies helped a whole quasi-bohemian sub-cultural milieu to come into existence, shaped styles, dress, attitudes, music and so on. The alternative institutions of the Underground emerged, basically, from this matrix. . . . [Hippie culture] permeated student and ex-student culture. It was then crosscut by influences stemming from the more political elements among middle-class youth — the student protest movement, radical social work, community action groups, the growth of the left sects and so on. . . . The two most distinctive strands flow one way, via drugs, mysticism, the "revolution in lifestyle", into a Utopian alternative culture; or, the other way, via community action, protest action and libertarian goals, into a more activist politics.[4]

With some local variations and differences of emphasis and a bit of a time lag, this offers some indication of the milieu out of which the Popular Theatre Troupe and Street Arts emerged. What held this broad alliance of disparate groupings together was a generational break, between a group whose formative years coincided with the Depression and the Second World War and a group whose adolescence was experienced through a period of apparent affluence and opportunity. The "politics" which emerged from this were characterised by a broad rejection of conventional social order, and an embrace of a utopianist egalitarianism exemplified most notably in a new grass-roots politics of participatory democracy.[5]

The Popular Theatre Troupe and Street Arts

The differences between the modes of operation and characteristic products of the two companies, and the arguments between them, are both a factor of the different strands of counter-cultural activism from which they emerged and of the working on each of them of the social, cultural and political milieus in which they worked, the Popular Theatre Troupe in the 1970s and Street Arts in the 1980s. The demise of the Popular Theatre Troupe and the emergence of Street Arts in the early 1980s, to some extent brought about by the loss of Australia Council funding by the former and the gaining of it by the latter, led some to deduce a bureaucratically-driven evacuation of politics from the Queensland theatre scene, and draw attention to the differences between the two ventures. These differences tend to be over issues of strategy rather than ideology, as the easy movement of members from one company to the other would indicate, but they are nonetheless important, and indicative of a more general shift, both in Australia and overseas.

The central difference is exemplified in the following from Street Arts founding member Pauline Peel on attitudes to the company's plans for its most important early venture, a long association with the community of Inala, an isolated

Housing Commission area on Brisbane's southern outskirts. The company was consistently told, she says, that

> . . . what we should be doing was going to Inala and giving them a Marxist analysis of what their situation was. And we just argued that you're better to get them talking about their situation and find ways of directing them so that they make their own conclusions. . . . You don't change people by . . . telling them you've got all the answers, you just don't.[6]

While this may overstate the case a little (and thus indicate the heat of the debate at the time), it pinpoints the core of disagreement. The Popular Theatre Troupe saw itself as a "left wing theatre group"[7], which places it in a particular tradition which predates the essentially counter-cultural forms and strategies of Street Arts, although the tradition was sufficiently resilient to offer much to the emergent groups of the later 1970s and 1980s. Street Arts, on the other hand, emerged from a set of notions about grass-roots politics and community activism which was much more distinctively counter-cultural, and saw itself more as a facilitatory organisation using theatre as a tool. An account of two projects characteristic of the early work of each company — the Popular Theatre Troupe's first show *The White Man's Mission* and Street Arts' Inala project — and of their respective lineages, indicates the differences.

THE POPULAR THEATRE TROUPE AND "THE WHITE MAN'S MISSION"

The White Man's Mission is a play about the white invasion of Queensland and its effects upon the indigenous population, and was written by Richard Fotheringham and Albert Hunt, a British writer, director and animateur who was instrumental in the establishment of the company. It was designed to be performed by a small group of professional actors and toured widely to non-theatregoing audiences, as was typical of the work of the Troupe. Equally typically, it was based on material gathered through a process of historical research, which was then framed within the broad parameters of a basically Marxist analysis. This material was then theatricalised via the appropriation of a range of popular entertainment forms, in this case predominantly that of the old touring religious revivalist show, but drawing also from traditions of agit-prop, political satire and vaudeville. This allowed a theatrical form which included a variety of items or sketches, a presentational performance style which embraced broad comedy, song and direct audience address, and a fast moving sweep through an extended period of history through the use of representational figures rather than "characters". All of this was held together by the controlling metaphor of the revivalist show which made its own satirical comment on the operations of Christianity within the colonialist venture.

The White Man's Mission has its direct origins in the experiences and understandings of political theatre of its co-writers, Fotheringham and Hunt. Fotheringham describes his as the experience of touring with the Queensland

Theatre Company in productions of two shows of some importance to the development of the theatrical styles and approaches of the Troupe — *Oh What a Lovely War* and an Australian descendant of the style, *The Legend of King O'Malley* by Michael Boddy and Bob Ellis.[8] The first of these, the original performances of which date back to 1963, is probably the best known product of Joan Littlewood's work with Theatre Workshop, a company which had been devoted to the creation of a popular political theatre since its establishment in England in the immediate post-war years.[9]

The lineage of this work can be further traced back to the political theatre experiments of the 1920s and 1930s, particularly those of Brecht and Piscator in Germany and Meyerhold in Russia, and also to the most vital element of popular political theatre of the period, the agit-prop movement[10]. Agit-prop, or theatre for agitation and propaganda, emerged initially in Russia but quickly spread throughout the capitalist west under the impetus of the political radicalisation which followed in the wake of the Depression in the 1930s. It was a populist form designed for performance to working class audiences in non-theatre spaces, ranging from the street to the gathering places of working people. Throughout the non-communist world, agit-prop was characterised by some basic enduring stylistic features. Troupes were small and predominantly amateur with members drawn from the politically active sector of the working class rather than the theatre. Performances were short and required a minimum of stage settings, props and costumes, which allowed troupes to perform almost anywhere at short notice, and run away from the police if necessary — as it often was (police reports are an important source of information about agit-prop performances). They did not take the form of "plays" as the term is conventionally understood but rather of a series of items, performed in a range of styles and using a number of different popular culture forms, from song and dance acts to gymnastics displays. The circumstances of performance necessitated that they be attention-grabbing, loud — the Red Megaphones was a particularly popular group name — and sufficiently entertaining to hold the attention of large numbers of people gathered for reasons other than watching a play, in the street or at a union rally, for example. The characters of conventional drama were replaced with typifications (the capitalist, the worker etc.) and figures representative of social forces (political parties, big businesses, the church etc.). The central reason for this was obviously related to the necessity for a speed of performance which precluded any possibility of careful development of character, but was more importantly based on an assumption that mainstream theatre forms, particularly those which fell within the ambit of naturalism, made social and political analysis impossible because they concentrated attention on the details of surface reality and individual psychology, and thus disguised the *structural* realities of capitalism under a welter of irrelevant detail. Agit-prop was the dominant left-wing theatrical form throughout the western world for a brief period in the 1930s. Many of its techniques were drawn into political theatre forms designed for more conventional performance circumstances, such as the documentary theatre of Piscator and others, and the "epic" theatre of Brecht.

Theatre Workshop stands as one of the only continuous links back to this tradition, and *Oh What a Lovely War* is a central factor in the development of a particular strain of documentary theatre, utilising "found" material and elements of popular performance styles, which became a standard repertoire item in the newly emerging British regional theatres of the 1960s. The best known of this work is probably that of Peter Cheeseman at Stoke-on-Trent, which is represented in print by two of the most famous shows *The Knotty* and *The Staffordshire Rebels* but there are many other examples such as Alan Plater's *Close the Coalhouse Door*, written for Newcastle-upon-Tyne in 1968. The style had already spread to Australia and was well in evidence in a spate of documentary or historical shows produced in Melbourne by Jack Hibberd, Barry Oakley and John Romeril with the Australian Performing Group, and in Sydney at the old Nimrod Street Theatre (now the Griffin) in plays like Ron Blair's *Flash Jim Vaux* and *The Legend of King O'Malley*, which was originally staged there after emerging from a workshop at NIDA.

For Fotheringham, touring rural Queensland in Queensland Theatre Company productions of these two plays indicated some of the limitations of the "real" theatre. The audiences for which the populist forms of these plays were intended seemed much more interested in the Slim Dusty concerts with which performances occasionally clashed on tour, which led him to a different notion of a theatre company and a different approach to audiences than that of the QTC. For him it became a matter of 'identifying specific communities and performing to them':

> We started with two ideas. The first was that we would study popular entertainment forms and try to discover effective and familiar means of communicating our ideas. The second was that we would avoid wherever possible formal theatres with all their social implications, and try to seek out ordinary people in their places of work and leisure and try to be entertaining and stimulating enough to win their acceptance.[11]

As part of this process, he grasped an opportunity to invite Albert Hunt to Brisbane to direct fringe theatre activities for an Arts Festival in 1974, with an eye to tapping his experience in establishing what became the Popular Theatre Troupe.

Hunt had a wealth of experience as a writer, director and animateur, particularly through his best-known work, *John Ford's Cuban Missile Crisis*, and gave of it generously both with the early work of the Popular Theatre Troupe and through his involvement in several projects in Melbourne with the Victorian College of the Arts. What he was particularly able to contribute was a knowledge of the styles, techniques and modes of operation of an emerging group of British left-wing touring companies[12] like Red Ladder and 7:84, the latter in particular through founder and writer John McGrath, strongly influenced by the popular documentary techniques of Theatre Workshop. McGrath's diligence in theorising the work of 7:84 (the name of which is a reference to a statistic published in the *Financial Times* in 1971 which indicated that 7% of the population of Britain was in control of 84% of the wealth) offers us easy access to some of the basic principles of this movement.

McGrath saw "mainstream" theatre as the enemy in a class war, as part of a bourgeois "culture" built upon a 'legitimating ideology . . . which penetrates all areas of the individual consciousness in order to legitimate class rule and maintain it'.[13] This led him to see the role of the oppositional theatre worker as assisting in the development of a counter culture, a "working class" culture capable of opposing and overthrowing this dominant "bourgeois" culture. As such, he saw a genuinely oppositional theatre as needing to do two things: align itself with the organisational arms of a broader "working class" political movement; and assist in the establishment of a distinctively "working-class" culture of opposition and dissent.

To McGrath, this suggested the necessity of making theatre in a "language", broadly defined, appropriate to these audiences, and he developed a detailed account of a language of working-class forms of entertainment, ranging from club entertainment to television variety and comedy shows.[14] This language is characterised by the use of comedy, popular music and a variety of kinds of performing, and also draws on the techniques of a range of earlier popular political theatre forms, from the documentaries of Theatre Workshop to agit-prop. He was also concerned to tailor the forms and styles he used to the specificities of particular audiences. This is clear in the most famous of the 7:84 shows, *The Cheviot, the Stag and the Black, Black Oil*, designed to be performed to a Scottish Highland audience. While the play utilised the sorts of popular, working-class entertainment forms he describes, in this case they were framed within the broad structures and techniques of the ceilidh, a form of informal entertainment still current in the Highlands and Hebrides.

The work of the San Francisco Mime Troupe in the 1960s and 1970s indicates a similar approach in America. In this case the work involved an exploration and adaptation of earlier forms of popular theatre, most notably commedia dell'arte, an Italian comic street theatre form of the renaissance, and also the American touring minstrel show and nineteenth-century melodrama. Other companies chose different popular theatre models, ranging from the British Red Ladder's initial espousal of a version of agit-prop forms to CAST's (Cartoon Archetypal Slogan Theatre) use of rock 'n' roll and stand-up comedy, but all operated on principles related to those of 7:84. Capitalism was the enemy, Marxism was the appropriate analytical tool and the working class, or more generally "the people", constituted the appropriate audience.

The theatre necessitated by these shared understandings was to be "popular", in both the sense of being enjoyable and accessible and the sense of being *for* and *of* "the people". Part of the commitment to accessibility meant performing in places where people normally gathered, ranging from outdoor public spaces to factory canteens, community halls, clubs etc. The commitment to popularity meant utilising the "language" of popular entertainment forms, but also viewing the world through the perspective of its intended audience and continually ensuring the maintenance of writing, production and performance standards of the theatrical "product" — something revealed in the script of *The White Man's Mission*, which is crisp, intelligent, funny and demanding on the performing skills of its small cast. It had two basic purposes: to explain and clarify issues and to assist in developing a sense of class consciousness or at least solidarity in its audiences. To this extent it duplicates many of the basic assumptions and techniques of agit-prop, although usually in more elaborated forms.

The Popular Theatre Troupe was not the only group in Australia engaged in this sort of venture but it was one of the first, one of the most accomplished and one of the most successful. It was also the first to receive consistent funding from the Theatre Board of the Australia Council, which made it a model for others entering the area. Its formal techniques, styles and strategies re-emerged in the work of other companies, most notably Junction Theatre Company in Adelaide (which produced a string of agit-prop pieces for trades union audiences in the mid- to late-1980s) and the outdoor performances of Sydney's Death Defying Theatre in the 1970s and early 1980s, and the work was carried on by Order By Numbers in Brisbane. It was, though, engaged in a form of popular political theatre which, it has been argued, has been overtaken by history. As Richard Seyd, a founder member of the British company Red Ladder, wrote:

> If people don't think that capitalism is an absurd and damaging way of organising society, then very little that one does in an agit-prop piece is going to change their minds. . . . In our experience, unless the audience is already relatively class conscious, agit-prop falls on deaf ears.[15]

As the political polarisations of the early 1970s broke down, agit-prop based forms appeared to have less political purchase on their intended audiences, which led to their often being superseded by an emergent community theatre movement, with increasingly a different set of strategies.

STREET ARTS IN INALA

To some extent these strategies are represented by Street Arts' Inala project, a piece of cultural and political activism conceived in very different terms. The Inala project was in fact three projects based in a suburb dominated by Housing Commission homes. Its most obvious difference to the mode of work represented by the Popular Theatre Troupe was that the performance pieces which it generated were not designed to be performed on tour by a small troupe of professionals but within the community by local people themselves, and that they were not written *for* them but *with* them. As a venture, the Inala residency is characterised by what became three essential principles of the early work of

Street Arts — firstly, never go where you are not invited (although this may entail fomenting an invitation); secondly, never do one project when you can do three; and thirdly, always ensure you leave something behind. The company's involvement in Inala thus followed an invitation from a welfare agency and consisted of three projects — a series of circus skills workshops in a local primary school and evening workshops with interested adults which produced *Inala In Cabaret* in 1983; a huge outdoor show incorporating more than 150 locals called *Once Upon Inala* in 1984; and a smaller project with twenty local women called *Kockroach Kabaret* in 1985, which eventually led to the establishment of Icy Tea (Inala Community Theatre) as an autonomous company. *Once Upon Inala* took on almost as legendary a status in Australia in the 1980s as *The White Man's Mission* had in the 1970s, and became a model within the community theatre scene. Its status as a model was assisted by the fact that the Community Arts Board of the Australia Council sent a message to its clients by making it the subject of an issue of *Caper*, an occasional CAB publication used to highlight the exemplary or air experiments particularly in accord with its own developing funding agenda.

Once Upon Inala emerged out of the *Inala In Cabaret* project which, according to Steve Capelin, was envisaged as 'a time of talking and finding out about each other, gaining trust, giving encouragement'[16] and Pauline Peel points out that, while the show had been less than a total artistic success, its legitimation lay in the larger strategy of the venture:

> *Inala In Cabaret* gave the participants a chance to see what was possible — it excited them and it raised the community's awareness. But it is crucial to this form of community theatre that it not be seen as a one-off event. The Inala project was seen by us as part of a long-term involvement with that community.[17]

As she points out, this was a decision taken at a very early stage:

> . . . we decided that to do one project was crazy . . . especially for the adults. So we made a decision that we'd go back until we got to a point where it was more appropriate for them . . . to take control.

Once Upon Inala, then, was a substantial project directed towards the production of a play but was, more importantly, a second step on the way to that point, which was reached in the establishment of Icy Tea.

Central to the project which produced *Once Upon Inala* was what writer Nick Hughes (formerly of the Popular Theatre Troupe) described as

> . . . a basic ideological commitment . . . that Inala people working with us would be in real and effective control of the decision-making process, including the writing.[18]

Thus the script was the result of a consultative process which included the substantial criticism and rewriting of a first draft. Similar consultation on other aspects of the production assured the sense of community ownership of the finished product on which its success ultimately depended. According to Denis Peel, the facilitatory process had its justification in the fact that it 'helped people's confidence and sense of their own personal power'.[19]

This sort of project is thus not to be measured solely in terms of its *artistic* success, although it must achieve some measure in the eyes of its participants if it is to be seen by them as of value. The real measure of success comes later, in the ways in which the skills learnt or honed by the participants, *be they artistic or organisational*, are put to use by the community constituted by it in the achievement of its own ends, either artistic or social or political.

For Pauline Peel, the big community show, while a useful means of consolidating and skilling a community, has substantial limitations and the real work commences after it,

> . . . when you start targeting communities more specifically. . . you make the one statement [of community] and then you get underneath, to the underbelly — a community is made up of a whole lot of target groups — and then you start to determine where you need to do affirmative action.

In Inala, this meant *Kockroach Kabaret*, a smaller project with twenty women, funded, significantly, by the Human Rights Commission and not by an arts funding agency. In 1981, 24% of Inala households were single-parent families, almost exclusively being held together by women leading difficult and isolated lives on social welfare. This smaller, more focussed project, made possible by the larger one which had preceded it, cleared the ground for the establishment of Icy Tea as an autonomous women's theatre group, which is still running a decade later.

What should be noted in this account is that this three-phase project is continually legitimated, not just in terms of the *aesthetic* worth of its products, but in the *social* worth of its processes, with the "product" of each phase as a stepping stone in the continuing process of the establishment, consolidation and skilling of a "community." What it thus represents is an almost purist version of the emerging practice of community arts. Like the work of the Popular Theatre Troupe, this has a lineage which stretches back to the counter cultures of the 1960s and 1970s, and most notably to the "radical social work" and "community action groups" referred to by Stuart Hall *et al.*[4] and to the grassroots politics of participatory democracy which were so characteristic of counter-cultural political activism.

Community Arts and the Craigmillar
Festival Society

In the case of Street Arts, it is possible to trace this work to a quite specific point of origin. Both Pauline and Denis Peel had worked for the Craigmillar Festival Society, a pioneering community arts venture in Scotland, and Steve Capelin had briefly worked with WEST Community Theatre in Melbourne under the directorship of Neil Cameron, who had also worked at Craigmillar. Helen Crummy, a major figure in establishing the society and its original secretary, has recently written an account of its history which offers a version of social activism through cultural activity which was widely influential on the development of community arts all over Europe and on the founders of Street Arts.[20]

As Helen Crummy describes it in her book, Craigmillar was a housing estate built in 1929 as the first of a series of "experiments in social engineering" around the fringes of Edinburgh, and initially occupied by a small community of miners and rural workers (the original inhabitants) and thousands of people cleared out of inner-city slums. By the end of the 1960s, the seven breweries and two coalmines which had been the major sources of employment in the area were all closed, leaving a population of 25,000 living in poverty in houses described as far back as the 1940s by a visiting politician as looking more like "barracks" than homes. Craigmillar, being the first and worst of these experimental estates, was the bottom of the heap, and a quarry for sociological researchers from Edinburgh University looking into the social effects of "multi-deprivation". Helen, indignant at the fact that her son could not get violin lessons at the local school in a city that hosted one of the most famous arts festivals in Europe, joined the Mothers' Club and fomented the establishment of the Craigmillar Festival Society in 1964. It then went on to run activities for local kids and, among other things, to stage an annual community play, usually written and always performed by locals.

By the mid-1970s the Festival Society had grown into a grass-roots self-help social welfare organisation, working in collaboration with government welfare agencies, which ran an annual local arts festival on a shoestring budget as well as a few arts-related activities throughout the year. Helen describes its activities as 'a partnership between politics (with a small "p") and local culture'.[21] By fairly effectively blackmailing the Edinburgh University sociologists — they told them that unless they did something for the community they were busily researching, the locals would spread the word and sabotage their research by lying to them — they elicited their support in making an application to the Council for Cultural Co-operation of the Council of Europe in 1976 for a huge grant under a pilot program in community development in selected sites of extreme poverty in Europe.

The Council for Cultural Co-operation, a general committee of the Council of Europe consisting of representatives of ministers of European governments with a responsibility for culture, had been engaged in exploring the possibilities of cultural activity as a means of community development for some years. Prior to 1970 discussions had centred on the notion of the "democratisation of culture", by which was meant making culture — defined as the high arts — more accessible to the socio-economically underprivileged or "ordinary people". When converted into government policy this had tended to mean subsidised ticket prices to the opera, the establishment of theatre buildings and art galleries in less fashionable suburbs and the like. By 1970 it had become clear that the policy had failed to alter the basic privileged audience for such activities, and this led to a major change in thinking. The notion of "democratisation of culture" was cast aside in favour of the much more radical notion of "cultural democracy". This entailed broadening the definition of "culture" far beyond just "the arts", which was seen as a minority culture enjoyed by a privileged few, to a more sociologically-based definition of it as

> . . . a continuous process creating the behavioural patterns, the attitudes, values and interdicts, and the common stock of intellectual and affective data that form the framework of life for any man or woman anywhere, at any time.[22]

"Culture", then, defined in this broad sense as "a way of life", is not singular; there is not *one* culture but there are as many as there are communities, and no one of them is necessarily "better" than any other. It is also not a set of dead artifacts but is *activity*.

These notions have several ramifications, many of which are reflected in the Council's general endorsement of a policy of "socio-cultural animation". What this entails is not the attempt to impose a dominant sense of culture defined as "art" but "animation"

> . . . which facilitates access to a more active and creative life for individuals and groups, and which increases capacities for communication and adjustment and ability to participate in community and societal life.[23]

These were all argued at the Council for Cultural Co-operation on the grounds of the broader democratisation of society at large, and it fairly quickly became clear that such a cultural policy *necessitated* social change, that socio-cultural animation was potentially "subversive".[24] It was at that stage that a brave attempt to put cultural activism for social change on the cultural policy agendas of European governments appears to have met a brick wall. The emerging community arts movement, from whence these notions came, had failed to pull off what would have been an impressive and unlikely coup, but community cultural development remained part of the policy debate, particularly in Australia.

The community arts movement in Britain, which had been an important player in this attempted coup, had its origins, once again, in the late 1960s. In the words of one of its major historians and theorists, Owen Kelly, it 'was woven . . . from three separate strands'.

> Firstly there was the passionate interest in creating new and liberatory forms of expression . . . Secondly there was the movement by groups of fine artists out of the galleries and into the streets. Thirdly there was the emergence of a new kind of political activist who believed that creativity was an essential tool in any kind of radical struggle.[25]

What this entailed was the establishment of a facilitatory mode of work for arts workers, whereby, as in the example of Street Arts' work in Inala, they act as the imparters of skills to specific communities which are then able to voice themselves. The point of this, according to Kelly, was 'to enable working people to be creative in ways that would make their creativity socially effective,' because

> . . . people's new-found effectiveness in the area of creativity would raise their morale and lead them to seek to empower themselves in other areas of their lives; and secondly [community arts workers] believed, as a matter of principle, that it was everybody's right to participate in the shaping of the world in which they lived.[26]

The task was, then, to work with a collection of people drawn together by factors ranging from geographical proximity to a shared interest or experience, assist them to discover what they shared, consolidate their sense of themselves as a community, and at best set them on the road of fighting for their shared interests with an enhanced ability to express and organise themselves.[27]

This was the sort of spirit which imbued the work of the Craigmillar Festival Society and, when it got the grant from the Council for Cultural Co-operation to turn the local initiative into a full-blown pilot program, it quickly became the administrative centre of a community-run social welfare system built around arts activity, and the biggest employer in the district. As a result, it became a model for the operation of a number of community arts organisations, not just in Scotland but also in Europe, Africa, the USA and, via the spread of its alumni, in Australia as well. Arts work, in this context, was essentially viewed as *functional* — it offered people an opportunity for a fuller participation in the life of the town, it assisted in the construction of a genuine sense of community via celebrations of local talents and strengths, it introduced people to modes of organised, communal self-help, and it drew people into group action to serve the needs of the community (Helen Crummy's politics with a small "p"). The Society ran arts-based workshops, staged locally-generated performances and outdoor pageants, and facilitated public art projects, all of them as local initiatives for which artistic expertise was hired if needed, and not imposed upon them by outsiders who felt they knew what Craigmillar people needed. As well, it ran a number of more clearly welfare-oriented programs for a range of groups in need, from kids at risk to the elderly and the disabled. It also lobbied successfully for the supply of basic amenities, such as a library and a community hall, for an estate which was designed and built in 1929 with none at all. The Society takes pride in the fact that it has contributed to the betterment of the lives of local kids in particular, who have tended to avoid the traditional dangers of growing up on estates like Craigmillar and have achieved in ways previously considered impossible. Helen Crummy's youngest son Andrew, for example, is now a community muralist in London, has a Master's degree from the Glasgow Art School, and has recently completed an Australian tour, guest lecturing at various tertiary institutions.

Street Arts and Arts Funding Policy

The influence of all this on Street Arts' approach in Inala is clear. Less clear, but undoubtedly there, is the influence of the Inala project on the development of funding policy within what was the Community Arts Board of the Australia Council, which became the Community Cultural Development Unit in 1987. The consequences of the shifts implied by this name change have been far-reaching in terms of community theatre practice, making much of it conform more to the Street Arts model as reflected in Inala than to the model established by the Popular Theatre Troupe, variants of which dominated practice in the early 1980s.

Gay Hawkins, in a recent book on the history of the community arts program within the Australia Council from its introduction as a funding category in the mid-1970s, describes it as having developed along two axes — firstly, in shifting from seeing its intended constituency as the "culturally disadvantaged" to the "culturally different" (which mirrors the shift from "the democratisation of culture" to "cultural democracy" within the Council of Europe debates); and secondly, in shifting from essentially "aesthetic" to "social" criteria of value. These developments are reflected in the name change which replaces "arts" with "cultural development". Interestingly, the point at which she sees these policy changes as taking place (1983-1985) corresponds with Street Arts' Inala project. Prior to the mid-1980s, most community theatre work in Australia manifested its radical intentions by making theatre *for* "disadvantaged communities", be they disadvantaged by class, gender or race, or by their lack of access to a political understanding of their situation, "high" culture or whatever. This had substantially been the approach of the Popular Theatre Troupe and the companies that emerged in its wake. In the second half of the 1980s, the Street Arts approach increasingly emerged as standard practice, to some extent because it had the firm approval of the major source of funding for most companies engaged in community theatre, and that approval had been won, through protracted debate between Street Arts and the Community Arts Board, in the company's fight for funding of what they saw as innovatory work in the Australian context.[28]

Hawkins sees the establishment of these "social or non-aesthetic discourses of value" as the "greatest achievement" of the community arts program in the Australia Council, in that it placed on record for the Council as a whole discourses which

> . . . remain as a significant alternative to the idea of art as a minority of "excellent" forms at the top of a universal cultural hierarchy.[29]

As a result of these changes, community theatre practice has moved away from, at worst, a patronising process of offering "art" or, in Pauline Peel's previously cited terms, 'a Marxist analysis of what their situation was' to an undefined "mass" of social and intellectual inferiors. Community theatre has increasingly become, at best, sensitive and responsive to the needs and cultural differences of the communities with which it is constructed. This, in part, is a result of the development of a range of community consultative mechanisms. It is usually now measured, by those who are professionally involved in making it, on the basis of the extent to which it alters and improves the social circumstances of its varying constituencies. It has shifted from being predominantly *about* politics to actually *being* political activism itself, even if only with a small "p".

Hawkins sees, though, some problems in this position with which many companies, including the Street Arts of the 1990s, are wrestling. For her the major problem results from the power of a bureaucracy, the Community Cultural Development Board, to construct a practice by choosing to fund it to the exclusion of other possible practices. The inclusion of "social" criteria of value has made "product" no more than a phase of "process". This, she claims, has produced 'a fundamental contradiction' whereby the 'obsession with the social often worked to devalue or dismiss the cultural or aesthetic results of community arts projects'.[30]

Some community artists, particularly those of an activist bent, may see the making of communities as dynamic, self-affirming and self-assertive entities as quite enough to expect of their work; may in fact have no trouble with a whole-hearted acceptance of social criteria of value. What Hawkins highlights, though, is the loss of some important opportunities in what amounts to the surrender of the aesthetic. What gets jettisoned, she claims, is the whole arena of "progressive art":

> While the 1970s and 1980s have been characterised by a phenomenal expansion in cultural theory and debate, community arts — and by implication community theatre — has been generally blind to these developments, preferring instead to develop communities rather than a dynamic aesthetic able to explore and critique the nature of social order.[31]

In many ways this brings us full circle, back to the disputes which arose between the different approaches represented by Street Arts and the Popular

Theatre Troupe in the early 1980s. Clearly a prime concern for companies taking the Popular Theatre Troupe position lay in what we may describe as the realm of the *aesthetic*, which is manifested in the artistic quality and production values of the shows which they toured so widely to a broad constituency of "working people", "ordinary people" or just "the people". These shows were designed to entertain so as to inform, to crystallise a political analysis *for* their audiences. Street Arts, on the other hand, was more concerned with the making of performance events *with* carefully defined and thoroughly explored and known communities as part of a broader strategy of community development.

The differences should not disguise the shared political perspectives and aims of the two companies, just as they reveal the very different responses to those political perspectives in terms of strategy. The former is a "top down" approach, which assumes the superior knowledge of the company, and thus runs the risk of patronising its audiences. The latter, a "bottom up" approach, assumes that a community knows its own circumstances best and merely needs to be "voiced," which runs the risk of never moving beyond the political under-standing with which it started. Both approaches have strengths and both present problems as political activism. The struggle to bridge the gap or amalgamate the strengths of the two positions has not been successfully resolved in the 1990s any more than it was in the 1970s, and will no doubt continue to preoccupy companies like the new Street Arts for some time. If Brisbane's record of innovation in political and community theatre can be sustained, the company could again have a central role in the continuing development of a radical theatre practice in Australia.

REFERENCES

1. Much of this work is recorded in
    Henry Lesnick (ed.) *Guerrilla Street Theater* [Avon, New York, 1973]
    Arthur Sainer (ed.) *The Radical Theater Notebook* [Avon, New York,1975]
    Catherine Itzin, *Stages in the Revolution* [Methuen, London, 1980]
    Theodore Shank, *American Alternative Theater* [Macmillan,London,1982]
    Eugene van Erven, *Radical People's Theater* [Indiana University Press, Bloomington, 1988]

2. Robert Hewison, *Too Much: Art and Society in the Sixties 1960-75* [Methuen, London, 1986] p. xvii.

3. David Edgar, *The Second Time as Farce: Reflections on the Drama of Mean Times* [Lawrence & Wishart, London, 1988] pp. 200-202.

4. J.Clarke, S.Hall, T.Jefferson and B.Roberts, "Sub Cultures, Cultures and Class" in S.Hall and T.Jefferson (eds.) *Resistance Through Rituals: youth sub-cultures in post-war Britain* [Hutchinson, London, 1976] p. 61.

5. Baz Kershaw, *The Politics of Performance: Radical Theatre as Cultural Intervention* [Routledge, London, 1992] pp. 35-40 — offers a similar, much more thorough account of the period in his definitive book on the evolution of the development of the community theatre movement in Britain.

6. From an unpublished interview with Pauline Peel, Brisbane, July 1989.

7. See, for example, Errol O'Neill in "Acting Politically: An Interview with Errol O'Neill on Politics, Actors and the Theatre" by Gary MacLennan, *Social Alternatives*, Vol. 4, No. 4, 1985, p. 66.

8. From an unpublished interview with Richard Fotheringham, Brisbane, February 1994.

9. See Howard Goorney, *The Theatre Workshop Story* [Methuen, London,1981] for an account of the work of the company, and Ewan McColl, 'Theatre of Action, Manchester,' in R.Samuel, E.McColl and S.Cosgrave (eds.) *Theatres of the Left 1880-1935* [Routledge, London, 1985] for an account of the company's pre-war origins in the British agit-prop movement in the 1920s and 1930s.

10. The agit-prop movement is well documented by R.Stourac and K.McCreery in *Theatre as a Weapon* [Routledge, London, 1986] and in R.Samuel, E.McColl and S.Cosgrave (eds.) *Ibid.*

11. R. Fotheringham, "Alternative Theatre: The Popular Theatre Troupe", *Social Alternatives*, Vol. 1, No. 2, 1978, p. 27.

12. This is documented in
    Catherine Itzin, *Stages in the Revolution* [Methuen, London, 1980] and
    Sandy Craig (ed.) *Dreams and Deconstructions* [Amber Lane, London,

1980] as well as in the pages of *Theatre Quarterly* which published on the work quite extensively throughout the 1970s.

13. John McGrath *A Good Night Out* [Methuen, London, 1981] pp. 20-21.

14. *ibid.* pp. 54-59.

15. Richard Seyd "The Theatre of Red Ladder", *New Edinburgh Review*, No. 30, 1975, p. 40.

16. From an unpublished interview with Steve Capelin, Brisbane, March, 1991.

17. From an unpublished interview with Pauline Peel, Brisbane, July, 1989.

18. Nick Hughes, *Caper*, No. 24 [Community Arts Board, Australia Council] written by Tim Low, p. 7.

19. *ibid.*, p. 10.

20. Helen Crummy, *Let the People Sing: A Story of Craigmillar* [Newcraighall, 1992].

21. *ibid.*, p. 48.

22. J. A. Simpson (ed.), *Socio-cultural Animation* [Council of Europe, Strasbourg, 1978], p. 8.

23 J. A. Simpson, "Socio-cultural community development for a common type of housing area," *ibid.*, p. 86.

24. See, for example, Jacques Depaigne, *Cultural Policies in Europe* (Council of Europe, Strasbourg, 1978), p. 58.

25 Owen Kelly, *Community, Art and the State: Storming the Citadels* [Comedia, London, 1984], p. 11.

26. *ibid.*, pp. 21-2.

27. See D. Watt, "Interrogating 'Community'", in V. Binns (ed.), *Community and the Arts* [Pluto, Sydney, 1991], pp. 55-66, for an account of the political ancestry of the term, and its developing use within the movement.

28. Hawkins has been criticised for her downplaying of the influence of practitioners in the development of community arts policy, most notably in print by Rachel Fensham, "(Post) Community Arts?", *Continuum*, Vol. 8, No. 2, 1994, p. 191.

29. Gay Hawkins, *From Nimbin to Mardi Gras: Constructing Community Arts* [Allen & Unwin, Sydney, 1993], p. 138.

30. *ibid.*, p. 77.

31. *ibid.*, p. 164

PART TWO

●

POPULAR THEATRE TROUPE

THE HISTORY OF
THE POPULAR THEATRE TROUPE

by Errol O'Neill

●

INTRODUCTION

I joined the Popular Theatre Troupe in 1977 as an actor and toured for two years before becoming a resident writer and director with the Company. In this article I present an overview of the history and significance of the PTT which a reader previously uninformed on the subject may find to be a mixture of indisputable fact and personal assessment. Memory and the PTT archives have provided the fact, and the recollection of the passionate political and social context of the late seventies and early eighties have provided the personal assessment. I shamelessly declare that my judgments are not value free and probably carry with them the same partisan devotion to radical social criticism which ensured that my seven years of involvement with the Popular Theatre Troupe were so satisfying.

For an understanding of the two or three years of the Troupe's life before I joined, I called on the assistance of founding member Richard Fotheringham, whose comments I have incorporated.

Elsewhere in this book there is a chronological list of all the Troupe's shows and activities, listing the personnel involved, subject matter, and other relevant details. Other former Troupe members have provided some details which I had forgotten or which never survived in written form. This article will talk in more general and reflective terms about the work of the PTT.

1. HISTORY

The Popular Theatre Troupe operated for ten years as a Brisbane-based professional theatre company, producing original theatre of social comment on a wide variety of subjects. The Troupe did not confine itself to topics relevant to Queensland. More often than not, our sights were set on the national and global implications of issues which were of universal concern.

Between 1974 and 1983 the PTT wrote, produced and regularly toured to various parts of Australia with a total of twenty-five original shows. It organised ten large scale community events, and was instrumental in the encouragement and development of a number of community arts projects in disciplines other than theatre.

THE BEGINNINGS

The first project of what was to become the Popular Theatre Troupe arose out of an attempt to establish a Festival of Arts in Queensland during 1973-4, largely as a result of dissatisfaction with the commercial "decorated floats and community bowls tournament" approach of the existing Warana Festival.

The director of the Arts Festival, Lesley Gotto, asked Richard Fotheringham to organise what she described as "fringe" theatre, but in defining the Arts Festival against Warana, the emphasis was to be away from that Festival's then token arts component, which was based on listing the activities of existing professional, amateur and student theatre groups. She wanted new activities, a program of original work that would not have occurred without the Festival's initiative. She requested that all activities be as high profile as possible, and involve international figures of standing in the arts — both for their intrinsic worth and for the publicity which the new festival desperately needed in order to establish its credentials.

THE QUEENSLAND FACTOR

Another set of circumstances which led to the creation of the PTT was the existence in Brisbane at the time of a number of professional theatre workers who were dissatisfied with both state politics and the state of the arts in Queensland.

This was the early period of the Whitlam federal Labor government, yet what seemed then to be a revolution in politics and in the politics and aesthetics of the arts throughout the rest of Australia, was being resisted in Queensland, where in 1972 the Bjelke-Petersen government had declared a state of emergency over the Springbok rugby tour, and had set out to frustrate changes in education, black-white relations, gender issues, labour relations, and the arts.

Theatre workers in Queensland were reading of the creation of new venues, and of plays and playwrights in Sydney and Melbourne, yet they were living in a political environment actively hostile to such innovation. The local theatre industry seemed too insecure to respond to new challenges, and obliged to engage instead in self-censorship in order to survive.

Therefore, unlike many of the later community theatre companies, the PTT in its first years comprised in part experienced arts workers with a background in "mainstream" professional theatre who were reacting against a particular set of political circumstances, but who were otherwise relatively orthodox in their definitions of artistic "standards" and abilities.

At meetings which Richard Fotheringham called during 1973 to discuss options for the "fringe" of the first Festival of the Arts which was to take place in May 1974, a number of proposals were made. Richard's personal preference was for a new writing and performance venue — an idea he continued to try to push until about 1976, by which time La Boîte had clearly moved into that niche.

Perhaps the most influential arguments came at the end of 1973 from Margaret Bornhorst and Duncan Campbell who had worked somewhat unhappily that year for the Queensland Theatre Company (QTC), touring schools. They intensely disliked the very large audiences they had been compelled to play to in inadequate venues, and the fact that even a modest entrance fee had effectively ostracised the poor (including aboriginal) students from the experience.

Richard's own experiences during three years in the QTC main company, particularly when on Arts Council tours, suggested that what was evident in educational practice was also true in the wider community: that theatre was being used to create self-satisfied minorities rather than provide a forum for communal debates and the acknowledgment and accommodation of differences, and that professionalism was becoming synonymous with commercialism, with little or no thought being given to finding more sympathetic connections between scripts, venues, and performance styles.

TAKING THEATRE OUT OF THEATRES

Slowly the idea developed of free portable shows, using a mixture of professional and amateur performers, experimenting with popular entertainment forms to dramatise contemporary Australian political issues, and performing in non-traditional spaces. Significant influences were *Oh What a Lovely War* and *The Legend of King O'Malley*, both of which the QTC had done in 1971. At about the same time Richard read in *Theatre Quarterly** about the Yorkshire writer-director Albert Hunt, who had worked with Joan Littlewood at Stratford East (where *Lovely War* had originated) and with Peter Brook on the *US* project about the Vietnam War, staged by the Royal Shakespeare Company.

* Albert Hunt: "John Ford's Missile Crisis", *Theatre Quarterly*, January - March 1971, pp. 47-55.

Hunt seemed to be someone who was interested in taking further the possibilities for documentary theatre explored by *Lovely War*, which used a music hall format to analyse the history of the First World War.

Hunt's own play, *John Ford's Cuban Missile Crisis*, used a Hollywood western movie format to dramatise the USA-USSR confrontation over missile bases in Cuba in 1962 which had brought the world close to nuclear war. The Hollywood imagery arose after research for the show uncovered repeated tendencies by the politicians involved to imagine and to speak about the events they were involved in, in the language of popular movies.

Hunt, a lecturer at the Bradford College of Art, seemed an ideal choice as a visiting contributor to the project, and satisfied the Festival's request for an international presence. The English Department at the University of Queensland agreed to fund his visit.

Hunt Comes to Brisbane

Albert Hunt already had a reputation in Britain as a leader in the alternative theatre movement. When he arrived in Queensland he gathered a team of local people to work on fringe theatre activities, a significant number of whom had come out of the rough and tumble world of student theatre at the University of Queensland, and were already programmed to respond to the challenge of creating political satire in the marketplace.

Hunt worked on many activities with this group, the most enduring being *Star Trick*, a satire which brought the realities of then current political life in Australia into sharp focus. Using the popular *Star Trek* television program as a metaphor, the lampooning began. Crowds in shopping centres and other places unused to theatre were amazed to see real actors performing on a temporary stage, slipping behind curtains, making quick changes, talking directly to the crowd and using metaphoric props. This is the tradition of marketplace theatre, of course, but Brisbane audiences were not accustomed to witnessing people being funny — or satirical — in public. Street theatre had finally arrived in the sunshine state.

But this, and the shows which followed it for the next decade, was more than simply street theatre or shopping centre entertainment. This theatre had bite — a reflective, intellectual and satirical content which could take it into the auditorium, the classroom, the factory, the prison, the conference hall.

The elements of Hunt's style which were to influence profoundly the later work of the Troupe were all showcased in *Star Trick*. Ironies and contradictions in the world of*realpolitik* were pounced upon mercilessly, and metaphors were found in the vast cauldron of popular culture which was Hunt's laboratory. He was particularly fond of using old movies and songs — it was not until 1979 with *Viva Indonesia* that the Troupe would begin to routinely write its own music for shows.

Up until then, the standard format was to supply a show with a leavening of old popular songs, sung in an ironic context, to comment on the action and the ideas. These elements of style were part of the legacy Hunt would leave the Popular Theatre Troupe when it became formally established under that title the following year, 1975.

Theatre of Ideas

The more significant part of Hunt's legacy, however, was that he gave this group confidence that they could stand up in the marketplace and present a "theatre of ideas". His personal charm and wit were exemplary too, and gave the Troupe a sense of humour without which it may not have survived beyond an initial burst of activity. The larrikinesque, satirical, fearless aspects of this theatre were in accord with the best Australian traditions of ridiculing pompous authority, laughing in adversity, and generally telling the boss where to get off.

A theatre of ideas had been emerging in the national arena since the late sixties, but it seemed to be mostly happening in Sydney and Melbourne. Australian theatre had for a long time been spoken for by such legendary plays as *The Summer of the Seventeenth Doll* and *The One Day of the Year*, which took up worthy, but safe and respectable, cultural themes. But now there was a widespread yearning for a new voice to record the new sensitivities about our national identity which had arisen from the wave of protest against our involvement in the Vietnam war and other issues of the time. From the mid-sixties on, the national consensus about sentiments and values, once taken for granted, was being pilloried in public. There was a general loss of faith in the certitudes which had kept the country asleep and compliant during all the Menzies years of full employment.

If Australia was dragged screaming into the twentieth century by the Vietnam war and the handful of other issues around which the young baby-boomers were now mobilising on campuses and in city streets across the nation, then it was inevitable that the Australian theatre would begin to reflect this new social consciousness.

Of course, the new theatre movement reflected the difference between the histories and the moods of the states and, in particular, of the state capitals. Brisbane has long suffered under the notion that it was a branch office town. There was nothing here to parallel The Pram Factory or The Nimrod. It seemed we had neither the ideas, the practitioners nor indeed the audience, to support a vibrant alternative theatre movement.

However, we were sharp enough to know that we could stage the proven successes from Sydney and Melbourne, and in the early seventies Brisbane audiences enjoyed very competent local productions of *The Legend of King O'Malley*, *Don's Party*, and other shows which came out of the new robust irreverence which had been forged in the southern metropolitan culture.

The universities of Sydney and Melbourne were the well-spring of most of the writing and performing talent which constituted the new Australian theatre. However, the very active dramatic society at the University of Queensland during the late sixties and early seventies produced original material burning with the same fervour of social critique and tongue-in-cheek satire which had motivated our southern counterparts. And it was prominent members of this dramatic guerrilla force which were attracted to Albert Hunt and the Festival of Arts fringe project in 1974.

Establishment in 1975

After successfully applying for funding to the Community Arts Committee and the Literature Board of the Australia Council, the Popular Theatre Troupe was established in April 1975 as a fully professional company with five full time actors, a resident writer, and an administrator (Peter Sutherland).

In April, the Troupe rehearsed two one-act plays, *The Puny Little Life Show* and *Red Cross*, and presented these shows in Brisbane, South-East Queensland, Northern New South Wales, and Sydney. During June and July 1975, the Troupe, under the direction of Albert Hunt, created *The White Man's Mission*, a highly entertaining and thought-provoking history of the white man in Australia, which was compared favourably by Ian Robinson in the National Times to the best work of the country's leading alternative theatre, Melbourne's Pram Factory.

Indeed, the comparison was a natural one, given the shared political sympathies between the Pram and the Troupe. In following years, when the Troupe wanted to present a public season in Melbourne, the Pram Factory was the preferred venue.

Star Trick and *The White Man's Mission* were instrumental in establishing a theatrical modus operandi which the Troupe employed from 1975 to 1983 when the organisation folded due to lack of funding.

Some would suggest that the natural life of the PTT had "run its course" by 1983, that there is only so much air in the lungs. The Troupe had shouted its message at factory gates for the best part of a decade, and had, according to this view, run out of puff.

But this is a shortsighted argument because, as you will read in other parts of this book, some of the most talented people who had passed through the PTT, who had cut their teeth on the Troupe's shows, went on with the same mix of political and artistic passion to create other material in the same tradition, either as individual artists or with other groups and companies. A rose by any other name would shout as loud.

The fact that the PTT eventually lost its funding and folded says more about Australian society's lack of cultural sophistication than about the talents of the Troupe members or the quality of their product.

Stages in the Revolution

The history of The Popular Theatre Troupe could be said to have started with Albert Hunt and the 1974 Festival of Arts. Indeed, from that project right up to 1983, there was always a continuing membership with enough overlaps to ensure that the corporate memory and ideology of the PTT was continued. Some personnel stayed for long periods, some for short periods, some came back after an absence for a second tour of duty.

The Troupe kept going for such a long time, not because of any one person or single show, but because it was a natural gathering point for the forces of social critique which, at that time as at other historical moments, gathered together willing voices to shout as one.

The people who worked in the Troupe during those years had a common political commitment even though their talents, abilities and backgrounds were different.

People wrote, acted and organised for the Troupe not just out of selfless commitment, of course. It was a place where one could achieve a self-expression and a personal fulfillment which other parts of the theatre industry at that time were simply not providing.

What held the generic Troupe together over the period 1974 to 1983? The answer is probably *ideology*. A general belief in the need to promote social critique through the medium of theatre. I use the term "ideology" not in a pejorative sense, but in the sense of a body of ideas, thoughts, leanings which tend towards a broad political classification.

The Troupe was never torn apart by ideological differences in the way that several other political groups were, such as the Communist Party or the many left groupings which divided and redivided their membership on the basis of single issues or fine points of political theory.

There were, however, identifiable ideological elements in the writing of the PTT's shows, and often there was heated argument about points of interpretation and belief. But always, the common ground asserted itself. A feature of left arts practice is a commitment to the "popular front" concept.

A Marxist analysis of issues was common, but not obligatory, in the preparation of PTT shows. Such an analysis goes hand in hand with a commitment to satire, perhaps. If you want to achieve more than mere parody, you need to develop a probing analysis of the subject matter. And Marxist categories assist greatly in this process. After all, it was a theatre of ideas, not just of shallow belly laughs.

There was a general acceptance of the principles of gender equality in the Troupe's organisational structure, reflecting the belief in affirmative action which permeated our shows. Three men and five women occupied the administrator's chair over the Troupe's life, women putting in more person years at the job by a factor of three to one. The theatre industry features female administrators quite commonly, of course, particularly Community Theatre. However, it was in the membership of the acting company where the PTT's policy was most evident. We always set out to achieve a gender balance when hiring actors, and then wrote the shows to accommodate the talent lineup. This often led to very successful artistic outcomes, such as the extremely well-observed male parodies performed by Kath Porrill.

Richard Fotheringham considers that phases in the Troupe's history were more or less defined by the work of the writers who provided the scripts for the shows. Although it was common over the whole ten year period for writers to work in collaborative situations — many shows were group-devised — the writer bore the major responsibility in most cases for the bulk of the research and the formation of structural ideas. Workshopping with performers profoundly influenced the shape of the production, but the writer was usually the provider of the central argument.

This is a worthwhile method of analysing the Troupe's literary/artistic progress, but there are other factors also at work which influenced much of the general impact of the Troupe on the community, determining which audiences it developed, and having a deep effect on the assessment of its own successes and failures and its responsive plans for future work.

Administrators influenced the choice of performance venue. For example, Peter Sutherland pioneered rural community-based projects for which he successfully sought funding from what later became the Community Arts Board. Roslyn Atkinson spent several years building contacts with the trade union movement and organised the first factory tours. Jan Oates was the first administrator to succeed (for a time) in getting the shows into secondary schools on more than an occasional basis.

The songs composed by Ken MacLeod and Jane Ahlquist for *Viva Indonesia* in 1979 had a great effect on the impact of the Troupe as well. Ken stayed with the Troupe over the next three years, writing much more original music. Previously, we never looked on music as much more than an accompaniment to the verbal and visual message. Ken built up the idea of music as a vehicle for the delivery of message.

The Troupe's relationship with the trade union movement waxed and waned from 1976 to 1983, but it always had an effect on the frequency with which we visited worksites and the choice of subject matter.

Our relationship to schools was a considerable factor as well. We never wrote what could be called Theatre-in-Education, but insisted that our shows were written for a universal audience, and proved by experience that they won the respect and attention of school audiences because they were, in that context, challenging and provocative entertainments which stimulated the students' critical faculties and social imagination.

The "moment of performance" is also worth considering as a barometer of the Troupe's artistic success and general impact on the society it served. Some actors were forceful, imaginative, unforgettable and, in performance made the shows a success even when the writing and production elements were relatively uninteresting.

There were many changeables and many constants, therefore, in the theatrical history of the PTT. But considering that our major emphasis was on the *theatre of ideas*, it may be worthwhile to trace the history of the Troupe according to the work and influence of the writers.

The Ideas in Phases

The first phase was from 1974 to 1976. The main influence here was Albert Hunt himself. *Star Trick* and The *White Man's Mission* were landmark shows which not only told the community what they could expect from the future of this emerging band of players, but also instructed the players themselves in the possibilities of theatre which went outside the bourgeois auditorium.

The next phase was distinguished by the writing and direction of Richard Fotheringham, a founding member of Hunt's group in 1974 who later went on to write and/or direct half a dozen shows for the Troupe. He carried on some of the elements of Hunt's style but also brought a particularly Australian flavour and originality to the group's work. His most productive and continuous period was from 1976 to 1978 but he also contributed shows to the repertoire in 1979 and 1981.

The third phase began in 1979 with my writing and directing *Popular Theatre Troupe's Australia*. I had worked with Nick Hughes writing *$tampede* in 1977 when I first joined the Troupe as an actor, but from 1979 to 1982 I worked more consistently and centrally within the PTT's style, as established and consolidated by Hunt and Fotheringham, calling on research assistance and ideas from academics Pat Laughren and David Biggins for the five shows I wrote and (apart from one) directed.

The fourth and final phase was the brave, unfunded year of 1983. Writer Kerry O'Rourke, in *Limited Life*, produced a show which differed in style in many fundamental ways from what had gone before. *Wage Invaders* used many pieces of previous PTT shows. *As The Crow Flies* was written by Michael Cummings and Glenn Perry. Hugh Watson worked on *There's More to Life than Snogging, Barry* which had a short exposure at the end of 1983. Actors and administrative staff soldiered on, living on the door takings and what small donations they were able to gather. But without core funding it was impossible to continue, and the Troupe's exciting and colourful history came to an end.

2. THE PHILOSOPHY AND POLITICS

The philosophy of the Popular Theatre Troupe set it apart from most other theatre groups at that time, in that there was a definite political motivation involved in mounting each of its productions. Because of the cultural vision of the Australia Council's funding policies in the wake of the Whitlam expansion, we were enabled to say what we thought should be said about social and political issues which we considered important. We didn't have to make box office the choice-determining concern that it was among bourgeois theatre companies. Content ruled.

Given the largely uncritical nature of the media in Queensland and the general lack of critical intellectual life in the public arena — particularly the parliament — the Troupe was destined to become part of the extra-parliamentary opposition. We saw ourselves in this way, and so did the rest of the extra-parliamentary opposition. We often found ourselves performing at counter-cultural and alternative functions, as well as political demonstrations.

We made contact with appreciative trade unionists who commonly shared a Communist or left background and whose experience had taught them the value of taking critical theatre and thought-provoking entertainment to the shop floor.

Another of our most successful regular venues was the schoolroom. Here, with the assistance of progressive teachers, we were able to assist and contribute to the critical education values which were being developed in the more enlightened areas of education practice.

The anti-intellectual regime of Premier Bjelke-Petersen and the conservative public culture of Queensland ensured that the Popular Theatre Troupe developed a hard-edged philosophy of social criticism and a savage sense of purpose.

The Special Branch of the Queensland Police force kept an eye on the Troupe and its members — some of us had files before joining. Two shows were declared unfit to tour to government schools. *Crook Shop* was banned in 1981 and *The State We're In* was banned in 1982. Ironically, this was just a few short years before the Fitzgerald inquiry into police misconduct. The Queensland Education Department had banned both shows because "they did not encourage respect for law and order".

Even though few of the PTT's twenty-five shows dealt specifically with Queensland, the Troupe's location made us determined to sharpen our social critique, to produce effective satire and not lapse into parody. Parody, it seemed, was an ineffectual form of delivering social criticism as it merely laughed at, and thereby reinforced, the status quo rather than exposing it, analysing it, and calling for social change. The state government's hostility to social critique gave us a purpose in life.

Creative Tension

During the life of the PTT there were always arguments. Arguments about the content of shows, about the style and presentation of shows, about organisational details. This was no different to any other theatre company but, because the Troupe operated as a collective, the arguments and disagreements were handled in a particular way. First of all, there was a broad political basis which everyone in the Troupe shared. The paths that led to membership of the PTT created a sort of filtering process which ensured that everyone had a basic commitment to theatre of social criticism. The Troupe members took it for granted that the reason for doing a show was that we had something to say about the world.

Therefore, when there were disagreements, they were generally about *how* rather than *what*.

Nevertheless, the Troupe had its share of strong-minded members and some arguments went on for days. Collective meetings were held to sort out differences. Rarely did the differences necessitate a vote, although the fundamental understanding was that the collective was made up of equals whose ultimate defence against tyranny was the ballot. We could see other theatre companies plying their trade more smoothly and efficiently with a hierarchical decision-making structure, but we knew that it was far more important for *all of us* to be in control of the artistic direction of the Troupe. It was pointless making efficient decisions about artistic choices if there was no agreement about *why* we were doing things.

In all Community Arts activity there seemed to be interminable meetings and the PTT was no exception. We knew that we could not individually abdicate responsibility for collective decision-making. At stake was the ultimate product — our shows. We believed it was necessary for the actors to go on stage believing in what they were doing. We all took it as given that when we talked to audiences after our shows we must be able to continue by other means the argument we had just presented theatrically.

This aspect of the actor's work distinguished, for most of us, community from bourgeois theatre. It seemed that actors in the latter could sprout anything on stage and never be held to account for it. We took content more seriously.

3. MODUS OPERANDI

The Popular Theatre Troupe's Audience

The PTT was always looking for new venues and new audiences, following the brief that we wanted to take theatre outside the bourgeois auditorium to people who didn't normally "go to the theatre". Of course, we also played in theatres to habitual theatregoers, but it was the constant attempt to move out of theatres, to find new ways of exploring the relationship between actors and audience, that distinguished the Troupe from much of the rest of the theatre industry, even from much of the "alternative" theatre. This characteristic was a natural corollary of our fundamental political philosophy.

It was important to allow discussion of the matters raised in the show, and to this end we always allowed time after shows for the actors to talk to the audience. In the case of school shows, we built this discussion time into the schedule. From time to time, our planning and technique for school discussions got a bit sloppy, and incoming Troupe members with specific experience in TIE were called upon to help upgrade our collective skills. We tried, as is usual with TIE groups, to set up the discussion in ways which would prevent kids from asking questions about the personal lives of the actors and the perceived "glamour" of theatre. Instead, we tried to guide their attention to a further exploration of the subject of the show they had just seen. The students' response was generally indicative of the level of social awareness engendered by their teachers and the school. Some students were very well informed and either took issue with us over certain points or voiced their agreement. We tried wherever possible to hand the debate over to the kids themselves. Having done the show, we tried to avoid lecturing on the right way to think about the issues. We presented particular opinions in the show, in a spirit of lively debate, but made sure that the overall message to kids was to think for themselves, to develop their own critical faculties.

The best way to reach an audience of workers was to organise through trade union structures. On one memorable occasion we allowed a lunchtime show at a car factory in Elizabeth, South Australia, to be organised through the works' social committee. Most of the workers avoided us like the plague because, as we found out later, the social committee was largely a management group and functions which they organised did not enjoy the same support as things organised by the unions. As we were packing up after a poorly attended performance in a noisy canteen, we spoke to a delegate from the Vehicle Builders' Union who told us that when the social committee's notices went up about the show they thought we were just a Bjelke-Petersen propaganda team from Queensland!

We performed at conferences, seminars, functions organised by community organisations, fundraisers for political parties. There was usually some progressive angle in a conference which would act as an umbrella to invite the Popular Theatre Troupe in for a bit of pointed, relevant entertainment. We played to Labor Party faithful at big meetings, little meetings. On one occasion we performed before one of our biggest audiences in the Toowoomba City Hall as a curtain raiser to the very popular then-President of the ACTU, Bob Hawke. The crowd was really there to see Hawke, who observed us with amusement from the wings for part of our show while the eagerly expectant crowd gave us a very warm reception.

We did many performances in gaols. Usually these were minimum security, but at different times and in different states, we performed to maximum security prisoners as well, in both male and female prisons.

We also performed to classes at tertiary institutions where progressive lecturers realised the value of our research and our commentary to their students.

And so the Troupe found itself carrying on one of the great traditions of theatre — being town criers, court jesters, strolling players, soothsayers, social critics — going from marketplace to court, presenting satires with bite. Sometimes playing to the converted, sometimes playing to the uninformed, sometimes to the hostile. Very often to the truly grateful.

Social Change Reflected in Working Methods

There was a fundamental belief in the necessity of progressive social change, particularly among those members of the Troupe who did the writing and the organising.

Not only did we write about subjects in a way which contradicted the predominant concerns of bourgeois theatre, we also went about presenting our theatre in ways which attempted to go beyond the safe formalities normally encountered in middle class culture.

We set out to present a theatre of ideas. We accepted that one of our fundamental aims was to entertain, but we saw a further need — a *sine qua non* of good political satire — to base the entertainment on a sound political analysis of the subject matter.

All the shows PTT wrote and produced were aimed at particular issues. The issues were decided upon first, then the show began. Research, workshopping ideas, finding a metaphor in which to present the material. The metaphor was also part of the argument and was chosen because of the ironic resonances it carried. We didn't sit around deciding what were funny gags and then build these into a show. We first decided on the most pressing and appropriate issue to address, then developed our argument in relation to it. This was the hard edge which distinguishes political theatre from mere entertainment. Of course, some of the shows PTT produced had various weaknesses in artistry and entertainment value, but none were ever so boring that the audience shouted or yawned us off the stage.

As time went on, and each team of actors/writer/designer worked together, the artistic level rose. This was not necessarily a linear historical development. The artistic level varied for many reasons over the entire period of the troupe's existence and had more to do with how relevant was the social issue which the show dealt with, how clear were the ideas with which the team workshopped, how easy was the transition from a set of ideas to a theatrical performance.

Conferences on economics, history, social work, all provided a venue for our performances. Because our satires often touched on a collection of interconnecting issues, it was often possible to give a conference a choice of show which could be presented in a way that fitted the delegates' concerns. Keeping several shows in repertoire over a 12 to 18 month period assisted the Troupe to maintain a flexible "guerrilla theatre" approach.

When making contacts with groups in the community to arrange new audiences apart from middle class trained theatregoers, our natural liaisons were with alternative organisations, groups that were critical of much ordinary social process, such as environmental groups and trade unions.

After most shows, except where the payment of a fee for our performance had been pre-arranged, we passed the hat around. This was a custom which all Australian audiences recognised. Often we were surprised by the generosity of the people who saw our shows, and read their donations as heartfelt thanks.

4. ORGANISATION

Working Methods

The Troupe structured itself as a collective from the beginning. This often meant long meetings to arrive at democratic decisions, but it created a sense of involvement. From the moment someone joined the Troupe they knew they were on an equal footing with everyone else in terms of the usual democratic procedures. Votes were rarely taken in practice, but consensus was generally arrived at on difficult issues after long and exhaustive debate. People in the Troupe argued and disagreed as in most of the alternative organisational structures of the time, but no one ever felt that their views were not given an airing.

The method of creating shows varied but the usual process was something like this: there was a group decision about the subject matter and perhaps the overall style; then the writer did some basic research and began drafting a script; the actors assisted in the research and workshopped scenes through various drafts with the writer/director.

Gender equality was a working principle from the beginning. The Troupe always tried to establish as close as possible to an equal male/female ratio in choice of actors. However, few women emerged from within the company to write or direct, or came to the company to work in those roles. In 1982 Jan McDonald of Melbourne's West Community Theatre directed the second production of It's MAD. and Fiona Winning, who joined the Troupe as an actor, wrote and performed a one-person show. Fiona subsequently wrote and directed elsewhere and Therese Collie, who joined the Troupe as an actor for Viva Indonesia in 1979, later went on to write and direct in stage and film.

The Troupe made repeated attempts to involve non-actors (such as the children's activities coordinator Mick O'Byrne, the Aboriginal Health Centre director Ted Curry, the North Queensland carpenter and activist Greg King, the Brisbane lawyer Paul Richards) in the creative work of the Troupe.

There was also a circulation of roles: actors became administrators, and vice-versa. While recognising the importance of professional expertise, there was a real attempt to make cross-experience contacts. This enriched the shows — Ted Curry's involvement for example led to revisions of The White Man's

Mission — and also helped in placing the Troupe's work in appropriate social and political contexts.

Within the Troupe too, an administrator who had been an actor was able to organise show bookings knowing the problems the actors would encounter, while an administrator who became an actor had a reverse appreciation of the need to accept paying bookings, no matter how difficult they were to fulfill.

5. PERFORMANCE STYLE

Agit-prop and Satire

The Troupe's performance style was very much determined by the influence of Albert Hunt as well as the type of venues we usually played in. The style changed very slowly over the decade.

Shows were necessarily presented in a two-dimensional style. There was a need for actors to face the audience in acoustically difficult situations — open air, large sheds, echo-filled cafeterias, the factory floor during relatively quiet lunch breaks with generators and machinery humming in the background — simply so they could be heard. Actors had to develop strong projection techniques.

Delivery in this agit-prop style was usually straight out front, and we had to have props which were quite visible. We sometimes had to lift them up in non-realist fashion, simply so they could be seen, because the audience was often on the same level as the performers.

Quick changes were common, and usually took place behind a plywood proscenium arch with a curtain, a sort of parody of bourgeois theatre itself, which we carried with us and erected before each show.

The head was the highest and most visible part of the actor. Therefore, hats were used routinely to denote class, and type of characters. Actors would more often than not represent several characters in the one show, by costume and hat changes. In much of the Troupe's work, the actor played a symbol more than an individual character in the Stanislavskian sense.

We were borrowing from or discovering anew the essential elements of popular marketplace theatre. Big symbols, refined ideas. There was no time, particularly in a lunch time factory show, to develop a complicated lengthy argument. The refinement of the ideas took place during the research and development process. By the time we got to performance we needed to have concise ideas, well integrated into the theatrical style, and reinforcing the ironic power of the particular metaphor.

The Troupe's use of music was, initially, borrowings from popular culture. Old songs were sung in an ironic context to underline the message. But with *Viva Indonesia* in 1979, this aspect of the Troupe's shows changed drastically. Of the musical team for that show, Ken MacLeod was the only one to stay with the Troupe for a longer period. He wrote music for several Troupe shows and often, as in the case of *Cockatoo Rock* the following year, surreal lyrics of great power. We wondered why no one had thought of writing songs before.

The soul of the Troupe's work was satire. Quick, witty, guerrilla attacks on the funny bone and the intelligence at the same time. Most of the work was then done by the audience in reaction and subsequent reflection. Satire was the great weapon, with which even conservative audiences could be made to laugh while they listened to our arguments.

6. FUNDING

The Troupe was funded from 1975 to 1982 by the Community Arts and Theatre Boards of the Australia Council. Apart from a small amount of funding in the very early years of the PTT, we never received any money from the Queensland Government. This, presumably, was a direct result of the Bjelke-Petersen Government's antipathy to critical culture. We never had proof, of course, but we operated on advice that our submissions to the Queensland Government for funding were lifted out of the usual process and became a concern of Cabinet, from which a directive was issued to the Division of Cultural Activities that we were never to be funded. This, along with the Queensland Police Force, Special Branch surveillance of our activities, put us firmly in the ranks of the extra-parliamentary opposition. Humphrey McQueen pointed out that this refusal to fund us was a sign we were doing something right.

Theatre companies in the rest of the nation which received Australia Council funding had a joint annual meeting with their state arts department and the Theatre Board representatives in conjunction with their submissions. In the Popular Theatre Troupe's case, we went through the motions, talking to some purpose with the Theatre Board while the Queensland Arts Director sat as a non-contributing and impotent observer. Arts office directors in Queensland were put in a very awkward position. None of them ever had the intestinal fortitude to object to the Government's blatant and clearly unfair treatment of a theatre company which in the view of the Australia Council was artistically sound and worth supporting. The Bjelke-Petersen Government's intention, as carried out by a series of arts directors, amounted to political censorship. But there was no redress — the press in Queensland, then as now, was largely ineffective as an organ of social critique.

Occasionally word would come through that it was the time to make a new submission and ask for a bold amount of money, as someone had assured someone that they could get it through Cabinet, but we never had any real success. Always, the dead hand of the Bjelke-Petersen directive was there, preventing us from getting any funds. In no other state of the nation was there a theatre group funded by the Australia Council which was not receiving corresponding funding from its state government.

7. THE PTT AND THE THEATRE INDUSTRY

The social and political context in which the Troupe operated from 1974 to 1983 is an important factor in assessing its relationship to the rest of the theatre industry. This assessment necessarily falls into two parts: theatre in Queensland, and theatre in the rest of the country (at least in eastern Australia).

Because of the more lively tradition of alternative theatre in Sydney and Melbourne, the Troupe was always well received by the theatre community in those two cities. Indeed the theatre community itself there had been influenced by the radical ideas emanating from such places as the Pram Factory and the Nimrod, so that it was common to find actors in main-stage theatre who were quite responsive to the style and content of political theatre.

But the theatre community in Brisbane was, and largely still is, conservative. The Popular Theatre Troupe and the groups which carried on alternative theatre in its wake were generally regarded as of inferior quality by most of the practicing theatre workers whose aspirations were, socially and politically, quite narrow. This was unfortunate for the Troupe members, because it meant that not only was the Government stacked against us, but our "natural" industrial allies were alienated from our work as well. It has been said by some that the siege mentality consequently adopted by the PTT produced good, even if solitary, theatre.

At the same time that the Troupe was passing out of existence, Bjelke-Petersen's gerrymander — inherited from the Labor Government of the previous generation and much improved since that time — allowed him to increase the National Party's support to the point where he could govern without his traditional partner, the Liberal Party. This meant things could only get worse for the Troupe, if it was to survive. But, as we pointed out several times in our satires, Bjelke-Petersen even at the peak of his power never commanded more than forty per cent of the popular vote.

For some of us, this single party minority government was a bitter pill to swallow. All those years in the wilderness and the PTT went to its grave without the scent of victory in its nostrils! Again, another Queensland Left tradition.

54

Crossing Theatrical Boundaries

The dominant theatre culture in Queensland mostly ignored the work of the PTT. Very few actors worked with ease in both alternative and main-stage theatre. Some practitioners crossed over, but most didn't. Many main-stage actors, who could have greatly improved the Troupe's artistic standard, regarded us with disdain. We therefore never had the joy of using their talents and they never had the joy of discovering the real social purpose of theatre!

At end of each year the collective (sometimes making a frightening interview panel of five or six!) interviewed applicants for the positions vacant for the following year. We often had to choose between talented actors with no politics and not so talented actors with good politics. And they were hard choices. Sometimes, wrong choices were probably made. Sometimes, actors who joined the Troupe with a low level of political commitment came out at the other end of their tour of duty with a completely changed outlook and set of opinions, largely as a result of the collaborative research methods and the familiarisation with political analysis which were integral to the development of Troupe shows.

Community Theatre

According to some definitions of Community Theatre, a necessary element is a geographical community. PTT never saw itself as this type of Community Theatre but rather as one serving a wider community in the realm of ideas. We toured constantly and therefore it was impossible to relate to a particular place and community. Our "community" was workers in factories in all parts of Australia, students in schools everywhere, prisoners in all sorts of prisons, people engaged in different pursuits both at work and at leisure.

The term *community* has an interesting history and has been used widely and with several different meanings in the last two decades. As a "category" it came from the social reform agenda of the early seventies and was originally employed to make a distinction between the usually elitist "high art" of the grand edifices and the elegant audience profile on the one hand, and the critical culture of the common people on the other.

Community arts were emerging as the critical and celebratory voice of the ordinary people. In the vanguard were a lot of disaffected artists from the mainstream, in many ways assisting "ordinary" people to find their voice. And this new movement brought into critical artistic practice many people who otherwise would never have considered themselves capable of it. The Popular Theatre Troupe played its part in this process by enlightening and empowering new audiences created from those parts of the population which did not normally frequent the theatre.

As we move on into the mid-nineties, the class aspects of all types of art need another review. The vibrancy of much of the early community arts movement has subsided into yet another version of elitism, in terms of practice and audience appeal. Perhaps each generation must establish its own cultural equilibrium and each individual and group within it must decide which side of the fence their conscience impels them to stand on.

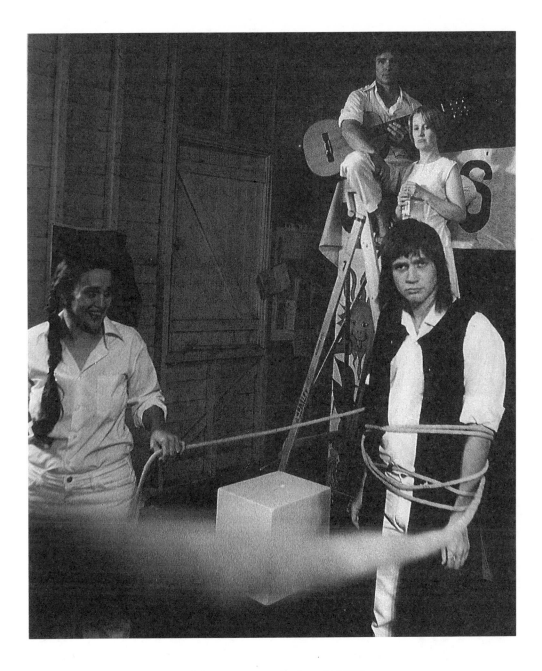

White Man's Mission (1975)

(at back) Duncan Campbell, Ros Atkinson
(at front) Kathryn Porrill, Nick Hughes

Millionaire's Handicap (1976)
(left to right) Nicola Scott, Janet Mahoney, Ros Atkinson, Duncan Campbell

Says Who? (1979)
(left to right) Therese Collie, Kathryn Porrill, Roger Rosser, Ken MacLeod

It's MAD (1981)
Michael Cummings and Julie Hickson

It's MAD (1982)
(left to right) Penny Glass, Fiona Winning, Nat Trimarchi, Allen Lyne

Crook Shop (1981)
(left to right) Julie Hickson, Ken MacLeod, Michael Cummings, Lynne Samson

A CHRONOLOGY OF THE POPULAR THEATRE TROUPE 1974 — 1983

by Errol O'Neill

1974

STAR TRICK
or
"SHE KNEW SHE'D SEEN ME ON TV AND SHE KNEW SHE LIKED ME, BUT SHE COULDN'T REMEMBER WHAT THE SHOW WAS"

Personnel:
Created and performed by Roslyn Atkinson, Ian Bauert, Roberta Bonnin, Duncan Campbell, Richard Fotheringham, Peter Clarke, Dick Freeland, Albert Hunt, Michael Macklin, Margaret Moore, Garrett Purtill, Peter Sutherland, Vicki Volkoff.

The Show:
Star Trick was an entertainment based on the idea that the American TV series *Star Trek* was being produced by the Australian impresario, Hector Crawford. A satire on current political events in Australia.

Development:
Star Trick began with workshops exploring the television characters and situations. The TV show was not being broadcast at the time, but was accessible through spin-off books. Initially the idea was to use a 'who are the aliens' sci-fi metaphor to write a show about aboriginal-white relations in Australia. This theme went forward in a different way into *The White Man's Mission* the next year. Just after rehearsals started, the 1974 federal election was announced, forced by a hostile Liberal Party controlled Senate on the newly elected Labor Government. This led to a radical revision of the nature and purpose of the show, which Richard Fotheringham rewrote in just a few days, using Prime Minister Gough Whitlam and the Liberal leader Billy Snedden as the principal antagonists. *Star Trick* was a relatively gentle satire compared to the harder-hitting later works, but succeeded in the challenge of successful performance in a wide range of informal venues, and helped the participants to build up a body of experience about what worked in such conditions. On this basis, the Troupe's performance style evolved — very cartoon-like two-dimensional

61

images, predominantly direct to the audience speech (even in dialogue with other characters), and the use of popular songs to punctuate and comment on the action.

Performance:
Brisbane — Shoppingtowns, hospitals, King George Square, Civic Centres, Town Halls, trade union clubs.

Comments:
This show was the forerunner to the formation of the Popular Theatre Troupe as such. Many of the actors remained and, with Albert Hunt the following year, produced and toured *The White Man's Mission*. In *Star Trick* the commitment of the ten actors, in terms of time and personal expense, was enormous. Only one actor received any remuneration whatsoever, and this was because she was a financial Equity member not in receipt of any other income. All the other actors had some alternative source of income but, in terms of travel costs, wear and tear on clothes and costume maintenance, were all well out of pocket. In a report on the project written for the Queensland Festival of the Arts by Richard Fotheringham we see the beginnings of some of the PTT's continuing concerns — the difficulty of performing in large and noisy venues, and the need for engaging visual content to attract and hold the interest of a passing crowd.

1975

THE PUNY LITTLE LIFE SHOW and RED CROSS

Personnel:
Directed by Brent McGregor.
Performers were Nick Hughes, Kathryn Porrill, Duncan Campbell.

The Show:
THE PUNY LITTLE LIFE SHOW by Roger McGough; and
RED CROSS by Sam Shepard. A double bill.

Development:
A number of members of the company had agreed to regroup in mid-1975 for another project, and the Australia Council agreed to fund another visit by Albert Hunt at this time. However, to secure funding to establish the Troupe professionally during 1975, the founding administrator, Peter Sutherland, obtained funds which had to be spent in the first half of the year, and suggested this project as a preparation for the larger program which commenced in June. Only Duncan Campbell of the previous year's acting group was available, but Kath Porrill had worked for another 1974 Festival of Arts group and knew the Troupe's style, while Nick Hughes had worked on similar projects in England before arriving in Australia in 1974. Brent McGregor was asked to direct the two plays — chosen as significant contemporary work and also because each

required only three actors. *Red Cross* was not a success and was quickly dropped from the repertoire, but *Puny* was a popular if lightweight piece which was regularly performed as a double bill with *The White Man's Mission* until *The White House Goes to the Movies* and *Dutch Treat* entered the repertoire in April 1976.

Performance:
Limited season at the Gallery Theatre in Bowen Hills in June.

Comments:
This was the only occasion on which the PTT produced work not written specifically for or by the Troupe or by Albert Hunt.

✼✼✼✼✼✼✼✼✼✼

THE WHITE MAN'S MISSION

Personnel:
Written by Richard Fotheringham and Albert Hunt.
Directed by Albert Hunt.
Performers were Kathryn Porrill, Margaret Moore, Roslyn Atkinson, Duncan Campbell, Nick Hughes.

The Show:
The White Man's Mission was a musical entertainment using the metaphor of a rousing revivalist meeting to present episodes in the history of Australia and the South Pacific. Racism, slavery and exploitation were examined in a bitterly humorous documentary about the fate of Aborigines after the arrival of the white man on the continent, and the fate of the 50,000 descendants of the South Sea Islanders still living in Australia today.

Development:
A large number of individual experiences went into the making of this complex and, for the Troupe, long (70 minute) show. Albert Hunt had grown up in the Pentecostal movement and knew many ideologically appalling but musically beautiful revivalist hymns; Nick Hughes had travelled around the Pacific on a tramp steamer and seen the effects of the US occupation of islands for atomic warfare testing; Kath Porrill came from North Queensland where about 40,000 people of South Sea Island descent still live; Richard Fotheringham and Roslyn Atkinson returned from work and study in London on alternative and political theatre techniques. Fotheringham did most of the basic research which he and Hunt shaped with the performers into script fragments; the overall metaphor and final scripting was principally Hunt's work, as was the direction.

Performance:
There is no doubt that it was the success of this show which gave the Troupe

national status and encouraged the Theatre Board to offer annual funding from 1986 to 1982. Seasons in Brisbane, Melbourne (at the Pram Factory), and Sydney (at the original Nimrod Street Theatre) attracted national publicity and were seen by, amongst others, Anthony Steele who contracted the Troupe to perform at the 1976 Adelaide Festival and to coordinate the Festival fringe activities that year. Another important series of performances were given at minimum-security prison farms in New South Wales, South Australia and Queensland, and a cut-down 25-minute section of the show (principally the section dealing with the Kanaka slave trade) was used for numerous factory lunch-hour performances. A North Queensland tour late in 1975 opened up new contacts and Townsville in particular became a major centre for Troupe performances and activities.

1976

THE WHITE HOUSE GOES TO THE MOVIES

Personnel:
Written by Albert Hunt.
Directed by Richard Fotheringham.
Performers were Roslyn Atkinson, Margaret Bornhorst, Duncan Campbell, Nick Hughes, Kathryn Porrill.

Development:
Albert Hunt proposed this project to the Adelaide Festival committee as a double bill with *The White Man's Mission*. It consisted of two of four short plays previously written by Hunt and performed by his Bradford company, based on some of Brecht's "learning plays" and on famous Hollywood movies. The two playlets each looked at an American presidency — Lyndon Johnson's, as if he were Longfellow Deeds, the simple country bumpkin who refuses to be corrupted by the city in Capra's *Mr Deeds Goes to Town* — and Richard Nixon's as if he were Marilyn Monroe in *Some Like It Hot*.

Performance:
A short Brisbane season preceded the Adelaide Festival season, but the show was rarely performed after that.

Comments:
Unfortunately, much of the humour depended on knowing the particular films and the Troupe, working without Hunt and with incomplete script fragments he forwarded, found the style and concepts difficult to stage. Hunt re-shaped the material immediately prior to the Festival performances in March 1976 but the shows were dropped soon after. This confirmed the general feeling in the Troupe that they needed to devise their own shows whenever possible, and was the last pre-written script used.

DUTCH TREAT

Personnel:
Written and directed by Richard Fotheringham.
Performers were Roslyn Atkinson, Margaret Bornhorst (to July 1976), Kath Porrill (to July 1976), Duncan Campbell, Nick Hughes, Judith James (from July 1976), Janet Mahoney (from July 1976).

Development:
The idea for this show came from the journalist Anthony Samson, who suggested in a book on the activities of multi-national companies that they were modern-day pirates in the precise sense of having allegiance to no nation but simply operating under flags of convenience. *Dutch Treat* had characters dressed as pirates but carrying businessmen's umbrellas and, in a Hollywood swashbuckling pirate-musical style combined with agit-prop placards and demonstration scenes, analysed the role of international capital in Australia, particularly after the sacking of the Whitlam government in November 1975.

Performance:
The play was workshopped in Adelaide and Melbourne early in 1976, and then joined the repertoire in April for a mid-year tour to North Queensland. It was after Laurie Carmichael and Fred Thompson of the Amalgamated Metal Workers' Union saw this show in Townsville that negotiations began which resulted in a major AMWU-sponsored tour of Sydney factory sites in September and October 1977.

Comments:
This show, the first scripted and directed by Fotheringham alone, was relatively simple and in a more agit-prop style, but its topical subject matter in the year when the role of international capital in destabilising the Whitlam government became widely known, and in the context of major protests and concern over the Fraser government's first actions, gave it an immediate impact with audiences.

****

THE MILLIONAIRE'S HANDICAP

Personnel:
Written and directed by Albert Hunt and Richard Fotheringham.
Performers were Nick Hughes, Roslyn Atkinson, Janet Mahoney, Duncan Campbell, Judith James.
The show was remounted in 1977 with the following cast: Janet Mahoney, John Lane, Nicola Scott, Greg King, Errol O'Neill.

The Show:
Based on a booklet published by Action for World Development about the activities of the Comalco Bauxite Mining Company in North Queensland, where the aboriginal people had been removed at gunpoint from their tribal lands. There was also evidence of transfer price fixing in Hong Kong to deny Australia a share of the profits resulting from the mining. *The Millionaire's Handicap* used training and racing horses as a metaphor for the treatment of different "races" of people by big business.

Development:
The show was the result of Albert Hunt's last visit as consultant and director for the Troupe and coincided with the beginnings of a major change of personnel. By the end of 1976 only Roslyn Atkinson and Richard Fotheringham were left of the original Troupe members, while Janet Mahoney had worked with the Troupe for six months. *The Millionaire's Handicap* was extensively rewritten and re-staged by the new company members at the start of 1977 as a short show specifically for factory lunch breaks.

Performance:
The show joined the repertoire in August 1976 and was played in Sydney and Melbourne (at the Pram Factory) and the next year through North Queensland.

Comments:
This was one of the Troupe's most accessible shows, with an easy to follow storyline and recognisable character types. (Roslyn Atkinson's 'The Little Punter' character was a particular favourite and she used it in several solo spots for community events.) A few scenes seemed to be dead spots, and it probably worked best after it had been shortened for factory lunch-break performances and it was extensively performed in that format in North Queensland mining towns during the first half of 1977.

1977

FALLOUT AND FOLLOW ME

Personnel:
Researched, written, designed and directed by Richard Fotheringham.
Performers were Greg King, Nicola Scott, Janet Mahoney, John Lane, Errol O'Neill.
Singing tutor: Mark Penman.

The Show:
A 25 minute script on the subject of uranium, the debate about domestic nuclear energy, and the work of large corporations such as Westinghouse and General Electric in trying to popularise domestic nuclear power stations in the

US and elsewhere, regardless of the dangers. The metaphor was that of a World War One recruiting rally. With songs from that era.

Development:
Actors started work with a relatively complete script. Some workshopping and further research by the actors.

Performance:
Season around Brisbane, then toured to North Queensland, New South Wales, Victoria and South Australia. Particular emphasis on lunchtime performances at worksites, including sugar mills in North Queensland.

Comments:
A good example of the PTT's analytical approach to the military industrial complex. Some school shows were memorable for awakening students to the harsh realities of corporate greed. Post-show discussions heard comments like 'But these big companies wouldn't build nuclear power stations if they weren't safe . . . would they?'

****

$TAMPEDE

Personnel:
Researched and written by Nick Hughes and Errol O'Neill.
Designed collaboratively.
Performed by Janet Mahoney, Nicola Scott, Greg King and John Lane.

The Show:
The history of trade unions in Australia and comment about the wages/inflation spiral. Wild West movies and pulp novels provided the metaphor and many old "western" songs were used, such as *Don't Fence Me In.*

Development:
Research and first draft by Hughes and O'Neill, workshop development with actors during early part of Central and North Queensland tour.

Performance:
Premiered in School of Arts, Moura. Then performed in the rest of Central and North Queensland, and in subsequent tour to New South Wales, Victoria and South Australia.

****

AN EVENT — ROSS RIVER PROVINCE (Townsville)

The Project:

During the NQ tour, a week was set aside for preparation of this one-day event, timed to coincide with Townsville's annual Pacific Festival. Many socially progressive groups in the Townsville area were contacted, such as the Conservation, Littoral and Wildlife Societies, the Aboriginal and TSI Legal Service (from Cairns), the Trades and Labour Council (TLC), The University Women's Group, the Movement Against Uranium Mining and the Youth Centre. These groups met nightly with Troupe members and other interested individuals in the basement of the Metalworkers' Union office to prepare their contribution to the event. Permission was gained to used the old Victoria Bridge across Ross Creek, just a short walk from Flinders Street, Townsville's main thoroughfare. The approach roads to the bridge had been cut off earlier so that, since the new bridge across the creek had been constructed, the old bridge roadway stood like an inaccessible platform over the water. We saw the possibility of creating an "island" out of the old bridge, and employing the imagery of the Hutt River Province of Western Australia. Ross River Province would secede from the nation and declare itself independent. With assistance from local tradesmen, and subject to regular health and safety inspection by the Townsville City Council, we built a broad staircase up to the level of the old bridge's roadway.

On the final Saturday of the Pacific Festival, when the city's streets were full of people, our week's preparation came to fruition, when all the various groups erected stalls along the length of the bridge roadway, much in the manner of a school fête. The overall satirical bent was reflected in the titles of the stalls. For instance, the Cairns Aboriginal and TSI Legal Service ran the Department of Caucasian and Mainlander Affairs, a reverse of the title of the then Federal department. Each stall was conceived of as a government department or facility, passports were issued to everyone as they entered the Ross River Province and people were encouraged to visit all departments and receive their particular visa-like stamps on their passports. The stamps — rubber and lino cuts — had been made during the nightly arts and crafts workshops conducted by the Troupe during the preceding week in the Metalworkers' basement. There were also food stalls and entertainment areas on the bridge.

The Troupe performed excerpts from its shows, and local musicians entertained the crowd of approximately 2,000 which passed through the event over the entire day.

****

AN EVENT — SUNSHINE SUPERSTATE (Brisbane)

The Project:
A comical, satirical extension of what Queensland might be like if it seceded from Australia and pursued its current trends more vigorously. As in The Ross River Province event in Townsville earlier in the year, passports were issued, visa stamps and certificates of citizenship were offered. The inventive ideas of the community groups involved contributed to the success of the day, which had been organised as a Warana/Queensland Festival of the Arts event in King George Square. Three thousand people passed through the event during the day. There were cane toad races, a darts board map of Queensland which you threw darts at to choose new National Parks (the dart board was made of tin), fertility cycle wheels of fortune, sewage disposal machines (it comes out just as it went in), displays, video programmes, an eerie ultra-violet nuclear reactor which you walked through and then came out giving a positive reading on a geiger counter, and a leaky Liberian oil tanker.

****

LADIES DAY

Personnel:
Researched, written and directed by Richard Fotheringham.
Designed by David Brinson.
Performers were Greg King, John Lane, Nicola Scott, Jo Caust and Errol O'Neill. In the 1978 remount, the cast initially was: Peter Murphy, Lindy Morrison, Jo Caust, John Lane, Errol O'Neill. Jane Ahlquist replaced Jo Caust at mid year.

The Show:
In a broad metaphor inspired by popular women's magazines and the television commercials which promote them, this show looked at women's place in society from an historical and economic viewpoint, focusing on the fact that social attitudes to women in the workforce had largely determined the lifestyle options available to women. A major source of information and argument was Anne Summers' landmark book "*Damned Whores and God's Police*" which dealt with the history of women in Australia. A sub-metaphor in *Ladies Day* was that of a ring event at the Royal Brisbane Show. This reflected the frequent historical references to women as animals — objects to be bought, sold, fattened, slimmed, trained, punished, rewarded and petted.

Development:
Rehearsed in mid-1977.

Performance:
The show played in various venues around Brisbane, then toured to New South Wales, Victoria and South Australia. Particularly effective in schools. The 1978 remount toured to North Queensland.

Comments:
The show was particularly well received in a number of private Catholic girls' schools, where the themes of women's social and economic independence from men seemed to accord with the career model provided by the modern wave of progressive nuns and women teachers. On the other hand, at the state school in the south-western Queensland town of Dirranbandi, the post-show discussion was distinguished by an outpouring of declarations supporting traditional gender roles. A male teacher, and some vocal male students, generally ridiculed the central argument of the show. Afterwards, in private discussion with the female teachers, we received earnest support and an assurance that the show had a great deal of meaning to some of the downtrodden girls at the school who didn't have the confidence to raise their voices during the discussion. Thus, the entire rationale of the show was vindicated.

****

THE WHITE MAN'S MISSION (in England)

The Project:
Six former members of the PTT formed a cooperative in England in September 1977, in order to mount a London season and English tour of the play [see notes about *White Man's Mission* in 1975 above]. The Arts Council of Great Britain provided a cash grant, the Calouste Gulbenkian Foundation provided a minibus and the Bradford College (where Albert Hunt was a senior lecturer in Community Media) provided "in kind" resources.

Personnel:
Directed by Albert Hunt.
Performers: Duncan Campbell, Kathryn Porrill, Nick Hughes, Janet Mahoney, Mick O'Byrne.

Performance:
Thirty three performances were given at 15 venues in London and other parts of England in the final months of 1977. A total audience of 1,519 saw the show.

OUT FOR A DUCK — The Story of Queensland

Personnel:
Researched, written and directed by Richard Fotheringham.
Designer was David Brinson.
Movement tutor: Bev Nevin.
Singing tutor: Mark Penman.
The performers were Peter Murphy, Lindy Morrison, Errol O'Neill, John Lane, Jo Caust.
At mid-year, Jo Caust was replaced by Jane Ahlquist, and extensive revision and expansion of the show took place, under the direction of David Gittins.

The Show:
Using the metaphor of Disney's comic characters, the show examined the history of Queensland since World War Two with particular emphasis on the exploitation of the state's natural resources by multi-national mining companies. Following the content of Disney comics (rather than the cartoons), we represented the Utah Development Corporation (and other multi-nationals) as Scrooge McDuck, receiving a warm welcome and a promise of assistance from his nephew Donald (Queensland Premier Johannes Bjelke-Petersen). Scrooge travelled all over the world to bring back money to his money bin in Duckburg, USA. He was even able to hoodwink Bjelke-Petersen's predecessors, the Beagle Boys (Labor governments up to and including that of Vince Gair).

Development:
A key source of information, and inspiration for our satire, came from *How to Read Donald Duck* by Dorffman and Mattelart, which described the insidious nature of the apparently harmless and widespread distribution of Disney comics among a largely illiterate population in South America. Disney comics, as well as the CIA and other American propaganda agencies, were winning the hearts and minds of the people while gaining tacit approval for the American economic mastery of their resources.

Performance:
After a varied season in Brisbane and South East Queensland, the show travelled to North Queensland.

Comments:
The Troupe was surprised that the presentation of this show, which mercilessly lampooned the Queensland Premier, was never apparently subverted by any state government agency. We had collected evidence that the Queensland Special Branch (Bjelke-Petersen's political police) was watching the Troupe's activities generally.

Ironically, the only two PTT shows ever banned by the Queensland Education Department were banned because they dealt with corruption and misbehaviour in the Queensland Police force. This was in 1981 and 1982, five years before the Fitzgerald Inquiry into police corruption.

****

THE GREAT AUSTRALIAN BITE

Personnel:
David Gittins, Lindy Morrison, Errol O'Neill, Peter Murphy, John Lane, Jane Ahlquist.

The Show:
This show was a compilation of bits from previous PTT shows put together by the performers.

Development:
The shortened versions of *Ladies Day* and *Out for a Duck* were not always appropriate for the short lunch break at factories. So, sketches from those two shows and others, including *The White Man's Mission*, were built into a new lunchtime show timed to last exactly twenty minutes.

Performance:
Various worksites around Brisbane and South East Queensland.

Comments:
The show was a satirical presentation of mainly economic observations about many aspects of Australian society. It didn't always meet with a warm response. Perhaps it was too varied and would have been better received had it taken up only one theme instead of several.

****

AN EVENT — THE (Non-stop Sunshine Superstate Shopping Plaza) MAZE (Townsville)

The Project:
An attempt to relive the success of *Ross River Province*. It wasn't quite as spectacular, but nevertheless was reasonably successful as a showcase of current social issues. A similar approach was taken — local groups meeting nightly under the Metalworkers' office. The old Victoria bridge was either not available or not desirable (I forget which) and a section of Flinders Street was set aside for us instead. With the help of rolls of black plastic and hessian we created a maze, with spaces for the local groups to set up stalls. The walls were

seven or eight feet high and the people walked through, meeting various performers (Troupe members and locals) and visiting the stalls. Again, it was during the Pacific Festival when the streets of Townsville were full of people. The maze had the feeling of sideshow alley, and the various groups that ran stalls were set up in all sorts of nooks and crannies.

****

AN EVENT — TREASURE ISLAND (Brisbane)

The Project:
This was the last big public event organised by the PTT. Similar to the *Ross River Province* and *The Maze* in Townsville, it was a gathering place for local oppositional forces wishing to promote debate on critical social issues. Various Brisbane groups prepared displays. During the preceding week Troupe members and volunteers built an enormous two-dimensional facade representing the side of a pirate ship. The large sections of the ship were built in the Troupe's base, an old wooden church hall at 60 Waterworks Road, Red Hill. The pieces were then assembled early on the final Saturday morning of the Warana Festival in King George Square. Truckloads of sand were ordered, and the pools and fountains of the square were used as various lagoons and coves of Treasure Island. One memorable issue of the event was the proposed bridge to Stradbroke Island. We were able to provide a graphic illustration of the ecological destruction of the island that would, it was argued, follow construction of a bridge, by asking members of the public to "walk the plank" — that is, to cross a section of water with a bag of rubbish and throw cans and bottles on a beach.

****

AN EVENT — THE MAZE
(Richlands State High School)

The Project:
Following the same principles as the Townsville *Maze*, the troupe worked with a group of high school students at Richlands, one of the two high schools serving the Inala area. The issues dealt with were slightly different, of course, given the teenage audience. Much emphasis was given to rock and roll in the presentation of ideas in the maze.

VIVA INDONESIA

Personnel:
Written and directed by Richard Fotheringham.
The performers were Jane Ahlquist, Ken MacLeod, Roger Rosser, Therese Collie, Clare McKenna, Kathryn Porrill, Roger Allen. Music composed by Jane Ahlquist and Frank Millward.
Lyrics by Richard Fotheringham, Jane Ahlquist and Frank Millward.
Musical director Jane Ahlquist.
Costumes by Anna Papas.

The Show:
An historical overview of Indonesia, focusing on the 1975 invasion of East Timor. In this landmark show, the Troupe departed from many of its former elements of style. There was satire, surely, in this dissertation on imperialism and the third world, but there were also many other things — shadow puppets in the traditional Indonesian style; compiled newsreel footage; songs written specifically for the show; an impressive line-up of seven performers, more than the Troupe had ever employed in one show up to this point. *Viva Indonesia* was a broad canvas, an exemplary piece of social critique in which political analysis, emotional reality, and intellectual observations were synthesised into a compelling two-act entertainment which signalled that the Popular Theatre Troupe had entered a new stage of artistic integrity.

Development:
Richard Fotheringham and several other writers had been invited by Rick Billinghurst, director of La Boîte Theatre, to contribute to a project called *Happy Birthday, East Timor* in 1977 to commemorate the suffering of the Timorese caused by the Indonesian invasion of 1975. *Happy Birthday* was a large, multifaceted theatre show which worked relatively well for the consciousness-raising project it was intended to be. But Richard Fotheringham still felt that the ideas could be expanded into something more powerful and tour beyond La Boîte.

Performance:
After a season in Brisbane and South East Queensland, the show toured to North Queensland, Darwin, Melbourne, Sydney and Canberra. *Viva Indonesia* broke new ground for the Troupe by touring to Mt Isa and Darwin. In Darwin, much closer to the political and geographical reality of the subject matter, it roused passions and caused arguments.

Comments:
For the first time, the Troupe wrote its own music for a show. From this show on it was normal, largely because of the songwriting ability of Ken MacLeod,

for the Troupe to write new material rather than reach back into the gallery of established popular songs to enhance our political arguments and dramatic presentation.

POPULAR THEATRE TROUPE'S AUSTRALIA

Personnel:
Researched, written and directed by Errol O'Neill, with assistance from Pat Laughren.
Performers were Teresa Wilkinson, John Lane, Duncan Campbell.
The show was remounted in the latter half of 1979 with Ken MacLeod, Therese Collie, Kathryn Porrill and Roger Rosser.
In the 1980 remount Malcolm Bell replaced Ken MacLeod.
Costumes by Anna Papas.

The Show:
Based on Manning Clarke's Short History, *Australia* was basically a satirical overview, looking at Australian history from a class perspective. Many traditional songs were used, ironically placed. The metaphor was primarily that of a travelling troupe of players, trying to decide what to perform and by chance falling into a telling of the story of Australia. Sub-metaphors were found in popular entertainment such as TV quiz shows, commercials.

Development:
Initial ideas were scripted and workshopped by the director and actors, with the participation of Pat Laughren.

Performance:
The show performed around Brisbane and then toured to North and Central Queensland, Australian Commonwealth Territory and New South Wales.

Comments:
The beginning of Errol O'Neill's period as resident writer-director for the PTT.

****

SAYS WHO?

Personnel:
Researched, written and directed by Errol O'Neill, with assistance from Pat Laughren.
The performers were Ken MacLeod, Roger Rosser, Kathryn Porrill, and Therese Collie.

In the 1980 remount, Malcolm Bell replaced Ken MacLeod.
Music by Ken MacLeod.
Costumes by Robby Billinghurst.
Set design by Bruce Wolfe.

The Show:
A documentary satire on the mass communications media and the psychology of the advertising industry. A series of metaphors served the production. A "radio play" with outlandish sound effects was performed to outline the link between the commercial media and capitalism. Kathryn Porrill, in the persona of Keith Murdoch, delivered a speech to the audience as if they were a journalism class, as a means of explaining why the Australian media are in the hands of so few people.

Development:
Initial ideas were scripted and workshopped by the director and actors, with the participation of Pat Laughren. A foundation source was Humphrey McQueen's *Media Monopolies*. McQueen, fortuitously visiting his home town of Brisbane during the rehearsal period, was able to attend some of the rehearsals and make a very valuable contribution to the development of the script.

Performance:
The show worked particularly well in schools where it provided a suitably analytical commentary on what was then becoming a very popular item on the school curriculum — media studies.

Comments:
Says Who? was revived for a Mass Media Education national conference arranged by Australian Teachers of Media (ATOM) in 1988 and was performed by students of Kingston High School under the direction of teacher Chris Hayward.

****

THE COMMUNITY ARTS CENTRE

In its early years, the Troupe used many rehearsal halls and stored costumes, props and sets in different places — usually under members' houses. In 1978, however, we were successful in finding a permanent home in the hall attached to St Barnabas' Church at 60 Waterworks Road, Red Hill. There was room there for an office as well as rehearsal space and some limited storage facilities.

After spending a year in these relatively luxurious surroundings, we felt confident enough to offer our material and organisational resources to a wider spectrum of community artists and activists. John Lane, who had been a Troupe performer (1977-79), initiated the move to open up 60 Waterworks Road as a venue for workshops and rehearsals for street theatre, street choir and other groups.

There was a perceived need for activities which offered more direct community participation in the sort of alternative arts which the Troupe was involved in. There was also a need to extend and consolidate the network of Popular Theatre Troupe supporters.

The Community Arts Centre began in 1979 with three part-time workers, John Lane, Bruce Wolfe and Lynne Samson, who coordinated activities for two years. In 1981 Chris Maver took over the role of coordinator.

The Centre opened with a celebratory Community Open Day in April 1979. The program included a Popular Theatre Troupe performance, kite-making, stilt-walking, face-painting and other outside activities conducted by Ian Reece of the Children's Activities Group, a bush dance with The Verandah Band, performances by the Street Choir and an evening of classic films. Food was supplied by a number of local community groups. Subsequent open days were held in a nearby park with an emphasis on participation.

The projects and activities of the Centre drew on local artists and long term supporters and members of the Troupe. Sunday film nights were established with assistance and advice from Pat Laughren and Rhonda Fadden. Films included classics and political and experimental works obtained through the Australian Film Institute. Workshops included silk-screening (Bruce Wolfe and others), dance (Bev Nevin), clowning, street theatre and drama (John Lane, Doug Anderson and others). A series of variety concerts in which local artists were invited to share their works included performances by Gerard Lee, Steve Capelin, Alex Black, Kath Porrill, Linsey Pollak, David Lord and a wide range of other artists representing ethnic community groups in Brisbane. The concerts presented a cross-section of musicians, story-tellers, magicians and clowns. The Verandah Band, which included former Troupe performer Roger Rosser, conducted bush dances on a regular basis at 60 Waterworks Road. The street choir and street theatre groups which used the Centre as a base performed at many protests and rallies in Brisbane.

60 Waterworks Road was an experiment in community involvement which demonstrated the potential for community arts activities in Brisbane. Its fortunes were always dependent on the fortunes of the PTT itself, so by the time the Troupe lost its funding at the end of 1982 the Community Arts Centre had ceased to function. But it had left seeds which went on to flower in other parts of Brisbane's alternative arts scenario.

OUT OF WORK, OUT OF MIND

Personnel:
Researched, written and directed by Errol O'Neill, with assistance from Pat Laughren.
The performers were Kathryn Porrill, Roger Rosser, Therese Collie and Malcolm Bell.
In the 1981 remount the cast was Michael Cummings, Julie Hickson, Ken MacLeod and Lynne Samson.
Design by Bruce Wolfe.
Costumes by Fiona MacDonald.

The Show:
Employment, unemployment, the nature of work, and the current economic recession provided the subject matter for this 45 minute documentary satire, which also widened out to explain a number of political theories by means of comic monologues delivered within the metaphor of a clown troupe trying to find something interesting to perform.

Development:
Substantial amounts of script were written and then workshopped by the director and actors.

Performance:
The usual PTT venues around Brisbane. Toured to Canberra, Adelaide (Australian Drama Festival), Melbourne, Albury in 1981.

****

COCKATOO ROCK

Personnel:
Initial impetus for the project came from Ken MacLeod and Roger Allen.
Directed by Robert (Bomber) Perrier, on loan from Murray River Performing Group.
Design and set construction by Bruce Wolfe.
Performers: Ken MacLeod on vocals and guitar; Roger Allen percussion, guitar and vocals; Alexandra Black lead vocals; Peter O'Brien on drums; David Osborne on violin and guitar; Terrie Kavanagh on bass.
Michael Fisher was the sound and lighting technician.

The Show:
At first, three 45 minute segments. Later, two one hour segments. The original idea was to use the Troupe's traditional tools of political satire within the context of a popular rock and roll show. Eight talented musicians and singers were enlisted. Difficulties of many kinds arose, however, and the envisaged satirical sketch content occupied less of the programme than the music. However, the excellence of the music and the challenging nature of the lyrics provided an unexpected degree of artistic and political impact. Marketing and logistical problems meant that the show, although very entertaining and artistically very strong, did not have the long run and the wide audience originally planned. The Troupe had no accumulated corporate expertise in managing and touring rock bands and so, as the *Cockatoo Rock* project came to an earlier than planned close, we realised that there was one more avenue of infiltrating popular entertainment which could be fruitfully explored if the requisite personal and material resources were available.

Development:
The original idea of *Cockatoo Rock* was conceived late in 1978. Although the Troupe knew it would be difficult to form and organise a show band employing seven people along with the large amount of sound equipment necessary for rock and roll, it was decided that we should go ahead with the project for the following reasons: 1. To counter the lack of political and social comment in Pub and Club entertainment; 2. To get the PTT known to a wider cross-section of the community; 3. To give musicians and writers an opportunity to express what they considered to be important material in their own medium. Ken MacLeod had spent some time writing music and lyrics, Roger Allen organised the production details, Bomber Perrier was engaged to give the project overall dramatic shape and direction, and attempts were made to develop sketch material to blend the musical numbers together. But the music was so strong and the dramatic ability of most of the performers so inconsistent that it soon became clear that the sketches were being overpowered in terms of audience pull. The venues where *Cockatoo Rock* performed were mostly pubs. Such audiences, attracted by rock and roll and alcohol, were not usually attentive enough to appreciate sketches. Even some of the sketches which did make it into the programme were eventually dropped for the sake of retaining the attention of the audiences.

Performance:
Pubs and similar music venues, as well as campuses, around Brisbane, South East Queensland, Central Queensland and the Bowen Basin, Mackay, Townsville, Rockhampton, and Northern New South Wales.

CROOK SHOP

Personnel:
Written by Richard Fotheringham.
Directed by Doug Anderson.
Music by Ken MacLeod with assistance from John Wilsteed and Sharon Raschke.
Set design by Bob Daley.
Performers were Ken MacLeod, Julie Hickson, Michael Cummings, Lynne Samson.

The Show:
The title was an ironic twist on *Cop Shop*, a long-running soap on commercial television. The TV show was used as the metaphor, with enough ironic references to maintain the running gag. But the substance of the show was significant, in that it dealt with police corruption and predated the Fitzgerald Inquiry by four years.

Development:
The script was entirely written before rehearsals commenced. A few minor changes were made during the rehearsal process. Some names were changed to prevent possible legal action. The major source was the Report of the Committee of Inquiry into the Enforcement of Criminal Law in Queensland, 1977 (The Lucas Report).

Performance:
The show performed around Brisbane at all the usual venues, except government schools. The Education Department banned the show on the grounds that it 'did not encourage respect for law and order'. Toured to Canberra, Adelaide (Australian Drama Festival), Melbourne, Albury, Central and North Queensland, Sydney.

Comments:
A good example of the theatre of social criticism. To incur the wrath of the then Queensland Government proved the Troupe was doing something important and socially beneficial. The show was shown to be prophetic a few years later when police corruption had become so bad that the Government had no option but to instigate the Fitzgerald Inquiry.

It's MAD

Personnel:
Written and directed by Errol O'Neill with research and script assistance from David Biggins and collaborative research and development by the performers.
Music by Ken MacLeod.
Design, set and props by Beverly Hill assisted by Jenny Brasher.
Costumes made by Kathryn Porrill.
The performers were Ken MacLeod, Julie Hickson, Michael Cummings, Lynne Samson.
For the 1982 remount, directed by Jan McDonald of Melbourne's West Community Theatre, the performers were Penny Glass, Allen Lyne, Nat Trimarchi and Fiona Winning.

The Show:
A 55 minute show about the history and present threat of nuclear war and the evils of militarism. Set in the metaphor of an insane asylum, the actors played a series of terrifying characters which arose out of their "MADness". The mad professor, regretting he had told anyone about his discoveries in nuclear fission, General Electric, the crazy inventor of domestic appliances; the American president; the CIA; and a host of other Cold War figures satirically illustrating the insanity of **Mutual Assured Destruction**. The military industrial complex was analysed and, towards the end of the show, all pretence at satire was quite purposely dropped for a dramatic monologue based on extracts from Wilfred Burchett's post-Hiroshima journalism and from the book on Hiroshima by J. Hersey. The actors removed their white smocks — the link between them and the insane asylum metaphor — and presented the final section in simple black clothes. The audience was left sometimes depressed by the description of the Hiroshima victims, but the company decided this was appropriate in view of the enormity of that bombing. The cast for the 1982 remount felt that the show should end with more of a sense of optimism, and some minor textual and production changes were made to this effect.

Development:
After initial research by the writer assisted by Pat Laughren, extra research was undertaken by the original cast. The show was workshopped and devised by the director and performers over an eight week period.

Performance:
All the usual venues around Brisbane. Toured to Sydney, Melbourne, Albury-Wodonga, Canberra in 1981. The 1982 cast took the show to Central and North Queensland.

HANDS ACROSS THE PACIFIC

Personnel:
Written by Errol O'Neill.
Designed and directed by John Watson.
Research assistance by David Biggins, Geoff Dow and Pat Laughren.
Collaborative research, scripting and development by the performers: Penny Glass, Nat Trimarchi, Allen Lyne, Fiona Winning.
Costumes by Kathryn Porrill.
Set construction by John Watson and Errol O'Neill.

The Show:
Starting with various economic facts, such as that 80 per cent of Australia's mineral wealth was owned and controlled by overseas interests, the PTT set out to examine the social, political and economic ties between Australia and the rest of the world, particularly the USA. The show looked at the effects of foreign control on our politicians and the decisions they made from World War Two to the present.

Development:
Commencing with some basic information and a few imaginative ideas about presentation, the actors, writer and director workshopped scenes and began to build the structure of the show.

Performance:
After the usual venues around Brisbane, toured to Newcastle, Sydney, Albury-Wodonga, Melbourne and Adelaide.

Comments:
The show, although entertaining and successful in its final form, had a difficult birth. Disagreements about content and form, as well as about working methods, arose during the rehearsal period. While the arguments and their resolution are now history, the phenomenon of disagreement is worth noting for analytical reasons. There was a significant break in the creative continuity of the PTT at the beginning of 1982 when *Hands Across the Pacific* was being produced. All four actors were new to the Troupe as was the director/designer. The actors in particular felt they were under pressure to conform to an established house style, and often resisted this perceived pressure. It is always difficult to assess the need for new directions without denying the value of the old forms and styles, and much of the argument hung on this question. So, while artistic disagreement was nothing new to the PTT, the signs began to appear in this case that the Troupe was now ready to explore new ideas about presentation and form, even about content and research methods.

****

TEA'S COMPANY

Personnel:
Written and performed by Fiona Winning.
Directed by Alexandra Black.

The Show:
A 20 minute satire which examined the role played by women in the workforce. Joy Jolly, tea-lady extraordinaire, delivered tea coffee and biscuits as she took up the issues of the time — women and unionism, the gender bias in occupations, apprenticeships, sexual harassment at work.

Development:
The writer/performer based her work on interviews she conducted with several older women unionists from the Federated Clerks, Meatworkers, and the Women's Auxiliary of the Seamen's Union, about their experiences in the workforce and in the union movement. Director and writer/performer collaborated on development of the script.

Performance:
Around Brisbane at various venues including worksites and women's shelters, then toured to Central and North Queensland.

****

THE STATE WE'RE IN
(A Revue of the Commonwealth Games)

Personnel:
Writer: Stephen Stockwell.
Performers: Nat Trimarchi, Penny Glass, Allen Lyne, Fiona Winning.
Director: Doug Anderson.
Set painted by Jamie Maclean.
Music by Nat Trimarchi and Penny Glass.
Choreography and dance tutoring by Bev Nevin.
Costumes by Life Line and Wenda Matthews.

The Show:
A 45 minute satire on Queensland politics and the way Queenslanders see themselves and want others to see them. The show also dealt with Aboriginal Land Rights. A response to the increasing oppressiveness of the Queensland Government, particularly the special police powers conferred during the period of the 1982 Commonwealth Games held in Brisbane.

Development:
Developed, written and produced collectively by the company in a three week period.

Performance:
Around Brisbane, then a tour to Central and North Queensland.

Comments:
This show was banned by the Education Department from performance in Government schools because it 'did not encourage respect for law and order'. Ironically, this ban was placed just a few years before the Fitzgerald Inquiry was instigated. But opposition to the Troupe's presentation of critical ideas came from the ranks of unionists as well. In Collinsville, traditionally a radical labour stronghold, interjections were made during the show and arguments developed later with some members of the audience — prompted by the Troupe's outspoken criticism of the then state government's attitude to the Land Rights question. This was seen by some of the Troupe members as an indication that the ties between the union movement and the Troupe could no longer be taken for granted.

1983

LIMITED LIFE

Personnel:
Written by Kerry O'Rourke.
Directed by Doug Anderson.
The performers were Nat Trimarchi, Katrina Devery, Maggie Nevins, Gavan Fenelon. Penny Glass replaced Maggie Nevins for a later series of special performances.

The Show:
A play which focused on the work hazards of asbestos, but which also commented on all occupational health and safety issues. It also celebrated working class culture through the use of songs and language that were familiar to and popular with the target audience.

Development:
The writer researched with the help of several trade unions concerned with the asbestosis issue, and worked with an asbestosis victim to develop a first draft which was then workshopped and developed with director and actors.

Performance:
After a main house season at Metro Arts in Brisbane, a shortened version toured to campuses and worksites.

Comments:
Helen Abrahams of the Workers' Health Centre linked up with the performers at some of the worksites to speak to workers about asbestosis issues. These public meetings, arranged by the Health Centre, were then followed by an abridged version of the show. The season at the Metro Theatre was successful, drawing small but responsive audiences, some of whom were families of asbestosis victims who appreciated the airing of the issues. The worksite shows were less successful because time was limited — usually to around half an hour — and workers seemed more intent on lunch and socialising.

****

WAGE INVADERS

Personnel:
Devised by the performers and Dee Martin with Glenn Perry in the key writing role.
Directed by Bernie Lewis.
Performers were Glenn Perry, Gavan Fenelon, Katrina Devery.

The Show:
Technology and its impact on the workforce. A compilation of relevant pieces from previous PTT shows were stitched together with a linking narrative. *Wage Invaders* used game show references and other devices to plot the status of the worker in the context of the growth of technology in modern working history.

Development:
Ian McLean of the ATEA (Australian Telecommunications Employees Union), an old friend of the Troupe, saw the need for a show which dealt with the effect technology was about to have on the workforce. He was instrumental in providing ideas for the development of the show and access to worksites for later performances.

Performance:
Campuses, worksites, La Boîte.

Comments:
A largely didactic piece of theatre which appealed to trade union audiences but missed the mark with campus audiences.

****

AS THE CROW FLIES

Personnel:
Script written by Michael Cummings and Glenn Perry in collaboration with Dee Martin and the performers.
Directed by Michael Cummings.
Performers were Katrina Devery, Gavan Fenelon and Glenn Perry.

The Show:
A cynical satire on both sides of politics. The Labor Party's role in introducing the gerrymander to Queensland was acknowledged. The show focussed on the invidious choice faced by voters who had to choose between a tyrannical Bjelke-Petersen regime on the one hand and an uninspiring Labor Party on the other. The state had been turned into one large theme park, Japanese investors were buying part of it and turning it into an enclave which excluded the natives. The sale of Queensland as a tourist mecca.

Development:
The writers provided a script which was then workshopped and developed collaboratively with the actors. Michael Cummings was chosen as director because of his stand-up comedy skills. There was a conscious desire to move beyond the constraints of the didacticism of some of the Troupe's previous shows. Narrative was less of a concern. Getting people to laugh and be captivated by the material was of greater interest. This was a fresh attempt to put politics into a language that ordinary people could relate to and enjoy.

Performance:
The show premiered at the first Community Theatre Conference in Adelaide, then toured to various places in South East Queensland.

****

THERE'S MORE TO LIFE THAN JUST SNOGGING, BARRY

Personnel:
Group devised by the performers and the writer, Hugh Watson.
Directed by Dee Martin.
Performers were Katrina Devery, Gavan Fenelon, Glenn Perry and Leah Cotterell.

The Show:
An exploration of gender issues, relationships, body image, sexual harassment and contraception. The show used a series of comic sequences and was even more sketch-based than *As the Crow Flies*.

Development:
The show was developed collaboratively within a very short time frame to take advantage of an offer from La Boîte's popular late night venue, La Bamba.

Performance:
A limited number of performances at La Boîte (La Bamba).

Comments:
Although it was received well at La Bamba, attempts to take individual sketches from the show to the emerging Brisbane comedy venues proved difficult. This was the last PTT show. The Troupe disbanded soon after and a huge garage sale was held at our Red Hill base. A number of pieces of Troupe equipment passed on to the emerging Street Arts Community Theatre Company including the company van, "Bluey", which saw further service not only with Street Arts but later with Rock'n'Roll Circus.

PART THREE

●

ORDER
BY
NUMBERS

ORDER BY NUMBERS, TEATRO UNIDAD Y LIBERACION AND THE NEW ACTORS COMPANY

by Hugh Watson and Penny Glass

Order By Numbers (OBN) was a collective of theatre workers that put on three shows during 1985 and 1986 — A Few Short Wicks in Paradise, *Tall Tales From The Altered State* and *Casualties* written for the Queensland Nurses Union. **Teatro Unidad y Liberacion** was a performance group that came together to put on a bilingual Spanish English play *Volcanes* in 1987. Both groups had a number of personnel in common, and were both administrated under an incorporated body called **The New Actors Company**. Although these shows all had political intentions, and although the majority of people involved were ex-members of the Popular Theatre Troupe, these projects were radically different in style from the old Troupe shows.

The final unfunded year of the PTT put an enormous strain on the people involved. Nevertheless it allowed workers to take risks with the established Popular Theatre Troupe style, something that many people had wanted to do previously, only to find themselves constrained by longer serving members, Troupe traditions, and audience expectations. But now, having shouldered the burden of keeping an unfunded company alive, and with little public expectation that they could do so, the members of the Troupe found themselves with unexpected artistic freedom.

The first of these PTT shows and in many ways the most radical departure was *Limited Life* which was written by Kerry O'Rourke, with original songs by Nat Trimarchi. *Limited Life* broke most of the Popular Theatre Troupe conventions in that it was a naturalistic drama with real characters. *As the Crow Flies*, while political satire, attempted a broader and more personal humour than previous Troupe shows. *There's More to Life Than Just Snogging, Barry*, a show about gender politics, included a speech by an unlikeable character who said politically repellent things in the most charming and likeable way, forcing the audience to assert itself and boo, or to sit tight and be seen to agree. The domestic intimacy and original music of *Limited Life*, the quirky paranoia of *As the Crow Flies* and the audience/actor brinkmanship of *There's More to Life than Just Snogging, Barry* were all to recur more strongly in OBN's *A Few Short Wicks in Paradise*.

A Few Short Wicks in Paradise was devoted to a range of issues, which were not so much analysed as commented on from various, sometimes contradictory, points of view. Humour was either slapstick or self-deprecating. The style of the shows drew from rock and roll and stand up comedy rather than more established styles of political theatre. Instead of rejecting the personal as the PTT did, the show embraced it, to the extent that the actors used their own names in performance.

The four productions that took place under the umbrella of the New Actors Company do not represent some mid-position between the old paradigm (The Popular Theatre Troupe) and the new (Street Arts Community Theatre Company). Instead they had a distinct vision of their own. This vision was strongly linked to what was going on in Brisbane at the time.

In 1985, the Electrical Trades Union went on strike against its employer, the South East Queensland Electricity Board (SEQEB). Over a thousand workers walked off the job. A few days later a fierce hail storm hit Brisbane causing blackouts, and the Union went back on the job to repair the damage and then resumed their strike. The National Party Government responded by firing all the striking workers, and this was done in such a manner that the workers would be denied their superannuation entitlements. The government would rehire them only if they signed an industrial agreement that prohibited them belonging to a union. The workers refused. The government then began to hire scab labour and brought down extremely oppressive legislation which, among other measures, made it illegal to picket outside an electricity installation. The penalty for an individual doing this could be as high as $1,000. The legislation also meant that unions could be penalised up to $50,000 for activities that had previously been legal forms of protest.

> I can see them sitting in a little room plotting out the year.
> 'Let's drop an Act in there and a State of Emergency here
> No, fuck the State of Emergency — let's make these bastards disappear
> Let's rule the power industry' — I hear the boardroom cheer
> Yeah, fifty thousand big ones is what you're gonna pay
> If you're a power worker and out on strike these days and
> If you join a picket you could be down a thousand bucks and
> If you tell 'em stick it they're gonna make you bankrupt 'cause it's
> No good throwing you in prison, that's just bad publicity
> That's the price you pay for your electricity.
>
> (from *A Few Short Wicks in Paradise*)

The founding members of OBN were Dee Martin, Penny Glass, Gavan Fenelon and Nat Trimarchi. This core group was responsible for the music, design, performance and content of the first show. The show also utilised material from two writers, Kerry O'Rourke and Hugh Watson, and the skills of sound recordist Kieran Knox. It was co-directed by Dee Martin and Michael Cummings.

What follows (in italics) are excerpts from an account of OBN/The New Actors Company written in 1994 by Kerry O'Rourke.

'All of us always went to the demos and the marches, though I always felt, heretically, that they were embarrassing opportunities for the more forward children to get attention — peculiarly wasteful, defusing, simple-minded, and absolutely necessary exercises that I will always hate taking part in. When we had any spare time, we had parties that were raw creativity drunk on rigour and invention, ganja and rum, but the time was walking all over us.

'So the compadres got edgy. We all got edgy. It was the time. Fear and fortitude filled all our days. Nat went overseas and came back crazed with the knowledge he had to convince them or kill them very soon or the entire operation would be a waste. I remember days of talking to him, calling off the guns, trying reason and logic, feeling like a coward, and old. He wanted action, and he was right. Penny was frenetically trying to pull the chaotic frenzy of Radio 4ZZZ into some kind of workable shape and coping with my radiopolitic journalist burn-out. Gavan was working on his music and his floating world of drawing and, for all I know, gesturing shapes from the sky. Hugh had begun to write nearby, silently, deeply, close to the page.

'All their visionary behaviour went finally into A Few Short Wicks in Paradise, the first Order By Numbers gig. I remember the hundreds of names that were drafted — by the others, I can't say but by myself, hundreds. All were rejected. They wanted to get this gig up in an ideological way, group-devising, but they also wanted to say it all their way. They wanted to be a group, and alone, simultaneously, with the kind of punchy madness that will come on some when they drink.

'Nat's fierce determination had joined with Penny's intensity and both had coupled with Gavan's sheer talent and integrity. They began to devise, develop. Hugh began to write with them. We all began to write. It flooded out and was bashed into shape with argument, insult, mind-link, near-assault, anger, excitement, worry and lust. The main material came directly from Gavan, Penny and Nat who felt alienated from and utterly bound to each other. They therefore perfectly reflected the state of mind of us all in Brisbane at that time. The show itself was patchy, but very good. It felt like Jazz, Punk, poetry, soap and even at times the old PTT, all at once and in every key. Maybe it was comedy but it was almost too intense for that. I've always felt it was more like crafted anger. It was political theatre all right but it was cool. It played everywhere and was just right for the times. 4ZZZ was doing late Punk and Jazz was coming on line. So with OBN they were getting sort of Pazz or Junk — like jazz, but nasty. As for comparisons, inside OBN on its best nights you could sense the shadows and flashes of those great moments in comedy and social commentary; the abuse from John Cleese, the wild rants from Lenny Bruce, the poetic hypnosis of John Cooper Clarke. Like so much that has happened in Queensland, none of it was captured on film — film, I said, not the blunted myopic eye of video.

'Thanks to OBN, theatre could finally compete at rock and roll gigs, and did.'

A *Few Short Wicks in Paradise* did a season at La Boîte and then appeared at rock and roll venues. The show was hired to be the support act at the John Cooper Clarke concert and excerpts were performed at many pickets and demonstrations. It twice went to Sydney, once as part of the Art in Working Life Festival. The full script may be found in this volume.

After *A Few Short Wicks in Paradise*, OBN went on to produce a sequel entitled *Tall Tales From The Altered State*. The cast was Penny Glass, Gavan Fenelon, and Leah Cotterell, with Hugh Watson contributing script. Because of the success of the first project, the second show attracted funding from the Theatre Board of the Australia Council and this allowed the company to employ Danny Fine as Director and Composer, and Brian Doherty as Designer. Despite the increased resources, the second show was not as successful as the first.

From Kerry's letter: *'Despite the new work of that wonderful voice, Leah Cotterell, and the continuing work of most of the original core group, it fell on its face into normal work. The characters, who had been so full of rage and the age in the first, became more like commentary on those characters in the second, even a soap starring those characters, even a sequel demanded under contract. It wasn't that bad, but Few Wicks had been so good, that it was simply a bloody hard act to follow. Exit OBN, but not the talent that had seen the time so clearly.'*

The final Order By Numbers script was *Casualties. Casualties* was commissioned by the Queensland Nurses Union and was one of Queensland's earliest Art in Working Life theatre pieces. The script of *Casualties* was written by Hugh Watson and the cast was Meg Kanowski, Leah Cotterell and Gavan Fenelon. The show was directed by Errol O'Neill.

'Penny and myself were not finished with political theatre', Kerry wrote. *'Through 4ZZZ and my interest in the literatures and films of Latin America, the Caribbean, and Africa I had been trying to learn Spanish, reading and, with Penny's guidance, talking to the Latin Americans in Brisbane about the situation back in their home countries. The main truth about the broad world through their eyes was that human beings are butchers who can cry over a phrase from Mozart.*

'Queensland at that time helped us to have some small inkling of the situation in Latin America, so a very real simpatico built up between us all. Finally we managed to secure funding for a project, a play. The Australia Council would not pay myself the writer because I was Anglo, but that is another story. The play had been an idea that came into being almost as soon as Limited Life had walked away, And by the time the funding came through we had managed to form a theatre company, Teatro Unidad y Liberacion. The company was Dee Martin (Director), Penny Glass (Producer, Translator, Actor, Musician), Therese Collie (Actor, Musician), Ovidio Orellana (Actor, Musician), Sergio Aldunate (Musician, Actor), Roger Rosser (Actor, Musician), Kate Harrison (Musician), Armando Soto-Viera (Designer), Elba Orellana (Costume Designer) and myself. The play was called Volcanes.

'Volcanes was a play that tried for a great sweep across the spirit within the world. In the original script, mythological, political and narrative links were established between Australia, Latin America and Africa. In the end, all that remained of the African influence was the smell of burning and a ritualistic piece that closes the play that I moulded out of Yoruba ritual, from which voodoo is derived.

The first draft of this section of the play was highly heretical, and understandably unsettled some of the actors. Each night, a different member of the ruling powers in the state and the world — targets, if you like — were to be named, and cursed, with real blood curses, on stage, to rhythmic chant. Perhaps one cannot play with that material with impunity, but I was prepared to try. After all, we had tried for over two decades to rid the state of Petersen and nothing had ever worked. I was prepared to try ritual curse seated within the heightened context of drama. As far as I am aware this is the first time this has been done in contemporary Australian theatre, perhaps elsewhere also. Such a shame it was so little witnessed.

The second draft of this scene was greatly diluted, but I left more structure to it than was obvious and, although less threatening, the relative potency was still there. At most performances I spoke some key words to myself, and mouthed completing phrases sotto sotto voce. Volcanes, as intended, remained as close to ritual as it did to politics.

The rest of Volcanes covered a lot of ground. Many stories from Latin America and Australia were interwound, including the obvious one of the Paraguay settlement, and slides and shadow puppets told of contemporary horrors and mythological tales updated, for children and adults alike. Music, drawing on Latin American, African, Latinamerican Indian, Aboriginal and Irish musics, much of it especially written and arranged for the play, filled the stage. It would have had film, but we couldn't afford it. I believe it was patchy, too long and, like a great deal of political theatre, it lacked good character development. Its strength was in its invention, poetry and humour and in the entirely new ground it broke in form, content and style for Australian theatre. As far as we know, it was the first professional bilingual theatre production in Queensland'.

Volcanes played a three week season at The Paint Factory in West End and, despite major media disinterest, many people came to see it because of the excellent word-of-mouth networks that exist in Brisbane. All of the artists who worked for OBN have continued to work in Queensland as arts organizers, activists and theatre workers throughout the eighties and nineties.

PART FOUR

●

STREET ARTS
COMMUNITY
THEATRE
COMPANY

STREET ARTS: A HISTORY

by Peter Stewart and Steve Capelin

•

Introduction — Setting The Scene[1]

by Pauline Peel

The Queensland of 1982 has been well documented. It was the 25th year of what was to be 32 years of conservative government in Queensland. This was an era marked by a "development at all costs" mentality, the anti-street march legislation, the electoral "gerrymander", the Special Branch, a corrupted police force and little regard for issues such as the environment, women or Aboriginal land rights.

For many Queenslanders, the conservative era was epitomised by Joh Bjelke-Petersen who was the National Party Premier from 1968 to late 1987. Ross Fitzgerald in his book *History Of Queensland, 1915 to the 1980s* describes him as 'a fundamentalist Christian, passionately anti-socialist and a fervent advocate of unfettered development'.[2] This was certainly reflected in the direction in which he took Queensland.

The impact of National Party policies can be seen in tangible ways such as the destruction of many of Queensland's natural resources, e.g. the rainforests and the mangroves. The urban sprawl of the Gold Coast and Brisbane's outer suburbs demonstrate the outcomes of years of poor planning and rampant development. Even the state's heritage buildings were not safe from the urge to develop. Many people will remember the overnight demolition of Brisbane's famous old Bellevue Hotel. This was despite a broad based campaign to save the Bellevue.

It is not surprising then that in this political climate there were a significant number of strikes, demonstrations and campaigns. The famous Mount Isa Mines Dispute of 1964-5 was marked by the extraordinary behaviour of the Nicklin Government in declaring a State of Emergency which eventually gave police almost unlimited powers. A State of Emergency was again called during the 1971 tour of the Springboks — the South African Rugby Union Team. The anti-Springbok demonstrations were notable for the brutality of the police in quelling them. The Queensland Council for Civil Liberties had been formed in the late sixties and gathered in strength over the years while the conservation movement gained momentum in the sixties and seventies. During the Brisbane Commonwealth Games in 1982, despite the draconian Commonwealth Games Legislation, a series of Aboriginal land rights marches were staged.

As might be expected, this was not an environment in which the arts, particularly the innovative or alternative arts, could flourish. This was a time when funding decisions were highly politicised. Arts funding decisions of over $10,000 had to be ratified by cabinet. Unfortunately for Queensland many fine artists, writers, performers and directors left Queensland for other states. A number of the leaders of the community arts and community theatre industry which was flourishing elsewhere in Australia in the seventies and eighties came from Queensland. This included people such as Jan McDonald and Bomber Perrier, founding members of WEST Theatre Company in Melbourne and the Murray River Performing Group in Albury-Wodonga respectively.

The Popular Theatre Troupe (PTT) was one Queensland theatre company which, despite the Queensland Government, had gained a national and international reputation for its repertoire of theatre of social criticism. Unfortunately, in 1982 the troupe's funds were withdrawn by the Theatre Board of the Australia Council and the company was disbanded in 1983. The work of the PTT was to be continued by companies like Order By Numbers and several PTT members would later work with and have a significant influence on the work of Street Arts.

Although the withdrawal of support from the Popular Theatre Troupe was a blow, there were some signs that things were changing in the Queensland arts arena in 1982. The Children's Activity Group with its unique approach to making the arts accessible to young people had been working in schools and communities throughout Queensland for many years. As an organisation it provided support and encouragement to fledgling groups and artists. The Queensland Community Arts Network was founded in 1981 and was to be an important advocate for community arts in Queensland. The first multi-cultural Fiesta was held in Musgrave Park in August 1982, by which time Queensland's first Community Arts Officers had been appointed.

'While Queensland's conservative Government worked hard to divide and rule, lots of Queenslanders were working to achieve community access to information and expression and to encourage community cohesion and participation in all areas that affect our quality of life.'[3]

Politically a great deal has changed since 1982. The Joh Bjelke-Petersen era finished when he was replaced by Mike Ahern in late 1987. The Fitzgerald Inquiry which opened in early 1987 revealed amongst other things corrupt elements within the police force, and helped change the face of Queensland politics including its electoral system. Finally in 1989 after 32 years in opposition a State Labor Government was returned to power in Queensland amidst great optimism for the future.

This then was the social context in which Street Arts Community Theatre Company was conceived.

Phase One: Circus, Families and Participation (1982 - 1986)

Musgrave Park, South Brisbane. Saturday 26th March, 1983. Three thousand people, young and old, gather around a thick rope laid in a circle. Second-hand sheets sewn together as backdrops carry the names "West End Wizards", "East Brisbane Dazzlers" and "Thrills'n'Spills Circus". An enthusiastic band of whistle and brass players, percussionists, a guitarist, a keyboardist and a banjo picker launch into the traditional Italian tune *Gobbla Madre*. "Aggrobats" tumble, jugglers fling scarves and coloured balls from hand to hand, clowns cavort and collapse, a fanfare celebrates a human pyramid. Queensland's first Community Circus Festival erupts in a blaze of colour and the local West End crowd loves it.

This first Community Circus Festival was the culmination of Street Arts Community Theatre Company's inaugural community project. Two years before, Pauline and Denis Peel had been involved in similar work in Edinburgh, Scotland[4], while Steve Capelin and Andrea Lynch were moving into a caravan in the western suburbs of Melbourne where Steve became a member of WEST Community Theatre's clown troupe[5].

At that stage, both couples were unaware of their common interests yet all had been educated in Brisbane and influenced, at one time or other, by the work of Ian Reece and his Children's Activity Group. And all, with the exception of Andrea Lynch, a speech therapist, had been teachers with the Queensland Education Department. None had formal qualifications in theatre, but all were significantly influenced by the work of innovative community arts director Neil Cameron — Denis and Pauline Peel in the public housing areas of Edinburgh, Steve Capelin and Andrea Lynch in the north-western suburbs of Melbourne.

In October 1982 Street Arts Community Theatre Company was founded in West End, Brisbane — Pauline, Denis and Steve were its first employees.

Pre-history

A number of fortunate circumstances played a part in the period immediately preceding the formation of Street Arts. While the Peels were in the urban backblocks of Scotland working with the Westerhailes Festival Society, Andrea Hull, then director of the Community Arts Board (CAB) of the Australia Council, happened to drop in as part of a tour of British community arts projects. She was most impressed and surprised to find a young Australian working alongside these working class visionaries. She invited Pauline to get in contact if and when she arrived back in Australia. As a result, twelve months later she was willing to lend a sympathetic ear to the concepts which Pauline and Denis described as their aspirations for the as yet non-existent Street Arts. Andrea Hull was nearing the end of her tenure as CAB Director and as luck would have it the incoming Director was Jon Hawkes of Circus Oz. A coincidental mutual interest in circus plus the positive reference from the outgoing Director gave the fledgling company the break it needed.

Pauline and Denis Peel had returned to Queensland from Scotland in October 1981. The lure of the political fight, with Joh Bjelke-Petersen's government still riding roughshod over civil liberties, cultural heritage, the environment and workers rights, was one factor in this decision. The attraction of a better environment, closer to family, in which to raise their expected child was another. Complementing these was the desire to implement the vision of community theatre they had developed in Edinburgh within their own community. They bought a two-bedroom house in multi-cultural West End and began networking.

Ian Reece and the Children's Activity Group (CAG) was an early contact. Denis Peel began to play sax and help out with their work at the Closeburn Markets while Pauline was soon doing office work for them. Meanwhile, Denis had discovered the Community Arts Centre in Edward Street, the City. There he met General Manager Bruce Dickson and, learning that the Queensland Community Arts Network had recently formed, the Peels attended a meeting at local "kids club" organiser Tony Hannon's West End house soon after.

In 1982 the Peels, at the invitation of the Hill End Kids Club, began to run circus activities with the rather wild bunch of primary-schoolers that attended the old Uniting Church hall in Mitchell Street, West End on a Thursday night. Denis Peel, meanwhile, had commenced teaching at Brisbane State High School in nearby South Brisbane and they both continued their involvement with Ian Reece's Children's Activity Group.[6]

Steve Capelin and partner Andrea Lynch, in the meantime, were keen to return to Brisbane. Steve had already received funding from the Theatre Board of the Australia Council for the Scrubby Creek Clown Project which was part of *Festival '82* that accompanied the 1982 Commonwealth Games. The project was conducted in Kingston, part of a sprawling public housing area to the south of Brisbane, ten minutes down the freeway from the QEII Stadium. Capelin wrote to the Peels through a mutual friend informing them of this project and his desire to work in Brisbane. They were interested and arranged to meet him when he moved back in July 1982.[7]

TWO FAMILIES

In an account of the history of companies such as Street Arts there is often a tendency to underplay some of the significant formative factors in the shaping of grass-roots organisations. In this case the presence of children in the equation (both the Peels and the Capelin/Lynchs had first born children in the year immediately preceding the emergence of Street Arts) was an element which influenced the early work of the company. At the simplest level this can be seen in the commitment to involving communities broadly, across generations, in community projects.

In August 1982 the two couples got together to discuss ideas and write their first funding application. This was to the Community Arts Board (CAB) of the Australia Council requesting funds for the Community Circus Festival held in March 1983.[8]

There was a sense of 'Let's do it!' amongst them; that the combination of their experiences and skills could both effect social change and make them all a living. They decided to give it a go for a year in 1983 and, if it was not financially viable, then they would give it away. They were idealistic and tunnel-visioned (or so Pauline Peel saw herself[9]) yet, being in their early thirties and with young children, pragmatic enough to make practical decisions and work with existing institutions.

To tide them over financially, Capelin developed a one-person show with local writer/director Sean Mee, *The Big Shot*, which toured to primary schools under the Street Arts banner at the end of 1982. Pauline Peel and Capelin concentrated on publicity during this period — getting the "Street Arts" name known by visiting schools, arranging photos in local newspapers and networking with a wide range of community development agencies. A social worker at Inala, an outer Brisbane public housing area, took a special interest in their ideas and introduced them to a range of people in that community. Later, Tony Carter, the principal of East Brisbane State School in a suburb adjacent to West End, and a strong supporter, introduced them to Neil Flanagan, the principal of Inala West State School who welcomed them with open arms.

Thus, by the time Street Arts commenced its first funded project in February 1983, the team already had one Arts Council approved tour behind it, the idea of a knockabout entertainment show, *The Manly Brothers*, under its belt, and a second target community, Inala, in its sights. The company also had strong links with its local West End community and very supportive individuals promoting its work.

Circus

Street Arts' founding members brought with them a belief in circus as an effective, all inclusive popular form of performance. Their own skills — influenced by Reg Bolton of Suitcase Circus fame, originally from the U.K. and now resident in Australia, and the New Circus and comedy movement centred in

Melbourne — were combined with their desire to explore new popular theatre forms.

The 1983 Community Circus Festival, Street Art's first project, was based in its home community of West End. As well as workshops at West End and East Brisbane State Schools, the project provided public workshops at the local Mitchell Street Hall. Here people who were to become key players in Street Arts had their first taste of community theatre. Tony Hannon, eccentric clown and whistle player later involved in community arts in Adelaide; Meg Kanowski, clown, comedian, writer, performer, director and company stalwart; Phil Davison, acrobat and performer; Peter Stewart, musician, performer, later musical director with the company; Derek Ives, schoolboy juggler, unicyclist and circus natural who has since worked with Rock'n'Roll Circus and Circus Oz to mention but a few. All were part of the first Thrills 'n' Spills Community Circus troupe which emerged from this project.

Others involved were local residents and/or workers. Some had connections with the House of Freedom, a Christian community group with a social justice focus, Hill End Kids Club, local alternative and anarchist groups, local schools or the large university student population in the area. Others walked in off the the street. Brought together by leaflets, media and word-of-mouth, this diverse group explored juggling, tumbling, clowning and music together.

Over the next three years the Thrills 'n' Spills Circus Troupe devised and produced five shows, often around themes common to popular culture or local events. They performed in parks, malls, gardens, halls, *La Bamba* late night cabaret at La Boîte Theatre, and even a central city synagogue. It was physical, tongue-in-cheek, irreverent family entertainment all performed to a big, brassy musical accompaniment with a minimum of equipment.

Street Arts saw itself as having a key role to play in nurturing new talent within the communities in which it worked. The philosophy was centred on the need to demystify the Arts process and debunk the Artist-Genius notion, thereby encouraging the possibility of genuine community-related artistic expression to emerge from the creative sources most attuned to community issues and community life — the locals.

METHODOLOGY

From the beginning Street Arts was not content to be pigeonholed as a "theatre company" only. The founding members were intent on utilising artforms which seemed to answer the needs of each new situation. Thus the work had a strong music and visual art component which supported the theatrical focus of the group. In effect Street Arts, as an organisation, became a defacto Community Arts Officer and the early concern with long term outcomes and relationships with communities meant that their work took on a cultural development role

104

well beyond the typical function of the Community Theatre Company of the time.

Street Arts' early community cultural development methodology did not rely on an invitation or inspiration from the community. Rather, it recognised that the company had ideas and skills that a community may never have experienced or imagined as possibilities, and which could, as they were described and enacted in that community, be a process for mutual development and community empowerment. The vision came from the company, but was shared with the community which then adapted it and made it their own with the company's assistance. The practice of community participation in all elements of the vision (i.e., the development of a piece of community theatre and the final product/event/show) gave flesh to this vision of inspiring, skilling and empowering a community. It was an approach relatively unknown and untried in Australia at that time.

At the 1984 Community Theatre National Conference held at the Mill Theatre in Geelong, Victoria, Pauline described the company's philosophy as follows:

> 'We believe that it is a basic right of all Australians to have access to theatre — more than that, we believe it is a basic right to be part of the *creation* of that theatre, that culture — a truly indigenous Australian culture.'[10]

How the company proposed to facilitate this "basic right to theatre" she summarised in the following aims[11]:

'Integral to our work is:

- finding new styles, new working methods, more relevant content and, in particular, styles of working outdoors;
- accessing more people to theatre;
- providing an alternative to television and packaged entertainment;
- giving people a voice through theatre.'

And Denis Peel emphasises the importance of "physicality" (and music) to each of these aims.[12]

PERSONNEL

The period 1982-1986 saw Street Arts involved in 28 projects. Some of these were short residencies, eight were company shows, including three Theatre-in-Education pieces, and ten involved large community production teams.

In terms of structure, the company maintained a core team of administrative and artistic staff (the collective) who were supplemented by guest artists as the need arose. Denis Peel and Capelin — and later writer/performer/director Therese Collie — while enthusiastic, skilled, and highly motivated, were generally aware of their limitations. The company developed a conscious policy of employing specific guest artists who would contribute to the ongoing skill and philosophical emergence of the group. These were often people that company members themselves wanted to learn from.

Amongst permanent collective members, there was the need for employees to share a similar philosophy, political analysis and social commitment, for the sake of both the work and the team.[13] Indeed, the issue of commitment to company philosophy and working methods versus perceived skills and standing in the arts world continued to dog Street Arts' employment choices over many years, especially when funding bodies, particularly the Performing Arts Board of the Australia Council (PAB), began in the late eighties to exert pressure on the company to produce more traditional mainstream product. This was a major issue because the company was pursuing a philosophy of theatre at odds with the dominant notions of "excellence" which many theatre-workers took for granted.

This was to become particularly evident in the role of company coordinator over the history of the company. Though describing itself as a collective, Street Arts nevertheless acknowledged the importance of a skilled and experienced organiser to help maintain direction and profile, not to mention basic financial and application and report-writing skills. These, plus a clear understanding of both theatre and the philosophy of cultural development, placed heavy demands on company coordinators. That all of these attributes were not always evident in equal proportions in the range of coordinators who held the position over a period of ten years is not surprising. Despite the rhetoric of collectivism, each of these people had a critical impact on the functioning and effectiveness of the company. The most notable of these were Pauline Peel and Fiona Winning, both of whom exhibited a total commitment to the company philosophy and a particular skill in leading a disparate group of politically inspired artists through some particularly difficult terrain. The company's ability to thrive and weather storms largely revolved around this key role and the fact that over a ten year period only four people, all women, held this position is an indication of the commitment each exhibited and the stability which this allowed the company. The PTT for instance had eight administrators over a nine year period. The coordinators to follow Peel and Winning were Kara Miller and Cynthia Irvine.

Given the incredible range of skills, political, theatrical and organisational, that membership of the collective demanded, it is not surprising that one also finds a number of ex-PTT members employed by Street Arts over the years. They had performance and organisational skills, political commitment, and were used to roughing it. Fiona Winning, Therese Collie, Kath Porrill, Gavan Fenelon and Roger Rosser were some of these.

West End, Inala and Beyond

Therese Collie joined the Street Arts collective at the beginning of 1984. She had just returned from Paris where she studied at the École Jacques Le Coq. She was a trained primary teacher and an accomplished performer with skills in comedy, directing and devising. Capelin and members of the management committee knew her work from PTT days. She was a natural choice.

During 1983 Street Arts had ventured into Inala, a Housing Commission suburb on the south-western outskirts of Brisbane which had been established in the 1950's. Inala had become the dumping ground for many of the housing problems of the government of the time. Deprived of public transport and with a high population of single parents and members of the Aboriginal and Torres Strait Islander community, the area had earned an unenviable reputation as a trouble spot. Once established, this urban myth was difficult to dispel.

Working on the premise that the most accessible point of entry to the Inala community was through the local schools and having been welcomed by one of the local principals, Street Arts set about making contact with a wide range of local groups and individuals. Initial contacts with groups including Inala Community House and local women's groups were encouraging and the team embarked on a series of workshops with children by day and with parents and general community members by night at Inala West State School. This pilot project explored the stories of the local residents, mainly women, and the natural design and performance skills of the young people. It culminated in a two night season of circus and topical sketches in a local Playground and Recreation Hall hastily transformed at minimal cost into a theatre venue. Everything in the show *Inala In Cabaret* was borrowed except the content which was totally original. Significantly, this project featured a number of women who would in 1986 become founding members of Icy Tea (ICT — Inala Community Theatre), a professional women's Community Theatre Company.

Del (McClymont) Cuddihy, Inala resident and a participant in *Inala In Cabaret*, was recruited to assist with administrative tasks. The invitation to Del to join the company was more than filling a need. It was the beginning of a conscious strategy to encourage members of the local community to develop skills and link the company in a grass-roots way to, in this case, Inala. Del was subsequently employed as secretary from January 1984 as Street Arts went from three to five employees.[14] The addition of Del Cuddihy and Therese Collie was integral to the development of the company's work with the Inala community and Collie then continued to work with the Inala community as writer and/or director on projects for some years.

The most significant project during Street Arts involvement in Inala was the large scale outdoor event *Once Upon Inala* in 1984. Written by Nick Hughes who had worked with PTT, it addressed the issues of "bad reputation" and the intrusive nature of the Housing Commission's relationship with its tenants. This rather mediaeval relationship between Government body and constituents was parodied in the performance, with the Housing Commission represented by a dragon and the whole performance played out as a mediaeval battle between good and evil. In a sense this may have appeared a simplistic representation of a complex situation but, judging by the response from those 1500 locals who braved a cold and blustery Sunday afternoon to witness the event, it represented their experience all too well. With large puppets, live band, food and a cast of over one hundred, *Once Upon Inala* was performed at a place known locally as Kev Hooper Park. It was generally described by locals and outsiders alike as a remarkable event.

CONSOLIDATION AND EXPANSION

Not content to "change the world" in key Brisbane communities, Street Arts took on a statewide brief and set out to service far flung communities that had expressed an interest in experiencing this version of "total immersion" community theatre. Work in West End and Inala continued as did the availability of a flexible range of workshops which the company offered to schools and interested groups. The company's work with schools also continued to expand with further shows and projects developed for high school audiences. This interest in working with young people survived right through this first phase of the company and in a sense had its culmination in the emergence of the professional Rock'n'Roll Circus company in 1987.

If 1983 had been the year to 'raise awareness, get people involved, and . . . get to know . . . [the] communities of West End and Inala'[15], then 1984 and 1985 were definitely years of consolidation and expansion.

There was more money and therefore there were more projects and more project workers. Community participants were more experienced and there was greater community acknowledgment and support generally. Collie's influence could particularly be seen in the themes and direction of the Theatre-in-Education (TIE) show *La Fa La Ful*, the direction of the large-cast outdoor production *Once Upon Inala* and the increasing sophistication of the performers in Thrill'n'Spills. The larger collective had a strong woman performer/deviser/workshop leader in Collie and the company's work was becoming more sophisticated in style and content.

Collie's employment also meant a closer link with ex-PTT workers, many of whom were skeptical of Street Arts' political commitment and working methods. While some were forging stronger links between popular theatre and ongoing political struggle as members of the company Order By Numbers, others began

108

to pick up work with Street Arts and experience a different approach to using theatre as a tool for social change. *Once Upon Inala* saw Kath Porrill from Innisfail, and a former member of Grin and Tonic Theatre Troupe as well as PTT, begin a long term association with the company as designer and performer.

Street Arts expanded into new communities as well. They were contracted by John Stanwell, Griffith University's Community Arts Officer for Brisbane South and Logan City, to work on a large high school project, *The Logan City Story*. This built on Steve Capelin's contacts with Kingston State High but included archrivals Woodridge High as well. Pat Cranney was the writer, Danny Fine musical director and Richard Collins directed a daring and hilarious analysis of the mores and rivalries of the teenagers of the community and their families. Teachers, professional actors and students performed alongside each other in the most public venue available — the centre court of Woodridge Plaza Shopping Centre. This choice of space was as inspired as it was difficult. Each evening as the shops shut at 5 pm the production team would begin the bump-in of sound, lighting and seating for a cast of eighty and an audience of three hundred, this whole process to be repeated in reverse again at 10.30 pm and everything stored in preparation for the following night. In script terms this was an opportunity Pat Cranney could not resist and as a result the climactic scene of the show was set in that very place, the shopping plaza centre court. In terms of community ownership this represented the ultimate level of recognition for the audience, many of whom would never be able to work or shop in the Plaza again without the memory of scenes of their own lives being enacted almost in their own homes. While this was perceived to be a highly successful project in artistic and process terms, it was to be five years before Street Arts returned to work in this community and then with a completely different set of young people.

The move into high schools continued into 1985 with the research and writing of *Rites, Wrongs and Off-beat Thongs* with Phil Sumner, formerly of WEST Community Theatre in Melbourne, as guest writer/director. The company was resident at St Thomas More College, Sunnybank and involved students in the writing of the show. As a TIE production, it then toured secondary schools. However, its exploration of sexual mores and the then-current SEQEB strike (a long-running industrial dispute over National Party legislation designed to reduce the power of the Electrical Trades Union) meant it fell foul of the Queensland Arts Council and the Education Department. 'The threat of censorship and its [political and budgetary] ramifications'[16] meant that this was the last TIE show produced by Street Arts until *Cityzen* in 1993 and Pat Cranney's *Busted* in 1994. This is a reflection of the degree of conservatism and political control in the area of Theatre-in-Education in Queensland during the eighties.

Regional work, begun in 1983 with Rockhampton Youth Theatre, continued in 1984 for the Capricana Festival, while an invitation to visit Home Hill for three weeks leading up to the 1984 Harvest Festival saw the production of *Artesian*

Yarns. This was the first regional show to involve adults as well as children and told the story of the Burdekin River in a mythical pageant form. In the years 1983-86 Street Arts toured, performed or were involved in residencies in Toowoomba, Coomera, Townsville, Rockhampton, Innisfail, Home Hill and Newcastle (NSW).

While helping to provide access to ideas, skills and alternative approaches to creating community events and theatre, this regional work, which was largely confined to one-off contact with the host community, ultimately felt less productive than when focussing energies on communities closer to home where long term strategies could be explored. Cultural development was at the core of the company's work and it became clear from these regional residencies that, while there was clearly an impact on the community in the short term, the company did not have the resources to follow up the promising beginnings made during these visits.

By 1985 Street Arts was far more than just its founding members. A larger collective, committed participants, regular guest artists and an inspired and supportive management committee were all stakeholders as well. Out of the success of the circus festivals and the reality of a committee made up of mainly inner city dwellers came a desire to explore in greater depth what it meant to be part of Brisbane's West End community.

WEST END — THE LOCAL COMMUNITY

West End became the testing ground for the fundamental set of ideas and beliefs upon which Street Arts based its work. As a long term resident company in the community, this was where the evidence of the impact of Community Arts practice would be most clear. Street Arts' vision was one of the Arts as an integral element of community life where it could facilitate, reflect on and respond to local issues and explore and celebrate a sense of identity in a public and participatory form.

The model which Street Arts developed in this early period and described in relation to Inala was evident in the company's developing relationship with its home community. There was a clear understanding of the need to establish a broad and vigorous network of personal and strategic contacts. This had begun well before the company came into official existence. Choosing to live permanently in the West End area facilitated this and allowed the Peels to seek out like-minded people who would be interested in supporting new initiatives as they emerged. There was a willingness to pitch in and become involved in pre-existing networks and activities as participants and contributors. Some of this was the natural inclination of the Peels but the other major influence was the revolutionary work of Helen Crummy in the desolate housing estates of Edinburgh in Scotland [see David Watt's chapter for a more detailed account of her work]. Pauline and Denis Peel were strongly influenced by her ideas during their stay in Scotland and her ways of working are reflected in the approach they took to the task of building trust and support in West End.

Thus, local support, public visibility, a constant dialogue with local community members, politicians, community leaders, traders, teachers and community organisations laid the basis for acceptance and understanding. This strategy of informally and formally introducing the company and its ideas to the locals took many forms. Public theatre skills workshops, particularly circus, were offered in local halls. Personal visits were made to many local citizens as well as the state funding body and other kindred organisations throughout the city. Street Arts would take their wares as often as possible into the streets with impromptu parades, music, circus acts — in fact any excuse to be seen as a visible presence in the main shopping precinct. These forays, often on a Saturday morning and often with community members emerging from the latest juggling, balancing or music workshop in tow, were initially met with some bemusement by local shoppers and traders but over time this quickly changed to inquiries of when the colourful team would next be enlivening the local area. Of course this wasn't merely a way of filling in a Saturday morning. These events served as a point of contact between the company and the community, allowed the distribution of company brochures and also represented the philosophy of the company in action — Art as part of daily life.

COMMUNITY ACTIVISM

These activities, of course, could easily have been dismissed as just a bunch of eccentrics showing off on Saturday mornings. It was important to demonstrate to the community how this concept of community art could be taken further. Thus the next strategy involved a series of ambitious and major projects which would clearly achieve a broad community involvement and develop a greater level of trust in, and understanding of, the aspirations of the young company of artists. These projects deliberately set out to be accessible across the community, accessible and initially non-confrontational. It was clearly a case of bringing the community together, building trust and then making judgments about the appropriateness of when and how to deal with contentious issues within the community.

It was here that the company came in for some criticism from some of the more politically militant members of the community and from current and former members of the Popular Theatre Troupe of the time. It appeared to these people that this form of community activism was inherently conservative and that the only acceptable role for a politically active arts group was to act as the social conscience of the community, presenting an alternative analysis of the issues of the times. The analysis of the process of change adopted by Street Arts was one of social change through individual experience and analysis, rather than the clear political line adopted by companies such as the PTT. Rather than people learning to act differently through being challenged as audience members to think, Street Arts asserted the importance of learning to think differently through the process of actively engaging in relevant issues, as generators of ideas and solutions. In these early projects the very act of identifying themselves as a community and daring to create their own artworks was in itself seen as a political activity. Street Arts was interested in reaching new audiences and wherever possible avoiding the comfortable situation of finding themselves preaching to the converted. Thus the early Circus Festivals set out to achieve a number of fundamental things — a high degree of visibility for the company, a sense of trust between the local residents and the company, and a demonstration of the positive energy the arts was able to bring to local urban life.

This difference in the sense of timing of political content is well illustrated by the work in the same years in Inala and West End. At Inala the issues and the level of anger and frustration were so clearly present from the very first conversation that this content demanded to be the central element in both *Inala In Cabaret* and in the subsequent *Once Upon Inala*. This was despite the fact that there were quite significant differences in the traditional political stance of members of the community. In West End in 1983-4 there was no equally strong single issue to galvanise the community into political action. West End was a diverse community whose strongest common bond was a preference for living in this diverse multi-layered, multi-ethnic community. It was not until 1988 and the advent of Expo '88 that the community was united by what was perceived to be an external threat to the peace and harmony of the area.

The first two major projects in West End were Community Circus Projects which allowed a wide range of age groups and ideologies to coexist and to collectively claim their identity as locals doing their thing. From this base the company then set about exploring the identity of the community in more depth. The next major project was a large scale dance/theatre production, *Next Stop West End*, which set out to acknowledge the multi-faceted reality of the local area.

Inspired partly by a large community dance production Pauline Peel had witnessed in Scotland, and drawing on the history of the South Brisbane-West End area, *Next Stop West End* told the story of West End from pre-colonisation to 1985 (and the feared future impact of Expo '88 on rental levels and the availability of low cost housing in the area) through dance, music and drama. It drew on the memories of many local people and their relatives for stories and tapped the creative well of dancers, musicians and performers in the community. It was truly an all-age production and its one-week season at West End's historic Rialto Theatre in June attracted rave reviews and full houses.

Roger Rosser, musician and former Popular Theatre Troupe actor, made his debut with the company in this show as master of ceremonies and, working with Meg Kanowski, had volunteers from the audience pouring onto the stage to join in the dances that linked the eras. In an attempt to acknowledge the multi-cultural nature of the West End community, efforts were made to involve non-Anglo-Saxon stories and performers as well. However, this proved more difficult than expected. There was a Murri presence in the opening and a Vietnamese refugee told her story, but apart from members of the rap dancing troupe (a trio of young Greek and Turkish boys), that was about it. The desire to include a broader spectrum of cultures in future shows remained however, and lessons were learnt.

Phase One Culmination, 1986

1986 proved to be the culminating year of Phase One in the life of Street Arts. Financially the company had its most successful year, earning an unequalled $88,714 of non-government income. (See Table 2) The company undertook its first "Art in Working Life" production, the very successful *Sweeping Statements*, and a second offshoot was spawned when Rock'n'Roll Circus, the company, was born.

In addition the company

- mounted a political cabaret, A *Few Bobs Short of a Quid*, affectionately known as The Bob Club — all the characters bore the name Bob or a derivative

- toured a new version of *Rites, Wrongs and Offbeat Thongs* to high schools

- spent seven weeks as company-in-residence in Innisfail, Far North Queensland

- created a touring show, *Postcards*, with students of Rochedale State High School about tourism in third world countries for the Queensland Development Education Committee

- initiated the inaugural Boundary Street (West End) Festival

- and, strangely, after a year of dramatic progress in developing the politics and sophistication of the company's work, found itself at Christmas in Bougainville, P.N.G. performing a Pidgin version of A *Few Bobs Short of a Quid*[17] as guests of CRA Exploration — a multi-national mining giant!

1986 was the year in which Street Arts began to act at times as a community arts production house. The annual Boundary Street (West End) Festival, for example, was inaugurated to meet the ongoing needs of West End for events that celebrated the sense of community and cultural diversity in the area. It involved shopkeepers, families, West End Community House, anarchists, schools and the Murri community. A key element of the first Boundary Street Festival and an example of Street Arts willingness to operate outside its theatre brief was the commissioning of a community mural. This was coordinated by visual artist Mark Crocker and involved a broad range of Murri and other local artists of varied experience in converting a local eyesore into a cultural statement.

"ROCK'N'ROLL CIRCUS"

From the beginning, Street Arts had attracted large numbers of young people interested in the mushrooming and accessible area of circus performance. Each year this interest grew as did the skill level of the participants. By 1986 this had begun to take on a life of its own with small groups developing their own material and with the company looking for ways to facilitate the flow of opportunities for further training and experience for this group. The Murray River Performing Group based in Albury-Wodonga had established The Flying Fruit-Flies, a circus troupe based around the young people of that rural community, and had initiated a series of national training programmes in Albury-Wodonga using guest trainers from Nanjing in mainland China. Street Arts had sponsored a number of its performers and community participants to attend these and had also begun to develop strong links with trainers and performers through these gatherings. This led to a rapid increase in the level of skill among the participants and also fed the imaginations of the local circus junkies with possibilities for circus which still lay untapped in Brisbane. 1986 then was not only the biggest year in the company's history in terms of projects undertaken but was also a turning point in the place of circus in the work of the company.

The Rock'n'Roll Circus Project was largely the brainchild of Lachlan McDonald, circus performer, Queensland University student and graduate of a Nanjing Circus training project in Albury-Wodonga. McDonald had joined the company on a one year CAB funded community theatre traineeship. This was the first of a series of traineeships which the company undertook over the next few years. Part of the traineeship included an agreement by the company to support an independent project of McDonald's design in the second half of the year. McDonald was a big thinker and, with a visionary's eye and a generous helping of idealism (and innocence), he proposed the biggest project the company had ever undertaken — McDonald planned to put up to one hundred circus performers and musicians on stage at the Rialto Theatre, West End after an eight month training programme.

Conceived as a skills exchange between circus junkies and musicians where participants would eventually end up accompanying each other in a combination of circus and rock'n'roll, the first workshops began in April. This project drew together eighty visual artists, musicians and performers, many of whom had been involved in previous Street Arts' work. In addition there was an injection of new talent from youth theatre, other community arts groups, local unemployed young people and a broad network of artists many of whom had worked at some stage with the PTT. After an eight month gestation period the two week season at the Rialto Theatre in November proved a sellout and set a number of people on the road to careers in community arts and/or circus. For not only arts skills were developed. Many of the participants worked long hours on organisation, construction, front of house, writing and devising as well.

At the end of the project a core group who were keen to continue on a full time basis emerged and Rock'n'Roll Circus, the company, was born. As with most births it was not without some trauma as by now there were up to eighty people with a stake in the concept, many of whom were interested in continuing circus work as a hobby. Despite the difficulties, Rock'n'Roll Circus leapt into existence with a series of smaller community shows during 1987 before becoming a full-time incorporated collective of six performers in 1988.

The Art in Working Life programme

"SWEEPING STATEMENTS"

By the end of 1985 Street Arts had begun to explore notions of community which went beyond the geographical definitions as represented by Inala and West End. This was partly an organic process and partly influenced by the growing sophistication of the Community Arts Board who had, in parallel with Street Arts, begun to shift from an arts project focus to a cultural development focus. One of the initiatives of the CAB was the identification of a series of programme priority funding areas. These were intended to promote community arts work in communities regarded as historically having had less opportunity to access funding and arts programmes in the past. One of these was the labour movement.

From the CAB's point of view the Arts dollar and the practice of the arts had tended to be skewed towards the middle classes and was often about middle class experience. Average Australian workers who had traditionally been involved in skilled and craft-based labour were seen to be largely excluded from mainstream cultural expression. This interest in broadening the scope of the company's work led Street Arts to approach the Federated Miscellaneous Workers Union (the Missos) with a proposal for a collaborative project. The resulting show *Sweeping Statements* dealt with the difficulties which this large and scattered union faced in terms of both its internal conflicts and the relationship of the workers with their employers. It was a very human show which set out to acknowledge the realities and the complexities of the world of industrial relations. It succeeded in mixing the personal with the ideological and was a clear illustration to the union movement of the power of good theatre to not just propagandise but to explore issues honestly. This was the first in a series of Art In Working Life projects for Street Arts which spanned the next four years.

Sweeping Statements broke new ground for the company on a number of fronts. It was the first show planned with a community-of-interest rather than a geographic community and it was the first bilingual production, featuring Guatemalan guest performer Leonor Orellana. The bilingualism, though not extensive, was probably a first for Queensland. Leonor and her family, refugees, brought a strong sense of social justice and grass-roots political struggle to the project.

Sweeping Statements proved extremely popular amongst the unionists and political activists who were new to the company's audience. Many saw it at their workplace during its post-season tour of south-east Queensland. Surprisingly, it also proved a hit with the critics and more traditional theatregoers, perhaps because its characters were more than just stereotypes and the satire was irreverent and infectious.

"THE REUNION SHOW"

Phase Two of the company's history (from 1987 on) saw the work with unions continue and expand. *The Reunion Show* was written by Gavan Strawhan, a young writer with a number of community/political theatre pieces to his credit in Adelaide. It was standard practice for writers to commence on projects before involving the rest of the creative team and, with the help of Trades and Labour Council Arts Officer Dee Martin, Gavan began by canvassing issues facing the seventeen unions who were to be involved.

Reunion was to be a more analytical look at the issues common to most unions in Queensland at the time. Those involved ranged from Street Arts' President Bill Yarrow's Professional Officers' Association to the Seamen's Union. The number and diversity meant that the project did not garner the same degree of hands-on support as *Sweeping Statements*, but regular feedback sessions attracted interested members and officials to view work-in-progress presentations at The Paint Factory. These provided significant input into the shape and content of the show, including the mandatory call to collective action at the end.

Reunion was an integration of naturalism, dramatised story-telling, music and puppets, skillfully directed by Therese Collie. Kath Porrill's stereotyped puppets of union officials were, in fact, the highlight of the show and provided a satirical critique of traditional male union culture. The season was very successful, which was just as well because it had already been decided to tour the show (and a workplace version) to regional Queensland in early 1989.

"TRADING HOURS"

The third Art in Working Life production was *Trading Hours* (1990). By now the company had developed a collection of processes and structures which it felt best supported this kind of community-based company show. Hilary Beaton, a local theatre worker and writer with Literature Board credibility and some community theatre background, began by researching sexual harassment and the attitudes of the white collar unions involved in the project.

Pat Rogers, women's branch organiser with the Public Sector Union (PSU), and Dee Martin from the Trades and Labour Council (TLC) had approached Street Arts with the idea for the project. As Hilary began researching, she and Kara Miller (Street Arts coordinator) put together a steering committee of union officials, workers and women's groups' representatives to feed into and out of the project. During the rehearsal period these and other interested members of the community attended work-in-progress sessions where they provided more specific feedback after viewing readthroughs or rehearsals of the developing script.

Director Sue Rider was employed in line with the artistic development strategy of using skilled theatre professionals from the mainstream to improve the artistic standards of company shows. She approached the script in a naturalistic style with the aim of allowing the performers to discover and present "the truth", despite their varying skill levels.[18]

The project always called for a character from a non-English speaking background. This role was given to Alexandra Ruiz, a relatively recent refugee from Chile with training in singing and music and some acting experience. At the time, late 1989, there had been differences in the collective over whether she or a second generation non-Anglo actor be employed. The conflict lay in a perceived need for professional performances on the one hand and an authentic link with and empowering process for members of a non-English speaking background community on the other.

As it was, Beaton drew the character of Raquel from Ruiz's English language skills and experience of Australian culture while devising her part from the stories of other Latin American women in the Australian workforce.

Trading Hours was well received by the community, theatregoers and reviewers. It had a successful Paint Factory season and, in its reduced form, a very successful tour of Brisbane workplaces and colleges. While it was criticised for an over-didactic script, a lack of cohesion between naturalistic scenes and characters bursting into song, and direction that did not make the most of the power symbolism inherent in Rose Claiden and Bernie Lewis' multi-levelled set, the show achieved pretty much what the planning process, with all its constraints, desired of it. For most of the audience, especially working women, it was an evocative and enjoyable night of theatre.

Phase Two: The Paint Factory Years (1987-1991)

The second phase of Street Art's life was characterised by an increased intensity in the political activity of the company's work, a continuation of the large scale community participation projects for which the company had by this time become justifiably famous and, with the transition from founding members to the next generation of workers, the beginnings of some confusing times regarding philosophy and focus. That is not to say that some truly remarkable work was not produced in this period, much of it in the company's new venue — The Paint Factory.

The importance of the transition from the first generation of workers to the next cannot be underestimated in the life of any company driven by a commitment to a collective ideal and where a political philosophy underpins the very existence of the team. Any company committed to shared decision-making processes is faced at various times in its existence with the challenge of redefining itself to best reflect the aspirations, skills and vision of its current membership. This vital process is one which, despite some painful experiences, enabled Street Arts to adapt to changing circumstances, and survive.

For Street Arts, this second phase was very clearly a case of building on established principles and working methodologies, and expanding areas of focus. There was significant development in the sophistication of the company's processes and output, and a willingness to pursue at greater depth themes and work initiated in the first four years. The relationship between the company and the Union movement was further developed through *Trading Hours* and The *Reunion Show.* The nature of the West End community was investigated more thoroughly through a series of developing relationships between the company and various subgroups. These included the local Murri (Queensland Aboriginal) community and members of non-English speaking background ((NESB) communities. There was also an emphasis on issues of critical importance to local people, particularly the impact of World Expo '88 on housing and the psyche of the community.

In this second phase of the company, work in the area of circus and in Inala took on less importance while work in Logan City, West End and with the trade union movement took a higher profile. The other work of particular interest during this period was with prisoners and the Corrective Services system in southern Queensland.

THE PAINT FACTORY

The expansion in the company's workload and workforce, and the increasing role that seasons of indoor productions were having, meant that Street Arts

118

had been outgrowing their base in Hill End for some time. An unhappy neighbour and the Uniting Church's decision to sell the hall forced the company to speed up its search for new premises. The importance of the close relationship which Street Arts had developed with its home community meant that location was a critical factor in the search for a new base. The desire to maintain a visible presence and an open relationship with the West End community made The Paint Factory, located close by the major shopping precinct, an ideal place from which to continue to develop this. The move was made in February 1987. The disused warehouse was a mess and lacked any facilities, but it had potential, plenty of space for office, storage and rehearsal, and an affordable rent.

The Paint Factory was never a long-term option due to its limited initial lease, its sale to a new developer early in 1988, and difficult ongoing sub-lease negotiations with their new lessee, the engineering firm next-door. Street Arts' minutes and "Venue" files are littered with new venue prospects, proposals and wish lists. Yet The Paint Factory, despite its lack of a kitchen and no toilet or washing facilities, was Street Arts' home and venue for almost five years.

This was Street Arts' first really permanent base (there had been no written lease on the Mitchell Street Uniting Church Hall). The advantages of a permanent venue were in the areas of company convenience and efficiency, audience and community identification, and the potential to generate a higher proportion of box office income. The Paint Factory became synonymous with Street Arts, Rock'n'Roll Circus and similar community-based social activist theatre groups. It was a valuable community resource for concerts, dances, benefit nights, market days and performances.

During its period as a venue, The Paint Factory hosted eleven Street Arts productions including four large-cast community shows and seven company productions; eight Rock'n'Roll Circus shows; seasons by Sydney's Sidetrack Theatre, Brisbane's Grin And Tonic, Kite Preschool Theatre, Fractal Theatre Company, Syntheatrix Women's Performance Collective and a number of productions by independent production teams. There were also numerous multi-cultural and "alternative" concerts and dance parties; play-readings by Brisbane Theatre Company; and at least twenty-five benefit concerts for groups as diverse as Gulumba Football Club, Radio 4ZZZ, and the West End Housing Cooperative.

There was only one large performance and rehearsal space, a barn-like shed with uneven wooden floor and two loading bays, and two other large storage rooms. One of the latter became office to Street Arts and Rock'n'Roll Circus, the other a backstage workshop, a dressing room and alternative rehearsal space. A sink with illegal plumbing was installed under the only tap (in the performance space) and "Porta-Loos" were hired as required.

This period at The Paint Factory saw an exciting mix of Brisbane's arts-related organisations working in close contact with each other. The mutual sharing of facilities, particularly between Street Arts and Rock'n'Roll Circus as joint tenants, allowed a number of groups all with limited facilities to pool resources and attempt work on a scale otherwise impossible.

THE SECOND GENERATION

The Paint Factory reflected changes in the operations of Street Arts. The emphasis on circus diminished, although the tradition continued through Rock'n'Roll Circus and Go-Karts workshops for primary schoolers at The Paint Factory. Likewise, there was less emphasis on outdoor performance and spectacle, although this strand continued through the second Boundary Street Festival in September into the Maroochydore Youth Arts Festival, Clermont residencies in 1988 and other smaller, mainly school-based residencies up to 1991's Carole Park Project. However, this was not where the skills and enthusiasm of the changing collective were focussed.

Times were changing. Because Street Arts had come into existence espousing a new way of working in theatre, the onus was always on the company to deliver. This was relatively easy when the work appeared fresh and new to audiences and communities, notwithstanding the hard work and long hours that went into producing it. Gradually, however, there grew an understandable internal desire to be exploring new forms, to reach new communities, to develop better practice and to increase the political analysis inherent in the work. There was also a desire for higher artistic and production standards.

From *Next Stop West End* on, there had been a stated aim to involve more ethnic and aboriginal members of the West End community. While there was increasing involvement from the Murri community over this period, it was not until 1990's *Jalalu Jalu; Land, Law and Lies* with its specific look at the environment from a Murri point of view and its commitment to the employment of Murri writers, that this aim began to be fully realised.

In the meantime, the most significant step towards this goal and a project which marked a shift in emphasis from Phase One to Phase Two of the collective's life was *Happy Families. Happy Families* saw the employment of Hugh Watson as writer on his first project of many with Street Arts over the next five years. The show, which had the theme of peace as its beginning point, consciously explored a more naturalistic style than previous shows and included an aboriginal account of the acceptance and rejection (by the broad Australian community) of their participation in the defence of their country. This step towards the aboriginal community was a significant move which was consistently pursued in employment policies and content over the 1987-1992 period. Two other key artists involved in this project were Peter Stewart, musician, and

Sally Hart, designer. Both continued to have an ongoing and influential role in the company's life for years to come.

It was not until the 1991 multi-cultural cabaret piece *Cabaret d'Esperanza (Cabaret of Hope)*, developed with the assistance of BEMAC (Brisbane Ethnic Music and Arts Centre), that Street Arts finally worked in partnership with West Enders of Greek and Vietnamese heritage. This shift over time towards less geographically defined communities acknowledged the need to address issues of particular concern to these groups in more depth. While this was a commendable goal it was also one which was not without challenge.

Dean Tuttle in "Street Arts: Counting The Community"[19] observes that, even as the company focussed more on these specific marginalised groups, there was still a tendency to name a broad range of other target groups within the aims of the project, in an attempt to draw disparate groups together on a common project.[20] The West End shows targeting the Murri, the aged, multi-cultural and other groups are an example. The Art in Working Life projects with their diverse workplaces and multicultural priorities are another. Even the highly specific projects with Logan City young people aimed to involve Murri and multi-cultural young people as well as the groups already accessed.

These "communities within the community" . . . increasingly over time conformed to what the Australia Council has termed its "priority areas"[21]. According to Tuttle, 'By taking over the role of defining different communities, the Australia Council allows people only to passively acquiesce to membership of one or another statistical group. Unable to define their own community identity, they are unlikely to be motivated to explore, reassess or celebrate it through community theatre'.[22]

Of course, while Street Arts was overambitious in targeting its priority groups, the company did often involve people from diverse backgrounds in projects, with varying degrees of success. A key factor was the desire to meet the needs of as many marginalised groups as possible. Another was the need to overwhelm the funding bodies with a project's worthiness.

1988

The Queensland government's resumption and development of a large riverfront section of South Brisbane for a six-month World Expo '88 international trade fair, coupled with the associated Australian bicentenary, heavily influenced Street Arts' plans for 1988. Expo was placing severe stress on the West End community through housing speculation. This resulted in short-term leases, reduced numbers of boarding houses (many being close to the site), rising rents and evictions as the area became more desirable to the middle classes and commercial developers.

Musgrave Park's proximity to Expo added to these pressures as the local Murri community found itself the target of a National Party Government move to 'clean up' the area. A strong local resistance to the celebration of the bicentenary of the invasion of Australia by the British helped fuel boycotts of Expo '88 and support for Land Rights rallies.

Not surprisingly, few local performers or theatre companies were employed in any substantial way during Expo or the associated Arts Festival. Street Arts, therefore, found its purpose in expressing and celebrating the strength of the local community in opposition to imposed cultural products.

The year began with a company cabaret piece, *High Rent Low Life*, built around issues of housing. Devised by the new ensemble, *High Rent Low Life* was a cynical look at the trials and tribulations of renters and would-be pursuers of the great Australian dream, home ownership. Immensely popular with community development workers, it lacked the innocence of the political cabaret *A Few Bobs Short of a Quid* without sufficiently grasping the emotional heart of the local housing crisis.

In contrast, the West End community show *Underwraps: City For Sale* was a genuine response to community disaffection with the state's imposed agenda, i.e., Expo '88 and associated urban renewal for development and profit. It would be untrue to say that there was universal resistance to these changes. Those property owners who saw the value of their investment soaring were able to see the positive side of this invasion. Despite this there was a predominant feeling across the community of having been done over by the state government. Most residents and resident home owners had chosen to live in this community rather than over the river for precisely the reason that it was both cheaper and had less of a "renovator's paradise" tag associated with it.

Written by Kerry O'Rourke and participants of the writers' group, *Underwraps* was a mishmash of idealised homeless people, Musgrave Park Murris and confusing theatrical conventions, but it seethed with the indignation, anger and strength of a community under threat. There was a large, brassy band, set dance and verse-speaking pieces, a choir-cum-chorus and a cast of twenty-seven. It was directed by Meg Kanowski in a very physical visual style which successfully focussed the emotional intensity.

A significant development during this period was the employment of Bill McPherson as an Aboriginal trainee. *Happy Families* had involved Murris in writing and performing some scenes, and further discussion with members of the Murri community suggested a trainee was the next step. Besides his liaison role, McPherson's presence in the collective placed Aboriginal issues constantly on the agenda. As a member of the performing ensemble, writers had to write a role for him in company shows. At times this was contrived and dramatically unsuccessful (see *Quick Quick Slow*) but at other times it provided a strength through its exploration of experiences rarely seen on stage.

The work with the Murri Community

"JALALU JALU: LAND, LAW AND LIES"

Jalalu Jalu built on the relationship developed with members of the Murri community over previous projects. At the same time, it was a West End community show, the first since 1988's *Underwraps*, with the south-east Queensland environment as its theme. Peter Stewart was particularly interested in the dialogue that could result if environmentalists were forced to examine this theme with representatives of the original inhabitants of the land, the Murri community. The employment of Murri arts workers was deemed necessary to ensure that Murri input was central to the project and not token.

As it turned out, mainstream environmentalists did not have the time or inclination to be involved in such an exciting dialogue through theatre, and the final participants were local Murris, Borallon Correctional Centre inmates, members of more fringe environmental groups, interested local people and Street Arts community participants.

After much negotiation with Murri arts groups it was decided to employ a team of Murri writers rather than one. Funding difficulties and a lack of available writers made this difficult. Murri writer Steve McCarthy (from *Underwraps*) was keen and organised CES funding for Cheryl Buchanan, a writer and publisher who had recently written a show for Icy Tea, and assistant musical director Chris Anderson, a local musician who had also been part of *Underwraps*.

Dancer Roslyn Watson was to be director and her unavailability at the last moment really put the company in a spin. A quick search of Australian Aboriginal directors found no one available. Local director Meg Kanowski was invited to step in at short notice. She had directed Buchanan's Icy Tea show, knew the company and its processes, had directed McCarthy's work in *Underwraps* and had credibility in the Murri community.

Kanowski's work on *Jalalu Jalu* was integral to its success. McCarthy had already commenced writing with members of the writing group before Buchanan was able to start, and differences in their approach to the issues meant that Kanowski played a crucial dramaturgical role as well as drama workshop leader. Murri dancers were employed casually to help choreograph large cast movement sequences and crucial narrative dance segments.

Designer Greg Clarke (a NIDA graduate) was employed more for his credentials in mainstream theatre than for his experience in community theatre. However, he proved very adept at working with a team of participants, a script that was not completed until dress rehearsal and a complex decision-making process. His set was clever, functional and cheap, and his costumes for the animal characters were wonderful.

Jalalu Jalu: Land, Law and Lies was a great community show which had a
sell-out season. The secret to its success was its emotional and political heart.
The cast's commitment was palpable to audiences and united the disparate
elements of the script, songs and dances into a whole greater than the sum of
its elements. McCarthy's animal totem characters provided humour, Buchanan
contributed the importance of law and women's business,

Chris Anderson and Dawn Daylight wrote some great songs, Bernie Lewis
organised technical miracles, and Meg Kanowski kept it all together.

The final success of *Jalalu Jalu* injected some hope into a company reeling from
the exhaustion of the previous five months, the loss of annual PAB funding and
the imminent departure of Peter Stewart and Bill McPherson.

"THRU MURRI EYES"

The second project focussing specifically on Murri issues originally took
Musgrave Park, a traditional gathering place for Murris in West End, as its
source of inspiration. With a working title of *Stories From Musgrave Park*, noted
poet, writer and storyteller Maureen Watson was employed in 1991 to develop
a draft concept for creative development later that year and production in 1992.
A professional Murri production had been the aim of Street Arts since *Jalalu
Jalu*. Street Arts hoped to supply the administrative support that would
eventually lead to the establishment of an independent Murri theatre company.

A lack of time and resources and insufficient communication during 1992
meant that Maureen Watson languished in an unproductive state for some
months. She had the stories, concepts and characters developed during the
creative development period, but there was no script. This was partly due to
inexperience and the mistaken expectation that the company wanted a traditional "play". However, cultural differences between the arts workers also
caused communication to become difficult at many stages of the project. Ainsley
Burdell, who was dramaturg on the initial stages, was unable to convince
Maureen Watson that the company envisaged this project in terms of storytelling through dance, drama and song, the very form for which her poetry seemed
particularly suited.[23]

The difficulties did not become apparent until production was due to start. Sue
Rider, who had worked with Watson's poetry in *You Came To My Country But
You Didn't Turn Black*, was called in as dramaturg. The result of her work was
a sweeping historical scenario that made no reference to the creative development material. Watson withdrew and the production became *Thru Murri Eyes*,
a combination of naturalistic contemporary drama and stylised invasion
history devised by director Kathryn Fisher and the cast. Joe Hurst's masks
were particularly effective in the historical sections and music played an
important low-key role, but the outdoor setting of Jagera Arts Centre at

124

Musgrave Park was underutilised. The piece, performed as proscenium arch theatre, no longer had Musgrave Park as its context.

Despite the expense and organisation that had gone into the staging of this mainly Aboriginal production, it was not a great success, even within its own community. Those Murris who saw it enjoyed seeing their issues and history on stage, but it was not the show to ignite the community behind the concept of a Murri Theatre Company. Despite the difficulties, a primarily Murri show had been successfully produced through the skills of local Murri actors, director, designer and technicians and this, in concert with the work of the previous four years, can be seen as contributing in a significant way to the emergence of Brisbane's indigenous performing company Kooemba Jdarra. Without the work of Street Arts in pioneering this work alongside Contact Youth Theatre, which had also developed a significant Aboriginal and Torres Strait Island programme, it is unlikely that this would have occurred as soon as it did.

Stepping Out

Fiona Winning followed Pauline Peel into the coordinator's role in 1987. She was enthusiastic and inspiring, always kept the long view before the collective, maintained personal links with the funding bodies, developed the company's links with the Murri community and the Community Arts Network, budgeted and lobbied for more appropriate levels of funding, and successfully managed the company within budget. She developed the relationships with communities that led to some of Street Arts' most successful cultural development projects and she successfully publicised a series of high profile seasons. She was a forward thinker.

Being principally involved in budgeting and liaising with funding bodies, it was Winning who relayed the demands of the PAB to company meetings. It was she who brought the ideas for possible projects to discussions of the following year's programme. The rest of the collective were either too inexperienced and/or too involved in the actualisation of the current projects to be visualising and synthesising future ideas much beforehand. These factors, combined with the need to get applications written in a hurry to meet deadlines, unfortunately meant that many decisions were not fully discussed before being agreed to.

While the collective continued to pay everyone the same wage ($20,000 p.a. in 1988) and maintained company meetings as the principal decision-making body, it was a far cry from the close group decision-making of 1983. People did not spend time outside of work hours socialising together over dreams for Street Arts' future. Some did socialise together, others had other networks of friends and/or families to be with. It was a different situation and Winning became, through circumstance, a *de facto* artistic director with the collective as her powerful but usually acquiescent reference group.

With mounting pressure from the Performing Arts Board for the company to conform to more mainstream notions of artistic excellence and with decisions being made in this less than ideal way during 1988, Street Arts, after eight and a half years of existence and on PAB advice, found itself doing its first non-original work in April-May 1989. Numerous scripts from Australian community theatre companies and from Aboriginal playwrights were examined, but Winning's advice was to stick to a small, professional cast. Options were limited. It was finally decided in early 1989 to do The *Ballad Of Lois Ryan* by Andrew Bovell with music by Irine Vela, a piece originally written for the Melbourne Workers Theatre.

Lois Ryan was very much a main-stage style production on a shoestring budget. Production values were very important, the performance style mainly naturalistic and community input minimal. The Textile Workers Union were contacted and provided access for cast and crew to a spinning mill and its workers, some of whom attended the show. It could not however be called an Art in Working Life project in that the level of genuine collaboration with unions was minimal. Set materials were scavenged from mills and factories. Winning's character was Italian and required bilingual performance, so links were made with the Italian community. However, there was not the sense of ownership by the relevant communities usually developed during Street Arts' projects.

The season was moderately successful.

Dean Tuttle explores the pressure of the dominant cultural ideology on the company at this time.[24] He argues that it came both from the PAB and the desire of company members to be taken seriously as artists, to fulfill their "artistic needs". The company was, after all, operating within the dominant ideological system. It is not surprising that the 'convenient and powerful myth that the established mainstream theatre provides the model for good product' gained currency in the company, though it was committed to empowering alternative voices, practitioners and practices in opposition to this ideology.[25]

Amongst all this concern for professional standards and maintaining favour with the PAB there emerged a series of projects remarkable in their daring and challenging in their processes and outcomes: the Logan City projects.

"CHARGED UP" IN LOGAN CITY

Within south-east Queensland, Street Arts' work focussed on three main geographical areas. Inala and West End were the strongest of these until 1989. In that year, after an absence of four years, Street Arts returned to Logan City on Brisbane's southern border. Logan includes many of the fast growing corridor communities surrounding the south-east freeway and arterial route connecting Brisbane with the Gold Coast. Although the company had been involved in two previous projects in the area (1982 and 1984) the 1989 foray was not in any real way connected developmentally with their previous work. Their presence this time was at the invitation of the Christian Brothers' run Centre Education Unit in Kingston, Logan City. Two major theatre projects and the emergence of the independent youth arts organisation, Feral Arts, resulted. The first project was with non-mainstream young people and titled *Charged Up*. Initially a combination of a community theatre company looking for some marginalised young people to work with, and a Logan City youth worker and teacher looking for theatre workers willing to do drama with young people, it became much more than that.

The Centre Education programme (an offshoot of the Christian Brothers' run Boy's Town) provided an alternative education programme for 12 to 17 year-olds who had dropped out of or been expelled from the state education system. Approximately 25 students voluntarily attended the Centre on the condition that they participated, respected the decisions of staff/student meetings, and acted safely and legally. Approximately eight staff taught traditional subjects plus living and technical skills to small groups.

Street Arts employed Hugh Watson as writer-in-the-community to work with these students and the group of slightly older young people who congregated at Mayes Avenue, a local drop-in house. Mayes Avenue was a project of Youth and Family Service, a community-based welfare organisation with strong links to The Centre. Youth worker Peter Browning was from West End and familiar with Street Arts' work.

Rebecca Lister, a youth worker, participant in Street Arts shows and resident of Logan was employed as project coordinator. She was instrumental in introducing Watson to the community, establishing understanding between arts workers and youth workers, organising parent support and a fundraising benefit night, and finding a venue. Watson, who had most recently worked with young people in The Valley on a Rock'n'Roll Circus show *Psst!* for the Brisbane Youth Service, produced his script from the young people's stories.

The choice of Sarah Moynihan as visual artist on the project was an inspired one. Moynihan had worked with Brisbane Youth Service and John Oxley Youth Detention Centre as full-time arts worker. She was able to involve any young people experiencing difficulty in the group workshops in meaningful individual projects that contributed to publicity or the set.

The writing of the song, *Charged Up*, at a Centre workshop was a breakthrough in the project. It signalled to the apprehensive participants, no strangers to failure, and their worried teachers that this project might just be possible. For, despite their enthusiasm and dedicated support, much of it after hours, teachers and youth workers were uncertain that what Street Arts said they would do, i.e., produce a show by and with these young people for a public season could actually be achieved. They were also justifiably concerned about the pressure it placed on the participants, and about the letdown that would occur after the pressure, the excitement and the artists disappeared at the end of the season.

The Street Arts workers were no more convinced of their ability to pull off the show than the youth workers. Dress rehearsals at the venue, a large shop in a vacant shopping mall, were disrupted by cast members being placed in custody, drinking, feuds, stage-fright, unlearnt lines and desertion. On the day of opening night it was like going through the motions. There was no certainty that there would be a show, or how it would be received in its unpolished state.

That night the cast told the story of their lives. At times inspired, at times stumbling, they performed to a capacity audience of young people, parents, supporters, youth workers and welfare bureaucrats. The atmosphere was electric, the tension palpable and the evident risk taken by the young inexperienced performers created a strange bond between the cast and the audience. The story was real and the audience responded with warmth, respect and good humour. It was a new experience for the participants and, by the end of the evening, the sense of accomplishment and pride in ownership had replaced the distress evident throughout the day.

There was by no means a unanimous sense of triumph amongst youth workers however. In evaluating the project there was a sense that, overall, the project was a more positive experience for the young people than negative. But the cost in terms of emotional support, disrupted programmes and post-show frustration was high.

Despite these difficulties, and in some ways as a response to the realities represented in these expressed concerns, Rebecca Lister, Hugh Watson and Sarah Moynihan formed a partnership with the intention of further pursuing a community arts programme in Logan City. They did this to fill what they saw was the gap left by Street Arts' withdrawal after *Charged Up*. The Centre Education programme was integral to the survival of this newly formed group and, although Street Arts had a commitment to return the following year, it was less directly involved in the formation of Feral Arts than it had been in the case of Icy Tea and Rock'n'Roll Circus. In each case it had been a willingness to take advantage of opportunities within a developmental consciousness which was critical, rather than the notion of working to some preplanned blueprint.

BACK TO LOGAN

Twelve months later Street Arts returned to Logan to undertake a follow up project, *Raise The Roof*, this time focussing on youth housing and related issues. Two members of the recently formed Feral Arts, Hugh Watson and Rebecca Lister, were included in the team as writer and assistant director respectively. Lister also filled the role of Logan City Coordinator. The aim was to build on the strengths of the 1989 project (songwriting, youth-worker and Centre support) and to introduce instrument-making as a physical, hands-on element that linked in with the Centre's manual arts workshop programme. It would also expand on the success of Sarah Moynihan's visual arts work, so effective during the *Charged Up* project. However, failure to gain funding for Denis Peel as music tutor and co-musical director meant that the role music could play was reduced.

Hugh Watson found participants less willing to talk about family situations and homelessness than about boredom and "hanging out" behaviour, and so was more dependent on information from youth workers than in 1989.

A full day was devoted at the beginning of the project to airing expectations and possible problems with teachers and youth workers. Unfortunately, changes in staff at Youth and Family Service had led to unsympathetic management at the Mayes Avenue drop-in centre. This undermined support during the project. Street Arts' tendency to develop broad, all encompassing goals desirous of embracing quite disparate groups within the community became a problem as slightly older young people and participants in the relatively distant Beenleigh workshops also became involved. Territoriality, gender issues and age differences all became difficulties during the project.

That a show did result was testimony to the commitment of the arts workers — in particular, visual artist Lisa Smith's creative involvement of young people, the Feral Arts team and the tremendous support of the Centre staff.

The script of *Raise The Roof* was witty and pithy. The set and location, a huge abandoned markets building, was stunning. The band was rehearsed and committed, but the cast unpredictable and disunited. Why? A combination of age and territory differences, a reluctance to own the stories in the script, demanding roles, an alien art form (most of the cast had not been involved in *Charged Up*) and too heavy a burden on director Ainsley Burdell — all contributed to the difficulties.

Despite it all, however, the show was well-received in the community and the media, and many young people took from it new skills and confidence. Importantly, Feral Arts were in a position to build on these successes with funding for follow-up workshops.

From 1990 onwards Feral Arts developed music, visual arts, performance and, particularly, video arts programmes aimed at the isolated young people of Logan City and Albert Shire. In that period they forged an approach to this work which proved to be highly successful and avoided some of the major pitfalls of the large scale theatre productions of 1989 and 1990. Hugh Watson's account of the 1989-90 work elsewhere in this collection of writings further explores some of the issues raised in these ambitious projects.

"QUICK QUICK SLOW":
LESSONS OF A COLLECTIVE

While much of the work of Street Arts was radical and challenging, it would be naive to pretend that every project was a triumph. With increasing pressure from the Australia Council in the late eighties, the company felt itself forced into a position of dancing to the tune of the funding bodies, much to the concern of the staff and ultimately to the detriment of the work.

Quick Quick Slow was an ambitious performance project which attempted to integrate cultural development ideas and PAB performance goals. The result was a salutary and costly lesson for the company.

The "Dance Marathon" project, as it was called, came out of a series of suggestions for future directions at a public meeting at The Paint Factory in early 1988. It was an attempt to unite in one project the schizophrenic elements of Street Arts' practice and funding situation.

Pauline Peel's recollection of a large community production in Scotland based around different dance styles and involving the audience on stage once again (*Next Stop West End*, 1985) caught the company's imagination. It was planned to use this model in a project targeting two fringe communities with strong working class histories but currently in economic decline. These were Ipswich and Redcliffe.

Links with trade unions were to be exploited, and the young unemployed, the aged, people from non-English speaking backgrounds and the local Murri communities were all to be targeted for their versions of the districts' histories. Local dance and music groups were to be accessed and the final show had the potential to tell the stories of two contrasting communities through a chronological framework of dance and music styles. Audiences would be invited to participate in dances and there would be space for performances by local participants in what would be principally a company show of high artistic standard.

To involve the communities in the project, an extended period of workshops in drama, music, dance, visual arts and writing would be offered in each town, culminating in a community concert. These workshops would provide the material and research necessary for the final show, impart skills to participants, and develop pieces for performance at a community concert and in the final show when it returned to their local hall.

The final show was to be rehearsed and performed at The Paint Factory before being toured to Ipswich, Redcliffe and suburban Brisbane halls where workshops would once again involve the local community during the week before

130

Friday and Saturday performances. A similar tour of four regional towns with previous Street Arts links was to follow in 1990.

It was an elaborate plan designed to give voice to communities the company perceived as lacking opportunities to express themselves against the clamour of Brisbane. And it was to do it in an accessible and innovative form of sufficiently high artistic standard to impress the PAB with the value of its goals.

The company had their work cut out convincing the PAB, the Queensland Arts Division, local government and the Community Cultural Development Unit (CCDU) of the Australia Council that it would work. Eventually the project was approved but with insufficient funding to include both communities. Thus the project as outlined above, minus Redcliffe, was commenced in early August 1989. That this coincided with a change in company coordinators (the beginning of the third generation of employees) was to place incredible pressures on the working team.

Key guest artists on the project proved difficult to select. Brisbane singer/musician/actor Carl Rush was employed as co-musical director, performer and music workshop leader. Designers were Sally Hart and Anna Bourke. The director, writer and choreographer however needed to be acceptable to the PAB or Literature Board — Street Arts was under increasing pressure from the PAB to achieve standards consistent with more mainstream companies whose philosophies, processes and aspirations were totally alien to those of a community based political theatre company. This demand coupled with the fact that this was a community based project meant that the company would find itself trapped in an impossible situation.

Local Murri classically trained dancer Roslyn Watson was funded as choreographer but finding the required combination of skills and experience in both a writer and a director proved to be a challenge which resulted in a complex and, as it transpired, difficult mix of personalities in a team with conflicting working methods and incompatible aspirations.

A number of women writers recommended by the Australia Council were approached in 1988 and early 1989, but none was available. On a trip to Sydney and Melbourne later in the year, Fiona Winning met James McCaughey who had earlier been recommended as a professional development leader by the PAB. After some discussion his colleague and fellow director at The Mill Theatre in Geelong in the early eighties, Neil Greenaway, was recommended as director for the Dance Marathon. Time and options were running out by this stage and Winning returned with the suggestion that Greenaway be employed alongside a young writer he had worked with on a number of devised-in-the-community shows. Julianne O'Brien had most recently caught the PAB's notice with a work for the Murray River Performing Group that had been toured overseas.

Company performers spent two valuable weeks in professional development with James McCaughey as O'Brien began her research in Ipswich. The large Dance Marathon team then assembled for two weeks planning and orientation.

Employing workers with no history with the company and in such crucial roles proved to be problematic though it must be acknowledged that it had been successful at other times in the past. There was not sufficient time available to induct the two workers into the Street Arts modus operandi and no effective conflict resolution procedures existed to facilitate the resolution of differences as they arose.

In addition, the lack of a clear invitation from the community and severe under-estimation of the parochial self-sufficiency of an old city like Ipswich with its distrust of Brisbane, resulted in a dearth of local participants. Inexperience at the planning stages, Fiona Winning's departure, new coordinator Kara Miller's lack of experience, and burnout and distrust amongst the arts workers combined to create a project that was at all stages a mere shadow of its initial vision.

In comparing this process and project with those of 1983 and 1984 it seems that either through bad management or circumstance the company misread the level of support which they expected to receive from the Ipswich community. As a concept it appeared to have all the ingredients of an (admittedly ambitious) exciting and ground-breaking project, bringing together a number of the types of groups that the company had been developing relationships with over a period of years. Here was an apparently marginalised community with a traditional working class history, crying out to have its story told. Unfortunately the foundations of trust between the company and the community had not been laid. The result was an arts company with one picture of this community in its collective head but one which did not match the community's picture of itself.

One of the skills which the early members of the company had apparently failed to pass on to subsequent generations was not so much how to work effectively in large community contexts (the second generation had successfully done this with *Happy Families* and *Underwraps*), but how to effectively establish the necessary groundwork in a major new community. In this case, unlike Inala or Logan City, the model of first establishing a presence, followed by a small scale pilot project, before launching into a major project was ignored. The other factor in this case was the loss of control of the process by the core collective through succumbing to the pressures of outside funding agencies who had little understanding of the complexities of community participative processes. Creating new material is complex enough at the best of times. It becomes infinitely more complex when the stakeholders include whole communities and where there is an attempt to combine notions of Art with visions of community development. Unless the whole team speaks the same language the process becomes well nigh impossible.

How was it possible for this to happen? How could the company allow such a clearly articulated vision to fall to pieces? Briefs and agreements prepared for the guest artists were obviously insufficient while the company trusted that the *process* would sort out any problems as they arose, with courage and sheer grit triumphing in the end as it had so many times in the past.

That the company was driven by ideals and not by traditional theatrical skills and technology now became a problem. Street Arts had begun life with a strong political analysis, an attitude of total belief in itself and a willingness to explore ways of working outside the constraints of traditional theatre making. Unfortunately, this became a liability when attempting to bridge that gap between funding body pressures for excellent product and best practice for the company given its skills and history. In some ways what had been its strength in its early years now became its Achilles heel.

Julianne O'Brien, supported by Neil Greenaway, reframed Street Arts' vision as a text-tied draft set in the Ipswich Workers Club during a miners' strike in the forties. No other historical period was explored; there was little celebration of community; naturalism was paramount; an incident to do with Murri history seemed over-contrived; and all the dancing was of the forties ballroom style with which Ros Watson was not all that familiar.

The seasons went as planned with modest audiences, people enjoyed participating in the dances and the standard of performance was in some respects higher than in the past. However, by the end of the dispiriting suburban tour, the only thing worth celebrating was Labor's historic win in the state election the very day of the last scheduled performance.

There were many lessons to be learnt from this project. The problems associated with employing artists without ensuring a compatibility of philosophy and approach was one. Equally important was the danger inherent in choosing a community as the source of stories and material without planning effective strategies to empower that community in the process. To go in uninvited, fail to meet most community cultural development goals, then leave to develop the product elsewhere was, at best, risking disinterest.

The Third Generation

David Watt describes a "third generation" in Australia's community theatre movement who see the work as 'an habituated practice confirmed by funding' and 'a career option for people who, in some cases, see themselves headed for more "respectable" work'.[26] Street Arts has been something of an exception to this because of 'the political polarisation the Bjelke-Petersen government sustained in Brisbane'[27] through to the late eighties. This resulted in the maintenance of a steady stream of politically aware artists committed to opposing an oppressive and anti-democratic government. The demise of the

National Party stranglehold on power and the emergence of an effective Labor government with an assumed commitment to social justice programmes threatened to change this.

The effect of this change in political climate coincided with the emergence within the Performing Arts Board of a return to a more conservative approach to funding. This was the result of the decline of radical and community theatre influence within the board and the fragmentation of what had been a committed and effective lobby force of community theatre companies throughout Australia. It also represented a concerted fightback by the larger mainstream companies which saw their position as the natural recipients of the majority of funding dollars threatened by the effective arguments of the CCDU and the radical theatre movement. This posed a major problem for Street Arts. In the past Street Arts had argued and often won their case for criteria relevant to the goals and philosophy of the company to be accepted as valid yardsticks. This time the company succumbed.

Employment decisions in the late eighties were made with the PAB firmly in mind. Rod Wissler, PAB representative and lecturer in drama at QUT, was present during auditions to discount perceptions that the company did not employ the best actors available. Ainsley Burdell, a mature-age graduate of QUT's BA (drama), was employed as a collective member and, while she had a strong interest in community theatre, her tertiary qualifications were definitely seen as an advantage. In a similar vein, impressive office and clerical skills, rather than knowledge of community theatre or theatre per se, were the key criteria in selecting support staff.

David Watt's definition of the third generation applies to Street Arts to the extent that the more people were employed purely for their skills, the less emphasis there was on a common philosophy and a commitment to Street Arts' community processes. In practice this sometimes resulted in decisions appropriate to a main-stage theatre company coming in conflict with the development needs of a community. Community participants who unwittingly interrupted elaborate set constructions requiring concentration and skill sometimes received a clear message that this was the *real* stuff of theatre and their presence was not wanted; communities were sometimes portrayed in ignorant and/or inappropriate terms in otherwise successful publicity campaigns; the provision of more sophisticated technical facilities at The Paint Factory resulted in higher rental rates and elaborate sets of conditions of usage which in turn led to a decrease in community usage.

The increased emphasis on professionalism, standards and skills led to a breakdown in the company's ability to work creatively and flexibly with diverse communities and a reduction in the company's commitment to the people of those communities because of a shift in fundamental philosophy. This contributed to a steady fall in general membership and community support.

PRISONS WORK: "OUT OF THE BLUE"

During this tumultuous period there continued a series of outstanding projects which further developed the artistic and developmental work of the company. These projects took the company into areas which had been touched on in earlier work but which had not been ready for significant development until this time. They included work with the Murri community, work at Logan City, and work with communities from non-English-speaking backgrounds in collaboration with the Brisbane Ethnic Music and Arts Centre (BEMAC). Each of these is referred to elsewhere. The other significant area of work was with the prison system and women prisoners in particular.

The Women in Prison project that resulted in *Out Of The Blue* in 1991 was a longer and more careful version of the "company show from a community base" process used for *Trading Hours* (Art in Working Life project 1990). It had its origins in 1989 planning meetings and sought to build on a relationship commenced with the Brisbane Women's Correctional Centre in 1988 and continued voluntarily by Terrie Kavanagh and Katie Harrison.

The process was divided into stages for funding purposes. Therese Collie conducted ten weeks of writing workshops as "writer in the community" in the prison during early 1990. These resulted in the production of a booklet of the women's work.

Therese was then commissioned to write a play about women in prison for production in 1991. Funding from the PAB allowed two weeks creative development on the script in December 1990. Auditions were held for performers to participate in this and Hilary Beaton was employed as dramaturg. Murri actors Kathryn Fisher (known to the company since work on *Happy Families*) and Marguerite Wesselinoff (a performer in *Underwraps* and *Raise The Roof*) joined Ainsley Burdell, Lisa-Jane Stockwell and designer Gavan Fenelon in the creative development phase.

At the end of the creative development and during rehearsal in 1991, interested public, prisoner support group members and prison staff attended work-in-progress sessions. Sadly, and perversely, members of the primary community, i.e., prisoners, were not able to attend but those in power over them were. Input from authorities did help flesh out the final script, but anger from prison staff over how they were portrayed in initial drafts meant that the touring version of the show never gained permission to be performed at the Brisbane Women's Correctional Centre.

Out Of The Blue received a PAB project grant and was produced with the largest production budget in Street Arts' history.

The season was successful and the tour to the six men's correctional centers in south-east Queensland was a triumph in terms of audience enthusiasm.

That the show was unable to return to its original community was the only disappointment. Therese Collie's analysis of this process elsewhere in this book gives some fascinating insights into this complex situation.

1991

From touring *Out Of The Blue*, the company moved to Rockhampton for a week's orientation on their next project, the Duaringa residency. Here Ainsley Burdell, Mark Shortis and Murri artist Vanessa Fisher were joined by Rockhampton writer Maria Porter. Fisher had been associated with the company since working on Boundary Street Festival murals, and was well-known for her work with Kamarga Arts. Porter was known from tours and workshops in Rockhampton and had written shows for Backyard Theatre Company and other Rockhampton community groups.

Duaringa Shire, just west of Rockhampton, was a keen proponent of community arts. The Women in the West project, an independent project targeting rural women in central Queensland communities, and a week of the *Quick Quick Slow* tour spent in Dauringa were stepping stones to this ten week residency.

In something of a return to earlier community development processes the team worked predominantly in schools and with women's arts groups, spending three weeks in each of the Duaringa-Dingo, Blackwater and Bauhinia-Woorabinda areas. Woorabinda is a separate local government based on the old Aboriginal Reserve and was included at Street Arts' insistence. Outcomes included school and community concerts, a booklet of stories and poetry, a mural and radio play produced with Blackwater High School students, and other plays, songs and dances.

Meanwhile the imminent departure of coordinator Kara Miller once again placed the company in the problematic position of selecting a replacement for this key position. Working conditions at The Paint Factory, which probably failed to comply with many of the most basic industrial health and safety requirements, may well have played a part in the lack of interest in the job despite a significant increase in the wage offered (thus ending the collective's equal pay regime). The limited number of workers throughout Australia with experience in the arts, community development work and administration constantly placed Street Arts and similar companies in the position of competing for a very small pool of talented workers. Cynthia Irvine, who took over from Kara Miller in May 1991, had a rich background in community and media work but a limited history of involvement in theatre as such. This was both an advantage and a disadvantage. It meant that she was well versed in working across sectors and could envisage projects with true community connections, but her approach highlighted the differences within the company between the theatre aspirations of some members and the community development aspirations of others.

Among the final work undertaken by Street Arts to be referred to in this book is that with members of Brisbane's non-English-speaking background ((NESB) communities. While these communities had often been acknowledged in previous projects (*Next Stop West End, Sweeping Statements, The Ballad of Lois Ryan, Trading Hours*) it was not until this ninth year that the company found time and the opportunity to work in depth with this significant group. *Cabaret d'Esperanza* was a co-production with BEMAC which set out to represent as directly as possible the lives and aspirations of these largely invisible "communities".

Therese Collie was employed as writing coordinator and she began by working with participants from BEMAC's writing workshops of the previous year. The company had been clearer with its aims this time and had planned a cabaret format to allow participants' different writing styles and the music to work together without having to be forced to fit a storyline. Collie therefore encouraged participants to write stories and skits that she later linked with songs, dances and an M.C.'s. narrative. After the project many of these writers continued to meet, giving their group the title 'The Scribbling Optimistics'.

Cabaret d'Esperanza may not have been as big as some community shows, but it successfully fulfilled the long-standing aims of involving the Greek and Vietnamese communities in a West End production. In major community productions there is often one particular outcome which is of special significance. In this case it was the emergence of a very talented story-teller, comedian and writer in Effie Detsimas. Born of Greek parents in Sydney in the early 1930s, she spent most of the first eighteen years of her life with relatives on the Greek island of Ithaca before being brought back to Australia and to Brisbane in the late 1940s. She subsequently wrote, with Therese Collie, a new script, *I Yitha — The She Goat* which has received substantial Performing Arts Board support.

END OF AN ERA

While the work continued unabated throughout the late 80's and into the early 90s, the accumulated pressures of maintaining a large venue (The Paint Factory), a shrinking annual level of grant money and ongoing internal difficulties eventually took their toll. Non-government and government income was down. Corporate sponsorship was not forthcoming. Urgent and major decisions were about to be confronted by the company and they were brought to a head when Rock'n'Roll Circus decided they no longer wanted to share tenancy of The Paint Factory. Street Arts could not afford to keep it themselves and there were perceived advantages in not having to maintain a venue. It would free the company to work where it wanted for particular projects, save money and labour, improve workplace health and safety, and allow the company to relocate to a more central position in the West End community with better access and visibility.

The *Last Blast at The Paint Factory* and a bumper garage sale heralded the end of an era as Street Arts moved to a new smaller office in Boundary Street West End in November 1991. At the same time three staff went off wages due to lack of funds and the administrative position was reduced to part-time.

There had been much discussion about whether to fold the company, and tensions within the ex-collective members and between staff and members of the management committee were aggravated by this and other change options. Street Arts was heading for its third phase in a demoralised state.

Phase Three: New Structures, New Horizons (1992 . . .)

At the Annual General Meeting of March 1992, Street Arts' members were invited to comment on their perception of the company's future. A number of long-term supporters, including Pauline Peel and Peter Stewart, felt that if the energy wasn't there to continue, then the company should end with a bang rather than a whimper. Ten years would be longer than the founders had imagined the company surviving and that anniversary would fall at the end of the year. There would be no disgrace if the company was to do what the depleted funding allowed in 1992, then bow out with a celebration of ten amazing years.

More recent participants were more optimistic. It was Therese Collie, however, who swayed the meeting when she asked why it was that the community/political theatre movement should be forced to set up new structures from scratch every time there was a change in funding policy. Recalling the demise of the PTT, she advocated change within the structure of Street Arts which would give it the energy to tackle new circumstances.

Who had the energy to effect this change? A number of people beyond the management committee volunteered to begin this major re-evaluation process and a series of meetings which spanned a number of months was initiated.

These meetings operated on a number of levels. There was a consultative committee (a mix of early company members, current employees and other experienced community cultural development workers) which undertook an organisational review of the company and began the writing of a new mission statement and three year plan. Making recommendations to this on the details of goals, structure and a model of cultural development were the ex-collective members who eventually evolved into the Artistic Working Party. The management committee, meanwhile, was asked to take a larger role in the company by contributing to these groups and ratifying and implementing their decisions. The Artistic Working Party, in fact, became a deliberate combination of arts workers, company staff and management committee members.[28]

The new mission statement exhibited a distinct shift towards the rhetoric of community cultural development and a harder political edge. The emphasis on "original, dynamic, entertaining theatre" of 1991 was replaced by a recommitment to empowering communities through theatre. However, this shift in emphasis was not necessarily a symbol of a new united understanding. Once again the company tried to strike that elusive balance between 'doing artistically satisfying things and doing worthwhile . . . projects'.[29]

"LIVEABLE STREETS"

The most significant projects of this period were the Aboriginal production of *Thru Murri Eyes* referred to elsewhere, and a most unusual project — *Liveable Streets*.

Liveable Streets was a new development in method. Employing a team of arts workers including Wollongong's Catherine Fargher, who had worked with Death Defying Theatre as writer/deviser, visual artist Kath Porrill and Pat Zuber, visual artist and co-founder of Wynnum's Mudflat Arts, the company moved away from the "large-inclusive-community-show" model of cultural development. Discussions with the grass-roots organisation Citizens Advocating Responsible Transportation (CART) led to a proposal for a project which would work towards a series of celebrations of "community" with an emphasis on people reclaiming their streets. A number of urban quality of life issues would be explored with different communities utilising a variety of artforms at different times and places. The project was no less ambitious than previous Street Arts' work in terms of target groups and breadth of issues, but it did not attempt to unite them all in one production.

Cultural products of the project included a "person-sized" town planning board game produced with a group of town planners, a series of posters developed with sex workers and housing groups, a variety of music and performance pieces devised for street theatre and specific community events, a collection of haiku poems screen printed on zebra crossings, a young mothers' rap song, harmony singing on buses and shop-front displays.

Two festival days framed the "performance" period of the project and each featured performance pieces or "rituals" as well as stalls, buskers and the freedom to be out on the closed-off streets. The first festival was in West End and featured a performance in which the local landmark Dornoch Terrace bridge was auctioned off to developers, supported by a choir of auctioneers and bidders. The second was in the inner northside suburb of New Farm. A rather elaborate closing ritual had been in rehearsal for some weeks for this event, but was washed out by a sudden storm. It had involved many community participants from the company's core West End support base, plus a smattering of others attracted by the project's theme.

Liveable Streets broke new ground in the variety of ways in which it involved people in exploring their attitudes and fears about the urban environment and their relationship with their street. For this it received an award from the Royal Australian Planning Institute's Queensland Chapter. However, while it had an effective community presence in a guerrilla-tactic fashion, it failed to attract the broad sweep of local support that could have made the festival days truly diverse celebrations of local community.

TEN YEARS ON: 1993

Street Arts survived 1993 principally because Arts Queensland did not want to see another professional Brisbane theatre company follow TN! (formerly Twelfth Night) Theatre Company to the wall. Arts Queensland's operational grant constituted 51% of total income and allowed time for consolidation and the implementation of new structures. Applications to the Australia Council for project grants were largely unsuccessful (see Table 1). However, the need for a project officer to focus on community cultural development work was recognised by the CCDB.

There was not the level of funding, therefore, to implement the full 1993 programme, let alone the three-year plan developed in 1992. In dollar terms 1993 had the lowest level of income since 1985. (See Figure 1).

Old supporters of the company were not going to let the prevailing despair prevent a proper celebration of the tenth anniversary, however. Steve Capelin and Pauline Peel wrote and compiled a short history of the company, and a committee that included Di Craig, Meg Kanowski, Katrina Devery, Ainsley Burdell, Pauline Peel, Steve Capelin and Bernie Lewis began to plan a suitable celebration.

The *Next Stop West End Magical Mystery Bus Tour* and *Street Arts Tenth Birthday Party* (the latter at South's Leagues Club) were self-funding events held at the end of March, ten years after the first Community Circus Festival. As the crowded buses left Musgrave Park — the very site of that first community project ten years earlier — on their entertaining tour of historical (Street Arts) sites, a new groundswell of enthusiasm for the company's work seemed possible.

On a more practical level, however, Street Arts was involved in the protracted process of appointing another new coordinator. In April 1993 Brent McGregor joined Project Officer Panos Couros and office manager Anna Fairley, heralding a new beginning for the company with fresh staff who, though fully aware of the history of the previous ten years, were relatively unaffected by the personal complexities and historical encumbrances of that era.

The twelve month period following 1993 saw the company take a low profile during which time a largely new core team set about redefining a role for the Street Arts of the nineties. During this period a professional production of *Daily Grind* written by Vicki Reynolds and directed by Meg Kanowski was mounted. Subsequently, the company developed project work which was a mixture of tried and true community collaborations with some of Brisbane's outlying communities, notably Carole Park and Deception Bay, and a move towards a new experimental element in the company's work. Project Officer Panos Couros developed connections with a number of artists involved in the "performance art" area which resulted in a season and a number of events featuring small

141

scale works of a decidedly non-mainstream nature. The company was also active in the Brisbane Fringe Festivals of 1993 and 1995. The most significant of these recent works has been with women of the Filipino community who have produced a broadcast-quality documentary video entitled *Ang Pilipina (The Pilipina Women)*.

These two streams have co-existed alongside the ongoing and more traditional theatre-making aspirations of the company, largely driven by Company Co-ordinator Brent McGregor. The latter have included a series of play readings and works-in-progress and two new plays, the first of which *I Yitha — The She Goat* will be produced in 1995 as a co-production with the Ethnic Communities Council of Queensland. The second, *Upsadaisy*, a commissioned work by Therese Collie, explores a woman's search for and discovery of her Chinese ancestry.

The third generation has taken some of the strengths of the early years of the company and combined them with a drive to explore new directions which reflect the interests of the current generation of workers within the company.

Funding The Vision

AUSTRALIA COUNCIL

The Community Arts Board's support of Street Arts' initial work has continued throughout the company's history via the CAB's successors, the Community Cultural Development Unit (CCDU) and Community Cultural Development Board (CCDB). Street Arts' willingness to take risks and their commitment to creating new local structures for ongoing cultural development in communities, such as Icy Tea in Inala and Feral Arts in Logan, has produced an enviable reputation with the CCDB.

However, the community cultural development (CAB/CCDU/CCDB) proportion of Australia Council grants budgets has always been small (13% in 1982-3, 9-10% throughout most of the eighties and 10.9% in 1992-3)[30], especially when compared to the Performing Arts Board (47.4% in 1992-3)[31]. The CAB/CCDU/CCDB has consistently seen its role as seeding new initiatives and supporting State Community Arts Networks rather than long term maintenance of arts companies.

Figure 1 illustrates the source of Street Arts' income over the twelve year period 1983-1994. The company's application to the Theatre Board in 1983 was successful, and $5,553 was received towards the 1984 programme. (See Table 1). This tripled in 1985, jumped to $40,000 in 1986 and continued to increase until it peaked at almost $89,000 in 1989.

While these figures include grants for creative and professional development, they consist primarily of grants for annual funding, a status achieved by the company in 1986. Always presented as a precarious privilege by officers of the PAB, Street Arts was "under review" or "on notice" from 1988 until it lost its annual funding status in 1991. This ensured that the company was continually struggling to impress the PAB with the importance and relevance of its work while at the same time attempting to find out just what it was about the work that was not acceptable. The irony is that much of Street Arts' work during Phase Two fulfilled more PAB funding guidelines criteria than most work of the main-stage companies. New Australian work relevant to Australian audiences exploring new theatrical forms was consistently a feature of Street Arts work. PAB project funding for 1991 was $54,253 ($52,000 for *Out Of The Blue*). In 1992 it dropped to $40,000 for *Thru Murri Eyes*. An application for 1993 was unsuccessful.

The areas raised as problems during the "under review" and "on notice" years were "artistic standards" and "box-office income". In relation to the former, the buzzword was "excellence" and, according to the PAB, Street Arts didn't have it. Requests to the PAB for definitions of their criteria were not answered. Excellence being such a subjective concept, the Performing Arts Board officers

TABLE 1: Street Arts Income (Annual Reports 1983-1994)

	1983	1984	1985	1986	1987	1988	1989	1990	1991	1992	1993	1994
Community Arts Board/CCD (Australia Council)	$ 19900	$ 34554	$ 42000	$ 66800	$ 59460	$ 90280	$ 74500	$ 76737	$ 45000	$ 35000	$ 23000	$ 36554
Theatre Board/PAB (Australia Council)		$ 5553	$ 15603	$ 40000	$ 55000	$ 57805	$ 88977	$ 83576	$ 54253	$ 40000		
Other Australia Council Boards		$ 3900	$ 4128	$ 4000	$ 14800	$ 31961	$ 31401	$ 25897	$ 16060	$ 27000	$ 9712	$ 328
Arts Queensland (State)		$ 9500	$ 12000	$ 15500	$ 18750	$ 43984	$ 55830	$ 77000	$ 106000	$ 105150	$ 91150	$ 130000
Other Government (incl. Local)	$ 2160	$ 10144				$ 9765	$ 15020	$ 19142	$ 10000	$ 5000	$ 26124	$ 10719
Queensland Arts Council		$ 12777	$ 10920	$ 19300								$ 26540
All Other (incl. Box Office, Fees, Membership, etc)	$ 23124	$ 25590	$ 39682	$ 69414	$ 58790	$ 65306	$ 42090	$ 59800	$ 46886	$ 21556	$ 19910	$ 49233
TOTAL	$ 45184	$102018	$124333	$215014	$206800	$299101	$307818	$342152	$278199	$233706	$169896	$253374

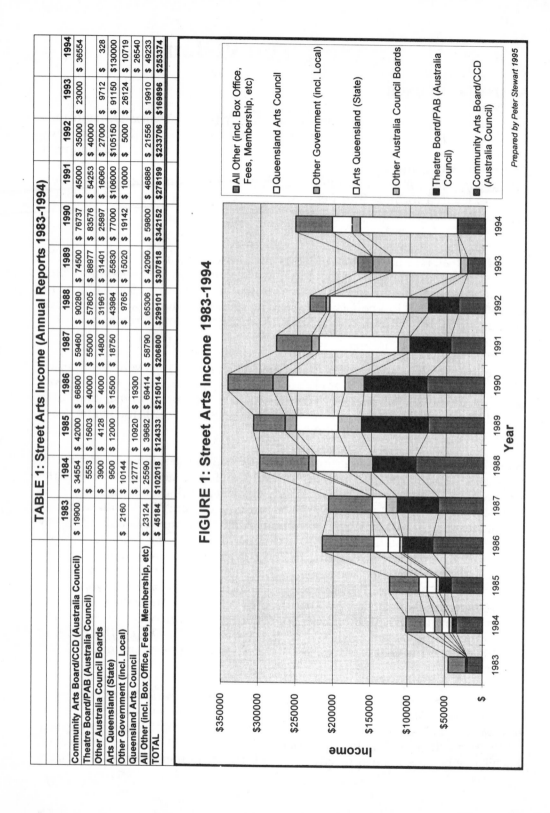

FIGURE 1: Street Arts Income 1983-1994

Legend:
- All Other (incl. Box Office, Fees, Membership, etc)
- Queensland Arts Council
- Other Government (incl. Local)
- Arts Queensland (State)
- Other Australia Council Boards
- Theatre Board/PAB (Australia Council)
- Community Arts Board/CCD (Australia Council)

Income / Year

Prepared by Peter Stewart 1995

TABLE 2: Street Arts Non-Government Income (Annual Reports 1983-1994)

	1983	1984	1985	1986	1987	1988	1989	1990	1991	1992	1993	1994
Box Office and Performance Fees	$ 11449	$ 4241	$ 12882	$ 49259	$ 33876	$ 38166	$ 23435	$ 24556	$ 16413	$ 12452	$ 8306	$ 10578
Workshop Fees	$ 5692	$ 15411	$ 4140	$ 7303	$ 5890	$ 2960	$ 1539	$ 6312	$ 3360		$ 3250	$ 33665
Queensland Arts Council		$ 12777	$ 10920	$ 19300								$ 26540
Corporate Sponsorship				$ 3555	$ 2940	$ 6620	$ 4462	$ 5076				
Paint Factory Hire								$ 5380	$ 11860			
Other (incl. Interest, Hire & Membership Fees, etc)	$ 5983	$ 5938	$ 22660	$ 9297	$ 16084	$ 17560	$ 12654	$ 18476	$ 15253	$ 9104	$ 8354	$ 4990
TOTAL	$ 23124	$ 38367	$ 50602	$ 88714	$ 58790	$ 65306	$ 42090	$ 59800	$ 46886	$ 21556	$ 19910	$ 75773

FIGURE 2: Street Arts Non-Government Income 1983-1994

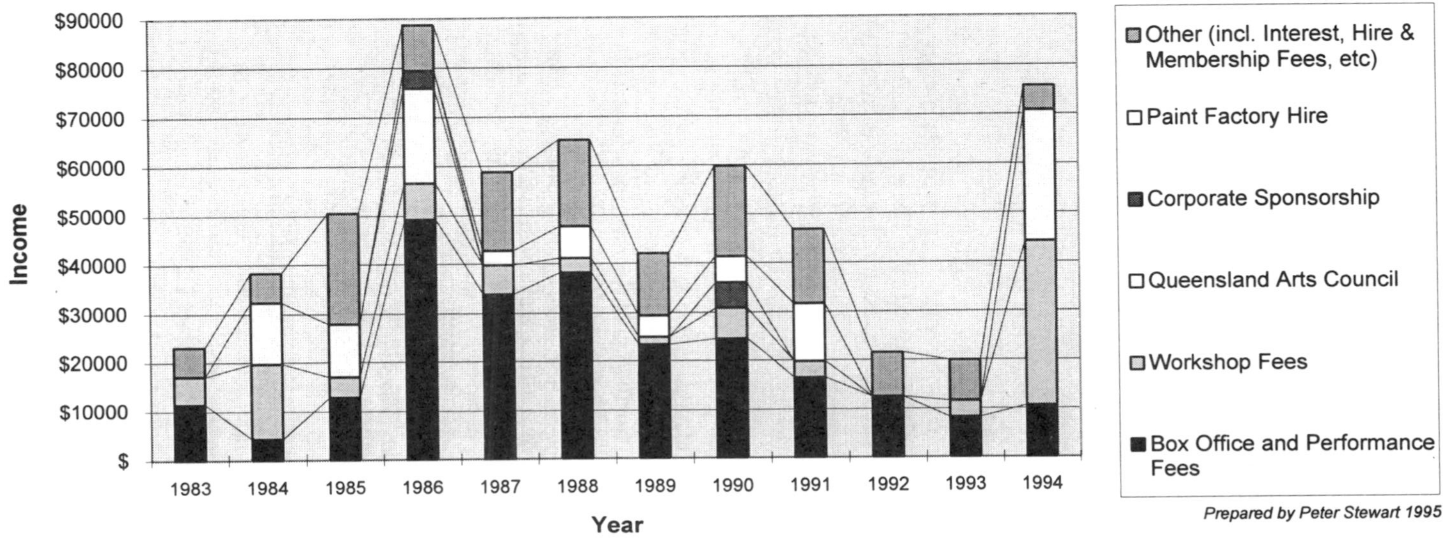

Legend:
- Other (incl. Interest, Hire & Membership Fees, etc)
- Paint Factory Hire
- Corporate Sponsorship
- Queensland Arts Council
- Workshop Fees
- Box Office and Performance Fees

Prepared by Peter Stewart 1995

and members seemed reluctant to engage in any meaningful dialogue or to identify their prejudices.

Anonymous performance reports spoke of uneven acting standards, poor production values and message-laden, non-naturalistic, unpolished scripts. While there was truth in some of these assertions, equally important for Street Arts were excellence in community process, integrity and relevance. These attributes rarely rated a mention in PAB performance reports beyond the calibre of 'the on-side audience loved it'. Moreover, constraints and contexts were usually ignored. A report of one show criticised for its acting did not mention that it was a community production with local participants performing. The constraints of limited funding on writing and rehearsal time (not to mention production values!) were unmentioned.

David Watt explores this tension between artistic excellence and community cultural development integrity in his papers 'Street Arts: Community Cultural Development and/or "Excellence"' and 'Street Arts and Bureaucratically Induced Schizophrenia'.[32] A broader Australian overview is found in his April 1992 article 'Community Theatre: A Progress Report'. [33] Watt explains how the PAB's lack of trust in Street Arts' ability to assess the needs of its work with particular communities led to funding shortfalls and second-best project plans that ultimately undermined the value of the work to the community, and diverted the company from its primary goals.[34]

It is important to recognise the political nature of these difficulties with the PAB, a body subject to a concerted backlash from main-stage companies and artists in the late eighties over its perceived shift, during the mid-eighties, towards funding smaller companies and community theatre at their expense. Street Arts was not alone in being regularly "under review" and then, in 1990, "on notice" of losing annual funding. Other companies with a focus on working with communities were also forced to apply for grants on a project-by-project basis. This meant more paperwork for the companies but made it far easier for the assessment committees to reduce companies' funding levels by rejecting a project or two.

BOX-OFFICE AND COMPANY INCOME

The PAB's second area of concern, box office income, was measured by the proportion of non-government money in annual income. In Phase One of the company, this varied from 51% in 1983 to 37.6% in 1984, but grew in dollar terms from $23,124 in 1983 to $88,714 in 1986 (41% of income) (see Table 2). This extraordinarily high 1986 figure has never been repeated and can only be explained by the enormous success of The Bob Club, *Sweeping Statements* and *Rock'n'Roll Circus*. Besides box-office and bar income, there were also fees for workplace performances of *Sweeping Statements*, the schools tour of *Rites and Wrongs* and *Xmas At The Bougainville Bob Club*.

During Phase Two of the company, as PAB grants became more significant, the non-government income fluctuated around $60,000, with peaks in 1988 and 1990 and troughs in 1989 and 1991. (See Table 2 / Figure 2). In percentage terms there was a decline in non-government income as a percentage of total income from 28.4% in 1987 to 16.8% in 1991.

In constructing annual budgets during this period there was a tendency to inflate expectations of non-government income by allowing for an unlikely degree of corporate sponsorship. Project budgets were then readjusted down to fit the level of income the company could be fairly sure of receiving. This was designed to ensure funding would meet the minimal needs of the company's work and to appease the PAB's constant and unrealistic demands for all performing arts companies to attract significant levels of corporate sponsorship.

Naturally, there were extensive efforts made to attract grants from sources other than arts funding bodies. However, they all had their price in terms of workload and labour-hours. The most successful initiatives were, not surprisingly, those related to welfare and community development issues or specific geographic communities. The Commonwealth Department of Education, Employment and Training sponsored wages for Aboriginal trainees; the Sidney Myer Foundation awarded grants towards community development work in 1986 and in Logan City in 1990; state government departments supported youth oriented projects; and local governments contributed to workshop programmes in Ipswich, Logan, Duaringa and Carole Park.

Private industry was really only interested in buying the odd programme advertisement and assisting projects in their local area and/or involving clear welfare goals with in-kind support. This often meant significantly higher production values than would otherwise have been possible, with venues donated; lighting, sound, and construction equipment discounted; and much set and visual art material donated. Bernie Lewis, employed in 1990 to be production manager and corporate sponsorship facilitator, was especially successful in attracting this in-kind support. However, he was not surprised by the lack of companies rushing to be corporate sponsors of a small community theatre company with a reputation for working with disadvantaged communities, trade unions and West End radicals — and operating out of an old paint factory. The Queensland Ballet it was not.

At the heart of this tussle was the inability of the PAB to acknowledge the validity of a community cultural development approach to theatre. They annually questioned the company's box-office prices, insisting that they were too low and audiences too small, while never affirming the company's role in introducing relevant theatre to brand new audiences in non-threatening venues (with limited seating) at accessible prices.

They questioned the reason for so few seasons per year without acknowledging the time required to work with a community in devising and then rehearsing a brand new script. They expected main-stage production values at a fraction of the cost. They suggested people to employ on company shows so that "artistic standards" could be improved. They invited coordinators to seminars where an executive officer of the Australian Ballet(!) would explain how he attracted a corporate sponsor.

QUEENSLAND GOVERNMENT

Fortunately, during Phase Two, the growing recognition of Street Arts' work from the Queensland Arts Division (later Arts Queensland) was translating into increased funding from this source. While there had been some individual support in the past (and cover stories in the Queensland Cultural Diary in 1984 and 1985) [35] the political climate of the Bjelke-Petersen era meant Street Arts could not expect much public funding support from the Queensland government.[36] The CAB/CCDU were sympathetic to this and funded accordingly. (See Figure 1).

However, as the company's public profile grew, state funding did grow to $18,750 in 1987 (Table 1). The combination of Fiona Winning's lobbying and the demise of Joh Bjelke-Petersen in late 1987 then produced a 134% increase to $43,984 in 1988. The defeat of the National Party government in late 1989 by Labor led by Wayne Goss, saw further increases. This was the result of a more accountable grants system, increases in overall arts funding, and priorities more in accord with those of Street Arts.

As Arts Queensland took up the bulk of Street Arts administrative funding, the CCDB reduced their contribution from around $75,000 in 1989 and 1990 to $45,000 in 1991. This cut, along with the $30,000 drop in the PAB's grant that accompanied the move to project-only funding, placed severe strains on Street Arts in 1991. Examination of Australia Council Annual Reports indicates that these cuts followed a $4 million reduction in the Australia Council budget for 1990-1. Small companies, naturally, bore the brunt of this.

Between 1991 and 1993 Street Arts increased its income from government sources other than arts funding bodies, but suffered successive cuts in PAB and CCDB support. 1993's annual income was in fact the lowest since 1985. Increased project and workshop income and successive increases in Arts Queensland funding have enabled more practical budgets and significantly more work in 1994 and 1995. The company began, during this period, to forge a related but distinctly different approach to the role of a community theatre company in the nineties. This reflects the aspirations of a new generation of artists who have pursued a policy of revitalisation and redefinition to ensure the survival of the company.

References

1. This is an edited version of Pauline Peel's Introduction in Steve Capelin, "Street Arts Community Theatre Company 1982-1993", *Network News*, first edition (1993), pp 16-18.

2, Ross Fitzgerald, *A History Of Queensland. From 1915 to the 1980s*, University of Queensland Press (1984), p 244.

3. Libby Sara, *Network News*, December (1991), p 1.

PHASE ONE

4. Pauline Peel interviewed by Peter Stewart, 30 November 1993, cassette side I, transcript p 2. Denis Peel interviewed by Peter Stewart, 30 November 1993, cassette side I, transcript pp 2-3.

5. Steve Capelin interviewed by Peter Stewart, 1-2 December 1993, cassette side A, transcript p 3.

6. Denis Peel interview, sides III and IV, p 5.

7. Capelin interview, side A, p 4.

8. Pauline Peel interview, side I, p 4.

9. *ibid*, p 3.

10. Pauline Peel, "Working With Amateurs" in *Community Theatre National Conference*, 9-11 November 1984 (Association of Community Theatres, 1984), p 35.

11. *ibid*, p 35.

12. Denis Peel interview, side V, p 7.

13. Capelin interview, side B, p 7.

14. Steve Capelin, "Street Arts Community Theatre Company 1982-1993", *Network News*, first edition (1993), p 19.

15. Pauline Peel in *ibid*, introduction: "Setting The Scene", p 17.

16. Capelin in *ibid*, p 22.

17. *ibid*.

18. Sue Rider, "Directors Report", in *Trading Hours Report*, an internal company report submitted to the Australia Council, 1990, p13.

PHASE TWO

19. Dean Tuttle, "Street Arts: Counting The Community", *Australasian Drama Studies*, 20, April (1992), p 40.

20. *ibid*, p 39.

21. *ibid*, p 34.

22. *ibid*, p 52.

23. Ainsley Burdell interviewed by Peter Stewart, 22 April 1994, cassette side 2, transcript pp 6-7.

24. Dean Tuttle, "Reds and Red Tape — the Politics of 'the Community': Street Arts Community Theatre Company 1982-1991", unpublished Honours Thesis (University of Queensland) (1991); and "Street Arts: Counting The Community", *Australasian Drama Studies*, 20, April 1992.

25. Tuttle, "Street Arts: Counting...", pp 40-41.

26. Watt, "Community Theatre: A Progress Report", *Australasian Drama Studies*, 20, April (1992), p 5.

27. *ibid.*

PHASE THREE

28. Ainsley Burdell interview, side 2, pp 14-15.

29. Cynthia Irvine interviewed by Clare Apelt, 18 January 1994, transcript p 4.

30. *1983 Annual Report, 1993 Annual Report*, Australia Council.

31. *1993 Annual Report*, Australia Council.

32. David Watt, "Street Arts: Community Cultural Development and/or 'Excellence'", unpublished paper, 1992; and "Street Arts and Bureaucratically Induced Schizophrenia", unpublished paper, 1993.

33. David Watt, "Community Theatre: A ..."

34. David Watt, "Street Arts: Community...", pp 13,14.16; and "Community Theatre: A...", pp 3-9.

35. *Queensland Cultural Diary*, 12, 4 (May, 1984) and 13, 11. (December 1985 - January 1986).

36. Pauline Peel interview, side II, p 5.

**West End Community Circus
Festival (1983)**
Musgrave Park, South Brisbane.

**West End Community Circus
Festival (1984)**
Musgrave Park, South Brisbane.

Once Upon Inala (1984)
Kev. Hooper Park.

(Photo: Sheena Dunn)

Next Stop West End (1985)
Rialto Theatre, West End.
(from left to right) Michelle Crocker Cathy Grimley Vicki Caldwell
Tracey Robertson Lisa Smith (Photo: Peter Young)

Rites, Wrongs and Offbeat Thongs (1986)
(left to right) Steve Capelin, Jane Brown, Katrina Devery, Denis Peel
(Photo: Courier-Mail)

Sweeping Statements (1986)
Ukrainian Hall, South Brisbane.
Lachlan McDonald, Leonor Orellana, Steve Capelin, Denis Peel,
Jane Brown and Katrina Devery *(back to camera)*
(Photo: Barry Trotter)

Happy Families (1987)
(left to right) Anne Onnim, Sally Hart, Fiona Winning, Mark Crocker.
(Photo: Queensland Newspapers)

Reunion Show (1988)
Rehearsal
Therese Collie (director) and Kathryn Porrill (designer)
(Photo: Fiora Sacco)

Charged Up (1989)

(back) Sciobhan Benstead, Missy Mancktelow, Jason Cochrane, John Knight, Peter Knight, Michael Bagley
(front) Silvana Luscak, Margaret Beard, Donna Anderson, Ben Kalotoi, Matthew McMurray, Fayaz Ali,
Chrissy Kampf, Jimmy Knight   (Photo: Fiora Sacco)

Underwraps (1988)
The Paint Factory, West End.
Kathryn Porrill and Sam Morrison
(Photo: Angela Bailey)

Reunion Show (1988-89)
Peter Stewart and puppet

(Photo: Fiora Sacco)

Jalalu Jalu (1990)
The Paint Factory, West End.
Vanessa Kessler   Mary Foster

(Photo: Fiora Sacco)

Cabaret d'Esperanza (1991)
The Paint Factory, West End.
(from left to right)
Lidia Vidovic Mark Shortis Larisa Chen Tiziana Miceli Warren McMillan
Kym McGregor Robert Donaldson James D'Ath
(Photo: Fiora Sacco)

Out Of The Blue (1991)
The Paint Factory, West End.
Kaye Stevenson   Marguerite Wesselinoff   Ainsley Burdell
(Photo: Fiora Sacco)

"ALL 4114 ALL":
WRITING FOR
STREET ARTS IN LOGAN CITY

by Hugh Watson

Good community theatre projects get set up in any number of ways; but in the best of them, there is always the feeling that synchronicity — *zeitgeist* — the spirit of the times, is taking a part.

Street Arts' interest in young people at risk began in 1988. The collective went to a youth theatre forum, and came away angry, having realised that the youth theatre industry was overwhelmingly aimed at young people from the middle class. The company decided that a theatre project with marginalised young people would be important and groundbreaking work.

But the company couldn't simply go out and organise such a project. Because Street Arts' policy was reactive, they believed community artists shouldn't devise projects out of their own values and then foist them on communities. They should wait for communities to ask them in.

Enter the *zietgiest*. Within months, the company was contacted by Peter Browning and Brother Paul Wilson, two youth welfare workers from Logan City. Peter Browning worked for Youth and Family Services (Logan City) an agency that ran accomodation services for homeless young people and a day program for unemployed teenagers. Brother Paul, a teacher, worked for the Centre Education Programme, an alternative school that catered for young people with a history of offending and truanting. Both men were experimenting with adding art and theatre workshops to the programmes they ran with young people. Independantly, both men contacted Fiona Winning, Street Arts' administrator, and asked the company to come down to Logan and run drama workshops. They encountered a company that was far more than tepidly interested. Fiona met with both men, and suggested that Street Arts work with the agencies to produce a full scale show with and about Logan City's young people.

It was a bold, perhaps over-ambitious, idea; but Peter and Paul were adventurous, and agreed.

I was contacted and asked if I would be interested in being the writer on the project. I was. A submission was prepared, funding was granted by the Australia Council and the project got under way in April 1989.

LOGAN CITY, YOUTH AND FAMILY SERVICES, THE CENTRE EDUCATION PROGRAMME AND THE CHRISTIAN BROTHERS

Street Arts had worked in Logan City before, in 1984, but the workers who had been involved in that project had all left the collective. Before the project started all we knew about Logan was as follows: that its Postcode was 4114; that it was a satellite community twenty-four miles south of Brisbane; that although it had been a city for only seventeen years, it was the second largest and fastest growing city in Queensland; that it was underserviced; that it had a high rate of unemployment and high proportion of single parent families; that of the 186,000 people who lived there, forty nine percent were eighteen or younger; and that the young people we would be working with would be amongst the most needy and difficult in Logan.

The two organisations, Youth and Family Services (YFS) and the Centre Education Programme, were founded by members of the Christian Brothers. Catholic Order; and it's worthwhile examining the history of these organisations because these institutions had an enormous effect on Logan City and therefore on the Street Arts projects as well. As I understand it the Christian Brothers, like many other monastic orders in the late seventies and early eighties, were faced with the problem of dwindling numbers. Older members were retiring while fewer and fewer younger men were joining. The Christian Brothers, a teaching order, were forced to employ lay staff in the schools that had once been run entirely by their own members and, by doing this, they inadvertently challenged the basis of their own vocation. If lay people could run Catholic schools, then what was their particular mission, especially in light of the fact they might not survive another couple of generations? Reflecting on the life of their founder, who had given up a career in business to educate and work with street kids in Ireland, and influenced by Liberation Theology they decided that their role was to work with young people in poverty and distress — 'to seek', as one of them said to me, 'Jesus Christ among the faces of the poor'.

The first of the brothers to explore the needs of young people in Logan City was Mick Devlin. He moved to Logan in the early eighties and, by pounding the pavements and by attending juvenile court, he made contact with a large number of young people who were divided from their families, in trouble with the law or developing problems with drug and alcohol. Mick, with a number of local people, founded YFS. It's primary mission was to give young people legal and other support when they were involved in the justice system. Mick was the organisation's first coordinator.

Since the young people who YFS was trying to serve had invariably dropped out of school and since they were, still, a teaching order, Brother Terry Kingston moved to Logan City. His idea was to complement the Youth and Family Services' programmes by setting up an alternative school. In this way young people could be encouraged to stay at school while working out their other difficulties. Within a year he had founded the Centre.

When Street Arts first came down to Logan City, Youth and Family Services had already, as it were, begun to liberate itself from it's origins. Mick Devlin had left. Members of religious orders still worked for the organisation, but the organisation had expanded and the majority of the staff were professional youth workers and social workers.

The Centre, on the other hand, was still being administered by it's founder, Brother Terry. Of the seven other people who worked there, four — Sister Cathy, Sister Greer, Brother Paul and Brother Jules — were Christian Brothers and Presentation Nuns. They were living in Logan City with other members of their orders. They lived on tiny budgets, worked at the Centre during the day and responded to young people's crises pretty much round the clock.

The Centre had only twenty students, but they were always the most difficult young people around. The three lay staff were Tony Kelly, Dale Murray and Kay Dart.

"CHARGED UP"

My work in Logan City started in mid April 1989, five weeks before Street Arts Theatre Company arrived to do workshops. It was thought best that I start my research early so as to avoid the hustle and bustle of rehearsals and workshops.

In fact I was anxious to start as soon as I could — I thought a bit of extra time might help the job. But Rebecca Lister, who was to be the Logan City coordinator of the project and who was at the time helping teach drama at the Centre, kept on leaving me messages like, 'Don't come down this week, the kids are out of control'. As a result my "early introduction" took place on the Friday before my first official Monday.

At that time the Centre Education Programme was located in Mary Street, Kingston, right next to the railway line, two allotments down from a pet food factory, in the shadow of an overpass. It was housed in a small shopping centre whose businesses all went bust when the overpass was built. The shop fronts became classrooms; a bitumen car park surrounded the building and a high wire fence surrounded the car park.

I arrived in time for the first drama class. I was met by Brother Paul and Rebecca Lister who had an air of rueful good humour which was really nervousness on my behalf. Drama was done in the "big" room which is mostly used for meetings. A long blank rectangular space, carpeted and with sliding glass doors at one end, the big room held nothing except twenty or thirty large cushions.

Class began with a series of delaying tactics. No matter how loud Paul shouted, students just drifted in. The first to arrive picked up as many cushions as they could, and piled them into elaborate sofas. One against the wall, two to sit down on, one for the feet, one to hold against the chest. When the last students trailed in, there were none left.

'Give us a cushion, Troy!'
'Piss off!'
'F— you then, I'll take it!'
'Ben, you c—, give it back!'

The cushions became the subject of mock battles, they were hurled and swung, weapons as well as prizes. Finally, there was some sort of order and five boys sat facing Rebecca and Paul and me, their expressions wary or indifferent or resentful.

That class was fairly unproductive. No one wanted to do anything — the project was feebly discussed and I had the feeling of being checked out. The next class, composed of four girls and two smaller boys, was just as bad and although Rebecca, in particular, tried to motivate them, they also refused to do anything. In the middle of the period, a small baby-faced boy stared me straight in the face and, with a gentle smile, began to curse me at great length in his native language. Rebecca and Paul were furious. This was obviously something he did to visitors all the time.

I stayed for morning tea before going back to Brisbane. In the kitchen another boy flew into a rage about the lack of decent food in the place. He was so incensed, he waved a knife in front of one of the Brothers. The gesture was an unconscious one and it was only a butter knife . . . but . . .

I did very little at the centre for the first week — just hung around. The kids started to call me "psycho" and one morning, when I said good morning, told me that I was "f—ing weird". They also found out I was a soft touch for a cigarette. In the meantime, I brought down my computer and people were amazed at how fast I could type — 'Hey, Torti! Dr Who types just like a cop!'. Dr Who, or Dr Hugh, was my alternative nickname.

I also spent that first week moving into the neighbourhood — a spare room in Tony Kelly's and Rebecca Lister's house.

I had first met Tony while working on a project with street kids in Fortitude Valley and our already established friendship proved to be a big advantage as Tony had strong links with a large number of Logan City kids. He invited me along when he did street work — which really only meant wandering through the teenage hangouts and introducing ourselves to unknown kids. On Thursday nights we would go down to the Woodridge Plaza. Because there was so little to do in Logan City, the shopping Plaza was an important meeting place for young people, and every Thursday night they would go down in groups and roam around. It's like some television game show without a climax — all the wealth of our society displayed on either side of a circular path and teams of kids going round and round between them but never seizing a prize. One night we went to the skate board bowl, part of a local park, one of a number of late night drinking spots. We arrived just as a good dozen half-pissed adolescents were leaving to do a break and enter. A little while later they came back with spray cans and graffitied the bowl. Generally, though, street work wasn't that exciting; mostly just an opportunity to make contacts and to take in the local scene in a low key, relaxed way.

When ten days had gone by, I was ready to make my move on the Centre students and took over three of Brother Paul's English classes. Using an exercise I'd learnt from Gavin Strawhan, an Adelaide writer, I divided each class into two teams and gave each team a Nikko pen, a sheaf of loose paper and a roll of masking tape. I then asked them what they'd like to see in a play about Logan City and invited them to stick on the wall as many different topics as they could, as quickly as they could — they were, after all, in competition with the other team. After five minutes, I declared the game finished. Then, after removing repetitions, I counted the topics and declared the winner. After that I went through each topic, and asked the person who wrote it to say why. Finally I grouped the topics together by association.

At the end of the day, I had a list of topics which included:
Drugs, sex, alcohol, abuse in the family, anger, breaking and entering, thieving, stealing cars, skateboards, teachers, homelessness, runaways, gangs, crimes, pigs, parties, weapons, pubs, 'charge ups', privacy, poofs, lezzos, transport, sport, and 'what goes on after hours'.

Over the next two weeks I used this list as a starting point when I taped interviews with young people. I taped three. One was with the teenagers who were attending Youth and Family Services day programme at Mayes Avenue. They were fifteen to eighteen year olds, and all but one had finished school. Being older, having experienced more, they seemed better socialised than the Centre kids. They treated me more as an equal and tended to look at their lives in a more analytical way. They saw the problems for young people in Logan City in terms of superstructure, lack of transport, lack of entertainment facilities.

I then taped an interview with two young women who were residents at Atkinson Street Youth and Family Services medium-term accommodation programme. Much of our discussion dealt with leaving or being kicked out of home. Finally three young women whom Tony, Rebecca and I met while street working, came by the Centre and consented to be interviewed. They were either fifteen or sixteen years old and each had only recently left school. School was very much on their minds. Their discussion about schools, stiffs and night life is the basis of much of the "bowling alley hill" scene in the resulting show, *Charged Up*.

After four weeks had gone by, I had mixed feelings about what I had accomplished. I had talked at some depth with young women and to the older and more socialised young men. However there were still the mid-teenage boys at the Centre who had remained a closed book. Much of the material I had gathered felt ephemeral — so many people had talked about juvenile crime and the juvenile justice system as a major Logan City issue but, in most cases, their stories were very old or second-hand. The boys at the Centre, however, were still offending. I'd had no luck in talking to them. They were still checking me out and, for my part, I was still afraid of their pint-sized machismo and volatility. At this point, fortunately, Brother Paul stepped in and arranged for me to meet with one of them, Fayaz, at the Centre over the weekend.

When I arrived the Centre was closed and Fayaz and his friend Che were waiting outside the gate. I hadn't expected two of them and immediately felt slightly defensive. Nevertheless we went inside and they played pool while I set up my dictaphone and composed myself. By this time I knew that at least part of the show should be on crime and the juvenile justice system. I knew that Che and Fayaz had a lot of experience and background in these areas, but I was experiencing my role as intrusive and I feared they might resent my questions. As it turned out they were unexpectantly open and I felt very comfortable with the process. Fayaz, who had a gift for abstracting things, gave me a kind of potted life history of adolescent crime. Starting out stealing chips from the supermarket shelves, he had progressed to car theft and break and enters. Now, at sixteen, he was beginning to regret it. Meanwhile his younger brothers and their friends were following in his footsteps and behaving even worse than he did.

After an hour of conversation, the whole gang arrived. Fayaz's younger brother, Che's friends and several other of the more imposing characters of the Centre's student body. They swarmed over the fence. They weren't supposed to be there, the school was closed, but there wasn't any way to stop them. An argument broke out over possession of the pool table. Since Fayaz was here at my invitation and the rest had gate crashed, Fayaz had no intention of sharing it. It was his by right. Voices were raised.

As for me, I was on the point of getting on the phone and calling Tony or, if not him, any one of the Brothers — Terry, Jules or Paul — to come down and bail me out. But it had been such a good afternoon, I decided to push my luck. I told them that they could stay but I hinted that if things went amuck I'd get into more trouble than they would. I suggested they share the pool table on a rotation basis and that those who weren't playing should come into the administration office and talk to me. To my surprise that was exactly what happened. Over the next hour, three more kids came in and were interviewed.

I remember that afternoon as the most satisfying period of a very satisfying project. By the end of the afternoon, John, Jimmy and Alleyaz, as well as Fayaz and Che, had all given me their stories, and these stories became the basis for the male characters in *Charged Up*.

At the day's finish, I wrote the following:

> Flushed with success, I round them up and take them on the train to MacDonald's for a burger feast courtesy of Street Arts. On the way there, the kids pick a fight with some better dressed kids and, chasing after them, I leave my briefcase behind on the platform. At McDonald's one boy, with the deep instincts of a gentleman, offers to get me stoned to pay me back for the treat, while another, who was arrested at twelve for uprooting a bush in a parking lot, re-enacts the offence with a plastic MacDonald's shrub — he pulls it right out of its pot — in order that I might get a clearer grasp of what happened. Soon they're quizzing me. Can I fight? No. They're puzzled by this. Haven't I ever met anyone I could beat up?

> When the meal is finished I find that my cigarettes, unaccountably, have gone too and by this time we're all dying for one. I agree to buy a packet and share them round before everyone goes their separate ways. Down at the petrol station, they follow me into the little kiosk. I hear rustling behind me, and I find that I'm staring deep into the eyes of the shop assistant, willing her not to look past me. Back outside I line them up and give them a cigarette each, and then I formally thank them (and they thank me) for the pleasant afternoon we've spent together. They trail away, their pockets filled with stolen Kit Kats and Crunchy bars, down Wembley Road and disappear like smoke.

That was the end of my research. Replete with information, I began to write.

AFTER "CHARGED UP"

Readers of Peter Stewart and Steve Capelin's essay will have gleaned that the project was a considerable success. In many ways it was. It was success for the young people who stuck with it, a success for the company and a success for the community. But our pride and pleasure were quickly taken away.

More so than any other participant, Fayaz had been a key part of the project. Fayaz introduced me to the hard core young men. Fayaz wrote the lyrics to the show's title song. Fayaz performed the role of narrator. Save for Peter Knight (who played the judge) Fayaz worked harder than any other actor. In fact he used to complain that other people weren't taking the project seriously enough.

This was remarkable, given his history. Fayaz and his friends were known to be some of the most difficult boys in Logan City. But it was Fayaz who had the courage to come into the Centre and ask if he could be a student. Other Centre students were referred by youth agencies: Fayaz was one of the first to self-enrol. When Fayaz became a student, many of his mates did too.

He wasn't always an easy person — at fifteen, who is? — but what Fayaz did for *Charged Up* impressed everyone. Street Arts, wanting to keep his involvement in theatre alive, offered him a work experience position for later in the year. Without being conscious of it, we assumed that Fayaz had stopped offending, stopped taking risks. We were wrong. Within a month of the closing night, he was dead — killed when he drove a stolen car into the side of a bridge.

There was something satisfying, even joyous, about doing *Charged Up* in Logan City. And it had a lot to do with the Centre, where energy and spirit were produced, as if alchemically, by the combination of Religious staff, lay staff and kids. We workers from Street Arts tapped into this energy and when the project finished we walked away enriched, feeling good about ourselves, and rightly so. But when Fayaz died we realised what a lot of people in Logan already knew — that although there may be incidental pleasures and successes in this kind of work, there are no final outcomes, much less victories.

"RAISE THE ROOF"

When an organisation or movement is young it can sometimes stay open, responsive and alive because its original founders are still involved. The visionary aspect of the organisation is based in them and they have the authority to alter the vision and keep it flexible. But when they leave, the vision has to be codified and it risks becoming written in stone, inelastic.

When we first came down to do *Charged Up* Mick Devlin had already left YFS, but I guess his example and vision still permeated that agency. At any rate the lay youth workers and social workers at both YFS and the Centre were all very much interlinked, socialising together and sitting on each other's management committees and, as a group, it was my observation that they were strongly influenced by the values of the Religious — both the ones who still worked at YFS and the larger number concentrated at the Centre. The decision the Brothers and Sisters made to live in Logan was probably a significant example to people like Tony Kelly, Rebecca Lister and Helen Renny, who did the same themselves. The way the Religious immersed themselves in the community, not just by being on call for kids outside of work hours but also by simply being visible — shopping, driving, whatever — encouraged, I believe, the youth workers to relax the barrier between being at work and being off duty.

This state of affairs had a lot to do with the success of *Charged Up*.

We didn't realise it at the time, but when we asked the youth workers to come to rehearsals — both to maintain order and to help coach the young people — we were asking an enormous amount, far more than what they were professionally obliged to do. As it happened, many of these youth workers, were planning to leave YFS within the near future. And I think that for them *Charged Up* became an event that would mark the end of their tenure. A big finale, a full stop.

When we came back to Logan City in 1990, the culture at YFS had changed. There were new workers and a new administration — and they were both hostile to the previous youth worker "culture". The new YFS (members of which occasionally referred to young people as "clients") were more interested in being "professional". One of the defining qualities of this "professionalism" was that a youth worker should basically be able to satisfy all the demands of their job within a nine-to-five framework (and get back home to Brisbane). In this view of the world, spending some of your free time with young people doesn't prove you're dedicated to your work — it proves that you're sloppy, inefficient.

When Street Arts came down to do *Raise the Roof* we got caught in a war between the old guard and the new guard. One of the people we most trusted and enjoyed was sacked within a week of our coming down. At least one case of defamation (between youth worker and youth worker) was threatened and, by the end of the project, Youth and Family Services and the Centre Education Programme had largely broken off relations.

Unwilling to work outside a nine-to-five routine and suspicious of us because we were so closely connected to last year's status quo, Youth and Family Services failed to support us in producing *Raise the Roof*. Unfortunately, before coming down, we had decided to rely on them more than the previous year to give the Centre a break. Similarly, I had decided not to live with Tony Kelly and Rebecca Lister (although I had been invited to do so) and instead moved in to Mayes Avenue as unpaid caretaker — a ring side seat from which I watched the situation deteriorate.

Youth and Family Services were happy for us to do daytime workshops at Mayes Avenue and the first six weeks of the project went all right, although one could feel ripples of suspicion which were soon to mount into waves. But by the time rehearsals started, we'd been completely abandoned. Only Brother Paul and Sarah Moynihan from the Centre came along to support the company, and they weren't enough. Consequently members of Street Arts had to work as youth workers as well as arts workers. We weren't trained to do it. There was a certian amount of violence and a great deal of threatening behaviour — a small group of young people terrorising the others — something we failed to control and were barely able to limit.

When the play was put on, YFS policy was not to attend — they claimed that we had allowed the young people to run out of control, and the area wasn't "safe". At the debriefing sessions at the end of the project, we were accused of encouraging the young people to practice black magic — some kids had vandalised a local graveyard — and it was said that *Raise the Roof* had given them the idea.

Of course, despite these things the play got up, and it's possible that the tension between YFS and Street Arts even contributed something to the script. In the play, the heroine, Kerri, has a rather aloof youth worker, Bill. Bill dies of a heart attack and is reborn as a dog. Kerri, now homeless, adopts the dog. So at least in the fictional world, there was one Logan City youth worker who would never again knock off at five or go home to Brisbane but would instead spend a dog's allotted span trotting at Kerri's knee, being "among the poor, poor — amongst the filthy, filthy too".

In the script's second draft, Bill's job was changed from "youth worker" to "child guidance officer" so as not to offend sensibilities.

Street Arts left, but the tensions between youth workers in Logan City continued long after. Eventually (I gather) many of the new staff at YFS left to work for another Logan City organisation and the situation between YFS and the Centre reverted to something like it had been before. But there's a poignancy to this. The Christian Brothers had been, for many generations, a group of people whose job it was to provide a Catholic education within schools their forerunners had founded. Faced with their own mortality they heroically redefined themselves and undertook a different kind of mission. In Logan City that mission must have seemed, at times, overwhelming — overwhelmingly rewarding, disturbing, challenging, exhausting and sad. Founding institutions such as YFS and the Centre was a part of this new mission but their relationship to these institutions was different to what it had been in the past. Instead of being maintainers and custodians, they saw themselves as catalysts. In Logan City they hoped their organisations would be taken over by the community and that they themselves would be replaced by lay staff. It must have been a painful irony when they succeeded and saw YFS filled with workers of such a different spirit — whose attitude was hostile to, and perhaps even a mockery of, the original vision.

"RAISE THE ROOF" COMPARED TO "CHARGED UP"

As in other genres, so in community theatre: it's always harder to write the sequel. In *Charged Up* we had the luxury of taking on any and all subjects that the young people suggested, and we took the ones most interesting to them and ourselves. When it came time to develop *Raise The Roof* we didn't want to repeat subject matter and so decided to concentrate on issues of accomodation.

This seemed, on first consideration, a dry subject for a play. But after I talked with some of the youth workers, I realised that "accomodation" could be thought about on a deeper level — being kicked out of home, or being fostered out, were also issues of accomodation.

The difficulty occurred when I started interviewing young people who had left or had been thrown out of home. Although they could tell me the sequence of what had happened to them, they couldn't or wouldn't reveal their feelings about it. It was as if they were too painful to share. It took me a while to realise I would never break through this barrier and by then it was too late to change topics. I had an extremely rewarding interview with a number of Child Care Officers which gave me two of the main themes of the play — that no matter how badly behaved a young person is, being thrown out of home is something no one can ever *deserve:* and, conversely, no matter how blameless a young person is, they will always feel responsible for any bad thing that happens within their families. Out of these two ideas the character Kerri was born. Kerri is a prickly, difficult child who does her best to make life difficult for her sister and mother. But when circumstances get out of control and she is forced to leave home, Kerri overreacts, and comes to believe she has a "voodoo mouth", a capacity to blight everyone she cares about.

The trouble with the material was that it came from adults, welfare workers, rather than from the young people. The views of the Child Care Officers were, I believe, perfectly accurate. But that wasn't the issue. When the kids read the script of *Charged Up* they knew they were the ones who'd informed it. When they read the script for *Raise The Roof* they knew I'd got my information somewhere else — and they didn't feel they owned it.

I exacerbated the problem by writing a script which was plot driven, and was focused on two characters, Kerry and Bill the Dog, who are constantly in front of the audience. Had I been more thoughtful, I would have realised these roles were too big for inexperienced actors. Director Ainsley Burdell cast and recast young people, but they all eventually refused to take the parts which in the end were performed by adults — a big disappointment.

On a more positive note, in 1991 Feral Arts, a community arts company then composed of Sarah Moynihan, Norm Horton and Rebecca Lister, mounted a third performance piece called *Bloodlines*. *Bloodlines* incorporated video footage of Logan City's young people and had a much looser non-narrative structure. The way *Bloodlines* developed allowed more ownership of the material and allowed young people to work in smaller more independent groups. Only a year after *Raise the Roof*, *Bloodlines* was fully supported by both the Centre Education Program and Youth and Family Services.

As a writer, I'm pleased with the script of *Raise the Roof* but in terms of community work, I'm infinitely more proud of *Charged Up*. I look back on the time that Street Arts spent in Logan City as some of the most significant months in my working life.

FROM PRISON TO PERFORMANCE "OUT OF THE BLUE"

by Therese Collie

All too often in community theatre the role of the writer is to produce to order. And quickly. While these are important skills and much great work has been produced on the run, this rarely enables any in-depth exploration of character or more detailed observation of place.

Out of the Blue (A Jailbird's Story) offered me the comparative luxury of being part of a 12 month process. The play was one result of Street Arts' well designed Women in Prison Project which commenced with writing workshops at the nearby Brisbane Women's Prison in 1990 and culminated in the first production of *Out of the Blue* in 1991.

In 1987 and 1988 Street Arts held theatre, music and dance classes for Brisbane Women's Prison inmates. Because the women's first question afterwards was, 'When are you coming back?', the Education Officer Jill Spring and Street Arts negotiated with the prison authorities to run a ten week writing course in 1990.

As the writer, I was to work each afternoon with small groups of women developing their writing skills and at the same time use their stories and perceptions of prison life as research for a play to be produced by Street Arts in 1991.

By the time the course was due to commence in March 1990, much had changed. The supportive lynchpin of the project, Jill Spring, had left and there was no immediate replacement. Since the Kennedy Report and the setting up of the Corrective Services Commission, the Queensland Prison System had been undergoing a process of review and reform which made everyone even *more* wary of outsiders. On top of all that, the murder of a maximum security inmate meant a complete restructuring of the prison timetable so that the women were not available for classes during the day and maximum security prisoners were kept strictly isolated. This division eventually became a central issue in the play.

After consultation with the acting manager of the prison, Miss Stack, a notice was placed in the library which elicited responses from one woman from maximum security ("max") whom I arranged to meet on Friday nights from seven to nine, and from three women from medium/minimum security ("up top") whom I was able to meet during visiting hours. They had told me weekends were boring as they didn't get visitors often, so I agreed to come in Saturdays from one until four, which caused one woman to comment, 'Gee, you're keen!'.

171

I felt good once I had met the women. Until then I had only encountered a system which frustrated attempts to contact potential writers and inspire their interest in the project.

INSIDE

Working inside a prison — an agent of social control with its gates, locks, uniforms, cameras and security passes — presents particular problems. There is the length of time it takes to get to know the ropes and to establish familiarity with the staff. Depending on the prison officer, it can take up to half an hour to be let in for your session. One afternoon I was kept waiting but, rather than let it eat into my classtime, I said, 'Other officers let me walk up by myself.' I was accused of sounding just like the prisoners — '"So-and-so said I can!" That's one of our pet hates.' What could I say? I was powerless because I didn't want to lose any more precious time. I was beginning to understand how the women felt.

Once inside I was not allowed to move freely, so I had to wait for the classroom officer to contact the appropriate block's prison officer to tell someone I was there. If a woman didn't feel like coming, there was no way I could find out why, quell her fears and then perhaps convince her to come after all and enjoy herself.

An unhealthy environment — physically, mentally and emotionally — a prison can suppress a woman's motivation to learn. As one woman ironically put it, 'Getting anything done in here is like moving the Statue of Liberty!'

When the women *do* come, they find it difficult to work as a group because they are living in an atmosphere of mistrust. 'Will this get back to someone who can make my life hard for me?' Often the women have been disadvantaged educationally resulting in poor communication skills. Also they are bored. Pinching a cigarette can cause a hell of a fight. Old and young women are thrown together. There is no personal space except in their cell ("slot") at night. Even then, the officers can watch the women through the window in their doors. One young woman I met used to fog up her shower, rush into her toilet and then scurry back and sit in the corner of her shower to wash.

As if that weren't enough to prevent any sustained group dynamic, our classroom was the recreation room, always crowded with women either sewing, typing, playing the piano or, on Saturdays, blasting us with their rock boxes (cassette players).

CLASSES

At first my classes drew largely on Hilary Beaton's *WRITE!* — a booklet designed to aid teachers of the writing process. Based on the principle that everyone has a story to tell, it uses the characters and plot in fairy tales to analyse the structure of the participants' own work.

This analysis of the structure of stories provided ways of understanding experiences, which built confidence and self-esteem. In discussing *Hansel and Gretel*, the following exchange took place between two of the women:

M: Their father didn't love them.
K: No! Just because he was weak and wouldn't stand up to the stepmother doesn't mean he didn't love them.
M: I used to say, if my pop comes to see me, that means he loves me. Now I see that it was just in my head.

"MAX"

The sole woman from "max" was committed to writing and had a high level of literacy. She attacked my classes enthusiastically. Because of her interest in the film *The Company of Wolves*, I introduced her to Angela Carter's books and used them instead of a traditional fairy tale to discover how to establish plot and identify dramatic principles.

I also took in published works, such as *In the Vegetable Patch*, a collection of poems from Boggo Road Men's Prison next door and Nawal el Sa'adwi's *Memoirs from Prison*, which inspired her at a time when she was writing submissions about prisoners' needs to the Corrective Services Commission.

From her I derived the central situation of my play — a woman from "max", seen as a heavy, who comes "up top" and tries to motivate the others to change things. A media junkie, she provided me with a quick, witty language peppered with references to films and television shows.

"UP TOP"

Working "up top" was a different story. It was soon obvious that in minimum security the make-up of the group would vary from week to week as women with short sentences were released and others entered.

It the main, this group wanted to improve their grammar and increase their vocabulary in the hope that this would help them get jobs when they got outside. I developed exercises for them based on *Lily on the Dustbin (Australian Women's Slang)* by Nancy Keesing. Discussing the meaning of expressions such as, 'You can wish in one hand and wee in the other and you know which one will be full first', proved to be very popular with the women.

Because the women's difficulty in relating to each other in a group disrupted our work, I introduced some games from *Reaching Out (Interpersonal Effectiveness and Self-Actualization)* by David W. Johnson. Activities such as writing three adjectives to describe yourself, talking about it in pairs, and then reporting back to the group about your partner, stimulated productive focussed discussions which the women appreciated.

I was turning into a cross between an English teacher and a psychologist but I was gaining the trust of the women and learning a lot about their lives, inside and out.

DEVELOPMENT OF THE PLAY

I made it clear from the start that a play would be the outcome of my work inside the prison, so the women knew I was listening to their stories as research. At home I kept a diary of everything that happened at the jail. After I had gained the women's trust they allowed me to take notes in front of them as they talked. They wanted and needed to talk, particularly to someone who was outside the system. They also wanted us outsiders to know what was gong on inside. Desperate for communication, they would often slip me poems, short stories or letters they had written. I would type them and return them to the women with a copyright © at the end. This, and encouraging the women to read their work out to the others, validated it. Soon other women were sending in their work via those who attended my classes.

This part of the project extended beyond the planned ten weeks to six months. More time was needed to establish good working relations with the women, particularly the Aboriginal and Torres Strait Islander women who Street Arts specifically wanted me to encourage, since they comprise a disproportionately high percentage of the prison population.

ABORIGINAL WOMEN

On the fifth Saturday, the first Murri (Aboriginal) woman came to the workshops. By week ten, she had encouraged another Murri woman to come along. By then I had established contact with other people and resources coming into the prison with whom I could work in tandem to interest more women in writing.

I had originally gone in on Wednesday nights with an Adult Literacy tutor in the hope of making contact with some Murri women she was seeing. However, she was teaching English as a Second Language (ESL) to three migrant women and the Murri attendance had dropped off. Nonetheless I persevered and the two Murri women from Saturday started coming Wednesday nights as well.

Eventually, after two months — that's how slow it is in prison — I learned that Stuart McFarlane, a Life Study Skills Program tutor from the Aboriginal and Torres Strait Islander Unit at Queensland University, was going in on Thursday nights. After negotiations with the Unit I was allowed to join in these sessions with Stuart. In this way I met Murri women who would never have come to a writing class and I heard stories, experiences, language and jokes I would otherwise have missed out on. Stuart also taught me another way to cope with the place. I used to scuttle in in my black clothes trying to look as unobtrusive as possible, whereas Stuart used to walk in with his guitar saying 'Gidday' to everyone and laughing loudly, really breaking up the fear and intimidation of the place and opening up a different avenue of communication for the women.

PRISON OFFICERS

I felt that any portrait of the prison community must also tell the story of the prison officers. I observed them at work and interviewed one woman, the only one willing to talk to me — and that was when she was outside the prison on court duty. She was one of the "new breed" who, as the name suggests, are the ones just out of training, the ones who think that imprisonment is punishment enough: 'There's no need to make their lives more difficult'. The "oldies" who refused to be interviewed are the ones who have been at the job a long time, the ones who resist change mainly because they see it as a threat to their job security.

THE PLAY

Out of the Blue is a two-act play with 7 female characters (played by 5 women) and one male character (a prison officer). It tells the story of 5 prisoners — Rachel, Toey, Nancy, Delma and Kris — and 2 prison officers — Jemmy and Shepherd. Rachel and Delma are Murris. Toey and Kris also play Jemmy ("new breed") and Shepherd ("old breed") respectively. The roles of the prisoners and prison officers were doubled due to the company's financial restrictions. Happily, this heightened the dilemma of just who are the real prisoners of the system — the keepers or the kept!

Out of the Blue is a play committed to the exoteric, the everyday, the common-place, not the clichés of sensationalism. In the play I tried to show the human face of prison life as I had met it. Not the horror stories, not the statistics, not a program of prison reform, but the routine boredom of day after day and the humour and courage it takes to live without freedom.

Research:
Not much is heard of prisons in our society and even less is told of women in prison. When we do hear of prisoners, it is in the media content of controversy or as a social problem. Despite this taboo, in Brisbane, local community

responses to the prison system are substantial in the form of organisations such as the Catholic Prison Ministry, Radio 4ZZZ Prisoners' Program, Women's Legal Service, Prisoners' Legal Service and IPCHAC (Incarcerated People's Cultural Heritage Aboriginal Corporation).

As part of my research for *Out of the Blue*, I contacted these community agencies who saw Street Arts as a theatre company committed to giving a voice to the issues facing a forgotten community — women in prison.

The workshops and research produced the first draft of *Out of the Blue* in August 1990. A second draft was written following work with the dramaturg, Hilary Beaton. This draft strengthened the storyline, introduced a sub-story for the prison officers and further developed the characters.

Creative Development:
The next funded stage of script development was the two weeks Creative Development phase in December 1990, where the writer, the dramaturg, the designer Gavan Fenelon and the actors — Ainsley Burdell, Kathryn Fisher, Kara Miller, Lisa-Jane Stockwell and Marguerite Wesselinoff — and QUT student Lisa Smith — workshopped the script. A reading of the second draft was presented to invited representatives from the prison, the Corrective Services Commission, the community agencies and theatre companies in an attempt to consult with and accommodate responses from people involved in relevant areas.

The main result of this feedback was the development of the representation of the prison officers from over-simplified good and bad characters to more complex human individuals.

I had not been allowed back into the prison to get the women's feedback on the first draft script. I was told my course was over. End of story. As it was, I had stretched the limits of the proposed course, staying six months instead of ten weeks, working three nights a week and Saturday afternoons.

Following the creative development and three weeks rewriting, the draft for production was completed. The script development continued during rehearsals and further cuts were made after the show opened. Actors from the creative phase — Ainsley, Kathryn and Marguerite — were joined in the cast by Bernadette Ryan, Kaye Stevenson and Mark Shortis.

The writing workshops and the commission to write the play were funded by the Literature Board and the creative development, production and tour of the play were funded by the Performing Arts Board of the Australia Council and the Queensland Arts Division.

Season and Tour:
Out of the Blue enjoyed a three week public season from 26 February to 16

March 1991 at The Paint Factory, Donkin Street, West End and positively revelled in a two week prison tour which required a shortened version of the show — ninety minutes, no interval — to fit prison timetables. The prison version gave an intensity of duration, a real-time effect. The prisoners responded to the play both as an entertainment and a recognisable portrait of their situation.

In a scene towards the end of Act I, Toey and Officer Shepherd have an argument which separates into two short punchy rhyming monologues that overlap. Following this, Toey is put on a "Section 39" (solitary confinement). The general public who saw this scene were usually reduced to tears. However, at the Sir David Longlands Maximum Security Prison the men laughed. One of the men explained, 'They laugh because it's real. It's happened to them and they can appreciate that Street Arts got that bit right'.

Though able to tour successfully to most of the men's prisons in South-East Queensland — Borallon, Moreton, Sir David Longlands, Numinbah, Palen Creek and Woodford — *Out of the Blue* was not allowed into the Women's Prison. We fell prey to one of the risks of the consultation process. The representatives of the prison felt that the reading highlighted negative aspects of the prison and that many of the situations were no longer relevant. The Women's Prison was the focus of media attention as the model for the Corrective Services Commission's restructuring of prisons, so the management was extremely sensitive to public comment. Unfortunately, the period of consultation also coincided with sensational news stories about the management of the prison and no amount of offers to rework the script would change their minds.

It was a bitter disappointment to us all that Street Arts was not able to fulfill its commitment to take back to the women in prison a story of their community. However, it has been published in the October 1992 edition of *Australasian Drama Studies* (a journal published by the Queensland University), a copy of which is in the prison library, so at least some of the women I worked with have read it.

In prison you learn to speak another language — not just the jargon of the nick but the language you use to communicate under surveillance. You must be clear about what you are saying and when to say it. Prisoners get confused if you don't. They are so desperate for support and information that they latch onto the smallest shred and worry at it. It's a big responsibility. I didn't realise how much I was being affected by my work inside until I stopped. Then it was as if something was missing, some intensity of experience that you don't have outside. You take so much for granted, your family and your friends and your freedom. The women I met inside don't have that luxury. They've lost their freedom, contact with their loved ones, but not their sense of humour.

The script of *Out of the Blue* is presented elsewhere in this book.

PART FIVE

●

SCRIPTS

THE WHITE MAN'S MISSION

by

Richard Fotheringham and Albert Hunt

THE WHITE MAN'S MISSION

Originally created
and performed in 1975 by
the Popular Theatre Troupe:

Roslyn Atkinson
Duncan Campbell
Richard Fotheringham
Nick Hughes
Albert Hunt
Margaret Moore
Kathryn Porrill
Peter Sutherland
with the assistance of
The Literature and Theatre Boards of
THE AUSTRALIA COUNCIL
THE BRITISH COUNCIL
and
THE QUEENSLAND FESTIVAL OF THE ARTS
under the direction of
Albert Hunt.

The songs used in the play are all traditional hymns (mostly associated with the Pentecostal movement) except for the few lines of *"Bye Bye Blackbird"* and for *"Uncle Ned"* which is an old Stephen Foster number. None of the tunes or lyrics has been altered in any way except for *"Hear the Pennies Dropping"* where the words are our own.

Enquiries regarding performance rights should be addressed to:

Richard Fotheringham
c/- Department of English
Queensland University,
St. Lucia, Q. 4067

THE WHITE MAN'S MISSION is a musical political
entertainment which relates to the history of the
white man in Australia and the Pacific.
The Bible says,
' Go ye into all the world and preach ye the gospel . . .'

This show tells the story of many who have gone and
returned, and many more who have gone forever as a result
of . . .

THE WHITE MAN'S MISSION

*I speak of the Christian religion, and no one need be
astonished. The Church in the colonies is the white
people's Church, the foreigners' Church. She does not call
the native to God's ways but to the ways of the white
man, of the master, of the oppressor. And as we know, in
this matter many are called but few are chosen.*

Frantz Fanon
The Wretched of the Earth

INTRODUCTION

(a) The Play Itself:

THE WHITE MAN'S MISSION was created during June and July 1975 by the Popular Theatre Troupe under the direction of the English Fringe director Albert Hunt, who also scripted most of the scenes before they were worked on in rehearsal. It was first performed at the Festival of Australian Student Theatre at Sydney University in August. Since then, the original production has received critical acclaim in both Sydney and Melbourne, and has been performed throughout the eastern states of Australia. Most rewarding, perhaps, have been the performances in north and central Queensland where reprisals against aboriginals and the Kanaka slave trade are very real memories to many people.

There are up to 50,000 South Sea Island descendants still living in eastern Australia. Since all the Kanakas were supposedly sent home after Federation in 1901, their existence as a separate ethnic group in Australian society has never been recognised by any state or federal government. In the face of that kind of deeply entrenched belief in maintaining a white Australia, which has washed its hands of the sins of the past, the documentary story of the white man's physical, cultural and economic slaughter in the world needs to be presented to people again each generation. Those of us who are fourth or more generation Australians have to face the fact that we are the descendants of mass murderers and slave drivers; that the prosperity of our lucky country is derived directly from that barbarity; and that the unvarnished consequences of their actions can be seen on every aboriginal reserve in Australia.

(b) Notes on Production:

Albert Hunt, the director and co-author of THE WHITE MAN'S MISSION is the chief inspiration behind the form and style of the play. His background explains this style. He is senior lecturer in Communications at Bradford College of the Arts in England and he is as active in video and film as he is in theatre. His plays, therefore, are a series of carefully planned visual images, two dimentional pictures as if seen on a screen. In THE WHITE MAN'S MISSION, images are repeated for cumulative and ironic effect at successive points in the story; the result is visual theatre. It is an exciting but demanding discipline for actors, since posture, gesture, positioning and movement are all experimented with, an image arrived at, and that image tightly drilled to communicate a total effect of people, props, set and dialogue.

The working method involves games, improvisations, and a rich junk-strewn environment where strange objects can be picked up off a scrap heap and turned into the visually bizarre. "This is a flag", the script might say, but it's a broom or a vacuum cleaner. Again not every wild invention is adopted, but a few selected for maximum effect. Almost every object referred to in the play is a real object, some literal (a missionary collar), some symbolic (a U.S. flag which flips over to become a can of Coca-Cola), some bizarre. But everywhere the visual reinforces directly or ironically the dialogue ('How many Kanakas have you got in that hold', asks the outraged liberal Christian missionary as he absent-mindedly passes a gun to a crew member who goes off and shoots the lot with it).

(c) Documentary Facts?

THE WHITE MAN'S MISSION doesn't pretend to be fair to any individual man, but the events of history are true or false. The real Captain Arthur Phillip agonized over the problem of convict cruelty to aborigines and aboriginal reprisals far more than the actor in the play. But the result is true, Phillip hanged ten aborigines as a warning after his gamekeeper was killed. The facts of escalation are the truth communicated in the play, not the delaying agony which accompanied it.

Secondly, the play makes no attempt to be literary, poetic or directly documentary. In almost every instance the direct quotations proved to be flaccid, and superfluous, and were pared down in rehearsal. It's a process of translating the way they talk on T.V. or on the political platform into the language of the home or the pub. Groucho Marx is the only God whose words survive verbatim.

RICHARD FOTHERINGHAM
Brisbane, 1975

CAST

There are five characters in the play, but these characters also play at times historical personages. Where they are identifiable as such, the script indicates this. Elsewhere the roles are indicated by the first names of the actors who played them in the original production:

Roslyn Atkinson
Duncan Campbell
Nick Hughes
Margaret Moore
Kathryn Porrill.

Duncan played guitar, Margaret the accordion and guitar in the final song and Kathryn played the flute. Some songs were unaccompanied.

THE WHITE MAN'S MISSION

The cast enters.

DUNCAN Good evening, brothers and sisters, and welcome to the White Man's Mission. We're very pleased to see you at our missionary service tonight, and we hope you'll all receive a blessing from God. We'd like to open our service this evening with a song. It's an appeal for people to join the White Man's Mission, to go and save sinners, and it's called "Throw Out the Lifeline". We'd be happy for you to join in the chorus.

(sings) Throw out the lifeline across the dark wave,
There is a brother whom someone should save,
Somebody's brother, oh who will then dare
To throw out the lifeline, his peril to share?

(chorus) Throw out the lifeline, throw out the lifeline,
Someone is drifting away,
Throw out the lifeline, throw out the lifeline,
Someone is sinking today.

KATHRYN Throw out the lifeline to danger-fraught men,
Sinking in anguish where you've never been,
Winds of temptation and billows of woe
Will soon hurl them out where the dark waters flow.

(chorus) Throw out the lifeline . . . *(etc)*

MARGARET Soon will the season of rescue be o'er,
Soon will they drift to eternity's shore,
Haste then my brothers no time for delay,
But throw out the lifeline and save them today!

(chorus) Throw out the lifeline . . . *(etc)*

DUNCAN Brothers and sisters, Jesus said . . .

KATHRYN Did you hear the one about the boong who stole mission soap to wash his sins away? 'Course they've got no moral sense these boongs, no sense of property whatsoever. Take wife swapping for instance. There was this boong who lived in St. Lucia . . .

DUNCAN Jesus said . . .

MARGARET I've been very hard done by. People say I'm a sinner just because I found myself alone, in the moonlight, on a desert island, with this beautiful native girl . . .

KATHRYN There was this boong who lived in St. Lucia . . .

DUNCAN Jesus said . . .

ROSLYN Brothers and sisters, I'd like to open our service tonight by taking up a collection. Every year, on the anniversary of the Queen's birthday, we give blankets to the natives . . .

MARGARET With this beautiful native girl . . .

KATHRYN There was this boong who lived in St. Lucia . . .

DUNCAN Jesus said . . .

NICK	Jesus said, 'Go ye into all the world and preach ye the gospel', and He gave unto his disciples the power to work miracles. Brothers and sisters, for my first miracle tonight we shall need a ship *(a toy ship)*, an undiscovered island *(a map of Australia)*, a flag, a missionary *(himself)* and a comparitively passive native population.
	(DUNCAN *puts on a black cloak which indicates "black man" role).*
DUNCAN	What do I get out of it?
NICK	You get the island. Give him the island. Brothers and sisters, this trick is called "Discovering an Island".
KATHRYN	Hey mister, want to show me a place to land my ship?
DUNCAN	Why should I do that?
MARGARET	You want to be discovered, don't you?
DUNCAN	Why should I want to be discovered?
NICK	Try appealing to his need for salvation.
MARGARET	We've heard the voice of the Lord saying, 'Go ye into all the world and preach ye the gospel'.
KATHRYN	Only we can't preach it to you because you haven't been discovered yet.
DUNCAN	Why should I want to be preached at?
NICK	Try appealing to his native curiosity.
MARGARET	You're all alone, in the moonlight, on this undiscovered island, when all of a sudden you look out, and see a beautiful white ship!
DUNCAN	Gee, I've never seen a ship like that before.
KATHRYN	Want to put it in Botany Bay for a while?
MARGARET	I'll hold Australia.
NICK	Now this is where you claim possession. When you've landed, raise your flag and say:
ROSLYN	By this ceremony of the raising of the flag, I claim this land and all its inhabitants for God and the King of England.
	(MARGARET *tears Australia into four pieces)*
NICK	Now this next trick is called, "Teaching the Natives Religion". Watch this closely.
	(makes the sign of a cross. MARGARET gives him pieces of Australia)
KATHRYN	You watch this, boong.
	(the three kneel, make the sign of a cross. NICK gives them each a bit of the map of Australia, keeps one for himself)
	It's your turn now.
	(DUNCAN *goes to NICK, makes the sign of cross, puts hand out. NICK kicks DUNCAN. He rolls back to KATHRYN)*
	Here you are, boong, *(holds up Bible)* to wash your sins away. *(gives him Bible, turning it round as she does so. It is a packet of Surf washing detergent)*

DUNCAN	*(sings)* We have heard a joyful sound,
(chorus)	Jesus saves, Jesus saves,
	Spread the gladness all around,
(chorus)	Jesus saves, Jesus saves,
KATHRYN	Send the news to every land,
ROSLYN	Climb the steeps and cross the waves,
MARGARET	Onward 'tis the Lord's command,
(chorus)	Jesus saves, JESUS SAVES.

(all leave except DUNCAN)

DUNCAN   Brothers and sisters, Jesus said, 'Go ye into all the world and preach ye the gospel, for the fields are white until harvest, and the labourers few'. Well, brothers and sisters, we're lucky enough to have with us tonight four labourers in God's harvest fields, who are going to tell us gospel stories from far and wide. But, brothers and sisters, the Bible also warns us to beware of false prophets, and so tonight, as we listen to these travellers' tales, we invite you to play with us the game of "True or False?". And the first testimony tonight comes from the founder of the first penal settlement in Australia, Captain Arthur Phillip!

KATHRYN   *(enters)* Yeah. Well, I'm coming in to land and I see this old boong jumpin' up and down as if he's pleased to see us, and pointing to this spot on the beach. Of course, I'm very careful, you know you can never trust a boong, for all I know he's trying to run us on the rocks. But in fact, he's showin' us the deep water. So I leave a couple of packets of Square Deal Surf on the beach, and he goes off and eats himself sick. That night, we're roasting some meat over a fire on the beach, when he comes nosing around.

Well, I'm not having that. I mean, how would you feel if a boong or a sheila came and sat beside you while you were having a counter lunch with the boys? So I pick up a spade, and I draw a circle round the fire, like this see. And I say to him, 'You stay outside the circle, Jackie'. And after I've booted him a few times, he seems to understand. But I happen to have left the spade on the beach, and the next thing I know, he's walked off with it as if it were a packet of bloody Surf or something!

Well, I'm not having that, so I decide to teach him a bit of British law, a bit of respect for personal property. So I bash him. Not a real bashing, just a few slaps. And he goes off and sulks like a spoilt kid. Soon after that, some of his mates go out sailing in their canoes, and they leave their spears on the beach, and some of my convicts they see these spears, and pick them up as souvenirs. Then the black fellows come back and treat us as if we were a bunch of bloody thieves!

So I say to the boys, 'Look boys, I know this seems unreasonable after all we've given these savages, but they don't like you taking their spears, and their fishes, and their wives'. So I tell the boys to lay off, and I hope things are gonna improve. Then, for no reason at all, my gamekeeper gets speared by one of the boongs! Unless it was one of my convicts. So I pick ten boongs at random, and hang 'em, just to show they can't get away with bloody murder!

190

DUNCAN	Thank you, brother, for that stirring testimony. And now, brothers and sisters, True or False? Personally, I find it very hard to believe that a British officer would condone the kidnapping, and order the random execution of hostages, as if he were a murdering, torturing, raping Japanese! But all that about the natives and the square deal surf on the beach, that had a ring of authenticity, so I'd say True, and I'd be right! Ten points to me for the hanging of ten aborigines.
	The next testimony tonight, brothers and sisters, just to show how open minded we are here at the White Man's Mission, is from an aborigine. Come along brother. (NICK enters) Don't be hesitant.
NICK	My name is . . .
DUNCAN	Excuse me, brother, are you a Christian?
NICK	What do you mean a Christian?
DUNCAN	I'm sorry, brothers and sisters, but this boy isn't a Christian. That means he doesn't know how to take the oath. And that means we can't accept his testimony. But I'm sure his testimony, if he had been allowed to give it, would have been true, and I'd be right. Ten points to me for the thirty thousand aborigines massacred in New South Wales. The next testimony tonight, brothers and sisters, is from Mr Thomas Coutts.
	(MARGARET enters)
MARGARET	Yeah, well I think I've been very hard done by. I'm a squatter, sheep farmer, see. Had this little station at Kangaroo Creek, back in the 1840s. Nice little station. Five thousand sheep. The only trouble was the bloody boongs. They were everywhere, like bloody spiders. They used to break into my stores and pour flour and sugar all over the floor, just for the sake of being bloody minded. And that's not all. The buggers used to kill sheep. Two and a half thousand of mine they killed in eight years, not to mention two shepherds and a boy.
	Well, all the squatters in that area got together. Whenever they heard of a boong camp they'd ride out at night, surround the camp, and as soon as it was light, shoot the lot — men, women, kids — got rid of a lot of boongs that way, protecting your property, see.
	Me, I had a different method. Harvest of 1848 I persuaded the boongs to come and work for me, and afterwards I paid them with food. Only I put poison in the food. Had a good laugh over that one — but I laughed out of the other side of my face when my mates refused to back me up. They said poisoning boongs wasn't cricket, not playing the game. You'd have thought I'd broken the hunting laws or something. The only decent, law-abiding way of killing boongs was to go out and shoot them in the bush. So I was arrested, and sent to Sydney, and no one would help me with the bail. Bloody criminal it was the way I was treated. 'Course I was never brought to trial, but when I went back up to Dawson a few years later, the bloody boongs remembered me, and killed off my shepherd and stock again. And that's why I think I've been bloody hard done by.
DUNCAN	Thank you, brother, for that moving testimony. And now, brothers and sisters, True or False? Personally I find it very difficult to believe that a decent hard-working Australian would poison his workers, no matter how sharp the provocation. But all that stuff about the totally

unprovoked, senseless, mindless savagery of the natives, that sounded only too likely to me, so I'd say True. And I'd be right. Ten points to me for the seventy-five thousand aborigines massacred in Queensland.

The next testimony tonight, brothers and sisters, comes from the founder of the Presbyterian Church in Australia, the Very Reverend John Dunmore Lang!

(enter ROSLYN)

ROSLYN   The end of the aboriginal race is by the general appointment of divine providence. *(exit)*

DUNCAN   True, true! Ten points to me for the end of the aboriginal race.

(KATHRYN and MARGARET hold rope across the stage. NICK is wearing "black man" cloak)

KATHRYN & MARGARET
See the natives dropping.
See the natives fall,
Everyone for Jesus,
He shall have them all.

KATHRYN   Help God. Leave a barrel of flour around. Put a steel-jawed trap in it just below the surface. When the native comes to steal the flour, it cuts his arm off and he bleeds to death!

KATHRYN & MARGARET
(as they wind NICK up in rope)
Dropping, dropping, dropping, dropping,
See the natives fall.

MARGARET   Help God. Take two pistols. One empty and one loaded. Put the empty pistol to your own head and pull the trigger. Give the loaded pistol to the native. These natives have a wonderful sense of mimicry.

KATHRYN & MARGARET
(another wind)
Everyone for Jesus, He shall have them all!

KATHRYN   Help God. Put strychnine in their meat.

KATHRYN & MARGARET
(another wind)
Dropping, dropping, dropping, dropping,
See the natives fall.

MARGARET   Help God. Take a hint from Governor Arthur of Tasmania.

DUNCAN   In 1830 I assembled a line of men from the east coast of Tasmania to the western highlands. Five thousand soldiers, fifty yards apart, beating the bush from Bass Strait to the southern tip of Tasmania.

(KATHRYN and MARGARET search and, in the process, untie NICK and tie themselves up so that NICK is in charge)

In my mind's eye I saw hundreds of thousands of cunning and dangerous blacks fleeing south before the relentless advance of my soldiers, fleeing south over a narrow strip of land on to the Tasman Peninsula, where they could be imprisoned forever more. How many did you catch?

NICK   Two. *(exits, dragging them by the rope)*

DUNCAN	True or False, Brothers and sisters? The fact is, the story is false. The line of soldiers across Tasmania caught no one. But the way they tell it in the history books, they caught two. So I'd say True, and I'd be right. Ten points and Tasmania to . . .
NICK	(enters) That was called the Tasmanian rope trick. And now I'd like to do a little number called "Killing by Kindness or If the Devil Doesn't Get You, Jesus Will". Now for this we shall need a missionary who can play the flute. (KATHRYN enters), an island (ROSLYN enters with map of Tasmania), a ship to get the native population to the island (MARGARET enters with a toy ship), and a cunning but frightened native population (MARGARET tries to put the black cloak on DUNCAN).
DUNCAN	Stop. I've seen this trick before. You tear up the island, divide it amongst yourselves, and I get kicked.
NICK	No, in this one you get the island.
DUNCAN	I get the island?
NICK	You get the island.
DUNCAN	I don't get the Square Deal Surf?
NICK	You get the island!
	(DUNCAN accepts the black cloak, makes sign of cross and puts his hand out. MARGARET kicks him)
	Not yet. I haven't shown you the trick yet. Now this here is the Reverend George Augustus Robinson, and he can play the flute. Show them how you can play the flute. (KATHRYN does so, plays "Hear the Pennies Dropping") Now the cunning but frightened native population are charmed by the Reverend George Augustus Robinson's flute, aren't they, Gus?
KATHRYN	I can charm a boong at fifty yards, like a cobra.
NICK	Now Gus here is going to play his flute, and you're going to be charmed. (KATHRYN plays the flute. DUNCAN is unimpressed) I said you're going to be charmed.
DUNCAN	I don't know how to be charmed.
NICK	Use your imagination.
DUNCAN	I haven't got any imagination.
NICK	Listen. You do want this island, don't you?
DUNCAN	I want the island.
NICK	You don't want the Square Deal Surf?
DUNCAN	I want the island.
NICK	Then bloody well be charmed! Right, let's try it again, Gus. (DUNCAN is charmed) That's better. Now Gus here plays his flute up and down Tasmania for about five years, and you follow him. (DUNCAN doesn't move) I said you follow him! (DUNCAN moves) It's very dangerous. You can't cross a road at dusk without being shot at.
DUNCAN	Murderous blacks.

NICK	No, murderous white settlers. Now after five years Gus leads you to the seaside. You step on board a ship, you step off the ship, and you're given an island. *(DUNCAN makes sign of cross)*
ROSLYN	Here you are, brother. *(tears off tiny bit of map)* Flinders Island!
NICK	True or False, brothers and sisters? You'd say True, and you'd be right. Ten points and Tasmania to me! *(takes Tasmania and exits)*
KATHRYN	Right. Now you've got an island of your own, we're going to teach you Christianity. Who made you, boong?
DUNCAN	The land? *(he is kicked)*
KATHRYN	God made you, boong. And who's God?
DUNCAN	God? *(he is kicked again)*
KATHRYN	God is love, boong. *(kick)* Who made you?
DUNCAN	God?
KATHRYN	Right! Now you're ready to be civilized.
	(ROSLYN and MARGARET pick DUNCAN up, look at him, then scream)
KATHRYN	What's the matter?
ROSLYN	He's naked.
KATHRYN	Then give him some trousers.
	(they put the Union Jack on him, he falls to the floor and they scream again)
MARGARET	He's getting his trousers dirty.
KATHRYN	Well, give him a chair. *(they do so and scream)*
ROSLYN	He's starving.
KATHRYN	Well, give him some food. *(they do so and scream)*
ROSLYN	He's eating it with his fingers.
KATHRYN	Well, give him some utensils. *(they do so and scream)*
MARGARET	He's spilling food on his trousers.
KATHRYN	Well, give him a table. *(they do so and scream)* What's the matter this time?
ROSLYN	He's getting it all for nothing!
KATHRYN	Well, take it off him. *(they do so)* If you want all these products of civilization, you're going to have to learn to work. *(beats drum 4/4 time)*
MARGARET & ROSLYN	Work for the night is coming, Work through the morning hours, Work while the dew is sparkling, Work 'mid springing flowers. Work while the day grows brighter, Under the glowing sun, Work for the night is coming, When man's work is done.

KATHRYN	Get up. Get fed. Get out. Get to work. Get back. Get to bed. Get up. Get fed. Get out. Get to work. Get back. Get to bed. Get up. Get fed. Get out. Get to work.

(DUNCAN *continues mime through song*)

ROSLYN & MARGARET	Work for the night is coming, Work through the sunny noon, Fill brightest hours with labour, Rest comes sure and soon. Work till the last beam fadeth Fadeth to shine no more Work for the night is coming When man's work is o'er.

(DUNCAN *dies*)

NICK	*(enters)* The massacres in Tasmania left alive two hundred of the original twelve hundred blacks. After forty years civilization on Flinders Island, all two hundred had died out. True or False?
DUNCAN	*(sits up)* See King Billy dropping See Truganini fall, Everyone for Jesus, He shall have them all!

Anybody want to buy four thousand acres on Flinders Island? Going very cheap.

(NICK *makes sign of cross, takes island. All but* NICK *leave stage*)

NICK	As we reach the end of the first part of our missionary service for this evening, brothers and sisters, I'd like to remind you of the words of the prophet Marx who said of one of his brothers, Chico, 'He may look like an idiot and talk like an idiot, but don't let that fool you, he really is an idiot'. Let us remember that a lot of the first missionaries to Australia not only looked like thieves and talked like thieves, they really were thieves. Which is why they'd been sent out from England in the first place. As missionaries. By other missionaries who called themselves high court judges. But who were really thieves. Brothers and sisters, for the second part of our service this evening we are pleased to be able to introduce you to one of God's thieves. That famous blackbirder, Bully Hayes!

(enter MARGARET *with accordian, and* KATHRYN)

MARGARET	Naught have I gotten, but what I've received; Grace has bestowed it since I have believed; Boasting excluded, pride I abase, I'm only a sinner, saved by Grace.

Yes, brothers and sisters, that's what I am. A sinner saved by Grace. But I think I've been bloody hard done by. People call me a blackbirder, just because I take the poor benighted heathen from the South Sea Islands and sell them to sugar planters in Queensland. I was the best captain in the South Seas. After I'd wrecked four ships, I found myself stranded with my supercargo here, without a vessel, without a cent. But the Bible says, 'Ask and ye shall receive'. So I raised my voice to the Lord and I said, 'Lord, send me a sucker'.

KATHRYN &
MARGARET   Lord, send us a sucker!

(enter DUNCAN with a bag of money)

DUNCAN   What a friend we have in Jesus . . .

MARGARET   Saved by Grace!

KATHRYN   Hey mister, want to buy a ship? Tip top condition.

DUNCAN   Why should I want to buy a ship?

NICK   Try appealing to his sense of moral purpose.

MARGARET   We've heard the voice of the Lord saying, 'Go ye into all the world and preach ye the gospel'.

KATHRYN   Only we haven't got a ship.

(DUNCAN is not impressed)

NICK   Try appealing to his nineteenth century sense of progress.

KATHRYN   Have you never heard the parable of the man who was given ten talents, traded with them, and gained another ten?

MARGARET   A hundred per cent pure profit.

DUNCAN   How much does this ship cost?

KATHRYN   Four thousand pounds.

DUNCAN   You're sure I'll make a hundred per cent profit?

MARGARET   You're not questioning the truth of the Bible are you? I tend to take great offence at anyone who questions the truth of the Bible.

DUNCAN   Where can I buy this ship?

KATHRYN   You give my Captain the money, and I'll give you the ship.

(they do so. The ship is battered)

DUNCAN   I thought you said this ship was in good condition.

MARGARET   That's all right. We'll have her refitted.

KATHRYN   At our expense.

NICK   Now here you need a new ship, and a bill for the repairs. You give the new ship to Bully Hayes and you pass the bill to the owner.

MARGARET   I'm only a sinner, saved by Grace.

KATHRYN   And the word of the Lord came unto Bully Hayes and to many other ships' captains, saying, 'Follow me, and I shall make ye fishers of men'. So they followed him to the Polynesian Islands where they fished for Kanakas.

(puts black cloak on DUNCAN)

MARGARET   Kanaka. The Polynesian word for man.

KATHRYN   They were big. They were strong. They were black.

196

MARGARET	They had a peculiar glandular system which enabled them to work with impunity in the unimpeded rays of the tropic sun.
KATHRYN	They were timid, inoffensive, docile, hard-working.
MARGARET	And unlike the Malays, the Tamils, the Chinese or the Japs, they were not protected by a strong foreign power. *(kicks* DUNCAN*)*
KATHRYN	And what's more, they worked almost for nothing! *(karate chops him)*
NICK	Now this is where your history comes in. You need a few revolutions in Europe, and an Englishman, Captain Ben Boyd!
	(enter ROSLYN*)*
ROSLYN	Bloody hell!
MARGARET	What's your problem, matey?
ROSLYN	I came out here from England to make a packet out of sheep and cattle. But now the bottom's fallen out of the market. I've had to cut my shepherd's wages, and now I can't get any bloody shepherds. Bloody Australian workers!
KATHRYN	*(indicating* DUNCAN*)* Sell you sixty-five men from the Melanesian Islands.
MARGARET	A strong, healthy class of men of a copper coloured caste, with fine flaxen hair.
KATHRYN	Three pounds a man.
ROSLYN	Make sure they know how to bloody well work.
	(they kick DUNCAN*)*
NICK	Now you need a civil war in America and the founder of Townsville, Captain Robert Towns.
ROSLYN	Bloody hell!
MARGARET	What's your problem, matey?
ROSLYN	There's a boom in cotton. I've opened up bloody great cotton plantations in Queensland. But I can't get any white workers. Bloody layabouts.
KATHRYN	Sell you a hundred men from the New Hebrides.
MARGARET	A strong, healthy class of men.
KATHRYN	Five pounds a man.
ROSLYN	Make sure they know how long they've got to bloody well stay.
	(they kick DUNCAN*)*
NICK	Now you need someone to discover that the tropical climate of Queensland is very good for growing sugar cane. Captain the Honourable Louis Hope.
ROSLYN	Bloody hell!
MARGARET	What's your problem, matey?
ROSLYN	I've had the boongs cutting down the cedar forests in Queensland. And I've opened up bloody great sugar plantations. But now the boongs have gone and got themselves ki. .., and I can't get any white workers to work in the flaming tropics. Bloody bludgers.

KATHRYN	Sell you a hundred and fifty men from Tanna.
MARGARET	A strong, healthy class of men.
KATHRYN	Seven pounds a man.
ROSLYN	Make sure there's a bloody Government agent on board the ship. I don't want to be accused of being a blackbirder.
NICK	Now you need a Government agent (ROSLYN), a ship's captain (MARGARET), canoes full of natives (DUNCAN *with guitar as paddle*) and a ship.
	(NICK, ROSLYN *and* MARGARET *form ship.* DUNCAN *paddles.* KATHRYN *beats time on drum*)
ROSLYN	Look Captain. Canoes full of natives paddling out to welcome the ship.
MARGARET	How many would you say, Mr Government Agent?
ROSLYN	About ten canoes. Five or six men in each. What'll we do this time? Throw stones on them to smash up the canoes?
MARGARET	No, we'll use the harpoons. Harpoon the canoes, tip the natives into the water, send a boat to pick them up, and then dump them in the hold. Do they seem hostile?
ROSLYN	No, they seem very friendly to me. One of them's waving his paddle.
MARGARET	You can never trust a native. When he seems most friendly, that's when he's most treacherous. Wave back and get the harpoons ready.
ROSLYN	Look, Captain, there's a kid on board one of the boats.
MARGARET	This is no place for kids, they're too young to work. You shoot him and I'll harpoon the canoes.
ROSLYN	I hope I kill him with the first shot. I'd be in bloody agony if he took a long time to die.
MARGARET	Harpoons ready? Fire!
DUNCAN	I was sailing along on life's pitiful seas, When cruel waves threatened my ruin to be; When there at my side I dimly espied A stately old vessel, and loudly I cried:
(chorus)	'Ship ahoy, ship ahoy', And loudly I cried, 'Ship ahoy'.
KATHRYN	'Twas the old ship of Zion just sailing along, All aboard her seemed joyful, he heard her sweet song; And the Captain's kind ear, ever ready to hear, Heard his wail of distress as he cried out in fear:
(chorus)	'Ship ahoy, ship ahoy', As he cried out in fear, 'Ship ahoy'.
MARGARET	The good Captain commanded a boat to be lowered And with tender compassion we brought him on board.
DUNCAN	And I'm happy to say all my sins washed away, In the blood of the Saviour, and now I can say:
(chorus):	'Bless the Lord, bless the Lord', From our souls we can say, 'Bless the Lord'.

MARGARET	Get that nigger on board the ship.
	(all exit except NICK)
NICK	And it came to pass that there was a missionary stranded with all his goods *(shows bag)* on an island, trying to teach the natives *(enter DUNCAN)* about salvation. Now this is very important. You are a sinner. Bad. Born bad. We all born bad. Me born bad too. All people born bad go to hell. But Jesus born good. Jesus big God's son. Big God love Jesus so much that He send Him to die. So that blood can wash badness away. It seemed reasonable enough when I learnt it at the London missionary school. Listen. Me saved, you lost. Me white, you black. Red blood wash you white . . . And there was cast upon the island Bully Hayes *(enter MARGARET)*, a Government agent *(ROSLYN)*, and an interpreter *(KATHRYN)*.
MARGARET	What's your problem, matey?
NICK	I'm stranded on this island. I've got three hundred pounds worth of goods in this suitcase — just look at this jacket. And I don't seem to be able to communicate anything about the doctrine of atonement to this poor sinner.
MARGARET	Perhaps you're using the wrong methods, brother. Hey, Supercargo, show our English brother here how to teach the natives religion.
	(KATHRYN makes sign of cross and puts hands out. DUNCAN imitates her. She gives him a bottle of rum)
NICK	Thank heaven you're Christian brethren. I thought you might have been one of those blackbirders.
MARGARET	Blackbirders?
NICK	Yes, you know. One of those villains who kidnap the natives and take them off to Queensland as slaves.
ROSLYN	There are no slaves in Queensland, brother.
KATHRYN	The laws in Queensland are very strict.
ROSLYN	Every Kanaka must sign a contract.
KATHRYN	Every Kanaka has to be paid a wage.
ROSLYN	Ten shillings a month.
KATHRYN	In goods.
MARGARET	You can't call that slavery, brother.
NICK	I'm very relieved to hear that. You're told such wild rumours about people harpooning canoes. I'd like to warn this poor native but I can't speak his language.
MARGARET	Well, that's a real blessing, brother, because my supercargo here speaks the language. He'd be only too happy to interpret anything you say.
NICK	Tell him that I'm a man of God, and I've got his best interests at heart.
KATHRYN	My Captain and I have come to invite you back to our island. We've got your best interests at heart.
DUNCAN	I've heard stories of your island. People go there and bring back guns. I'd like a gun.

KATHRYN	He says he's heard of Jesus and wants to be saved.
NICK	Tell him to believe in Jesus who will save his soul, and not to trust the white man who will steal his body.
KATHRYN	You can trust us. If you come and work for us for a little while, we'll give you a gun to bring back.
DUNCAN	What's "a little while"?
KATHRYN	He wants to know what you mean by "soul".
NICK	Tell him that part of you that goes on living forever.
KATHRYN	A little while. Three years.
DUNCAN	What's "three years"?
KATHRYN	He wants to know what you mean by "forever".
NICK	Forever? Eternity.
KATHRYN	Three years. Three moons.
DUNCAN	I'll come with you for three moons.
KATHRYN	He says he wants to join.
ROSLYN	Make sure he signs the contract.
NICK	Contract? What contract?
MARGARET	It's a local tribal custom. Whenever a native wants to pledge himself to something, he touches the pen.
KATHRYN	He wants to pledge himself to Jesus. Listen. This is a pen. That's a piece of paper. It's white man's magic. Once you touch the pen, the white man's God who lives over the mountain starts making your gun.
DUNCAN	Let me touch the pen!
MARGARET & ROSLYN	Praise the Lord.
MARGARET	And thank you, brethren, for bringing another soul to Jesus.
KATHRYN	Right. You're signed on now. Let's get moving. (grabs NICK's bag) Can I carry your bag for you, brother?
ROSLYN	Climb up on the bridge with us, brother.
	(MARGARET, ROSLYN and NICK climb ladder)
KATHRYN	Get into the hold, scum. (exits with DUNCAN)
NICK	Why is that native convert coming on board the ship?
MARGARET	You know, brother, I reckon this vogaye is going to do me a lot of good.
ROSLYN	Let's hold a service on board.
MARGARET	And don't be afraid of making it loo long.
	(backstage sounds of fighting, yells)
ROSLYN	Let's sing a hymn, brother.
MARGARET & ROSLYN	Whiter than the snow, whiter than the snow, Wash me in the blood of the lamb, And I shall be whiter than snow.

200

KATHRYN	(enters) The Kanakas in the hold, they're fighting.
MARGARET	Well, fire a few warning shots over their heads. (exit KATHRYN)
NICK	How many Kanakas have you got in the hold?
	(sound of rifle shots. A prolonged scream)
ROSLYN	Sing up loudly, brother.
MARGARET & ROSLYN	Whiter than the snow, whiter than the snow, Wash me in the blood . . .
	(DUNCAN falls onstage through the curtain, wrapped in a red cloak)
KATHRYN	(enters) I'm afraid there's been a bit of an accident down below. One of the boys cut himself and there's a bit of blood on the decks.
MARGARET	Well, let's clean it up, matey. Get out the whitewash.
	(KATHRYN and ROSLYN lay white cloth over DUNCAN)
KATHRYN & ROSLYN	Wash me in the blood of the lamb, And I shall be whiter than snow.
NICK	(to KATHRYN) How do you come to be wearing my jacket?
DUNCAN	True or False, brothers and sisters? The fact is, the story is false. The massacre in the hold took place on the s.s. KARL, 13th September 1871. And the captain wasn't Bully Hayes, it was a certain Dr. Murray. After the massacre he whitewashed the decks of his ship to hide the bloodstains. A prowling British warship which inspected Dr. Murray's vessel complimented him on the clean state of his ship. So I'd say . . .
MARGARET	False, brothers and sisters. I'm getting tired of taking the rap for everything everyone did in the South Seas. I mean where would Queensland be today but for people like me? Full of bloody cedar trees. So get back in the hold, you scum. (all leave except KATHRYN) Me and my supercargo here are going to sing a sacred song.
KATHRYN & MARGARET	Pack up all your cares and woe. Here we go, singing low, Bye, bye, blackbird.
KATHRYN	I say I say I say. How did Bully Hayes die?
MARGARET	I don't know. How did Bully Hayes die?
KATHRYN	One of his sailors hit him over the head with a boom-crutch.
KATHRYN & MARGARET	Where somebody waits for me, Sugar's sweet, so is she, Bye, bye, blackbird.
KATHRYN	I say I say I say. Why did the white socialist workers of Queensland show such love and compassion for their black brothers by demanding the end of slave labour?
MARGARET	I don't know. Why did the white socialist workers of Queensland show such love and compassion for their black brothers by demanding the end of slave labour?

KATHRYN	Because the blacks were undercutting their wages.
KATHRYN & MARGARET	No one here can love or understand me, Oh what hard luck stories they all hand me . . .
NICK & DUNCAN	*(enter, together)* My name is Sir Robert Mackenzie.
DUNCAN	I'm the Premier of Queensland and a well known reformer.
NICK	I'm also an agent for importing Kanakas.
DUNCAN	I'm introducing a Bill to end abuses and give the Kanakas a fair go.
NICK	Why am I doing that?
DUNCAN	Because the Kanakas are getting wise to us and they won't come to Queensland unless we make a pretence of fair play.
NICK	What an astute business man we are.
DUNCAN	High minded, too. *(they exit)*
KATHRYN & MARGARET	Make my bed and light the light, I'll be home late tonight, Blackbird, bye, bye. *(they exit)*
NICK	*(enters)* Saint Paul said, 'We wrestle not with flesh and blood but with principalities and powers'. Brothers and sisters, the first bout this evening is between the wicked white planters of north Queensland on my left (KATHRYN *enters*), and the white socialist workers of Brisbane on my right (ROSLYN *enters*). The wicked white planters will be seconded by the evil blackbirders (MARGARET *enters*), and the white socialist workers of Brisbane will be seconded by the Brisbane Government (DUNCAN *enters*). I represent the highly principled and deeply humane British Government, and I shall be the entirely impartial referee. *(shakes hands with DUNCAN)* Round one. The Indentured Labourers Act of 1871.
	(ROSLYN and KATHRYN fight. DUNCAN and MARGARET speak between the punches)
DUNCAN	The Government in Brisbane forbids the sale of all firearms to natives in the islands.
MARGARET	But they'll only come for guns.
DUNCAN	We'll bribe them with tobacco.
MARGARET	They won't take tobacco.
DUNCAN	Well, bribe my customs officers and smuggle the guns out of Queensland.
NICK	*(using gong to indicate start and end of rounds)* Not much in it so far, brothers and sisters. It looks like it's going to be a hard, clean fight. Round two. White workers campaign against black labour.
DUNCAN	Kanakas, like all cheap articles, are nasty.
	They adopt the worst of the white man's vices, especially drink.
	They foam at the mouth with malevolent desire for white women.

What with the yellow peril and the black scourge, Queensland is fast becoming hell on earth.

NICK (to ROSLYN) Well, I think you gave him a drubbing in that round, brother. Now just get in there and finish him off. Round three. Planters attempt to reply.

MARGARET North Queensland's too hot for white workers.

They won't do nigger's work.

If you send the Kanakas home there'll be no cheap labour.

Unless you want to turn white men into niggers.

(ROSLYN is knocked out)

NICK One . . . Two . . . Three . . . Four . . . Five . . . (slips gong striker to DUNCAN and puts hands over his eyes) Six . . . Seven . . . Eight . . . (DUNCAN hits gong and slips striker back to NICK) Saved by the bell! Well I thought that was a fairly even round, didn't you, brothers and sisters? (KATHRYN menaces them)

DUNCAN Still, I think we'd better let them keep the Kanakas for a few years yet, otherwise we'll all go broke.

(MARGARET and KATHRYN celebrate. NICK whispers to the audience so that they don't hear. ROSLYN is in position to swing at KATHRYN)

NICK Round four. 1901. The new Commonwealth Government orders all Kanakas to be deported by 1906. (KATHRYN leaps up and is floored by ROSLYN) Eight, nine, out! And the winner is human decency, and a white Australia! (exit ROSLYN triumphant) Now you have got to get all the Kanakas back to their islands by Christmas.

DUNCAN Bloody hell!

MARGARET What's your problem, matey?

DUNCAN I've got thirteen thousand Kanakas in north Queensland and I've got to get all of them home by Christmas.

KATHRYN Hey mister, want to buy a ship?

DUNCAN I've already got a ship. What I haven't got is a ship's captain.

KATHRYN (indicating MARGARET) Hey mister, want to buy a ship's captain?

DUNCAN Oh no. The only ship's captains who know where Kanakas come from have been declared blackbirders and have lost their master's certificates.

MARGARET Yeah I know. I was declared a blackbirder and they took away my master's certificate.

KATHRYN (indicating MARGARET) Hey mister, want to buy a ship's pilot?

DUNCAN How much does this ship's pilot cost?

KATHRYN First class master's monthly wages.

DUNCAN (nods head) I want you to make sure that these poor people get home safely.

NICK And now for my next trick, (ROSLYN enters with black cloak and guitar) we shall need a Kanaka (puts cloak on DUNCAN) and a canoe. (gives him guitar)

(DUNCAN *paddles*, KATHRYN, MARGARET *and* ROSLYN *go off*)

Brothers and sisters, "Sending the Kanakas Back Home".

DUNCAN Sailing home, sailing home,
Over the ocean deep and wide,
Over the stormy tide.
I'm sailing home, sailing home,
Jesus shall my pilot be,
I'm sailing home.

ROSLYN *(enters as another black man wearing a cloak)* How was Australia,
Kanaka?

DUNCAN Very hot. Very hard work. But they gave us goods.

ROSLYN Did you get any guns?

DUNCAN No. No guns.

ROSLYN Well go back to Australia. Nobody wants you here.

(MARGARET *and* KATHRYN *rush on. All freeze*)

NICK Of course, brothers and sisters, it all happened a long time ago. We're
looking at it through modern civilized eyes . . .

KATHRYN There was this boong who lived in St. Lucia . . .

NICK I mean, not all the white blackbirders had black hearts. And there were
plenty of black men who behaved as badly as the whites. They sold black
men to the white blackbirders as if they had been white blackbirders
selling black men to the white planters — who were not entirely black.
Brothers and sisters, let us sing a hymn.

ROSLYN When upon life's billows you are tempest tossed,
When you are discouraged, thinking all is lost,
Count your many blessings, name them one by one,
And it will surprise you what the Lord has done.

(*chorus*) Count your blessings, name them one by one,
Count your blessings, see what God has done,
Count your blessings, name them one by one,
And it will surprise you what the Lord has done.

(*all leave except* NICK *and* DUNCAN)

NICK Brothers and sisters. For my next trick which is called "Cementing the
Bonds of Friendship", we shall need the South Pacific (*enter* MARGARET
with map), a ship (KATHRYN *enters with the good toy ship*), an emergent
United States of America (ROSLYN *enters with U.S. flag*) and we shall
need . . .

DUNCAN You don't need a comparitively passive native population? (NICK *shakes
head*) You don't need a big strong Kanaka? (NICK *again shakes head*)
Then what do you need?

NICK *(taking cloak off* DUNCAN) We need a big, strong, independent white
Australia.

DUNCAN *(starting to make sign of cross)* Do I get the South Pacific?

NICK You don't have to go through that rigmarole. This is the twentieth
century. 1908.

DUNCAN	I don't get kicked?
NICK	Of course you don't get kicked. You're a big, strong, independent white Australia. Give him the South Pacific.
KATHRYN	They were big, they were strong, they were white, they were independent.
MARGARET	They had a peculiar insular brand of socialism which said that all men were equal, as long as they were white Australians.
KATHRYN	They were threatened by the coloured hoardes of Asia.
MARGARET	And deserted by the nigger lovers in Britain. *(kick)*
KATHRYN	And what's more, they were entirely defenceless. *(karate chop)*
NICK	Now this is where your emergent United States of America comes in.
ROSLYN	Hey mister, want to buy a ship?
DUNCAN	I've seen this trick before. I give you the money, and you give me a rotten old hulk.
ROSLYN	Show him the ship, brother.
KATHRYN	There you are. The great white American fleet of 1908. Sixteen battleships, all in tip top condition.
DUNCAN	How much does this fleet cost?
MARGARET	It's completely free, brother. Part of the bonds of friendship.
KATHRYN	Want to put it in Sydney Harbour for a while?
DUNCAN	Gee yeah. I've never seen a fleet like that before.
MARGARET	I'll hold the South Pacific.
NICK	Now this is where you make a speech. You say, 'This visit invites the people of America to admit the common trust between the two white races whose destinies are bound up in Pacific dominance'.
DUNCAN	Brothers and sisters, for my next turn this evening I'm going to make a speech . . .
NICK	You say, 'With America our friend and ally neighbourly predominant in the Pacific, Australia has nothing to fear from Asia'.
ROSLYN	A toast. To the common trust.
ALL	To the common trust.
ROSLYN	To American naval predominance.
ALL	To American naval predominance.
ROSLYN	To the White Man's Mission.
ALL	To the White Man's Mission.
NICK	Brothers and sisters. In this moving moment of history, I'd like us to remember some of those who have made our two great nations great. To the American Indians, and the Australian Aborigines, who by so generously allowing themselves to be exterminated, and by giving so freely of their land, have made possible the fulfilling of the white man's manifest destiny.
ALL	To the injuns and the boongs.

NICK	To those Africans and Polynesians whose generosity in labour has laid the foundations of our common wealth.
ALL	To the niggers, and the Kanakas.
NICK	Brother, would you give us a song for the departed blacks?
DUNCAN	There was an old nigger And his name was Uncle Ned, But he's dead long ago, long ago. He had no wool on de top of his head, In de place where de wool ought to grow.
(chorus)	So lay down de shubble, And de hoe, de hoe oh, Hang up de fiddle and de bow. There's no more hard work for poor old Ned, He's gone where de good niggers go. There's no more hard work for poor old Ned, He's gone where de good niggers go.
KATHRYN	Well, time we were off. Thanks for your hospitality. You Australians sure gave us a visit to remember. *(grabs boat back)*
DUNCAN	Hey. You said I could have the South Pacific.
NICK	You know the rules.
	(DUNCAN kneels, makes sign of cross. KATHRYN kicks him. He rolls over to ROSLYN)
ROSLYN	Here you are, brother, a reward for your hospitality.
	(turns flag over and gives it to DUNCAN. It is a two-dimensional can of Coca-Cola)
KATHRYN	We'll be back — for the second World War.
	(all exit except DUNCAN)
DUNCAN	And so we come, brothers and sisters, to the closing stages of the White Man's Mission. But before we go any further, I'd like to make a personal statement. Now I don't wish to appear critical of my missionary brothers and sisters but, as a modern rational scientific preacher of the gospel, I can't altogether go along with these emotional methods of instant salvation. Putting poison into flour, harpooning canoes — I can't altogether believe that these are the most simple and effective ways of bringing about the kingdom of heaven — of winning the hearts and minds of a simple and primitive people. But I'm sure that Jesus understands, and I'm sure that when our missionary brothers and sisters come up for judgment before that great white throne, He will say, 'Father, forgive them, for they lived at a time with very different values from those of the mid-twentieth century'.
	And now, brothers and sisters, at a time when God's kingdom has spread all over the world, we bring you one last chance to play the game of "True or False?". But for reasons of security, we have to be careful about names and places. And so we bring you the testimony of a humble officer in God's army, somewhere in the mid-twentieth century.

KATHRYN   *(enters)* Yeah, well I'm in some army or other, wearing some bloody uniform or other — Nazi, American, British — they all look the same to me — when I get sent to this bloody foreign boong village in France, Vietnam, Northern Ireland, some bloody foreign boong village — they all look the same to me. Well, at first the boongs are very friendly and they give me their wives and I leave a few trinkets on the mantlepiece — the odd bottle of schnapps, or scotch, or bourbon — they all taste the same to me — and the boongs go off and drink themselves sick. But I happen to have left my rifle by the bedside, and the next thing I know one of the buggers has walked off with it. Well, I'm not having that, so I bash him. Then for no reason at all my batman gets shot. So I decide to teach 'em a bit of twentieth century civilization and shoot ten of the buggers at random, just to show that they can't get away with bloody murder.

DUNCAN   Thank you, brother, for that stirring testimony. And now, brothers and sisters, True or False? Personally I find it very difficult to believe that a white officer in the mid-twentieth century would condone random executions. But all that about the mindless treachery of the civilian population had a ring of authenticity, so I'd say True, and I'd be right! Ten points to me for the massacres at Ouradour, My Lai and Londonderry.

My next testimony tonight, brothers and sisters, comes from a humble mid-European public servant who prefers to remain anonymous.

MARGARET   *(enters)* Yeah. Well, the reason I wish to remain anonymous is that people say I'm a mass murderer, and I think I I've been bloody hard done by. I had a few stations east of the River Oder, the only trouble was the bloody boongs. They were everywhere like bloody spiders. Now this was back in the 1940s, and at that time everyone was killing boongs. A group of squatters out in Russia called the Wafen S.S. used to line up Russian boongs, shoot them, and then dump their bodies in lime pits. Another group of squatters in England got together and formed a vigilante unit called the R.A.F. Bomber Command. They used to go out at night, find a German city full of German boongs, and set fire to it. Burn the lot. Men, women, kids . . . got rid of a lot of boongs that way. About half a million. Me, I had a different method. I used to go round Europe rounding up the Jewish boongs and putting them in cattle trucks, and when I got them to my stations I offered them a hot shower. Only I put poison gas in the showers instead of hot water. Well, by the time we'd done away with six million in 1945, everyone decided it was time to stop killing boongs. And me mates turned against me. They said it wasn't cricket, not playing the game. You'd have thought I'd broken the bloody hunting laws or something. The only decent law-abiding way of killing boongs was to go out in bombers and burn them alive. Well, I wasn't brought to trial, at least not at first, 'cause I shot through to Argentina. But then some Jewish boongs found out where I was because I bought my wife some flowers on our wedding anniversary. Bloody criminal it was the way I was treated. They kidnapped me, took me to Jerusalem and had me hanged. And that's why I think I've been bloody hard done by.

DUNCAN   Thank you, brother, for that moving testimony. And now, brothers and sisters, True or False? Personally I find it very difficult to believe that a civilized mid-European public servant would round people up as if they were cattle, and kill them with poison gas. But all that about the terrorists who had him kidnapped and executed — that sounded only too likely to me, so I'd say True, and I'd be right! Ten points to me for the six million Jews gassed at Auschwitz. The next testimony, brothers and sisters, comes from a man who, like a prophet of old, rained down fire from heaven. Brothers and sisters, I give you Colonel Etherley!

NICK	*(enters)* I helped to drop an atomic bomb at Hiroshima. Since then, I've been feeling very guilty, and . . .
DUNCAN	Excuse me, brother, but isn't it true that you've been certified insane? I thought so. I'm sorry, brothers and sisters, but this boy is in no fit state to give a testimony. But I'm sure that if he had been in a fit state that he would have been proud to have taken part in a mission that worked so well. In which case his testimony would have been true. So I'd say True, and I'd be right! Ten points to me for the eighty thousand people incinerated at Hiroshima. The next testimony, brothers and sisters, and the last, comes from the Commander of the American Joint Chiefs of Staff in 1948.
ROSLYN	*(enters)* Bloody hell!
MARGARET	What's your problem, matey?
ROSLYN	I've made a whole lot of atomic bombs, but during the war I only had time to drop two. On cities. And what I want to know is, can they sink ships?
KATHRYN	Sell you the great white fleet. Knocked about a bit at Pearl Harbour, but nearly as good as new.
ROSLYN	Where would I sink this fleet?
MARGARET	Sell you the Bikini Atoll.
ROSLYN	What about the inhabitants?
DUNCAN	You don't want a big strong Kanaka?
NICK	No. No Kanakas.
DUNCAN	You don't want a big strong independent white Australia?
NICK	That's the last thing we want.
DUNCAN	It's just that I'm tired of getting kicked and not getting the island.
NICK	In this one you start with the island. Give him the Bikini Atoll.
MARGARET	Twenty-seven islands scattered along a coral reef enclosing a blue lagoon.
NICK	With a hundred and sixty-seven inhabitants. *(puts cloak on DUNCAN)*
KATHRYN	They were simple, they were friendly, they were harmless.
MARGARET	They had a peculiar accent caused by their lack of contact with the world.
KATHRYN	They were the last of the Marshallese to be missionized.
MARGARET	And the last to adopt a Europeam form of dress. *(kick)*
KATHRYN	And what's more they'd only just been liberated. *(chop)* Hey mister, want to buy an island?
DUNCAN	I've already got twenty-seven islands.
MARGARET	Sorry, brother, Harry Truman needs these — to blow up the U.S. Navy.

KATHRYN	There you are. Rongerik. Good class of island. With poisoned fish in the lagoon.
ROSLYN	Harpoons ready? Fire!
	(MARGARET *tears map of Bikini into four*)
MARGARET	Thou Christ of burning cleansing flame,
(chorus)	Send the fire, send the fire, send the fire.
KATHRYN	Thy promised blessing now we claim,
(chorus)	Send the fire, send the fire, send the fire.
KATHRYN & MARGARET	Look down and see this raging host, Give us the promised Holy Ghost, We want another Pentecost,
(chorus)	Send the fire, send the fire, send the fire.
ROSLYN	'Tis fire we want, for fire we plead,
(chorus)	Send the fire, send the fire, send the fire.
ROSLYN	The fire will meet our every need,
(chorus)	Send the fire, send the fire, send the fire.
DUNCAN	To burn up every trace of sin, To let the light and glory in, The revolution now begins,
(chorus)	Send the fire, send the fire, send the fire.
ALL:	God of Elijah, hear our cry, Send the fire, send the fire, send the fire. Oh make us fit to live or die, Send the fire, send the fire, send the fire. Oh see us on thy altar laid, Our lives, our all, this very day, To crown the offering now we pray, Send the fire, send the fire, send the fire.
KATHRYN	Help God. *(the rope trick again)* Send six hundred thousand troops to Vietnam.
MARGARET	Help God. Declare South Vietnamese villages free fire zones and make everybody leave.
KATHRYN	Help God. Pour burning petrol on those who are left behind.
MARGARET	Help God. Bomb Hanoi back to the stone ages.
KATHRYN	And turn the Vietnamese into abos.
KATHRYN & MARGARET	Dropping, dropping, dropping, dropping See the natives fall. Everyone for Jesus . . .
	(DUNCAN *has tied them up*)
DUNCAN	Well, there I am in my own country, Indochina. When along comes this pack of white boongs. Well, at first they're very friendly. They gave us presents. A few packets of Square Deal Surf, a few cans of Coca-Cola.

But then they started pushing people around as if they were cattle, and bombing villages flat, and burning my kids. Well, I'm not having that. So I draw a circle around Indochina. And I say to them, 'Look here, you white boomgs. You stay on the other side of this line'. And after I've booted them, I think they begin to understand.

(exit dragging KATHRYN and MARGARET by rope)

NICK	For my last trick this evening, we shall need a progressive white politician with a reformist policy *(indicates ROSLYN and gives her a copy of "The Australian" to read)*, a typical Australian voter *(enter KATHRYN drinking a can of beer. MARGARET also enters with guitar)*, and the last remnants of the people from whom we stole Australia *(enter DUNCAN)*. Brothers and sisters, the White Man's Mission presents, "Soothing the White Conscience".
ROSLYN	Bloody hell!
MARGARET	What's your problem, matey?
ROSLYN	I'm in agony. I can't cope with all the suffering.
NICK	You mean the suffering on the aboriginal reserves?
ROSLYN	No, no. The suffering in my heart. The thought of all those kidnappings and massacres. I'm going to make a gesture of repentance. I'm going to give them land rights.
KATHRYN	You can't do that. I've got a string of houses across their so-called sacred bloody places.
ROSLYN	I suppose you're right. I can't steal your land. I'll have to give you safeguards. *(tears newspaper in half and gives half to KATHRYN)* I'll give them some land of their own, out in the bush. They can have the mineral rights.
KATHRYN	You can't do that. There's a world shortage of minerals. There's a lot of money to be made out of digging up Australia.
ROSLYN	I suppose you're right. And we'll need a lot of money to help the urban blacks. You can keep the mineral rights *(tears again and gives half to KATHRYN)*. I'll give money to the urban blacks to help them build houses.
KATHRYN	You can't do that. They'll spend it all on grog.
ROSLYN	I suppose you're right. I'll set up a white committee to handle the money *(tears and gives half to KATHRYN again)* and I'll declare a crash program of medical care. Treat it as though we were fighting a war.
KATHRYN	You can't afford it. The commies have just captured Saigon. You're going to need it to put missiles around Brisbane.
ROSLYN	I'll have to ask the electorate about that one. *(gives all but a tiny bit of paper to KATHRYN)* I'll give them a little something just to tide them over. Here you are, boong. It'll make me feel better.

(DUNCAN takes scrap of paper)

KATHRYN	Hey mister, want to buy some beer? *(gives DUNCAN some beer in exchange for the scrap of paper)* Told you they'd spend it all on grog.

Brightly beams the Father's mercy,
From his lighthouse ever more,

But to us he gives the keeping
Of the lights along the shore.
Let the lower lights keep burning,
Send a gleam across the wave.
Some poor sinking struggling seaman
You may rescue, you may save.

DUNCAN   Brothers and sisters, thank you for joining us in our White Man's Mission. Good night, and may God bless you all.

ALL   Let the lower lights keep burning,
Send a gleam across the wave.
Some poor sinking struggling seaman
You may rescue, you may save.

END OF PLAY

FALLOUT
AND
FOLLOW ME

by
Richard
Fotheringham

A 25 minute script on the subject of Uranium, as performed by
The Popular Theatre Troupe during 1977, particularly in factories and mining towns
throughout Queensland.

Researched, written, designed and directed by Richard Fotheringham

Actors:

Greg King
Nicola Scott
Janet Mahoney
John Lane
Errol O'Neill

Singing tutor:

Mark Penman

A Community Theatre Project in association with the
QUEENSLAND FESTIVAL OF ARTS.

Assisted by the Theatre Board of the AUSTRALIA COUNCIL
and the QUEENSLAND GOVERNMENT.

CHARACTERS

COMPERE   who also plays Hiroshima in the first scene, and Westinghouse during much of the play. 2 I/C to the General. Also plays guitar.

GENERAL   usually General Electric, the leader in military matters.

SERGEANT   lackey to the other two. He is a Soldier in the first scene, then Rio Tinto Zinc, and later the American Atomic Energy Commission.

         All three wear army trousers and boots, scientific lab coats with medals, etc. attached. Their hats are changed according to the specific role they play in any scene.

NURSE   traditionally attired, who plays the various governments of the Free World, and a peaceful scientist.

The original idea for a "uranium plant" gardening speech came from a Melbourne-based performer who developed a longer scene which he performed in a show commissioned by Monash University in 1976 and workshopped by Richard Fotheringham. As revised in Scene Five, it was performed by Nicola Scott as a solo routine at demonstrations, rallies, etc. against nuclear proliferation. She also recorded it for ABC Television in 1977.

FALLOUT AND FOLLOW ME

A sign **"RECRUITS WANTED"** *hangs over a back curtain. Two cutout trees are on stage —
these are used for hiding behind as in war movies and Burnham Wood.*

*Enter COMPERE carrying 2-sided cloth bag — Australian flag on one side, Rising Sun
on the other — and a guitar.*

COMPERE   Good afternoon, ladies and gentlemen. We present "Fallout and Follow
Me". Part One, the Invasion of Japan in 1945.

Scene One   Hiroshima and Nagasaki

*Enter GENERAL and SERGEANT, throwing grenades. AMERICAN GOVERNMENT also
enters, with drum. Soldiers carry machine guns.*

SERGEANT   We've lost ten thousand men taking Okinawa, ma'am. The Japs will
never surrender.

GENERAL   If we're going to set up a ballot box democracy in Japan, then we're going
to have to use the atomic bomb.

GOVERNMENT   Couldn't we explode a bomb on a desert island and show them how
terrible it is?

GENERAL   No — blast 'em. They started this war.

*(drum beat. They advance, COMPERE sits up, puts bag over head with
Rising Sun showing)*

SERGEANT   Watch out, ma'am.

GENERAL   It's Hiroshima and Nagasaki. You'd better let us blast 'em.

GOVERNMENT   But what about the women and children? *(indicates figure)*

GENERAL   Blast 'em. She's probably the mother of the Nip who used my best friend
for bayonet practice.

(drum beats, advance. COMPERE starts playing guitar)

SERGEANT   They're re-arming, ma'am. The situation's getting desperate.

GENERAL   The Russians want to help us, ma'am. We've got to stop them.

GOVERNMENT   We fire-bombed Tokyo and killed eighty thousand. Isn't that enough?

GENERAL   No, ma'am. They still want to keep their emperor.

SERGEANT   We've got to bomb them, ma'am — to save American lives.

GENERAL   We've got to bomb them, ma'am — for the sake of Democracy.

SERGEANT   We've got to bomb them, ma'am — before the Russians arrive.

GOVERNMENT   All right, bomb them.

(drum beat. Soldiers react to blast. COMPERE stops playing)

SERGEANT   One hundred and forty thousand dead, ma'am.

(COMPERE starts playing guitar again)

GENERAL	Too late. The Russians have joined in. There goes China.
GOVERNMENT	Bomb them again.

(drum beat, reaction, COMPERE stops playing)

SERGEANT	Another eighty thousand dead, ma'am.

(COMPERE plays two or three notes to finish. Puts hands up)

GENERAL	They've surrendered.

(all advance cautiously. GOVERNMENT takes bag off COMPERE's head. Machine guns point at bag)

GOVERNMENT No one regrets more than the U.S. Government the tragic loss of civilian life at Hiroshima and Nagasaki. However a balanced view of history must surely point out that it was probably the only way to convince the Japanese that Ballot Box Democracy is the only humane form of government.

> *(sings)* I don't ever care to rise to power,
> I would rather be with you an hour.
> For the things that one can buy,
> Are not worth a lover's sigh.

ALL
> I don't want to set the world on fire,
> I just want to start a flame in your heart.
> In my heart I have but one desire,
> And that one is you, no other will do.
> *(hum next four lines under GENERAL's speech)*

GENERAL Ladies and gentlemen, welcome to today's recruiting rally. We're going to show you some highlights of the war, sing you some songs that we in the trenches sing to keep our spirits up, and bring you the personal histories of some of those who've fought in the struggle for a better world — the world of nuclear power.

(all sing. COMPERE moves behind NURSE, turns bag round to show Australian flag while soldiers point machine guns at flag)

> Believe me,
> I don't want to set the world on fire,
> I just want to start a flame in your heart.

(All exit except GENERAL)

Scene Two   The General explains World Power

GENERAL At ease. Now not many of you I'm sure realise just how serious this war the nuclear energy companies are fighting is. Some of you may not even know this was exists. But it does. That's why we're here today — to win your hearts, minds and signatures for these companies in their gallant struggle — the struggle to put nuclear energy in every home, and atomic missiles around the globe.

Ladies and gentlemen, it hasn't been an easy fight. First we had to persuade President Roosevelt to let us make a bomb. Then we had to lie to President Truman. We told him that if we dropped a couple on Japan, the Japs would surrender. But the Japs tricked us — they did surrender. So before long we had a whole lot of bombs and nowhere to drop them. So we dropped them on the Bikini Atoll in the Marshall Islands — and the islanders tricked us. A couple of hundred got in the way of some H-bomb fallout and started dying of leukaemia, so we had to confine them to barracks for thirty years to stop the world from finding out. Then we wanted to drop bombs on Korea and Vietnam — and the free world tricked us. They wouldn't agree to it. So we had to use low-grade weapons like Napalm instead. And we lost the war.

So we turned to atoms for peace — and India tricked us. We gave them peaceful atoms, and they turned them into a bomb. Israel, Pakistan, South Africa, Japan — they're all doing it. What right has the Third World got to take power into its own hands?

Ladies and gentlemen, that's why we need your signatures. Oppose the spread of nuclear weapons and prevent these irresponsible governments from getting the bomb — by selling your uranium to us. Remember, they're the ones who want to set the world on fire and, if we have to do so, it'll be your fault. *(exit)*

Scene Three   The History of Rio Tinto Zinc in Australia

COMPERE | *(enters)* But let's not get depressed, ladies and gentlemen. Even in the blackest days of the Blitz there were some companies which stayed true to the cause. We'd like to continue this recruiting rally by bringing to you some episodes in the life of one of the staunchest fighters in the front line — The Rio Tinto Zinc Corporation of England.

(enter SERGEANT as RTZ. In this scene COMPERE is a Walter Winchell type reporter, spying on the action)

SERGEANT | *(sings)* There'll always be an England
While there's a country lane . . .

COMPERE | Rio Tinto Zinc took the King's Shilling in the days after Japan fell, and fought in Canada, Australia and South Africa.

SERGEANT | Wherever there's a cottage small
Beside a field of grain . . .

COMPERE | One of its major concerns was to make sure that the governments of these countries *(pause, enter NURSE carrying three dainty handkerchiefs)* appreciated what RTZ was doing for them. In the early 1950s RTZ moved in on Canada's uranium.

SERGEANT | Excuse me, ma'am. Haven't we met somewhere before?

NURSE | I don't think so. *(moves away)*

(RTZ follows her, takes a large handkerchief out of his pocket, drops it, and then picks it up)

SERGEANT | Pardon me, ma'am, is this your handkerchief?

NURSE | Why no, it isn't.

218

SERGEANT	Are you sure? It's a vast Canadian uranium deposit. I felt sure that, as the Canadian Government, such a beautiful handkerchief could only belong to you.
NURSE	I'm afraid you're mistaken.
	(she takes one of her dainty hankies and drops it. Both go to pick it up but NURSE gets there first)
	Is this yours? It's a permit to mine the uranium and pay me very little for it indeed.
SERGEANT	Why yes, it is. *(takes it)*
BOTH	*(sing)* Red white and blue, what does it mean to you? Surely you're proud, shout it out loud, Britons awake! *(they freeze)*
COMPERE	At the same time, RTZ was moving in on Australia's uranium. First Rum Jungle, then Mary Kathleen.
	(SERGEANT and NURSE break tableau and take up the same positions as before)
SERGEANT	Excuse me, ma'am. Haven't we met somewhere before?
NURSE	I don't think so.
SERGEANT	Pardon me, ma'am, is this your handkerchief?
NURSE	Why no, it isn't.
SERGEANT	Are you sure? It's a vast Australian uranium deposit. I felt sure that, as Bob Menzies and the Australian Government, such a beautiful handkerchief could only belong to you.
NURSE	I'm afraid you're mistaken. Is this yours? It's a permit to mine Mary Kathleen for ten years and pay me nothing at all.
SERGEANT	Why yes, it is. *(takes second handkerchief)*
BOTH	The Empire too, we can depend on you, Freedom remains, these are the chains, Nothing can break. *(freeze)*
COMPERE	Later RTZ met the South African Government in similar fashion, taking over the Rossing uranium mine in South West Africa in spite of objections by the United Nations. With mines in three countries, RTZ was able to close Mary Kathleen and work the other two first.
	(SERGEANT and NURSE break tableau. NURSE reacts to COMPERE's words)
NURSE	What will become of me?
SERGEANT	Frankly, my dear, I don't give a damn.
COMPERE	But then in 1970, RTZ heard about the rich Narbalek deposit discovered by Queensland Mines.
SERGEANT	Excuse me, ma'am. Haven't we met somewhere before?
NURSE	Twice.
SERGEANT	Pardon me, ma'am. Is this your handkerchief?
NURSE	Why no, it isn't.

SERGEANT	Are you sure? It's a vast Australian uranium deposit. I felt sure that, as John Gorton and the Australian Government, such a beautiful handkerchief could only belong to you.
NURSE	I'm afraid you're mistaken. Is this yours? It's a permit to buy out Queensland Mines.
SERGEANT	Why yes, it is. *(goes to take it but . . .)*
NURSE	Then, as the Gorton Government, I intend to see that this project stays in Australian hands. *(whips hankie away)* And, as the McMahon Government, I intend to put strict controls on foreign investment, *(grabs second hankie)* And, as the Whitlam Government, I intend to make all mining Australian owned. *(grabs third hankie)*
COMPERE	For a time, things looked grim. *(the other two jump into battle positions)* But after the 1975 coup, a more favourable government came to power.
SERGEANT	I told the new Australian government — just because I own four out of your eight largest companies and a hundred smaller ones, doesn't mean I have more control over your economy than you do. And they all cheered *(he kisses the NURSE)* and devalued the dollar. *(takes a hankie)* And I told the unions — just because I'm making record profits doesn't mean I can afford to give you higher wages. *(kiss)* And they accepted wage indexation. *(grabs second hankie)* And I told the Australian public *(kiss)* I'm working for your benefit. *(grabs third hankie)* And they believed me.
BOTH	*(sing)* There'll always be an England And England shall be free, While England means as much to you As England means to me.

(picks up NURSE and walks off with her)

COMPERE	That, ladies and gentlemen, was a few pages from the war history of Britain's Rio Tinto Zinc Company — the largest mining corporation in the world. But there are other soldiers — America's General Electric and Westinghouse Corporations for example — for whom the war hasn't been quite that easy. Although they used to control eighty per cent of the nuclear energy business, in 1961 both were courtmartialled by the U.S. Government and accused of cowardice in the face of free enterprise. We'd like to show you now how these two gallant soldiers shook off these slurs on their characters and proved themselves heroes in the field of battle. *(exit)*

Scene Four   Two Episodes in the
History of General Electric and Westinghouse

A. THE 1961 COURT CASE

Enter SERGEANT.

SERGEANT	The Court will rise. Ladies and Gentlemen. The U.S. Government *(enter NURSE)* versus General Electric *(enter GENERAL)* and Westinghouse *(enter COMPERE)*. The prisoners, your honour.

NURSE	General Electric and Westinghouse, you are charged under military law with having conspired to fix the price of your electrical equipment and so swindled local governments out of millions of dollars. Have you got anything to say?
GENERAL	Yes, ma'am. I'm the sixth largest company in the world. Do you think I got that way by doing anything illegal? *(COMPERE kicks him)*
COMPERE	We're just small-time crooks, your honour. Why don't you courtmartial the Atomic Energy Commission? *(kicks SERGEANT)*
GENERAL	Good idea. *(kicks COMPERE)* Pass it on. *(COMPERE kicks SERGEANT)* They allowed uranium mining to go ahead without adequate ventilation even though they knew two out of every five miners would die of lung cancer.
NURSE	We're not talking about killing uranium miners. We're talking about criminal activities.
GENERAL	Bad idea. *(he and SERGEANT kick COMPERE)*
NURSE	Swindling governments is a serious business.
COMPERE	We're guilty, your honour.
GENERAL	Sorry, ma'am.
NURSE	As the American Justice Department, I'm going to have to send seven of your top executives to jail.
	(SERGEANT grabs COMPERE)
COMPERE	It's no more than we deserve, your honour.
NURSE	As the local governments concerned, I'm going to have to fine you five hundred million dollars.
	(SERGEANT grabs GENERAL as well)
GENERAL	We can take it, ma'am.
NURSE	And, as the White House, I trusted you to run the nuclear energy business — so, as the President, I'm going to have to throw the book at you and let you write off the five hundred million dollars as a tax deduction *(GENERAL and COMPERE kick SERGEANT)* for ordinary and necessary business expenses.
	(they kick SERGEANT again. He is vanquished)
GENERAL & COMPERE	Thank you, ma'am.
NURSE	And in future I want to see harmony between government and private enterprise. No squabbling in the ranks.
GENERAL & COMPERE	Yes, ma'am.
	(SERGEANT groans)
NURSE	Case dismissed.

(the three soldiers break and hide behind trees)

And so General Electric, Westinghouse and the Atomic Energy Commission went back to the trenches, and they proved their gallantry in battle. They remembered the story of the trench in the Crimean War where one wounded and dying soldier had a full water bottle, while the bottles of his thirsty and starving compatriots were empty. 'Here,' he gasped, 'this could ease my suffering but it's more important that you should live to fight again.' And so the water bottle was passed around the circle of thirsty men and was returned to the dying soldier — still full to the brim. Ladies and gentlemen, we present "The Battle to Make the Uranium Business Pay" *(exit)*

B. GOVERNMENT ASSISTANCE to the NUCLEAR ENERGY BUSINESS in AMERICA

COMPERE *and* GENERAL *(Westinghouse and General Electric) are crouched behind one tree, the* SERGEANT *(the Atomic Energy Commission) behind the other.*

GENERAL	We're pinned down by heavy fire.
COMPERE	I know, sir. I'm being sued for two billion dollars worth of uranium I haven't got.
GENERAL	Courage, lad. I'm six billion dollars in debt over my nuclear reactor contracts.
COMPERE	I can't take any more, sir. I'm only flesh and blood . . .
GENERAL	We'll find a way to win, lad.
COMPERE	I can break like other companies, sir.
GENERAL	Don't lose your nerve, boy. Other companies don't have government assistance. Call in the Atomic Energy Commission.
COMPERE	Yessir. Hey you. Work your way over here.
GENERAL	We'll give you covering fire.
SERGEANT	Whatever you say, sir. I'm ready. *(weaves his way over to them)*
COMPERE	Well done. We've got an important mission for you.
GENERAL	Now listen good. You're an independent adviser to the American Government on Atomic Energy, right?
SERGEANT	Right, sir.
COMPERE	And who recommended you for the job?
SERGEANT	Why, you did, sir, when you were talking to the President.
GENERAL	Right. And who did you work for before you got the job and who are you going to work for after you leave the job?
SERGEANT	Why, I'm going to work for you two, sir.
COMPERE	And what happens if we die?
SERGEANT	I'll be unemployed, sir.
GENERAL	There's nothing like a careful briefing before an important mission.
COMPERE	Good. Now go and find the U.S. Government and give her some independent advice.
GENERAL	And tell her there's a couple of wounded soldiers here.
SERGEANT	I'm ready, sir. And I'll go alone. *(he weaves his way offstage)*
COMPERE	He doesn't know what fear is.

GENERAL	He's got a mind of his own, that boy. That's why I chose him.
SERGEANT	*(off)* Don't shoot. It's the Red Cross.
	(enter NURSE carrying a watering can)
NURSE	Water for the wounded.
	(GENERAL and COMPERE groan)
	Oh dear, so many soldiers and so little water.
	(groans)
SERGEANT	*(enters)* Two wounded soldiers over here, ma'am.
	(more groans)
NURSE	Poor lads. Have some water.
GENERAL	Why, thank you, ma'am.
COMPERE	Much appreciated, ma'am.
NURSE	I'm afraid I can't give you any more, boys.
GENERAL	We wouldn't think of it, ma'am.
COMPERE	There are others more needy, ma'am.
NURSE	Such fortitude. *(gives can to SERGEANT)* Here, take this to my great society health programs.
	(GENERAL collapses, groaning terribly. SERGEANT leaps to his side, offering water)
SERGEANT	May I, ma'am?
COMPERE	I think he's going, ma'am. He built a sixty million dollar uranium reprocessing plant which doesn't work.
NURSE	But what about others in need.
GENERAL	*(faintly)* Water . . .
COMPERE	He's lost a lot of money, ma'am. And nuclear energy is vital to the U.S. economy. I think we can pull him through.
NURSE	Oh, very well. *(SERGEANT gives GENERAL water)* So many soldiers and so little water . . .
SERGEANT	We've saved him, ma'am.
NURSE	God is merciful. Here, take this to my great society welfare programs.
	(COMPERE collapses)
SERGEANT	May I, ma'am?
GENERAL	I think he's going, ma'am. He tried to meet his uranium contracts by buying out Queensland Mines, but Whitlam stopped him.
NURSE	But what about others in need?
COMPERE	*(faintly)* Water . . .
GENERAL	He's lost a lot of money, ma'am, and nuclear energy is vital to the U.S. economy. I think we can pull him through.
NURSE	Oh, very well. So many soldiers, and so little water . . .

SERGEANT	We've saved him, ma'am.
NURSE	God is merciful. There's still a little water left. I'll take this myself to my great society housing programs.

(both GENERAL *and* COMPERE *collapse)*

SERGEANT	Quick, ma'am. *(grabs can)* The whole industry could collapse. *(starts pouring water)*
NURSE	But what about education, community aid, child cars . . .?
GENERAL	You've saved us, ma'am.
COMPERE	History will remember you, ma'am.
NURSE	I can't stand to hear men in pain. So many soldiers — and no water. Oh well, life wasn't meant to be easy. *(exits)*
SERGEANT	*(sings)* Every day, In the park, When the troops are marching by,
GENERAL	There's a nurse, What a nurse, And she catches every eye.
COMPERE	What a style, What a smile, Can you wonder why they fall,
ALL THREE	From the Colonel, To the Private, You'll hear the army call . . .

(NURSE re-enters for dance routine)

Nursie, come over here and hold my hand,
Nursie, there's something I can't understand,
Round my heart, I've got a funny pain,
Oh oh oh oh, it's coming on again.

Nursie, come over here and hold my hand,
I feel awful shy,
Nursie, when I look at you,
My heart goes goo goo,
Nursie, Nursie, I'm a-getting worsie,
Watcha gonna do?

(exit all but COMPERE*)*

Scene Five   Digging for Victory

COMPERE	Well, after seeing that heartrending scene, ladies and gentlemen, I hope you'll be moved to support our army, or perhaps even enlist yourself. But those of you who are in ill health or in essential occupations can still serve your companies. Napoleon said, 'an army marches on its stomach', and during the Blitz even the moat around the Tower of London was turned into a vegetable garden. So remember, if you can't carry a rifle, you can still Dig for Victory. *(exit)*

(enter NURSE *wearing gardening hat and pushing a wheelbarrow which contains a garden gnome, a pot of geraniums including one blue flower, fertilizer, a sprinkler and a piece of coal)*

NURSE Hello, there. Well, the problem we're facing today is that many of our old energy foods *(coal)* are dying out, and we're trying to find something to replace them with. One of the most promising new energy foods these days is the fast-growing nuclear reactor plant *(geraniums)*. You can get these from a few small nurseries in Canada and France, but most come from bulbs supplied by the two big American nurseries, General Electric and Westinghouse.

Now if you want to help the war effort, I'd strongly advise you to plant a row of these — but be sure to site them properly. Uraniums need a sunny well-drained position well away from other plants. Many farmers like to put them right down the back of the farm or even over the neighbour's side of the fence. *(throws a flower behind tree)*

Once your uraniums have sprouted, with the stalk and early leaves out of the ground, they have to be fertilized. The most popular fertilizer *(packet of "Thrive" Fertilizer)* plutonium is, unfortunately, highly poisonous to the gardener — in fact a packet this size could poison the whole world. The plant, however, thrives on it and gives, as they say in the trenches, a bigger bang for a buck — so all in all, I think it's worth the risk.

If it does get a bit hot, however, you can always install an irrigation system *(sprinkler)*. Liquid sodium is ideal for this although the Russians have had a few problems with this one. One of our spy satellites has reported that their giant sodium coolant plant has disappeared, leaving a large hole in the ground. Critics of uranium say this indicates a major accident, but I feel sure they've merely uprooted it for replanting at a more favourable site.

Now you may be asking yourself why this energy food instead of simpler foods such as sunflower seeds and so forth. Well, there are two major advantages with this one. The first is that the dead leaves and seedpods of the reactor plant are too dangerous to use for mulch or compost, and have to be stored in a completely dry 1000 foot hole under close supervision for about half a million years *(puts leaf under gnome)*. This will help to solve your unemployment problem as it's clearly a career with a future. The second advantage is that the plant gives off suckers such as fuel fabrication and uranium enrichment plants which use up just about as much electricity as the plant itself produces, thus making for a near perfect ecological balance.

Let me make one thing quite clear. This peaceful plant is an entirely different species from the noxious atomic bomb weed *(removes blue flower from pot)*. The atmospheric fallout from this weed used to kill half a million children every year. But the introduction of the atmospheric test ban beetle in 1963 has largely brought this problem under control — with only about thirty major fallout outbreaks since.

But as I say, this delightful plant is an entirely differnt species with less than one in a million chance of producing the noxious fallout. So you can happily start digging away, knowing there are no mutants *(indicates gnome)* at the bottom of your garden. *Cheerio. (exit with wheelbarrow)*

Scene Six   Mining in Australia; The Ranger Report; Conclusion

Enter COMPERE.

COMPERE   Meanwhile, back at the front, the war had begun on a number of new battlefields in Queensland and the Northern Territory. And so it was that a group of daring commandos parachuted into the dead heart of Australia, intent on sabotage. *(crosses to battle position)*

The strain of battle is deadly. It puts a man's body and spirit on the rack. It flays every bruised muscle and shrieking nerve. There comes a point when it seems flesh and blood will break under the strain. What holds a man or an army together then is — leadership.

(enter the other three. NURSE has drum, three soldiers each have one of the gardening scene objects which they use as mines. GENERAL also has a book)

GENERAL   Right, men. We're going to cross this paddy field under heavy public attack. There are strong defences concealed here somewhere, so keep your eyes open, and plant your mines carefully. All set? Then let's go.

(they advance to drum beat. Before they can put down objects —)

NURSE   Watch out!

(all retreat)

SERGEANT   England's launched an enquiry, sir.

COMPERE   Australia's done the same, sir.

NURSE   Even America's stopped helping us, sir.

GENERAL   Keep going, men, keep going.

(they advance again but before they can put down objects —)

NURSE   Watch out!

(all retreat)

SERGEANT   I want to turn back, sir.

COMPERE   I can't take it any more, sir.

NURSE   It's murder, sir.

GENERAL   We can't stay here, men. Forward!

(this time they succeed in planting mines and reaching safety)

Right, men, we'll shelter here. *(all rise. GENERAL produces book)* Now this Ranger Uranium Enquiry Report isn't good enough. It says that the nuclear industry is highly dangerous and that the Australian public should decide whether or not Australia mines and exports its uranium. Now I want a volunteer to carry this Report across that minefield to prove to the Australian public that nuclear energy is the safest form of electricity known to mankind. *(applause)* Any volunteers? *(all step back*

226

a pace) No, then we'll have to vote on it. *(all hold out fists)* One potato, two potato, three potato, four. Five potato, six potato, seven potato, more. *(he counts himself out.* NURSE *applauds)* I did it wrong. Anyway, as a corporation I wouldn't dream of influencing public opinion one way or another. I'll start here *(counts himself first)*. One potato, two potato, three potato, four, five potato, six potato, seven potato . . . *(realises he is going to count himself out again. Turns on* NURSE*)* more!

*(*COMPERE *puts academic trencher on* NURSE's *head,* SERGEANT *gives her a businessman's umbrella,* GENERAL *gives her a Report)*

SERGEANT	Congratulations. As the Australian Government *(gives her Australian flag from first scene)* you've got private enterprise, a balanced Report *(puts it on her head)* and Sir Philip Baxter on your side.
COMPERE	And remember, while you're out there risking life and limb, we'll be in here thinking what a sucker you are. *(pushes* NURSE *towards mines)*

*(*NURSE *prepares to cross minefield, hesitating before stepping across each mine and balancing Report on her head. Others call encouragement and one beats a drum as a circus tightrope stunt)*

GENERAL	Come on. There's only one in a million chance of a major reactor accident.

*(*NURSE *jumps over first obstacle. Staggers)*

COMPERE	Three out of five uranium miners **don't** die of lung cancer.

*(*NURSE *jumps again)*

SERGEANT	And plutonium is less toxic than nerve gas.

*(*NURSE *reaches other side. All cheer)*

NURSE	Ladies and gentlemen, nuclear energy — the hope of mankind! *(sings)* Fall in and follow me, Fall in and follow me, Fall in and never mind the weather, All together, Count on me, boys.
ALL	I know the way to go, I'll take you for a spree, You do as I do and you'll do right, Fall in and follow me.
NURSE	Ladies and gentlemen, the Ranger Inquiry has called for full public participation in the debate and in making the decision whether or not Australia mines and exports its uranium. So as you go about your business today, each of us here . . .
GENERAL	General Electric.
COMPERE	Westinghouse.
SERGEANT	Rio Tinto Zinc.
NURSE	And the Australian Government — we all urge you to take away with you this thought. *(holds Australian flag in front of her as in first scene)* "It all depends on me" . . .
SERGEANT	And me . . . *(leans over, arms around* NURSE *and takes flag)*

227

COMPERE	And me . . . *(points gun at flag)*
GENERAL	And me . . . *(points gun at flag.* NURSE *puts up hands in surrender*
NURSE	And you?
ALL	*(sing)* You do as I do and you'll do right, Fall in and follow me!

END OF PLAY

It's MAD
by
Errol O'Neill

A short play concerning militarism, war, and the nuclear arms race, written and produced by the Popular Theatre Troupe, Brisbane, June-July 1981, and performed by them in various parts of Australia after that date.

Researched and developed collaboratively by the Troupe

The actors

Julie Hickson
Lynne Samson
Michael Cummings
Kenneth MacLeod

Writer

Errol O'Neill
with special research and script assistance by David Biggins

INTRODUCTION

Mutual Assured Destruction (MAD) was a phrase used in the cold war of the fifties and sixties to describe the outcome of any contemplated nuclear exchange. Since then, with scientists at the service of war-mongering military machines, both East and West are developing surveillance systems with a view to achieving the ability to knock out the other side's "aggressive" weapons with what would presumably be identified, by themselves, as "defensive" weapons. A first strike kill capability is talked about seriously, rather than an international disarmament movement. It doesn't take long to figure out that this is MADness. Laughable but for the fact that this madness could cost the lives of a large part (if not all) of the world's population. America's use of nuclear bombs on civilian targets in 1945 is the only wartime use of such weapons so far. Meanwhile, conventional warfare has done a roaring trade in a hundred wars since World War Two.

It's **MAD** looks at life in the armed forces, who makes weapons and who profits by them, the dilemma of scientists involved in weapons production, the role Australia plays in the confrontation between the two superpowers and, using the historical evidence of Hiroshima, explores the grim reality of what a nuclear holocaust would be like.

It's **MAD** was based on wide research. Some of the most useful sources are as follows:

- E.P. Thompson & Dan Smith (eds.): *Protest and Survive*, Penguin 1980.

- J. Hersey: *Hiroshima*, Penguin 1966.

- J. Cox: *Overkill*, Penguin 1977.

- J. Cox: *On the Warpath*, Standpoints series, OUP 1976.

- A. Baran & P. Sweezy: *Monopoly Capital*, Pelican 1968.

- A. Roberts: Preparing to Fight a Nuclear War, *Arena*, No. 57, 1981.

- E.P. Thompson: Notes on Exterminism; the Last Stage of Civilisation, *New Left Review*, June 1980.

- *The War Game*, a film made for BBC TV in the mid sixties but not shown on TV because its nuclear holocaust scenes were too "gruesome".

It's MAD

The speech prefixes refer to the actors who originally played the parts. The set is all white, with four divisions. Each division, or cubicle, has a black chair and various unobtrusive pegs for hats and props.

The four actors come from behind the set, dressed in black tights, black t-shirts, which are covered by almost-knee-length white smocks, reminiscent of hospital patients. The atmosphere is that of an insane asylum.

At their first appearance the actors have bandages on their faces, one is using a crutch, one has an arm in a sling. Casualty ward images. They march out to centre stage humming a vaguely militaristic tune. They address the audience.

MICHAEL

Will you spend . . .

JULIE &
  LYNNE

. . . the rest of your life . . .

KEN

. . . in a boring, repetitive job?

MICHAEL

Is the coffee break . . .

OTHERS

. . . the biggest thrill in your day?

ALL

Or would you rather be out there on company time playing football, cricket, sailing, soccer, basketball, swimming, squash, tennis, waterskiing, polo . . .

LYNNE

Just to name a few.

ALL

Playing an active, rewarding, important, satisfying, exciting, responsible, fun-filled, vital role in Australia's defence?

KEN

How many companies can offer you a choice of thirty exciting careers, thirty exciting lifestyles, with the best possible training from the best possible instructors in the best possible conditions in the best possible buildings on the best possible pay you ever thought possible?

JULIE

If you're for Australia —

ALL

Then the NAVY's for you.

(they hum a navy tune and perform appropriate actions)

JULIE

The nation needs the Army and the Army needs you.

MICHAEL

We're currently looking for MEN. Tough men. Strong men. Men with an appetite for danger. Men who can look fear in the face and come back laughing. Men who can throw themselves into the jaws of death without thinking twice.

KEN

We want men who aren't afraid to take their shirts off.

MICHAEL

We want men who can kick start a tank.

BOTH

We want MEN who like MEN.

LYNNE

Think big.

ALL

Think ARMY!

(they hum an army tune and perform appropriate actions)

KEN	Now, if you prefer a more impersonal conflict, if you like to go to war at one o'clock and be home by seven to catch the details on Willesee, if you like to fly over the target, press the button, and be halfway home before the bombs even hit the ground . . . Wing Commander Williams is talking to you.
JULIE	We're currently looking for medical officers, engineering officers, legal officers, pharmaceutical officers, radiographers, a plumber, a couple of aircraft mechanics, and the HMAS Melbourne.
LYNNE	You can play an active, vital role in Australia's defence.
JULIE	Do yourself a favour.
LYNNE	Give your lifestyle a lift-off.
MICHAEL	If you want to fly,
ALL	Then the AIR FORCE wants you.
	(they hum an air force tune and perform appropriate actions)
JULIE	At ease. If you thought life in the armed forces was only for men, think again.
LYNNE	If you enjoy working with people, and you want a well-paid career with a free initial wardrobe of sporting clothes and uniforms, with a lingerie allowance, the WRANS lifestyle is your lifestyle.
JULIE	Or if you prefer the army, life in the WRAACS has got all the elements of a career that can take you right to the top. Accommodation on base is comfortable, with convenient amenities, with swimming pools, squash and tennis courts, games and television rooms, and a modern laundry.
LYNNE	For those modern girls who want to fly, there's plenty of pie in the sky. And if parachuting from 20,000 feet isn't your idea of fun, then you can find plenty to do around the base. And there's lots of time to play sport when you're a WAAAF. And lots left in your pay packet for the good things in life, like a car, travel, and great civilian clothes when you're on leave.
JULIE	You can play an active, vital role in Australia's defence.
LYNNE	Do yourself a favour.
KEN	Give your lifestyle a lift.
JULIE	If you want to fly —
KEN	Float —
MICHAEL	Or fight —
LYNNE	ENLIST!
KEN	'Tention. Left turn. Quick march.
	(MICHAEL and JULIE march up and down. KEN and LYNNE return to their cubicles and don white coats and hornrimmed glasses. They give the appearance of psychiatrists. LYNNE blows a whistle. MICHAEL and JULIE react as though someone is trying to stop their fun and reluctantly return to their cubicles)
KEN	Wilson and Lapsley were very troublesome last night. Had to be sedated and confined.

LYNNE	Oh really? Just when their treatment was achieving results. *(she looks at someone in the audience)* Calm down, Bobby. *(to KEN)* Did you sedate Bobby?
KEN	Results? Ah yes, results. Did you get the results of Singleton's tests yet? Scars are healing nicely, Tina.
	(MICHAEL *is putting on a white coat and a scientist's wig — bald head with side pieces of grey hair. He groans)*
JULIE	*(rushing forward)* Excuse me, can you get on with it? The professor's getting restless back there.
MICHAEL	*(coming forward)* I'm sorry, I'm sorry. I didn't know it would get out of hand. I should never have told them. I thought it was innocent research to improve the human condition. Ooh, I should have been a locksmith.
LYNNE	Not feeling too well today, Professor?
MICHAEL	No.
	(at LYNNE's *direction*, JULIE *hoists* MICHAEL *back to his cubicle)*
	Ooooh.
LYNNE	His deep guilt and remorse appear to be festering again. Singleton? Who's Singleton?
KEN	You remember Singelton. Paranoid scuba diver with the giant clam complex. Had your medication yet, Frank?
LYNNE	Oh yes, Singleton. We had him put down.
KEN	Put down, eh?
LYNNE	Yes.
KEN	Too good for him. Okay everybody, you all know what day it is today?
MICHAEL & JULIE	Yes - terday.
KEN	Right. That means today is analysis day.
MICHAEL & JULIE	Yes.
KEN	Well, last week's topic — what they put in our porridge — didn't create much stimulation, but this week's topic generated a lot of interest. The number who put their names on the board to speak in today's session is quite impressive. Before we get under way I must state the . . . er . . .
LYNNE	Rules.
KEN	Yes, I must state the rules. Now when somebody says they're Jesus Christ . . .
MICHAEL	*(jumping up on his chair)* I'm Jesus Christ!
KEN	Or Napoleon . . .
JULIE	I'm Napoleon.
KEN	Or that the Martians are coming . . .
OTHERS	The Martians are coming?

KEN

Or says anything else that's outrageous or defies common sense, they're labelled and locked up. Freedom of speech is only for normal people.

(LYNNE *has taken off her coat and comes forward with a small Australian flag*)

LYNNE

I love my flag I do I do
Which floats upon the breeze.
I also love my arms and legs
And neck and nose and knees.
One little shell might spoil them all
Or give them such a twist
They would be of no use to me.
I guess I won't enlist.

I love my country, yes I do
I hope her folks do well.
Without our arms and legs and things
I think we'd look like hell.
Young men with faces half shot off
Are unfit to be kissed.
I've read in books it spoils their looks.
I guess I won't enlist.

KEN

Thank you, Betsy.

(LYNNE *returns to her cubicle*)

Because of the nature of today's topic, which may appear to be irrational and totally outrageous in regard to common sense, we have decided that the only rule be freedom of speech. Shall we begin?

JULIE

(*comes forward wearing a gob cap*) Sorry about that, folks. This is where the show really begins. Realism. Stark truth. Danger. Excitement. Patriotic music please, two, three, four . . .

ALL

(*sing*) I'm a Yankee Doodle Dandy,
Yankee Doodle do or die — probably die.

JULIE

My name is Chuck Optimist. I am very glad to have been selected for the crew of a United States Trident nuclear submarine. Not many sailors are so lucky.

MICHAEL

(*wearing a flying cap*) Hello sailor. Ha ha. Sorry about that, ladies and gentlemen. This is where the story really begins. Realism. Stark truth. Danger. Excitement. Patriotic music, please.

ALL

(*sing*) Yo - oh - heave - ho. Yo - oh - heave - ho.

MICHAEL

My name is Igor Stanislav. I'm a pilot with the National Air Defence Forces of the Soviet Union. It's a job I've wanted for many years.

JULIE

When I was young I used to watch movies about the Navy and think, wow, that's the life for me. Life on — or below — the ocean wave seemed so fresh and clean. The uniforms so romantic.

MICHAEL

I can remember when the glorious Red Army successfully defended our homeland against the Nazi invasion of World War Two. I said, as soon as I'm old enough I'm going to be a pilot and defend my country. The day I was called down to the Kremlin for a briefing I was overjoyed.

JULIE	But life on a nuclear sub isn't all fun. We have to work hard, and we have regular medical checkups, especially when we glow in the dark.
	(KEN and LYNNE give JULIE a medical)
KEN & LYNNE	Knees? Green . . . Arms? Green . . . Eyes? Green. Let's GO.
JULIE	You have to be in good condition to spend three months at a time underwater. Always watching. Attentive to all communications.
MICHAEL	What I like about my job is the heavy responsibility. Here I am patrolling in my Backfire jet, vrooom, vrooom, just waiting for instructions, carrying nuclear missiles powerful enough to wipe out an entire city.
JULIE	One day the signal might come through — 'Fire all your nuclear missiles at the programmed targets in Eastern Europe. All systems go!!'
MICHAEL	We could be put on red alert at any time.
JULIE	We could be put on red alert at any time.
MICHAEL	So you have to keep your wits about you.
JULIE	So you have to keep your wits about you.
MICHAEL	Hey, Chuck!
JULIE	Yeah?
MICHAEL	Why did the Yankee chicken cross the road?
JULIE	I dunno. Why?
MICHAEL	To join the other side. Ha, ha, ha.
JULIE	Commies have no sense of humour.
MICHAEL	Ladies and gentlemen.
JULIE	Chuck —
MICHAEL	— and Igor's Limited Nuclear Theatre presents, for your entertainment and horror "The Superpowers' Game Over Europe".
JULIE	Brought to you by good old Yankee know-how.
MICHAEL	And good old Ruskie Pow-wow. Act 1, scene 1. *(he gets a message on his intercom)* What? You're joking, it can't be. *(he picks up a round black pantomime bomb)* I've just got orders to blow up London!
	(in this scene Igor and Chuck throw the bomb to each other across the stage to indicate the bombing of the cities they mention. KEN and LYNNE add SFX: "Boom")
JULIE	Act 1, scene 2. In retalliation, we blow up Prague.
MICHAEL	Act 2, scene 1. Kaputski Munich.
JULIE	Act 2, scene 2. Bye-bye Warsaw.
MICHAEL	Act 3, scene 1. Arrivederci Roma.
JULIE	Act 3, Scene 2. Say goodbye to Belgrade.
MICHAEL	Act4, scene 1. Au revoir Paris.
	(KEN shrieks, LYNNE steps out to catch the bomb. Both have donned berets and KEN has a waiter's serving cloth over his arm)

LYNNE	Waiter!
KEN	Yes, madame?
LYNNE	What is this nuclear bomb doing in my soup?
KEN	The backstroke, maybe?
BOTH	Hey! Boom, boom.
	(JULIE and MICHAEL groan)
LYNNE	I think this scene is overdone.
KEN	Shall I take it back to the chef?
BOTH	Hey! Boom, boom.
	(JULIE and MICHAEL groan)
LYNNE	Well, joking aside, who owns this bomb anyway?
JULIE	You do.
LYNNE	What?
MICHAEL	You bet your sweet babushka you do.
JULIE	We've got them all over Europe.
MICHAEL	East —
JULIE	And West.
	(pointing at each other)
KEN	But I don't want these bombs going off in my restaurant. Take your bombs and play with them elsewhere.
JULIE	Sorry, that's the price you pay.
LYNNE	What for?
MICHAEL	Protection.
LYNNE	Who from?
JULIE & MICHAEL	Us!
LYNNE	You blow up our backyards to save your backsides?
JULIE	You got it, baby.
MICHAEL	And you're holding the baby!
JULIE & MICHAEL	Boom, Boom!!
JULIE	Exit stage right.
MICHAEL	Exit stage left, taking iron curtain call.
	(JULIE and MICHAEL do a vaudeville hand-waving "Exit")
LYNNE	And I thought I was crazy!
	(LYNNE and JULIE take off their headgear and sing "Who's Next". At end of song, MICHAEL joins them. They frantically ask each other "Who's next?" KEN has meanwhile donned a military cap with the G.E. symbol on it.)

KEN	I am. I demand the right to have first say on this subject on the grounds that anything anyone else might say could prejudice the outcome and obstruct the passage of justice.
OTHERS	Yep. That's reasonable. That sounds fair . . . etc.
KEN	Not only that, but it's a subject close to my heart and close to —
ALL	*(sing)* The Wonderful World of General Electric.
KEN	On behalf of General Electric, General Dynamics, Westinghouse, Boeing, McDonnell Douglas, General Corporation, and every other Corporation and every other General with shares in the Pentagon, I would now like to make my very popular Heroic Speech. *(the others cheer)* I have made this speech in many countries of the world to what can only be described as deafening applause.
OTHERS	*(yawn)* Ho hum, etc.
KEN	My grandad, J.P. Morgan, fathered a corporation and a family tradition when he founded this business. He supported the Northern cause in the American Civil War. And it supported him. He made $92,000 selling guns. And my father, just like his father, supported the First World War. And the First World War supported them. They made $1.8 billion supplying England and France with arms.
OTHERS	*(sing)* From the Wonderful World of General Electric.
KEN	But I'm getting carried away. Back to my Heroic Speech. It's 1944 and the lights are out all over Europe. *(the others grope in the dark)* But not so in my brightly lit office in the USA. Imagine the scene. I'm talking to the top allied brass on a subject of concern.
OTHERS	What is going to happen to our war economy when the war comes to an end?
KEN	The funny thing is, I told them, that when the war runs out, no one will want another one. That means that people like you and me will face an economic slump, or be out of a job. The revulsion against war will be an insuperable obstacle for us unless we begin now to set the machinery in motion for a Permanent War Economy!
OTHERS	*(sing)* See them shuffling along . . .
KEN	And they believe me!
OTHERS	*(sing)* Hear them singing a song . . .
KEN	Since the dark days of World War Two, the United States Government has spent over one million million dollars on military budgets. If our boys are in the front line, I'll be in the back line supporting them all I can. If they need guns, I'll sell 'em guns. If the folks back home need toasters, I'll sell 'em toasters. Domestic industry can't stop just because there's a war on. Diversification! That's the secret of —
ALL	*(sing)* The Wonderful World of General Consumption.

(KEN *stands counting money, while* JULIE *and* MICHAEL *are back to back shooting at "the enemy")*

MICHAEL	These Indians are getting worse.
JULIE	Indians? I thought we were fighting Rebels.
MICHAEL	Rebels? That was over long ago. Here come the Germans.

JULIE	Germans? They look Russian to me.
LYNNE	*(she has put her white coat on, and blows a whistle)* General! General! This is no time for commerce. Our soldiers are getting shot at and they've forgotten what they're fighting for. They need a morale booster. Please continue with your Heroic Speech.
KEN	Certainly. Yes of course. Sorry. What a blunder. Blunder. What about a blender? Or a General Electric steam and dry iron? OUT THEY GO! Twin engine fully automatic General Electric washing machine bombers! Swoop on your enemy this washday. Surprise them with a direct-hit five megaton load of the cleanest radioactive socks they've ever seen. OUT THEY GO! It's General Electric's Summer Madness Sale! Hey, Chuck. Help me move this hardware.
JULIE	Sure, boss. Where's it goin'?
KEN	Give you two guesses. This one's got Moscow written all over it.

(KEN and JULIE chuckle fiendishly)

MICHAEL	Hey, you crazy or something? You trying to start a war?
JULIE	War? Who said war?

(KEN is urging JULIE on. She sees MICHAEL)

Why, you dirty commie.

KEN	Commie? Who said commie? *(he sees MICHAEL)* The Russians are coming! The Russians are coming! Everyone to your stations. Alert! Alert! Remember the drill . . .
ALL	Down on the ground, up in the air, under the bed, they're everywhere, it's the — "Let's get them before they get us, let's bomb them before they bomb us, let's kill them before they kill us" — rag.

(mayhem. KEN goes into the audience to sell electrical appliances. JULIE and MICHAEL notice this and babble. LYNNE as the Psychiatrist appears to be trying to calm everyone down. She finally gets KEN back to his cubicle and calms the others down. She addresses the audience)

LYNNE	Poor old Electric Charlie. The General, he calls himself. Been here too long, like the rest of us. Bad case of schizophrenia, and the biggest military industrial complex in the annals of modern ideology.

One day it's guns, guns, guns. The next day it's electrical appliances. Did he try to sell you a toaster? Hmm. I'm not surprised. Did it once before, to his own visitors. Next morning they went to have breakfast, plugged it in, and blew up three suburbs.

We thought of having him put down, but the law says you always need someone like him in a crisis. I mean, where would we be if someone declared war on us tomorrow and we had nothing to iron our uniforms with?

He'll quieten down now, but don't anyone mention war or he'll be all over us like a rash.

(JULIE, as Chuck again, is bringing her chair forward)

Oh, oh. Here comes the navy. That's all we need. *(LYNNE retreats)*

JULIE	The type of person who goes to sea in a nuclear submarine is carefully chosen to be cool in emergencies and convinced of the rightness in some circumstances of using powerful weapons of mass destruction. *(her chair has become the submarine)*
MICHAEL	*(as Igor — and his chair becomes his aeroplane)* Flying up there above the clouds over Eastern Europe, I often fall to philosophical reflection. This highly advanced technology all around me is powerless without a human being to operate it.
JULIE	We have two tasks. The first is to not let people go off their rockers. It wouldn't do if we started a nuclear war by accident. The second is to act quickly when necessary with no moral compunction. When I joined the Navy they said, 'You're here to fight, sailor, not to think'. The missile firing crews are issued with pistols and given instructions to shoot anyone who appears likely to fire missiles without proper authority.
MICHAEL	Military equipment gets more complicated all the time. We have to keep our wits about us. If we misinterpret a signal on our computer and read it as "The Americans are coming . . ."
JULIE	*(nervously reacting)* What?
MICHAEL	That's **you**, stupid!
JULIE	Oh.
MICHAEL	. . . and send our missiles off to attack their missile installations, well, I don't need to tell you the consequences.
JULIE	Each one of us knows that his companion has a loaded pistol which he has a right and a duty to use, should he believe . . .
MICHAEL	Or say he believes.
JULIE	. . . that his colleague has gone mad. **Say** he believes? Who said that?
MICHAEL	But rest assured that all Soviet pilots are carefully screened. Only those who are calm in the face of emergency are allowed up in the strategic bombers. And I'm sure the same applies to the American forces.
	At least I hope it does. Otherwise they'd be letting us down.
	And as I said before, the best part about being in charge of all these . . . fireworks . . . is the heavy responsibility.
	(JULIE and MICHAEL begin to get jittery. LYNNE in white coat comes out and tries to calm them, giving the appearance of a Psychiatrist patronisingly getting them back to their cubicles with "Come on, Igor. Fly back into your little hangar" . . . "Chuck, it's time to sail back into port", etc.)
LYNNE	Those two sure are jittery today. I wouldn't like to be in their condition.
KEN	*(he is not wearing his white coat and holds his General Electric cap)* What are they doing here, anyway? Why aren't they at their stations? This isn't the Mickey Mouse Club. We've got a war to fight.
LYNNE	We've got a war to fight?
	(JULIE, as Chuck again, is bringing her chair forward)
	Oh, oh. Here comes the navy. That's all we need. *(LYNNE retreats)*

JULIE	The type of person who goes to sea in a nuclear submarine is carefully chosen to be cool in emergencies and convinced of the rightness in some circumstances of using powerful weapons of mass destruction. *(her chair has become the submarine)*
MICHAEL	*(as Igor — and his chair becomes his aeroplane)* Flying up there above the clouds over Eastern Europe, I often fall to philosophical reflection. This highly advanced technology all around me is powerless without a human being to operate it.
JULIE	We have two tasks. The first is to not let people go off their rockers. It wouldn't do if we started a nuclear war by accident. The second is to act quickly when necessary with no moral compunction. When I joined the Navy they said, 'You're here to fight, sailor, not to think'. The missile firing crews are issued with pistols and given instructions to shoot anyone who appears likely to fire missiles without proper authority.
MICHAEL	Military equipment gets more complicated all the time. We have to keep our wits about us. If we misinterpret a signal on our computer and read it as "The Americans are coming . . ."
JULIE	*(nervously reacting)* What?
MICHAEL	That's **you**, stupid!
JULIE	Oh.
MICHAEL	. . . and send our missiles off to attack their missile installations, well, I don't need to tell you the consequences.
JULIE	Each one of us knows that his companion has a loaded pistol which he has a right and a duty to use, should he believe . . .
MICHAEL	Or say he believes.
JULIE	. . . that his colleague has gone mad. **Say** he believes? Who said that?
MICHAEL	But rest assured that all Soviet pilots are carefully screened. Only those who are calm in the face of emergency are allowed up in the strategic bombers. And I'm sure the same applies to the American forces.
	At least I hope it does. Otherwise they'd be letting us down.
	And as I said before, the best part about being in charge of all these . . . fireworks . . . is the heavy responsibility.
	(JULIE and MICHAEL begin to get jittery. LYNNE in white coat comes out and tries to calm them, giving the appearance of a Psychiatrist patronisingly getting them back to their cubicles with "Come on, Igor. Fly back into your little hangar" . . . "Chuck, it's time to sail back into port", etc.)
LYNNE	Those two sure are jittery today. I wouldn't like to be in their condition.
KEN	*(he is not wearing his white coat and holds his General Electric cap)* What are they doing here, anyway? Why aren't they at their stations? This isn't the Mickey Mouse Club. We've got a war to fight.
LYNNE	We've got a war to fight?
KEN	*(putting cap on)* Of course we've got a war to fight. The United States Government wouldn't spend over one million million dollars on military budgets since World War Two if we **didn't** have a war to fight!

LYNNE	That's a trillion dollars. How do you know it's that much? *(she puts on flying cap)*
KEN	'Cause my father won the contract, God bless him, and I've been handling it ever since.

(both adopt patriotic poses)

We, who have suffered from large military industrial complexes, have become alarmed at the heavy casualty rate during international conflicts, so we have poured some of the United States military trillion into weapons research to make war safer than ever before.

On the battlefields of the future, enemy forces will be located, tracked and targetted almost instantaneously through the use of data-linked, computer-assisted intelligence evaluation and automated fire control.

LYNNE	Wow!
KEN	With first-round kill probability approaching certainty and with surveillance devices that continually track the enemy, the need for large ground forces to engage the enemy physically will be less important.

I am the son of the father of the permanent war economy and if any of you ratbag agitators *(this is said to the audience)* dare call me or my dad a merchant of death, I'll blow you right out of your sandals.

After all, what's the point of going into war if you can't win?

JULIE	*(coming forward wearing an apron)* Goodbye, dear, have a nice day at the war. And try to stay out of trouble. You know how I hate bloodstains on your collar.
LYNNE	Don't worry, dear. I'm safe in my General Electric McDonnel Douglas Boeing bomber. All I do is press the button and the computer does the rest. I don't have to wait around while the Vietnamese peasants writhe in torment, or pick up the arms and legs after the explosion. But I'd better hurry or I'll miss my flight. Have a nice day, dear, and don't work too hard.
JULIE	Oh, I've only got the washing to do.
LYNNE	Do you need a hand?
JULIE	No, with my new General Electric washer all I do is press the button and the electronic brain does all the work. I don't have to stand around waiting for the final rinse. I've got more time to spend on other things.

Oh, and don't forget, you're bringing the General home to dinner

LYNNE	I'm bringing the General home to dinner.
KEN	How did you go in Vietnam?
LYNNE	We blew it.
KEN	That's my boy!
LYNNE	No, I mean we **blew** it.
KEN	What? You had ten years in Vietnam with the most sophisticated weaponry the world has ever seen, and you blew it?
LYNNE	Guess we did, General.

JULIE	Don't be too hard on them, General. You know how dirty these Asians fight.
KEN	You'll just have to get back there and do it again, only this time get it right. I don't get paid half the U.S. military budget to make weapons so that you can go and lose a war!
LYNNE	But we can't go back there. Our own people are against it.
KEN	Well, we'll have to find somewhere else. Give me the map. What about El Salvador? There's a nice place, closer to home . . .
JULIE	When you boys put your nose in the map and start talking shop, it's time for me to check the dinner.
LYNNE	Do you need a hand, dear?
JULIE	No, all I have to do is pop the roast in the General Electric microwave, press the button, and technology does the rest.
ALL	*(sing)* The Wonderful World of Toasters and Blenders.
KEN	We went to Vietnam to do the biggest commercial the world has ever seen. It was gonna be one glorious full-colour quadraphonic campaign for Truth, Justice and Free Enterprise. Everything that opens and shuts. Electronic, automated WAR! He comes home and says, 'We **blew** it'. That's the kind of thing that gives Free Enterprise a bad name.
LYNNE	I know.
KEN	There's only one thing for it. We'll turn our guns into plough-shares.
OTHERS	Hooray!
KEN	Then we'll turn our shares into profits and plough our profits back into guns and be ready for the next war even before it starts. Just another service to the free world from —
ALL	*(sing)* The Wonderful World of Conventional Warfare.
MICHAEL	*(coming forward as the Scientist)* Now if I could make a blender with the blades on the **outside**, about five thousand times larger than the domestic model, and we drop them from low-flying aircraft, we could clear the forest and take care of the enemy at the same time.
	But there wouldn't be a market for it. Unless . . . wait a minute! Where's that crazy electric general from the Pentagon?

(the following is a spoken verse piece accompanied with appropriate actions and a rhythm provided by small percussive instruments. JULIE and LYNNE join)

KEN	There are nuts who want to rule the world Show your flag and shake your fist. Take up your toolbox, physicist And the sleeves of your white coat.
OTHERS	You mean us?
KEN	Forsake all that has gone before Show your flag and shake your fist. Take off your glasses, join the war. Build me a big bomb.

OTHERS	He does mean us. We're working on a formula —
KEN	Show your flag and shake that rat.
OTHERS	If you promise not to go too far.
KEN	Cross my heart and hope to die.
OTHERS	*(sing)* Building a big bomb, shedoobiwah Building a big bomb, shedoobiwah Building a big bomb, shedoobiwah Ten times hotter than the sun —
KEN	Shake your money and shut your mouth.
OTHERS	And fallout fatal for everyone.
ALL	Hail, hail, mighty Science.
OTHERS	*(sing)* Building a big bomb.
KEN	Invest in the military scientific trust.
OTHERS	Shake your money and shut your mouth.
KEN	It's a business boom on the edge of bust.
ALL	*(sing)* Military scientific trust, shedoobiwah. *(then, in funereal tone)* Boom, boom, boom, boom, boom, boom, boom, boom, boom, boom, boom.
	(they are returning to their cubicles. They turn to the audience)
	Shedoobiwah.

(in the following scene, LYNNE plays the archetypal U.S. President. KEN plays the archetypal Secret Service man with the letters "CIA" on his cap. MICHAEL is a scientist with a bald-head wig and, later, Nikita Krushchev. JULIE is initially a Scientist and, later, a KGB agent)

LYNNE	Morning, Homer.
KEN	Morning, Mr President.
LYNNE	What's the news?
KEN	Autumn 1939. Germany has invaded Poland, the price of steel has gone up, and there's a scientist waiting to see you.
LYNNE	Who is he?
KEN	A refugee from Nazi Germany. We checked him out. He's on our side. And he's also one of the world's leading physicists.
LYNNE	Send him in.
MICHAEL	Mr President? *(he has a piece of paper, and refers to it as he speaks)*
LYNNE	*(turning sharply to him and pointing her finger at him)* Yeah!?
	(MICHAEL starts and raises his hands as though the fingere were a gun. KEN frisks him)
KEN	He's clean.

MICHAEL	Mr President, some recent scientific research which I know of leads me to expect that the element uranium . . .
KEN & LYNNE	Uranium?
MICHAEL	. . . may be turned into a new and important source of energy in the immediate future. This research could lead to the development of extremely powerful bombs of a new type. I believe that it would be to your military advantage to begin similar research.
LYNNE	Making bombs out of uranium? *(KEN and LYNNE laugh derisively)* Thanks for your information. Don't call us, we'll call you. Oh, Homer.
KEN	Yes, Mr President?
LYNNE	Give him a ticket to the White House Ball.
KEN	Table six?
LYNNE	The Alcove.
KEN	*(deferring)* The Alcove. *(he leads MICHAEL away, gives MICHAEL's paper to JULIE)*
LYNNE	Who is this guy trying to kid? Uranium? What's wrong with good old-fashioned TNT?
JULIE	*(comes forward reading MICHAEL's paper)* But, Mr President . . .
LYNNE	Anyway, what do we care if Germany makes a new bomb? They're still our best trading customers. General Electric has a big deal cooking with Krupp, the German arms manufacturer. It'd be bad for business if we tried to meddle in some European squabble.
JULIE	But, Mr President . . .
LYNNE	Besides, we're not supposed to join this war till 1941.
KEN	1941? That's just around the corner.
LYNNE	So it is! Get Professor BiggerAndBetter in here on the double.
	(LYNNE points her finger at JULIE who raises her arms. KEN frisks JULIE)
KEN	Real clean.
JULIE	But I am Professor BiggerAndBetter.
LYNNE	Good, I'm glad you dropped in. Now what have you got on this "Uranium bomb"?
JULIE	Well, according to our information, the German scientist was quite right. I think we should take his advice.
LYNNE	So Gerry's got a Big Bomb?
JULIE	That's right, Mr President.
LYNNE	Get back to the Scientific Division and get to work. If Gerry's got a new toy, we want something Bigger and Better, Professor.
KEN	*(leaning over JULIE menacingly)* Remember the Alcove?
JULIE	I'll get on to it right away.
	(all put on bow ties)
LYNNE	Evening, Homer.

KEN	Good evening, Mr President.
LYNNE	Read it out.
KEN	Spring, 1945. The Germans have been defeated and we've learned that they were nowhere near developing the Atomic bomb.
LYNNE	What?
JULIE	Four years of work on the bomb for nothing?
LYNNE	Take it easy, Professor. We may have lost the Germans but we've still got the Japs to worry about. But I don't want to talk business, I'm off to the White House Ball.
MICHAEL	Mr President. *(the other three congregate and make conversation noises)* I feel I must warn you of the dangers which would face the world from the postwar development of atomic energy. *(conversation noises)* There is no need to continue with the development of the bomb, since the only nation with whom we are still at war, the Japanese, have no uranium. *(conversation noises)* It would be the single most criminal act of history if you were to bomb Hiroshima and Nagasaki as this would result in the deaths of over half a million innocent people. *(a loud burst of conversation and laughter)* All the more criminal since the Japanese are making attempts to talk peace.
LYNNE	No need to continue with the bomb? *(she dismisses MICHAEL)* Who is this guy trying to kid? We've got a little secret, and we're gonna make sure no one else gets the bomb before we do.
JULIE	Yessir, Mr President.
LYNNE	Especially the Russians. *(KEN and LYNNE dance a tango to accompaniment provided by MICHAEL and JULIE)* And we're gonna make sure that no one else gets a bigger bang for a buck than we do, especially the Russians.
KEN	Don't worry. The Russians don't get the bomb till 1949. That gives us plenty of time to buy the best scientists in the world at bargain basement prices. *(more tango)*
LYNNE	And we're gonna make sure we surround the Soviet Union with **our** friends and **our** missiles by 1954, before anyone else surrounds us. Especially the Russians.
KEN	I get it. Kind of contain their aggressive threat with our peaceful threat even before they get a chance to make a threat. *(during this they finish dancing)*
LYNNE	Bright boy, Twenty-One.
KEN	Gee, you can see why America leads the world in diplomacy.
LYNNE	Sure can. *(they congregate as before)*
MICHAEL	Mr President, there is more bad news! Britain has bought some scientists and made their own atomic bomb. *(conversation noises)* Oh, I should never have told them, I should never have told anyone. They don't know what they are doing. I must stop them before more countries get the bomb.
	(he has a newspaper — headline: BRITISH N-TESTS A SUCCESS*)*
LYNNE	Why don't you write to the American President? *(the three laugh)*

MICHAEL	Ah, I have it. I shall call on my fellow scientists in all countries. Winter 1955. *(he addresses the audience)* Fellow scientists, we must learn to think in a new way. We must ask ourselves not how can we provide a military victory for whatever group we prefer. The question is, how can we prevent a military contest of which the outcome must be disastrous to all parties. Shall we put an end to the human race? Or shall mankind renounce war?
	(the three advance on him during this)
LYNNE	Not feeling too well today, Professor? *(they intimidate him)* His deep guilt and remorse seem to be festering again. *(she dismisses him and takes the newspaper. She opens it out in reverse and we see a large CND — Committee for Nuclear Disarmament — symbol)* Put an end to the human race? Who does this scientist think he's kidding? We're just protecting ourselves.
KEN	Yessir, Mr President. *(KEN holds an umbrella over LYNNE. They begin to "marcher sur place")*
JULIE & MICHAEL	*(sing)* Singin' in the rain, I'm . . .
LYNNE	Anyway, they started it all with their crazy scientific notions.
KEN	Yessir, Mr President.
JULIE & MICHAEL	*(sing)* Singin' in the rain.
LYNNE	Well, we helped 'em along a bit, but there was a war on. It was our duty.
KEN	Yessir, Mr President.
JULIE & MICHAEL	*(sing)* What a glorious feeling, I'm . . .
LYNNE	Now these guys could be dangerous for future security. I want you, as the CIA, to make life difficult for 'em, if you know what I mean.
KEN	Yessir, Mr President.
JULIE & MICHAEL	*(sing)* . . . happy again.
LYNNE	After all, anyone who talks peace is likely to be dangerous. And anyone who talks peace while we're talking war is likely to be a commie.
JULIE & MICHAEL	*(sing)* I'm singin' . . .
LYNNE	We gotta defend our national interests.
JULIE & MICHAEL	*(sing)* . . . and dancin' . . .
KEN	That's what I call democracy.
JULIE & MICHAEL	*(sing)* . . . in the rain.

(JULIE and MICHAEL have been miming a microphone. The microphone now turns into an umbrella. They turn to go back to their cubicles. At the same time, LYNNE and KEN turn back to their cubicles — all four whistling the tune "Singin' in the Rain".)

JULIE *puts on a fur cap and becomes Olga, a KGB agent. She picks up a telephone and makes ringing noises.* KEN *keeps on his CIA cap and picks up a phone.* LYNNE *retains her President's cap and waits in her cubicle.* MICHAEL *waits in his cubicle. He soon puts on fur cap to become Nikita Krushchev)*

(this scene begins with the Cuban Missile Crisis and ends — by showing the President as the craziest of all the inmates — with the current world nuclear situation. The President gradually gets more manic over the next three pages)

KEN	Hello, that you, Olga?
JULIE	Homer! Nice to hear you.
KEN	Nice to hear you, Olga. Er . . . Olga, I've been looking through our 1962 winter catalogue and I notice you're stocking up on Intercontinental Ballistic Missiles.
JULIE	Mmm.
KEN	My President tells me we're running low on ICBMs. I notice you have quite a few.
JULIE	Mmm.
KEN	Would you mind if we had a closer look at one of them? The photos in the catalogue are a bit grainy. You know how spy photographs are.
JULIE	Oh, Homer. Do you want us to send you one on trial?
KEN	Now, enthusiasm has its place, Olga.
JULIE	Homer, you took the words right out of my mouth. We're opening a store in Cuba. We could send you one at a moment's notice.
KEN	The only thing we'd like delivered from Cuba, Olga, are cigars.
JULIE	Oh, Homer, you want cigars? We'll send you cigars. Ha, ha.
KEN	Gee thanks, Olga. Very obliging of you. You meet a nice class of person in Intelligence, no doubt about it. *(they hang up)*
LYNNE	Morning, Homer.
KEN	Thay're sending us some large Havana cigars.
LYNNE	Good. I like Havana cigars.
KEN	*Large* Havana cigars?
LYNNE	I like large Havana cigars.
KEN	Large *exploding* Havana cigars?
LYNNE	What!? Get me the hotline. (KEN *gives her the phone)*
JULIE	*(still has Olga's cap on)* Are you there, Moscow? I have an urgent call from Washington, D.C. Person to person from a Mr J F Kennedy to a Mr N Krushchev. Go ahead, please.
MICHAEL	*(standing on his chair — Nikita has been caught in the shower)* Singin' in the rain, just singin' in the rain . . . Oh. (JULIE *hands phone to* MICHAEL*)* Hello.
LYNNE	Nikita, how are you?
MICHAEL	Mmm.

LYNNE	Look, Nikita, we're not interested in those Cuban missiles after all. We'd like you to take them back.
MICHAEL	Mmm.
LYNNE	We *want* you to take them back.
MICHAEL	Mmm.
LYNNE	We *order* you to take them back!
MICHAEL	Oh?
LYNNE	Look, I might have told the American people that you had more bombs than us, but the truth is that we've got more bombs than you.
MICHAEL	You mean you *lied*?
LYNNE	It's a sort of custom here. We do it to get into office.
MICHAEL	Yeah, I know. We do it to stay in office. *(then, suddenly)* You got more bombs than us? That true, Olga?
JULIE	'Fraid so, comrade.
MICHAEL	Okay, Jack. You're a businessman. I'll do a deal with you.
LYNNE	Now you're talking my language . . . comrade.
MICHAEL	You send us your winter catalogue every year, and we'll send you ours.
LYNNE	Mmm.
MICHAEL	That way we can keep up with what you're doing, and you can keep up with what we're doing.
LYNNE	Mmm.
MICHAEL	You believe in equal opportunity, don't you?
LYNNE	Mmm. *(affirmative)*
MICHAEL	Well, we want the same opportunity to start a nuclear war as you.
LYNNE	Now wait a min—
MICHAEL	*(cutting in)* We'll pull out of Cuba, but seeing as you continue to surround us in Europe with your missiles, just remember, Hank, we've already got enough bombs to wipe you out once and for all.
LYNNE	Oh yeah? Well, I wasn't going to mention this, but *we've* got enough bombs to wipe you out *twice*!
MICHAEL	Oh really? Why do you need to wipe us out twice? Isn't once enough?
LYNNE	It ain't *how* you get killed, but *how many times* that counts. But let's not get into an argument about war when what we really want is peace. Put your catalogue in the mail and we'll send you ours by return post.
MICHAEL	Okay, Hank, but just remember, you can fool all of the Ruskies all of the time —
JULIE	*(cutting in)* No, no. It's fool some of the Ruskies some of the time . . .
	(they argue for a short time, then)
MICHAEL	Ah! Forget it. Click! *(they both listen, pretending to have hung up)*
KEN	You rang up to threaten him and you end up exchanging catalogues?
LYNNE	Quiet! He might hear you.

*(she hangs up the phone violently. Olga and Nikita scream with agony —
they have had their ears close to the phone)*

Listen, dummy. If we have information on where their missiles are, we
can point **our** missiles at **their** missiles. Then, in the event of a war, we
can strike first and knock out their ability to retaliate.

KEN   But there won't **be** a war unless **somebody** strikes first.

LYNNE   But nobody's going to strike first if they don't know what weapons the
               other side have got waiting.

KEN   What's that got to do with peace?

LYNNE   The important thing is for us to keep coming up with new weapons
               systems so they'll know we're serious about trying to stop the arms race!

KEN   *(realisation dawns)* Then **they'll** come up with new systems to show
               they're **just** as serious about disarmament!

LYNNE   Right! The more weapons we can both develop, the better chance we have
               of making an arms limitation treaty.

               (the President is by now quite manic. Chuck reappears)

JULIE   Three months at a time underwater. *(to LYNNE)* How would you like it?

               (LYNNE is quietened by this and retreats, perplexed)

               I sometimes wish I could get out there and swab the deck like Dean
               Martin and Jerry Lewis used to do in their Navy pictures. Breathe fresh
               air, crack a few jokes. But I'm down here with all these other morons
               breathing down my neck. I can't get away from them. And they've all got
               guns.

               My bunk is right next door to the weapons storeroom. When I lay down
               to sleep, my head is only one metre away from a five megaton
               thermonuclear warhead. I sometimes imagine I can hear it breathing,
               whispering to me.

               (the others breathe loudly and whisper Chuck's name)

               I was born in the atomic age. I grew up with the bomb. I know I have to
               live with it. Here in my underwater world. I know I have to make it my
               friend. In this tub it's the only friend I've got. I'm going next door to kiss
               it goodnight. *(she retires)*

MICHAEL   *(as Igor)* Sometimes I want to get out of the armed forces and go back to
               civilian life. Breathe fresh air, crack a few jokes. But I have never had
               any other interest. I wouldn't feel right if I wasn't in uniform.

               Since the revolution in 1917, my country has always had enemies. No
               nation in the capitalist world wanted to see the birth or the continued
               existence of a socialist state. We have always had to fight, and be
               prepared to fight. Now it is part of us. Part of the air we breathe. I cannot
               conceive of peace. *(he retires)*

KEN   Sorry about that, folks. This is where the story really begins. Realism.
               Stark truth. Danger. Excitement. A sunburnt country. Land of sweeping
               plains. Patriotic music, please.

OTHERS   *(sing)* Tie me kangaroo down, sport, tie me kangaroo down.

250

KEN	My name is YesSirNoSirWhateverYouSaySir, and I'd like to make an Heroic Speech. *(jeering from the others)* But I've lost me bit of paper.
LYNNE	*(as President)* How many times have I told you never to open your mouth without instructions.
KEN	Sorry, sir, Whatever you say, sir. As I was saying, I express the American . . .
LYNNE	Psst!
KEN	. . . Australian Government's concern at the growth of Soviet military power. The USSR now has a strategic and military reach well beyond the established zone of American . . .
LYNNE	Psst!
KEN	. . . Soviet military interest. This concern has also been expressed by the defence and foreign ministers of the . . . er, NATO *(LYNNE nods approval)* powers who, in their communiques, have made it very plain that they are worried about the increasing offensive capacity of the American . . .
LYNNE	Psst
KEN	. . . Soviet forces, giving them a reach into every corner of the world.

[the following scene uses the split-screen effect as before. JULIE and MICHAEL are Mr and Mrs Average Australian at a barbecue. KEN and LYNNE go into one of the cubicles behind a screen which says, "THE AMERICAN-AUSTRALIAN ALLIANCE". Their heads appear above the screen. This is a puppet show)

JULIE	This looks like a nice little corner of the world.
MICHAEL	Good spot for a barbie.
LYNNE	Ladies and gentlemen, Ronald Sixgun and Sir Malcolm . . .
KEN	YesSirNoSirWhateverYouSaySir.
LYNNE	. . . peeping out from under the American Nuclear Umbrella, present for your entertainment and horror, "THE AMERICAN . . .
KEN	. . . AUSTRALIAN . . .
KEN & LYNNE	. . . ALLIANCE.
MICHAEL	We'd have to be in luck. These two funny buggers are puttin' on a play.
JULIE	Fair dinkum?
LYNNE	Act 1, scene 1. All the way with LBJ. We convince you that we'll protect you from attack.
JULIE	Did you bring the Aerogard?
MICHAEL	Oh, bugger!
JULIE	Oh, Bert!
KEN	All it costs us is a couple of pieces of real estate at North-West Cape and Nurrungar. In gratitude, we send some troops to help you out in Vietnam.
LYNNE	We only use five hundred of them and send the rest home alive!
MICHAEL	Did you get to the butcher's before they closed?
JULIE	Yeah.

KEN	We are grateful again and hand over more territory. This time at Pine Gap.
LYNNE	We are proud to have the people of . . . er, Australia . . . as our honest and loyal friends in a world where Freedom and Democracy are constantly challenged.
KEN	We agree to ask no questions about what you're doing with our real estate, because we've seen your old movies and we know that —
JULIE	A man's gotta do what a man's gotta do. Light the fire, Bert.
LYNNE	Act 1, scene 2. You wake up one morning to find that our bases are being used for strategic military planning.
MICHAEL	Crikey, it's getting warm.
KEN	Some fools let a Labor Government get into office. They start asking questions about whether they can control what you're doing on our territory.
JULIE	Eek! The place is swarming with bullants!
MICHAEL	Strewth! We're sittin' on a nest!
LYNNE	November Eleventh, 1975. We decide it's time to get serious about the American world-wide deterrent system. We make sure there's an Australian Government who believes in the Russian threat as much as we do.
KEN	Act 2, scene 1. We accept our responsibility as a major part of America's . . .
LYNNE	Psst!
KEN	. . . the Free World's defence system. We offer Cockburn Sound near Perth as a home away from home for U.S. nuclear subs, and Darwin as a base for B52s and, as soon as we test the water . . .
MICHAEL	How's the billy goin'?
JULIE	Warmin' up nicely.
KEN	Australian troops for the United States . . .
LYNNE	Psst!
KEN	. . . United Nations . . .
LYNNE	Psst!
KEN	. . . United Front?
LYNNE	That'll do.
KEN	Whatever you say, sir . . . peacekeeping forces in the Middle East.
LYNNE	It's a lot easier in the Third World. You don't have to worry about educated politicians. Get on with it.
KEN	Okay. Act 2, scene 3. Some people reckon that having U.S. military communication bases in Australia makes us a prime target for nuclear attack.
JULIE	Shouldn'a worn black. Attracts the flies.
MICHAEL	Get out of it!

LYNNE	But we allay their fears by reminding them that Americans and Australians have fought side by side in every major war this century . . .
MICHAEL	That's bloody right.
LYNNE	. . . and anyway, they haven't got any choice, 'cause if you're not with us you're a commie and you know what we do to commies.
MICHAEL	Great to live in a free country, isn't it? Smell that fresh air.
JULIE	(sniffs) One of the snags has fallen into the fire! And Trixie's run off with the T-bone.
MICHAEL	(picks up the pantomime bomb) Hey, Life Be In It, Olive. Get over there and let's have a chuck. (they throw the "bomb")
LYNNE	Could you quieten down? We're trying to do a serious play here.
KEN	What are you two maggots doing here anyway? Why aren't you at work? Do you think you own this country?
LYNNE	No interval. Straight into Act 3.
JULIE & MICHAEL	What's Act 3?
LYNNE	That's when the American-Australian Alliance pays off.
JULIE & MICHAEL	When's that?
LYNNE	When the nuclear war breaks out.
	(MICHAEL and JULIE make noises of disbelief and throw bomb back and forth)
	Look out, there's a Russian missile!
MICHAEL	Cripes!
JULIE	There goes Perth. (they continue to throw the bomb)
KEN	There's another one.
JULIE	Stone the crows.
MICHAEL	There goes Darwin.
LYNNE	And another one.
JULIE	There goes Canberra.
MICHAEL	Fair crack of the whip.
KEN	And one more,
MICHAEL	There goes Adelaide.
JULIE	Fair suck of the sav.
LYNNE	This one's for *(name of a local area).
JULIE	*(local area)! Hey, Bert. That might hit our place. Did you turn the gas off? Oh, and Mrs Saunders was coming over for spareribs tonight.
MICHAEL	(who has been attaching a sparkler to the bomb and lighting it) Hey, Olive!
JULIE	What's the matter, Bert?
MICHAEL	There's a nuclear bomb on the barbie.

JULIE	Pull the other one. It yodels.
MICHAEL	No, seriously. Where shall I put it?
JULIE	Where's it supposed to go?
MICHAEL	I don't know. Maybe they do. *(KEN is trying to sneak away)* 'Scuse I, cobber, where's this bomb supposed to go?
KEN	Well, here I suppose.
JULIE	Huh?
KEN	It's the price we pay.
MICHAEL	What for?
LYNNE	Being part of the Free World.
JULIE	You mean you blow up our back yard to save your backside?
LYNNE	You got it, baby. And Bert's holding the baby. Boom, boom!
MICHAEL	*(he has the fizzing bomb in his hand)* Crikey!

(a change of mood. JULIE divests herself of the Olive character and speaks plainly to the audience. MICHAEL continues to hold the fizzing bomb)

JULIE	We live with the bomb. It threatens our existence. It has taken over. At present, six nations have it, two more probably have it and, within ten years, forty other nations could easily have it. It has become an instrument of diplomacy. We avert our eyes from its gruesome reality. But we know it has already been used twice during war, on civilian targets.

(KEN plays music in the following scene. LYNNE and MICHAEL are the narrators. JULIE makes silent physical interpretation of the narrative. All four actors have taken off their white smocks and appear in black)

MICHAEL	The flash of light from an average-sized nuclear bomb will burn the eyes of people hundreds of kilometres away if they chance to look at it. It happens quicker than the eye can blink for protection. The effects of this were seen at Hiroshima.
LYNNE	He heard a voice coming from behind the bushes, asking for water. He went over and saw there were about twenty men, all in exactly the same state. Apparently they had their faces upturned when the bomb went off. Their faces were wholly burned, their eyesockets were empty. The fluid from their melted eyes had run down their cheeks. Their mouths were swollen pus-covered wounds which they could not bear to stretch enough for him to pour water into. One of the men said, 'I can't see anything'.
MICHAEL	The flash of light is followed almost immediately by a blast wave, the sound of which has been likened to an enormous door slamming in the depths of hell.
	The blast is quickly followed by a searing heat wave. Anyone in the open up to fifty kilometres away will be fatally burned. An enormous number of fires will start over the same area. These fires will coalesce into a gigantic uncontrollable firestorm, sucking in air at hurricane force to fan and feed the flames. Winds over two hundred kilometres an hour will

uproot huge trees and engulf everything into flaming tornadoes. At the same time people in fireproof shelters will be suffocated as all oxygen is expunged from the scorching atmosphere.

This firestorm will consume everything within a thirty or forty kilometre radius, but there will be a much larger area within which people will suffer horrendous burns.

This was the way in which tens of thousands died at Hiroshima.

LYNNE

That night he heard weak cries for help. He discovered that there were about twenty men and women on a sandspit in the middle of the river. They did not move and he realised that they were too weak to lift themselves. He reached down and took a woman by the hands, but her skin slipped off in huge, glove-like pieces. He felt sick and had to sit down for a moment.

He remembered uneasily the great burns he had seen during the day. Yellow at first, then red and swollen, with the skin sloughed off and, later, suppurated and smelly.

He lifted the slimy living bodies and carried them up the slope away from the tide. He had to keep consciously repeating to himself, 'these are human beings'. When he finished he had to rest, but he slept very poorly.

When he awoke, in the first light of dawn, he looked across the river and saw that he had not carried the festered, limp bodies high enough on the sandspit the night before. The tide had risen above where he had carried them. Having not the strength to move, they must have drowned. He saw a number of bodies floating on the river.

MICHAEL

At Hiroshima, a city of almost two hundred and fifty thousand people, nearly a hundred thousand were killed or doomed at a single stroke. A hundred thousand more were injured. There were a hundred and fifty doctors in the city. Sixty-five of them were dead, most of the rest were injured. Of seventeen hundred nurses, sixteen hundred were dead or too badly injured to work.

At the largest hospital in the city, six doctors and ten nurses were able to work, and ten thousand wounded people needed attention. In such a situation, most people are unlikely to get the medical care they need.

LYNNE

As he walked along he met hundreds and hundreds who were fleeing, and every one of them seemed to be hurt in some way. The eyebrows of some were burned off and skin hung from their faces and hands. Others, because of pain, held their arms up as if carrying something in both hands. Some were vomiting as they walked. Many were naked or in shreds of clothing. Almost all had their heads bowed, looking straight ahead, were silent, and showed no expression whatever.

A great number of people lay on the pavement, vomited, waited for death and died.

When he reached the park it was very crowded. To distinguish the living from the dead was not easy, for most of the people lay still, with their eyes open. The silence in the grove by the river, where hundreds of gruesomely wounded suffered together, was one of the most dreadful and awesome phenomena of his whole experience.

No one wept, much less screamed in pain. No one complained. Not even the children cried.

MICHAEL   For those who survive the initial blast and burns there is radiation. A journalist, who arrived in Hiroshima a month after the bomb was dropped, reported . . .

LYNNE   People who were uninjured in the cataclysm are still dying, mysteriously and horribly, from an unknown something that I can only describe as the Atomic Plague.

For no apparent reason their health begins to fail. They lose appetite. Their hair falls out. Bluish spots appear on their bodies. And then the bleeding begins from the ears, nose and mouth.

At first the doctors thought these were symptoms of general debility and gave their patients vitamin A injections. The result was that the flesh started rotting away from the hole caused by the needle. Eventually the victim dies.

MICHAEL   An average-sized nuclear explosion will render an area of a few thousand square kilometres highly radioactive. Radioactive substances enter the body, become incorporated into living tissues, bones and blood, causing cancer, leukaemia and bone tumours. And radiation causes genetic mutations which may spread over many more generations.

This year (1981) about a thousand more people will die from the effects of the Hiroshima bomb.

And the world's arsenal of nuclear weapons is steadily growing and expanding around the earth.

(there is a musical interlude here during which the actors pick up percussion instruments and arrange chairs to sit on, etc. The interlude is a mixture of sounds which draw their significance from the preceding speeches. Sirens, screaming voices, general confusion. Out of this a song emerges)

KEN   *(sings)* Who threw the fire at the girl inside the plastic?
And who are her friends?
You know, we can't count them all.
We'd like to know her name so that we can say
She has been identified.
And why we want to know her name is just
The parody of genocide.

Did she hold her breath when the siren
Flooded the streets and the crowded bars?
Did she look for an ambulance
A red fire truck
Or a getaway car?
Did she see the butcher's boy
Stop in the tracks of his daily rounds?
For who could have said that the siren said
Goodbye Mrs Pale
Hello Mrs Brown.

Who threw the fire at the girl inside the plastic?
And who are her friends?
You know, we can't count them all.
We'd like to know her name so that we can say
She has been identified.
And why we want to know her name is just
The parody of genocide.

(at the end of the song, the actors bow and leave the stage. They have all been on stage in view of the audience since the beginning of the show)

END OF PLAY

A FEW SHORT WICKS IN PARADISE

by

Hugh Watson

Written by

Gavan Fenelon
Penny Glass
Dee Martin
Kerry O'Rourke
Nat Trimarchi
Hugh Watson

Performed by

Gavan Fenelon
Penny Glass
Nat Trimarchi

Directed by:

Michael Cummings
Dee Martin

Sound Recordings

Kieran Knox

OBN Administrator

Julie Goodall

SCENE SEQUENCE

Scene One..Morning
A Few Short Wicks in Paradise (Song)
Scene Two ....Back Talk Morning Talk
Scene Three..................................Newspapers
Self Preservation (Song)
Scene Four........................... Depression Rant
Scene Five .... Cat Grinding
Cat Kicking (Song)
Scene Six....................................Plastic Cards
My Electric Chair (Song)
Scene Seven................................. Power Lines
Scene Eight ....Aerobics
Scene Nine........................Talkback Phonecall
Child of a Terrorist (Song)
Scene Ten................................Walking Home
Mamma's a Slave (Song + Phonecalls)
Scene Eleven .... Joh Rave
A Few Short Wicks in Paradise (Song)

NAT *and* GAVAN *snore on mike.* PENNY *(maliciously) does loud alarm — prolonged.*

GAVAN   Turn that fucking alarm off.

                 (NAT *begins to sing 4ZZZ-FM ID Spot while* PENNY *showers — mike up to
                 shower height, turns on taps, tests water, steps in, pulls screen, sings
                 along.* GAVAN *plays harmonica)*

NAT   Well I ride a mail train babe can't even buy a thrill.
                       I've been sitting up all night babe, leaning on the window sill.
                       Well I wake up every morning and cover my head,
                       Well you know I don't subscribe baby — to 4ZZZ.
                       Well I wake up every morning and cover my hea-ea-ead . . .

PENNY   Hey Nat . . .

                 (NAT *stops momentarily)*

                 . . . can you turn that radio down?

                 (NAT *continues softer.* GAVAN *plays louder, screeches on the harmonica)*

                 And Gavan . . .

                 (GAVAN *stops playing)*

                 . . . leave my budgie alone.

                 (GAVAN *does a few bird/harmonica noises.* PENNY *lowers mike.* NAT
                 finishes station ID)

NAT   Subscribe to Radio 4ZZZ, or you too might one day wake up a tormented
                 Christian. Send $30 to P O Box . . .

                 (GAVAN *becomes radio dial.* PENNY *makes radio static noise and turns
                 dial)*

PENNY   . . . at Indooroopilly Shopping Town at 9.00 am and your house is
                 odd-numbered and your licence plate begins with a B and your third
                 child's name is Rosie, you could win . . .

                 (NAT *does radio static and dial turning)*

NAT   Bongiorno, signori e signore . . . Bon venuto a questa programma
                 italiano . . .

                 (PENNY *does radio static and dial turning)*

                 Sixteen to eleven Brisbane 4BC. We'll take another caller. Good morning.

PENNY   *(holding nose)* Hello.

NAT   Yes.

PENNY   Is this me?

NAT   It is you.

PENNY   . . . Oh uh . . . Hayden, I always think we have an obligation to be cheerful
                 on talkback and I'm letting you down because I have a lament.

NAT	Ha, all right then.
PENNY	In a word . . .
PENNY & NAT	*(as themselves)* Queensland!!
	(NAT and PENNY laugh. GAVAN drops the dial and goes to mike)
GAVAN	Do we have to listen to that crap?
	(GAVAN moves back to being the dial while NAT and PENNY argue at him)
PENNY	You're never happy with anything.
NAT	Yeh, you've got rocks in your head.
PENNY	Fruit bat.
NAT	Ya little grunt.
	(NAT and PENNY together do radio static and turn dial until it's in GAVAN's face)
PENNY	*(as ABC announcer)* And now a preview of a forthcoming ABC radio serial.
	(GAVAN starts Russian theme music, which continues under serial dialogue. NAT and PENNY use Russian accents)
NAT	Comrade Dissidenski, for your crimes against the state . . . *(changes voice)* Oh no! Not the salt mines!
PENNY	Don't worry Dissidenski, the Premier's prepared to back you all the way on this one.
NAT	For your crimes against the state, we are sentencing you to a few short weeks in Paradise.
	(sound of kettle whistle)
PENNY	Tea's up!
	(NAT begins song)

A Few Short Wicks in Paradise

Introduction
There are sirens in the night time
There are sirens in my dreams
But the only sirens that I know
Are the ones I've never seen

Verse 1
You never see those sirens coming up behind you
It always takes a little blue light to find you
"Uh oh . . . only officer I should remind you . . .
That I surely know my rights
And they must be worth the fight . . .!"
'Cause there's . . .

(chorus)	More than a few short wicks in paradise More than a few short wicks in paradise . . . there's More than a few short wicks in paradise
Verse 2	I saw you sitting down in the city plaza You'd like to put a bomb up in the "Taj Ma- Hal" and make it turn to rubble Like they did to the Bellevue Like they did to Cloudland too . . . 'Cause there's . . .
(chorus)	More than a few short wicks in paradise More than a few short wicks in paradise . . . there's More than a few short wicks in paradise
	(Instrumental, Introduction and Verse 1)
(chorus)	'Cause there's More than a few short wicks in paradise More than a few short wicks in paradise . . .

Scene Two   Back Talk Morning Talk

PENNY	I had a really debilitating dream last night.
NAT	Give it a rest.
PENNY	That's just it. I didn't get any rest.
GAVAN	That's because your bed's polarised all wrong. Should be North-South.
PENNY	No, it's partly 'cause of my dream, and partly 'cause I was nearly asphyxiated by petrol fumes coming out of your bedroom at two o'clock in the morning.
GAVAN	Penny's gearing into aggressive mode for the day.
NAT	Not to mention the noise. What the fuck were you doing in there, Gavan? Tuning your car?
PENNY	And there were greasy rags outside my bedroom door this morning. Petrol head!
GAVAN	I had some friends over. We were making cocktails . . .
NAT	Oh, how Spring Hill.
GAVAN	For throwing . . .
PENNY	I wish I could be as productive as you are, Gavan. But petrol fumes give me debilitating dreams. Like last night. I was walking along Zillmere Road . . .
NAT	Oh yeah, where the fertilizer factory is and every time you go past you get a lungful.
PENNY	Yeah . . . it's okay, I was holding my breath.
NAT & GAVAN	Oh . . .
PENNY	And then I came to that horror intersection, where there's been a spate of fatal accidents recently.

264

GAVAN	Yeah, what . . . uh . . . how many? Six in the past twelve months? There's say . . . a million people in Brisbane . . . that gives you a 0.0006 per cent chance of being killed there sometime in the next year.
PENNY	Finished?
GAVAN	I could go on . . .
PENNY	*(getting more and more agitated)* So suddenly all the lights went out and I saw a SEQEB van speeding up behind. It tried to run me over, but I leaped to safety and hid in a Zupps Car Yard and John Zupp rolled out from underneath a Toyota Hiace holding ten $20 notes which turned into ten razor sharp knife blades attached like fingernails.
	(NAT does scary screeching noise effects and keeps going until the others stop him with a look)

Scene Three   Newspapers

NAT *makes the sound of a mini moke motor, skidding of brakes, dog barking.*

NAT	Get out of it you bloody mongrel!
	(NAT continues with the sound of a kick to the dog, a grunt, dog squeal, whistle, throwing of paper with a "hoik")
	I'll get it.
	(NAT tears off the comics section and gives rest of paper to PENNY)
	There you go.
PENNY	I'm not ready.
	(PENNY hands the paper to GAVAN who casts aside front page into PENNY's area and keeps Business section. GAVAN — business with paper. PENNY turns up collar, puts on sunglasses and opens out blinkers, and picks up the paper)
	Oh, the Joh pin-up.
GAVAN	I'll have it.
PENNY	No. I want it. You had it yesterday.
GAVAN	It doesn't count because it wasn't in colour.
PENNY	It's mine.
	(GAVAN rushes off and grabs the cornflakes packet)
GAVAN	Well I'm having the plastic Joh.
	(GAVAN roots around in the packet for the plastic Joh. PENNY takes pin-up section out, waits for GAVAN to find toy. PENNY then tears up the pin-up. Looks to GAVAN. GAVAN pauses, looks at toy then swallows it)
PENNY	You don't usually do that. You usually flush it down the toilet.
GAVAN	I'll be doing that tomorrow. After it's been through the legislative process.
NAT	I'd like to live in Juliet Jones' universe. One problem at a time, y'know?

PENNY	*(reading from paper)* Joh fires from hip. I'll sue Hawke — Joh. Why Joh will win. Joh fights back. *(throws down paper)* Joh, Joh, Joh, Joh . . . Joh who? His name's Petersen. Did the Jews call Hitler Adolf already?
GAVAN	Did the Jews call Adolf Hitler?
	(PENNY *puts blinkers back over eyes*)
NAT	No, they said don't call us we'll call you.
GAVAN	Cuppa tea. What d'ya reckon?
PENNY	And that's what you call self-preservation? Fruit bats.

(NAT *picks up newspapers and turns on backing tape*)

Self Preservation

Verse 1	Read the Monday papers on a Monday morning Let's you know you're still alive and that's how the week begins Getting out of bed before the desolation Strikes you in your bed sheets, keeps you down forever Well you wonder where you are and what you're doing
(chorus)	That's what you call self-preservation Self, self, self, self-preservation That's what you call self-preservation That's what you call self-preservation
Verse 2	Washington says it's only an illusion Don't worry your pretty head about all this confusion So you kick the pages and roll out of bed and tell yourself you couldn't do anything about it and anyway you're not the only one wishing
	You didn't read the Monday papers It hits you like a ton of lead It leaves you in exasperation Oh, if only ignorance was bliss
(chorus)	That's what you call self-preservation Self, self, self, self-preservation That's what you call self-preservation That's what you call self-preservation
NAT	*(indicating the tape recorder)* Let's hear it for the band.
	(PENNY *and* GAVAN *sit down*)

Scene Four — Depression Rant

NAT	Ladies and gentlemen, I'm here tonight to talk to you about a very serious subject that we all know about but rarely discuss — Depression. Not the sort of depression you get when you wake up on Monday and your whole weekend's been rained out; and not the feeling you get when your dole cheque's a day late. I'm talking about the full three-dimensional, solid black depression that they manufacture in Wacol and ship up here. The

266

sort of depression that visits you from out of nowhere for no reason, stays for a while and then leaves.

Ladies and gentlemen, I'd like to tell you about a period in my life when *I* was depressed. It was my first year out of school and I was studying out at Kelvin Grove and living up on Gregory Terrace with my lover, and both of us were living on TEAS. Well, my lover left me and I was, you know, crushed, depressed — y'know, really **low**. So I cashed my TEAS cheque and paid four weeks rent and went out and stocked up on flagons of red and tissues and cans of Big Sister self-saucing puddings and went to bed and didn't get up for weeks.

Well eventually my friends started to notice that I wasn't around anymore. And one day I get a knock on the door and I open it and it's my friend Hank. And he comes in.

(as Hank) Hey man! How've you been? I've been great! I've had the best week of my life. Just got back from this amazing twenty-first birthday party, up in Noosa. Spent the last two days surfing, sunbaking and doing a heap of drugs. Got back down here, put a bet on the TAB . . . Won two hundred dollars. My oldies have offered to buy me a car, got straight sevens in all my exams, and my case has been thrown out of court for lack of evidence. Hey Nat! You look terrible! What have **you** been doing?

(as Nat) Let's see. Nothing Monday. Tuesday nothing. On Wednesday . . . no, that wasn't me. *(pause)*

(as Hank) Well, what about Thursday?

(as Nat) On Thursday . . . Something did happen on Thursday. There was this man, walking around the neighbourhood knocking on people's doors. He had this tin can with a slit in it, and he told me he was from multiple sclerosis. So I gave him fifty dollars. I had to. Don't you know what the CIA's done to that country!

Anyway, Hank gave me a useful piece of advice. He said I should get out of the house more, do more things y'know, be more active. Now I've got to ask you people here for a bit of empathy — a bit of retrospective understanding. Because at this point in my life I wasn't just suicidally depressed. No, I was also becoming irrational, unhinged, really alienated. So I decided that what I wanted to be was a bikie, a tough guy. But I wanted to have politics as well. So I formed a far left political motorbike gang. And we called ourselves "Hells Engels". You know that slogan I put on my jacket? "Live fast, Stay pretty, Dialectic". It's still going but the I.S. took it over and I dropped out.

And you know, all this depression and misery I was going through — I didn't get that way all on my own. I suppose you've all guessed by now that I was, well, using. I was an addict, a junkie. It was just a big game to me at the start. I mean, before I got hooked. I was just doing it to impress people. Well, I thought nobody knew — I thought I had everybody cooled out. But my older brother Roberto found out somehow. And he came round one day, and I opened the door and he grabs me by the collar.

(as Nat — stoned) Hey Roberto, what's going on?

(as Roberto — angry) Don't give me that crap Nat. I heard out on the street that you've been using.

(as Nat) No Roberto, no. Somebody's been lying to you, that's all wrong.

And I'm terrified — I'm trying to stop him from coming inside. But Roberto pushes past me, goes into the living room and looks around. The whole household's there, bombed out of their skulls, and the **stuff** is all over the turntable.

(as Roberto) How could you do it Nat? How could you break Mama's heart like this . . .?

And then Roberto sees the records by the stereo.

(as Nat — panicky) No, Roberto. It's not what you think. Sure, I had a low period, and yeah I dabbled a bit — Janis, Ian, Tim Buckley — but I never touched the hard stuff! You gotta believe me!

But Roberto didn't say anything. He just picked up the record and held it out. It was the Leonard Cohen record.

(as Nat — in cold sweat) I swear — it's not mine! I'm just minding for a friend! I swear to it!

And still he didn't say anything. He just took the record out of its jacket, and slowly rolled up the sleeve.

(as Roberto) Bullshit, kid. I can see the needle marks. You coulda bin a contender!

. . . But ladies and gentlemen, after going through all these hard times — I wanted to tell you about them because I've discovered that it's not all personal — the place you live in has a lot to do with it.

(pause. GAVAN and PENNY begin a rhythmic pulse with electric bass and sticks)

Woke up in the morning, dropped the clock radio, fed the rat, swilled the hot water round the dregs of the coffee tin, looked out the window 'cross the river to the University. Thought . . . I should go to University. Then I realised that I'd been to University. That was a bit of a shock. But who wants to think about charismatic, Christian psychologists arguing bubble-gum politics with Young Liberal student union leaders who share houses with ex-private school law students who aren't really interested in law anyway and would rather be getting into Merchant Banks or tax evasion.
No, I didn't want to think about that.
Nor did I want to think about all the trees they had to chop down to print out my B.A. along with thousands like it just so as we wouldn't feel so bad about the pointlessness of squandering three years in an intellectual wasteland.
No, I didn't want to think about that.
I was going to be cheerful. I was gonna look on the positive side. So I took myself out for a walk to the city, cruised into Jo-Jo's, got myself a drink, got into a staring competition with three hundred All Hallows schoolgirls sipping Black Russians at three-fifty a pop, and trying not to be noticed by the Management who, of course, really believe that

they're all eighteen.
But I didn't want to think about that.
So I went down the up escalator, out into Albert Street, and walked towards King George Square past the Commonwealth Bank where all the methos are, sitting on benches sipping flagons of sherry, cheap at three-fifty a pop.
But I didn't want to think about that.
So I drifted down to Roma Street, ran into an old bloke who asked me for directions. 'How long you lived here?,' I said. 'All my life,' he said.

(NAT *gets more manic*)

'Well you are in trouble, where'd you want to go? Edward Street? Well you go past here where Redcomb House **used to be**, look to your right where Roma Street Station **used to be**. Go straight ahead. If George Street is still there you go into it. If George Street isn't there you go over it. That'll take you into the main drag, it looks like a parking lot, used to be a street, but it's now a Mall. Go through the Mall — if you need a landmark, your best bet, find yourself a crane.

(*pause. Sticks stop.* GAVAN *starts a riff on the bass*)

He said where do I go when I get through the Mall
I said what you looking for, he said Trades Hall
I said you gotta be joking mate don't you read the news
Then I looked him in the face again, I felt a bit confused
'Petersen!' you bastard and I grabbed him by the throat
He was having a go at me, having a bit of a joke
He knew Trades Hall had been pulled down, he knew unions were defunct
So I smacked him in the head, stole his money and his coat
Then I dragged him over to the Roma Street pit
And threw him in that jolly little moat.

(PENNY *begins to sing the riff along with the bass*)

'This one's for the Aborigines' as I sunk in one last boot
'And this one's for the ETU' as I spat at the little newt
Was it just a fantasy, well I don't really know
Could've been the Fourex, that's usually the go
All I know is that I read the rags that pass for newspapers in this town
And I know what makes me depressed
I know what makes me frown
'Cause every day in the Courier Mail
Another new disintegration
Another new push legislation by these fascist geriatrics
In a circus tent for a Parliament
His name is Gerry Mander — no not Gerry Connolly
No more jolly Joh ho ho
Anyone'd think it was Santa Claus
I can hear the National Party applause
Anyone hear the one about the SEQEB bunker
Anyone hear the one about the no-strike clause

No more impersonations of a devil. No more Mephisto gigs
Wonder when Hawke's gonna take the tumble
Wonder when the judge's are gonna burn their wigs . . .

(PENNY *stops singing and brings in long notes on the saxophone. Bass continues*)

'Cause you know our legislators have got an angle on it all right
I bet they stayed up all fucking night
I can see them sitting in a little room plotting out the year
Let's drop an Act in there and a State of Emergency here
No, fuck the State of Emergency, let's make these bastards disappear
Let's rule the power industry' — I hear the boardroom cheer
Yeah, fifty thousand big ones is what you're gonna pay
If you're a power worker and out on strike these days and
If you join a picket you could be down a thousand bucks and
If you tell 'em stick it they're gonna make you bankrupt 'cause
It's no good throwing you in prison, that's just bad publicity
That's the price you pay for your electricity.

(PENNY *and* GAVAN *do big sax and bass finish, four times of the riff*)

PENNY Let's have a big hand for Nat "He's So Angry" Trimarchi.

Scene Five   Cat Grinding

GAVAN Yeah Nat, I think I know where you're coming from. It's like you take a cat in one hand and a grinder in the other . . . or maybe you take the grinder in this hand . . . and the cat in this hand . . . or maybe . . .

PENNY Thanks Gavan . . . and now a song for pet lovers.

Cat Kicking

(chorus) Kick the cat in the morning, save me kicking you
Kick the cat in the morning, that's all I need to do
In this high pressure society
Need some cat kicking variety
It's the new wave thing to do . . .

Verse 1 Aaah cat came in in the morning,
I could not go on ignoring
So I kicked it in the teeth
Thought I saw it later
With my pet alligator
They were playing in the street . . . oh no
Kick them cats . . . meeeyow . . . take that . . . and that . . .

(instrumental & choreographed dancing)

Verse 2 Ooooh woke up this morning
Nothing I could do
Rolled over to your side
And started kicking you
Looked out my window

Thought I heard the blues
But that cat was tapping out a tune
In some alligator shoes...
In this high pressure society
It was the new wave thing to do . . .

(repeat chorus)

Scene Six   Plastic Cards

NAT   That reminds me Penny, where's that fifty bucks you owe me?

PENNY   Where am I gonna get fifty bucks at this time of night?

NAT   There's an automatic teller round the corner isn't there?

PENNY   *(scared)* All right . . .

(PENNY walks to centre mike. Presses GAVAN's button. GAVAN opens door like automatic teller, pokes tongue out. PENNY puts card in. GAVAN eats and swallows it)

GAVAN   Thank you for banking Commonwealth.

(GAVAN closes door. Pause)

PENNY   The other day one of those things spoke to me. It said, 'Thank you for banking Commonwealth'. And as an afterthought it said, '. . . and we know where you live you know'. I turned back. 'Oh yeah, we know where you live and we've told everyone'.

What!

'Oh yes, the banks, the advertising agencies, the Mormons, K-Tel, the Dianetics people and, of course, the Government. Have a nice day'.

And then it closed its door. I had an idea. I waved a fiver in front of it. The door came up again and it snatched the fiver and my hand into the slot. We struggled for some time. It trying to make a deposit. Me trying to withdraw. So we agreed on terms. I had to join American Express. It allowed me to sign with my other hand. Then it let me go. But that wasn't the end of it. No, I started to hear voices all over town. All the machines were talking to me.

NAT   Did you have a good time at the party the other night?

PENNY   What party?

NAT   Oh nothing.

GAVAN   What about those light bulbs you stole from the Night Owl?

PENNY   But that was two years ago.

GAVAN   So you did take them.

NAT   How's your mother's hysterectomy?

PENNY   She hasn't had one.

NAT   She will.

271

PENNY	They were everywhere. They knew where I'd been, what I'd been doing. They knew everything about me. I became bitter and twisted . . . Then the other day I went back and the machine just ate my card . . . And you know, I was relieved. I was free again. No one could track me down. My number wouldn't be on any computer. Life was suddenly beautiful. Until I realised I had no cash. I didn't even have enough for a sausage sanger. The machine had rejected me. I wanted to know why. And it just said . . .
GAVAN	You look like an intelligent sort of person, you work it out for yourself.
PENNY	Oooooh. *(scary paranoia)*

My Electric Chair

Verse 1
I'm the black sheep of the neighbourhood
Old ladies on the corner say that I'm no good
They say I graduated from the rough school
Better get yer suitcases and make yourself scarce
Don't think there's any room for your kind anywhere

Verse 2
Ours is such a lovely neighbourhood
With names on all the houses they all look so good
Sometimes I throw a stone they make me so mad
Sometimes I wish that I could be some kind of millionaire

(chorus)
But I'm the black sheep of the world
Of the world out there
So take away your comfort
Get it out of my hair
I don't wanna see your riches
I just wanna make a tear
In your comfort bubble
— It's my electric chair
— It's my electric chair

(instrumental

Verse 3
I'm the black sheep of the neighbourhood
And I deface the buildings that are standing new
Sometimes I wonder why — and then I don't care
Could it be because I'm not some kind of millionaire

(repeat chorus)

Scene Seven   Power Lines

GAVAN	Let's hear it for Nat and Penny, and speaking of electricity . . . the Electricity Commissioner came round the other day and told me I had to fix a power line. I said I don't know how to fix any power lines . . . I'm an actor . . . all I know is how to ponce around on stage . . . He said all right, I order you, under Section such and such of the Electricity (Continuity of Supply) Act to fix that power line and if you don't do it within the prescribed time, I'm gonna fine you a thousand bucks!!!

NAT	So???
GAVAN	So. I fixed the power line . . .
PENNY	How'd you manage that, fruit bat?
GAVAN	Easy, I reversed the polarity and made the power flow in the opposite direction.
NAT	So you had to climb up the telegraph pole . . . ?
GAVAN	No. I had to petrol bomb the Electricity Commissioner's car.
NAT & PENNY	Right!

Scene Eight   Aerobics

GAVAN   *(puts on sweatband)* Ladies and gentlemen, Order By Numbers not only aims to entertain and inform, we also aim to keep you looking good.

(PENNY and NAT put on sweatbands and track suit tops and start to jog on the spot)

So we've devised a series of exercises made for our special climate right here in Queensland. Now special instructor Penny . . .

(PENNY jumps with a 'Woop!')

. . . and Nat . . .

(NAT jumps with a 'Woop!')

. . . are going to demonstrate these exercises and you can try them later on at home. The first one's for all those situations where you feel you're just getting nowhere. All it takes is twenty minutes of your time, a little patience and a Besser brick wall. If you haven't got a Besser brick wall at home, any old weather board or brick veneer will do. It's quite simple. Stand about a foot away from the wall, relax your shoulders and bang that head against the wall.

(NAT and PENNY start banging their forehead against their mike)

Nice and hard, just as you see Nat and Penny doing here right now. Nice and hard.

NAT   Ooooh, it's hurting.

PENNY   It must be good for us.

GAVAN   That's so true. That's **so** true. It tones up the forehead and you can see the results almost immediately. Nat's been doing this exercise for quite some time and you can actually see his brain.

(NAT squeezes his forehead to make brain-like lines on it)

Now here's another one for all you picketers out there. The arm goes up behind the back . . .

(PENNY does this to NAT)

273

	. . . and off we go to jail. Just as you see Nat and Penny doing here right now. That's it Penny, nice and hard, make it hurt. Is it hurting Nat?
NAT	Yes, Gavan.
GAVAN	Fantastic. Terrific. I tell you what, you might like to try that one with the person sitting next to you. Reach across to that special friend you've brought along to the show tonight, grab their arm and push it up their back, nice and hard. That's the way, nice and high now, make it hurt. Terrific, fantastic. Now we're gonna have a bit of fun with what I like to call VOCAL AEROBICS. Great for loosening up the tongue and getting the jaw moving and lifting that soft palate. I think we'll divide the audience in half right up the middle there and we'll get special instructor Penny to take care of this side and we'll get special instructor Nat to look after the radical elements over here. Well, it's quite simple. What I want you to do is listen very carefully to the following phrase and we'll get you to repeat it with Penny after me. It goes like this — 'I arrest you under Section 5 of the Electricity, brackets, Continuity of Supply Act'. All together this side, with Penny.

(half of the audience repeats phrase with PENNY)

It's a difficult role to play, that one. What about this side over here? We're not going to let them get away with that are we? Of course we're not! You reply with an oldie but a goodie — 'Leave me alone you big fat copper!'

(the other half of audience repeats phrase with NAT)

Okay, Penny's side, your next tongue twister goes like this — 'Did you hear that sergeant?' All together now with Penny.

(PENNY's side repeats phrase with her)

Well, that's very good, but I'd like you to try it again, with a little bit more emphasis on the **that**.

(PENNY's side repeats again with her)

That's moderately better. Fantastic. Now, it's not looking too good for the picketers, but I tell you what, try and wrap your tonsils around this one — 'Ooooh, take your finger out of my eye!' All together with Nat.

(they repeat with NAT)

Just goes to show when you're in trouble you can always rouse yourself. Back to the other side.

PENNY	Well, we're looking a bit pitiful after that.
GAVAN	Never mind, your next one's particularly good for the tip of the tongue. Goes like this — 'Ay up, shove 'em in the back'. All together with Penny.

(PENNY's side repeats phrase with her)

Well Nat's side, it's looking pretty bad for you. But this next one's particularly good for dropping the jaw — 'You can't arrest me, I'm a journalist'.

(NAT's side repeats phrase with him)

Now, straight back to Penny's side, and you reply with — 'Ho ho ho ho, slam!'.

(PENNY's *side repeats phrase with her*)

Fabulous. And remember stay tuned next week when we'll be moving on to "Aerobics for Concerned Academics". And we'll be learning some really exciting new ways to massage your brain.

Scene Nine   Talkback Phonecall

[This scene was altered after the abortion clinic raids in mid-1985 — these are the two versions]

VERSION ONE

NAT	It's sixteen to eleven, Brisbane 4BC. We'll take another caller, good morning.
PENNY	Hello Hayden, I want to complain about that Telecom Union . . .
NAT	Oh yes.
PENNY	. . . not fixing the National Party's phones during the strike?
NAT	Oh yes that, that was highly irresponsible, wasn't it?
PENNY	Yes, and then there was that 24 hour blockade by the southern unions.
NAT	A child died waiting for a plane to Brisbane.
PENNY	I saw that on the telly. And another thing, when I went to the opening of our Cultural Centre, the Military Band wasn't allowed to play because they weren't in the union.
NAT	And what sort of parents would these unionists be?
PENNY	Irresponsible, I'd say.
NAT	That's right.
PENNY	And what will their children be like? You know Hayden, what they're doing, it's just industrial terrorism.
NAT	And that's the way our poll's been going. I couldn't agree with you more. Thanks very much for your call.

VERSION TWO

NAT	It's sixteen to eleven, Brisbane 4BC. We'll take another caller, good morning.
PENNY	Hello Hayden, remember me? I want to speak for the unborn children of Queensland.
NAT	Oh yes, you're referring to the abortion clinic raids. The women of Queensland have certainly won a victory there.
PENNY	Yes, I've hardly been able to sleep at night for the voices.
NAT	The voices?
PENNY	The unheard pleas of the unborn children, Hayden.

275

NAT	Oh those voices, yes it's a pity they didn't reach the right ears.
PENNY	Yes Hayden, and the left ones too. If only you could hear them.
NAT	And what are they saying to you.
PENNY	Oh it's very hard to understand them, they don't speak much English you know.
NAT	Oh . . .
PENNY	Yes it's more like . . . ee . . . ee . . . bloop . . . blip . . .
NAT	Thanks very much for your call, and we'll take a commercial break.

Child of a Terrorist

Verses

Mummy and Daddy are not home this evening
Mummy and Daddy left me all alone
And they said it was because
The world is bleeding from all sides

Mummy and Daddy are not home this evening
Mummy and Daddy are not home tonight
And maybe they have gone to South America
The world is bleeding from all sides

Mummy and Daddy are not home this evening
Just me and my little brother here tonight
Oh I hope they haven't gone away to Northern Ireland
The world is bleeding from all sides

(chorus)

Oh yeah, oh yeah
I'm the baby child of a terrorist
I'm the baby child of a terrorist

Verses

Mummy and Daddy would be pleased to meet you
Mr J'ovis Witness — was that your name?
But I'm almost sure they are in South Africa
The world is bleeding from all sides

Mummy and Daddy are not here this evening
But I'm sure they'd listen to your advice
Did you say we should pray for the Aborigines?
The world is bleeding from all sides

Mummy and Daddy don't go to church, sir
Mummy and Daddy say they're in a war
Oh all that I know is that it's in the world somewhere and
The world is bleeding from all sides

(repeat chorus)

Mummy and Daddy are not home this evening
Mr J'ovis Witness did you say that's a sin?
But they told me to tell you they are in the resistance 'cause
The world is bleeding from all sides

Mummy and Daddy said I'm only five sir but
Mummy and Daddy said I should say

While you sit in your sacristy and pray to end all war
The world is bleeding from all sides

Mummy and Daddy are not home this evening
Mr J'ovis Witness do you understand?
For the peasants that are dying in South America
Are Mummy and Daddy and me

(repeat chorus)   Mummy and Daddy said to watch the news sir
Mummy and Daddy said to watch all sides
And no matter what they show you, you must remember
The world is bleeding from all sides

Scene Ten   Walking Home

PENNY   I had this dream last night . . . it was sorta like the Twilight Zone . . . you know how in those shows the situation looks like it's got great possibilities but ends up being real debilitating. Anyway I dreamt there'd been this nuclear holocaust and everyone was lying dead on the ground. Actually it was sorta like a scene out of Woodstock, you know. The camera pans back and there's this field of bodies lying in mud. So anyway, I could hear Peter Garrett singing, you know from the Oils — oh really aware band. He was in the distance, so I followed the voice and found him. He knew me immediately, said 'G'day Pen, how y're goin'?' I said, 'Oh I'm great Peter, oh except for the nuclear holocaust.' 'Oh yeah', he said, 'it's really debilitating, isn't it?'

You know there's a set-up here in Brisbane. Not only is the lighting bad, the footpaths treacherous, the dogs unrestrained and vicious, the public transport non-existent, but even more debilitating are the Angels of Moral Displeasure. They may change their form and substance, but they're always with us. We live in their ethical ectoplasm.

NAT &
GAVAN   Oogie boogie . . .

(NAT and GAVAN start a heartbeat effect on mike)

PENNY   Take last Sunday night for example. It's the end of the weekend, I'm out of money and it's after 11 o'clock. All the buses, just like Cinderella, snuggled up in the depot with their mates, and there I am, my Self Defence class over for another week and faced with the terrible alternatives — hitch-hiking or walking. I decide to run.

(all three start to run on the spot)

Not a good idea. You know if you run in Sydney, you're a jogger.

(waves to NAT. NAT says 'Hi')

If you run in Brisbane they wanna know why.

(heartbeat stops. NAT and GAVAN sit down)

Choosing the route home to South Brisbane late at night takes a bit of working out. Dark streets mean I can't be seen by men cruising in cars or on foot, but I also won't be seen if I'm attacked.   Bright lights are great for seeing the deathtrap potholes in the footpath, but not so good for hiding from the cruisers. And then there's the direction of the traffic. I decide to walk down Stanley Street. Whoa, I don't have a PhD in orienteering though. Merivale Street one way that way. Cordelia Street one way this way. South Brisbane Station overpass. Stop sign. See what a difficulty Expo '88 puts people in my position in. And there are security guards crawling all over the place.

And then I hear this voice — it's Mama *(Yiddish accent)*. 'Watch out Penny, these pigs, they are not kosher, kosher, kosher . . . *(voice trails away like an echo)*

Fuck it, Mum, I'm heading off for Grey Street. Crossing the William Jolly Bridge I start to get pretty debilitated . . . light . . . shadow . . . light . . . hide behind a pylon while a Monaro screams past. Bright light . . . searchlight on top of the Pauls Ice Cream Factory at West End, and out of the searchlight a woman on a floating potato scallop. Looks like Botticelli's Venus, grinning wildly. It isn't, it's that Angel of Moral Displeasure, Silly Anne Atkinson and she's saying *(upper class accent)* 'I'm a woman and I understand your problems. My husband's going to be the Lady Mayoress. You're merely suffering anxiety that we won't get the Brisbane Olympics. Fear not, we're going to tart up the Botanical Gardens, put a car park in the foyer of the New York Hotel (leaving the facade of course) and take down the Nuclear Free Zone signs so you won't need to wonder which side we're on'.

And then I hear Mama — 'Oh boy Penny, are you a cynic! If you had eaten more chopped liver when you were younger you wouldn't hate Liberals so much, much, much . . .' *(voice trails away like an echo)* Oh give it a rest Mum, this has got nothing to do with my Vitamin B deficiency.

Finally I start along Grey Street. It's as desolate as the National Party's child care policy. Near Burleigh Marr's Fish House the ground starts to tremble. Oh just my luck I think. I'm here right at the moment they start to do 24 hour shift work clearing South Brisbane for EXPO '88. Vroom! A giant bulldozer comes screaming out of Ernest Street. And at the wheel, Flo Bjelke-Petersen in a Dolly Parton wig. She rips into fourth gear and drives straight through the Plough Inn (if it's still there), striking a blow for urban renewal. On her second victory lap she spots me and, uh, gleefully pins me up against a wall. This Angel of Moral Displeasure claims to be the symbol of progress for Queensland. She leans forward on her steering wheel. *(American accent)* 'I'm a woman and I understand your problem. But you brought all this on yourself. You know if you'd voted National you wouldn't be here at this hour, you'd be at home looking after the kiddies, and standing by your man, and anyway he would have bought you a nice little Ford Hatchback'. And she launches into some well-rehearsed speech and while she's frothing at the mouth I manage to slip away, dodging the bullets and the roadblocks, I beat it down Stanley Street. Past the Mater Hospital, past the Touch of Class, past the Shish Kebab.

'Oh Penny, didn't I warn you already. This is no place for a nice Jewish girl — Catholic hospitals, houses of ill repute, Lebanese restaurants,

rants, rants . . .' *(voice trails away like an echo)* Oh give it a rest Mum, I'm almost home.

You know how you get that feeling of relief when you turn the final corner, and home is only fifty yards away. You step on this morning's squashed cane toads, you smell the frangipanis and the freshly burned earth where the house next door used to be. Dogs are barking . . . dogs are barking? And there's this white Ford GL outside our house with a flashing blue light on top, and an incredible amount of activity going on in the house. Holy holy holy, shitburger and beans, I'm coming boys. *(runs off)*

Mamma is a Slave

Verse 1	She gets up early from the table Swallowed firsts to serve up seconds The men accept that she is able That's the call of nature calling Shut the window 'cause outside it's pouring Get the coffee now the water's boiling
(chorus)	Mamma is a slave but she won't admit it Mamma is afraid of what she doesn't understand So she waves goodbye to what the radical girls say Her ideas are too old to change Listen what the radical girls say Listen what the radical girls say Listen what the radical girls say
Verse 2	She laughs when I offer her a hand Swallowed pride is no concession and The men would never really understand Oh what you go and do that for You make trouble for us all And it doesn't matter . . . after all
(repeat chorus)	Mamma is a slave . . . listen what the radicals Mamma is a slave . . . listen what the radical girls say Mamma is a slave . . . oh she couldn't break the rules anyway Mamma is a slave . . . look boys Mamma is a slave oh Mamma is a slave . . . *(etc)*

(phonecalls to Mum during **"MAMMA'S A SLAVE"***)*

PENNY	Mum? . . . Yeh, yeh . . . I was going to write you a letter but I've been really busy. Pickles? . . . Pickles . . . Pickets, they're called pickets. Whaddaya mean, what's the point of having a daughter if she lives in Queensland? Yeh? . . . What a chutzpah! You've been doing it for thirty years. If they don't like undies on the line, it's their problem. Well, don't listen to me then!
NAT	Ciao Ma, che dici . . . Non, non . . . No I didn't get arrested . . . Hey how's Dad? . . . Listen Ma . . . you don't have to wash the clothes every day . . . E sempre a la cuccina . . .

GAVAN   Yes Mum, I've eaten today. What? Oh a little dish I call Pritikin Backlash. *(looking around)* The others here just love it. Look Mum, can't we talk about something else? . . . Yeah . . . Yeah. Oh yeah, I forgot to tell you — I think I've sold one of my inventions. Yeah, the Cat Grinder Theory. To the government patents office. But anyway, Mum, I'll tell you all about it when I see you. They told me to be careful about sprouting over the phone. Apparently Telecom's got left-wing terrorist connections.   Yeah . . . Mum? . . . Mum? . . . Mum? . . .

Scene Eleven   Joh Rave

NAT *and* PENNY *sit down, read newspapers etc.*

GAVAN   G'day, my name's Gavan— Gavan to my friends. Y'know shit, I like it here at La Boîte *(or whatever venue)*. The lights, the seating, friendly faces, cold beer. Someone's gone to a lot of trouble here. And I think it's great that you could all come along tonight . . . and . . . you know what else I think is great? I think it's great that you can all sit together so peacefully without any friction or tension . . . that's why I stopped the show.

(GAVAN moves to the centre of the stage. He looks up at the lights. He makes a gesture that includes the lights and himself)

Light . . .

(he points to the audience) Darkness . . .

(he points to himself) Standing up . . .

(he points to the audience) Sitting down. Paid to get in . . .

(he points to himself) Paid to be here.

(he thinks) Free to move around. *(he does so)*

(he points to each section of the audience in turn) Passive . . . passive . . . passive . . . passive.

(he points to himself) Active.

See, that's what I want to talk to you about . . . Everybody's equal here, right? But you can't deny the fact that there are differences. Like the fact that I'm free to move around and you're not. So what do we make of that? *(pause)* Well . . . we could say that because we're here on stage, that makes us your representatives. What I mean by that is . . . it's our job to bring you the kind of material that you want to see. And that gives us certain privileges that you're not allowed to have. But only so we can do the job properly. Fair enough?

(pause. We can see GAVAN giving it some thought himself)

Well, I don't think so. No, I don't think it is fair enough. I think you have the right to talk to yourselves if you want . . . to, um . . . come onto the stage and jump around if you want. To suddenly decide that you're going to . . . watch the rest of the show standing up. Now I'm just going to get somebody to demonstrate what I mean. Let's pick somebody at random

280

. . . You , what's your name? *(let's say Michael)* . . . would you please stand up?

(a member of the audience stands up. Pause)

Y'see. Nobody's interfering with Michael in any way . . . by which I mean . . . the stage manager hasn't rushed out here with a pack of thugs and forced Michael back into his chair. So I think it's plain that we do respect Michael's right to . . . not conform. But what I want to point out to you, Michael, is that by standing up, you've blocked the view of everyone behind you, distracted me, and split the audience's attention. And those are bad things. So what I want to suggest to everyone is this — that although you've all got certain rights . . . and we've proved that, haven't we? I want everyone to agree to not use those rights . . . at least until the skit is over. Okay? *(concerned)* Michael, do you want to sit down now? Does anyone want to stand up quickly, before I go on? No? It's your last chance!

(pause. GAVAN faces the stage, scratching his head, thinking out the next step)

So, what's the situation? Even though you've all got the right to do anything you want to, you've agreed not to exercise those rights because if you do, you'll interrupt me. Which means you're going to act like a traditional audience. That means that I'm going to have to act like a traditional performer . . . all the responsibility for entertaining you rests with me. But that's all right. I can cope with that. I mean, I've had seven years experience in the theatre. I know what entertainment is. I know what **sharp** entertainment is.

(pause. GAVAN beams at the audience)

And so tonight . . . to finish off the show . . . we're going to beat Michael senseless. Penny and Nat have the clubs.

(PENNY and NAT start to watch GAVAN)

But hold on . . . Michael's looking a bit distressed. What's the matter? Don't you want to be beaten senseless?

(GAVAN pauses. He doesn't offer the person in the audience the microphone. If they say something only GAVAN hears it)

(disbelieving) You object? But you can't start asserting yourself now. It's too late for that. I gave everyone a chance to have their say just a minute ago. And everyone agreed . . . that I'd make the decisions. That's democracy. *(angry)* For Christ's sake! Don't tell me you've forgotten! You helped me do it! *(pleading, in an undertone)* C'mon Michael, don't let me down — cooperate.

(GAVAN pauses. He doesn't offer Michael the microphone, so we don't hear Michael's reply if there is one, but it would obviously be 'No'. GAVAN is enraged, he moves to centre stage)

All right mate. But you're in my black book now. Nat, Penny, I want you to get a photograph of this one. *(placating)* Now, ladies and gentlemen, I don't want you to think that something's gone wrong — we've just had the bad luck to strike one of the small minority that exist in any community, who want to buck the system. That's Michael. Let's show Michael, and all the troublemakers like him, that we believe in democracy. Let's have some of you **volunteer** to be beaten senseless.

No, no, no one? Fair enough. The skit's running overtime anyway. State of emergency conditions — thanks Nat and Penny. Read them the Act.

(NAT *and* PENNY *go to their previous halves of the audience*)

NAT &
PENNY   *(together)* Section 1 of the State of Emergency Act empowers Order By Numbers to impose a seven dollar Theatre Exit Levy upon all patrons for the privilege of vacating the theatre.

(during the above, the microphones go off one at a time, and then, suddenly, the lights go out)

NAT   *(in darkness)* Oh shit, Gavan, you've done it again.

PENNY   I knew this would happen. Here, hold this, fruit bat. And hold it still, it's got a short wick.

(PENNY *hands* GAVAN *a kerosene lamp. She lights the lamp. The stage is once again flooded with light, as if it were all emanating from the lamp*)

GAVAN   I always go overboard in that skit . . . I dunno why.

PENNY   Yeah, well, you should know by now . . . the tech people don't like it.

GAVAN   *(agitated)* Well I'm sorry! I can't help it! I need a break from this crazy town.

NAT   No worries, mate. Tell you what, we'll take you on a holiday.

PENNY   Somewhere clean, sunny, relaxed.

GAVAN   Bribie?

NAT   Chile!

PENNY   Johannesburg!

GAVAN   Cairns? Managua. El Salvador. Great Keppell (*etc.*) . . .

A Few Short Wicks in Paradise

(introduction)   There are sirens in the night time
There are sirens in my dreams
But the only sirens that I know
Are the ones I've never seen

Verse 1   You never see those sirens coming up behind you
It always takes a little blue light to find you
'Uh oh . . . only officer I should remind you . . .'
That I surely know my rights
And they must be worth the fight . . .! 'cause there's . . .

(chorus)   More than a few short wicks in paradise
More than a few short wicks in paradise . . . there's
More than a few short wicks in paradise

282

Verse 2	I saw you sitting down in the city plaza You'd like to put a bomb up in the "Taj Ma- Hal" and make it turn to rubble Like they did to the Bellevue Like they did to Cloudland too...'cause there's...
(chorus)	More than a few short wicks in paradise More than a few short wicks in paradise . . . there's More than a few short wicks in paradise
	(Instrumental, Introduction and Verse 1)
(chorus)	'Cause there's More than a few short wicks in paradise More than a few short wicks in paradise . . .
	ALL THEY NEED IS TO BE LIT!

END OF PLAY

RAISE THE ROOF

by

Hugh Watson

****

with

Street Arts Community Company inc.

RAISE THE ROOF was first produced in 1990

Director:
Ainsley Burdell

Performers:
Elisa Brennoks
Mandy Brennoks
Jason Cochrane
Michael Ferguson
Steve Gartside
Elizabeth Gordon
Natalie Grisanti
Tanya Hill
Lisa Hollis
David Johnstone
Philip Jones
Jimmy Knight
Lindy Nilsen
Jim Powers
Alison Schache
Michele Smith
Jason Spires
Sharon Staib
Kevin Steltman
Roy Turner
Marguerite Wesselinoff

Opening — a movement piece involving tribes of kids, real estate agents, boarding parents, truckies et al. as well as dogs. At the end of the piece, one DOG is left on stage.

DOG   Good evening! Good evening to all you human beings! All you ladies, kids and gentlemen. And a very good evening to all the dogs who are with us tonight . . . all you poodles, pekes and dobermen. And can I just say it's great to see so many dogs here in the audience tonight. Woof! Woof!

(the DOG flashes a 'thumbs up' sign)

And welcome to tonight's show which is called "Raise the Roof". And it's a play about accommodation — about how hard it can be to get a roof over your head. As for me — I'm the mongrel who's going to be narrating the play. Now when I say I'm a mongrel, I'm not putting myself down or anything 'cause it's true. My mum, she was a pure bred German shepherd . . . but my dad . . . he was a kelpie labrador cross . . . at least I think so . . . at any rate the point is, I am a dog. A talking dog. Which brings me to the last thing I need say. This play has got a fair few songs in it. It's very musical.

music starts up

But it's also full of strange uncanny things . . . it's very magical.

music turns eerie

Of course, that won't bother us dogs. But it might disturb the human beings, so, ladies and gentlemen, if something happens that frightens or alarms you, please stay in your seats. You will be perfectly safe, and it will all work out for the best. Now as for the dogs, this will be the first time you've ever been to the theatre and so, a couple of pointers. Don't bark. It disturbs the actors. And, if you are enjoying the show, please try to control yourself. We don't want to have to clean the seats.

And now we will begin . . .

(the DOG turns to the left and barks once. Turns to the right and barks once. Turns upstage and barks)

ACT I   Scene Two

BILL HASLUCK *and his wife* JILL *at home.* BILL *enters l. wearing a shirt and tie. He is also struggling into a large overcoat and scarf.*

BILL   Jill? Jill? I'm off!

JILL   *(enters l.)* You going already?

BILL   First day back on the job. Want to be there on time.

JILL   How are you feeling?

BILL   Fit as a fiddle.

(he sees the expression on her face)

Ah, come on, Jill.

JILL   You were in hospital for a month. You only got out two weeks ago.

BILL   Which means I've had six weeks in bed! I'm fine.

JILL   *(doubtful)* All right. But take it easy will you? Don't get too stressed.

BILL   Jill, I'm a child guidance officer! Of course I'm going to get stressed. But I'm young, too, y'know. I can handle it.

JILL   Ah, wake up to yourself, Bill! You've got to start facing facts. You've had a heart attack, and you've only just got better.

BILL   I didn't have a heart attack. The doctors didn't say I had a heart attack. They called it a spasm. You heard them, Jill. They were calling it a heart spasm.

JILL   Yes, and they said if it happened again, I'd be calling you an undertaker. *(pause)* Now have you got everything?

BILL   *(pats pockets)* Yes, I think so.

(they kiss, he leaves. Music to cover his transition to his office)

ACT I   Scene Three

BILL's *office. He is at his desk.* LOCKIE *is facing him.*

BILL   Now, Lockie, the records show you've only been at school ten days in the last month. Do you think you can tell me why?

LOCKIE   Mr Hasluck, I come from a very ancient culture. Murris learn things in a different way to white people.

BILL   Lockie, it's not going to work. I know your parents.

LOCKIE   So?

BILL   I know what you are, and you're not aboriginal. You're a Tongan.

LOCKIE   Well, black is black.

BILL   Nice try.

(a knock on the door. KERRI comes in with the school NURSE. There is a big bandage on her face)

NURSE   Mr Hasluck?

BILL   Yes?

NURSE   Someone to see you.

(sees KERRI)

BILL   Whew. What happened to you?

KERRI   Already told her.

NURSE   She got bashed up at the railway station.

KERRI   It's true!

BILL	Alright, Lockie, you can go now.
LOCKIE	What, just like that? Jesus. *(he leaves)*
NURSE	I took her to the doctor's. She can go home but she said she wanted to talk to you.
	(BILL nods. The NURSE leaves)
BILL	You want to talk about what happened?
KERRI	Nah.
BILL	You've missed a lot of school. You want to talk about that?
KERRI	Forget it.
BILL	Been in trouble with the police?
KERRI	Nah.
BILL	Well, what do you want to talk about?
KERRI	Is that all you do . . . sit on your bum and talk all day?
	(pause)
BILL	When I'm very busy, I write a letter.
KERRI	Wouldn't mind your job.
BILL	Well?
	(KERRI makes up her mind to talk)
KERRI	Nah, it's home. You know my dad? You know how he left? Well, Mum's got a boyfriend.
BILL	Yeah?
KERRI	Tony, his name is. Well, he's a truck driver, right? And he thinks he's a real tough guy. And when he first came around I thought . . . well, he's only here for a feed and a . . . root, y'know? And I thought he was ripping Mum off, only she didn't know it, so . . .
BILL	So you didn't like him?
KERRI	Oh, I hated him. But I didn't hassle him 'cause . . . oh, I was probably a bit scared of him, and I didn't think he'd hang around. But he has. He's moved in with us. And now, me and him fight all the time.
BILL	Do you still think he's ripping your mum off?
KERRI	No . . . ah, no. See, he's paying a lot of the bills, more than he has to. And he's always home when he says he'll be home, which my father never did. And he's nice to Christine, that's my sister. An he'd be nice to me too if I let him. And he seems to really love Mum. I don't know why, 'cause she's seven years older than he is . . . and she's a bit of a dog, to be honest.
BILL	It sound to me . . . as if you're saying . . . that Tony's an alright sort of bloke.
KERRI	Yeah. I guess he is. But it doesn't matter. 'Cause every time I see him, I have a go at him. I'm always stirring him.
BILL	What, you mean you're rude to him?

KERRI	Nah, I'm rude to everyone, mate. Nah . . . I do things like . . . walk in on 'em when the bedroom door's closed. Like I'm trying to catch them at it. Drives Tony wild. Bit wierd, eh?
BILL	It's interesting.
KERRI	Oh, but I do the normal stuff too, like pinch his smokes, drink his beer . . . one night I tried to steal his truck . . . I would've too . . . 'cept I couldn't hold onto the steering wheel and reach the brakes at the same time.
BILL	Well now, Kerri, it seems to me that what you're saying now is that the problem is really your behaviour, the way you're acting. That's what's causing the problems.
KERRI	Yeah.
BILL	And so the question becomes, what are you going to do about it?
KERRI	Well, just let me finish telling you. Last night I did something really bad. I'm not saying what it was. But Tony, when he found out, he just hit the roof. Really lost it. We had a punch up. After it was over . . . like . . . we were both really shaky. He was really shaky because he'd hit me. And I was really shaky . . . not because I'd been hit but 'cause I'd treated him as a joke, and he wasn't. *(pause)* I don't really like it, y'know, him and Mum. But I don't think I really want to split them apart.
BILL	And that's how you got the . . . *(points to the bandage)*
KERRI	Yeah, but it's alright now. *(KERRI stands up)* Well, thanks for the advice.
BILL	I didn't give you any.
	(the NURSE comes back in)
NURSE	Well, Kerri? Do you want a lift home now?
KERRI	Yeah.
BILL	Can I speak to you for a moment, Nurse?
	(KERRI goes outside)
	How bad is her cheek?
NURSE	Well, she's fractured her cheekbone. Did she tell you which kid did it?
BILL	It wasn't a kid.

ACT I   Scene Four

Lights up on MEG RYAN's kitchen. CHRIS is ironing her K Mart uniform. KERRI is reading a Mutant Turtle comic book. MEG is applying makeup with a compact. MEG moves downstage.

MEG	Did you hear something?
CHRIS	No, Mum.
MEG	It wasn't a truck?
KERRI	It wasn't his truck!
MEG	Do I look alright?

CHRIS	Yeah, fine.
MEG	Kerri?
KERRI	Ah, yeah. You'd look alright if your bum was a normal size.
CHRIS	Jeez, you say some nice things.
MEG	You know who she's like? Every day, more and more . . .
CHRIS	Mum! Now, don't you start!
MEG	Sour and mean, just like . . .
KERRI	If you're going to say my father . . . you can't. He's not here to defend himself.
MEG	I'll talk about you, then. You're not very pleasant to be with, you know that? You treat this place like a hotel. Who buys the food you eat? Who buys the clothes? Who cleans up the mess you make? Not you, y'know. It's me and your sister.
CHRIS	And I won't be doing it for much longer. I'm moving out.
MEG	You're waited on, hand and foot. And you can't even be nice. No, every time you open your lips, you pour shit on someone or something. You got a real voodoo mouth, and sometimes I can't believe how like him you really are.
KERRI	See? Every time, Chris, every time . . . every time she has a go at me, she sticks the knife into the old man.
MEG	*(to CHRIS)* I didn't say your father. I said "he". Could've been talking about anyone.
CHRIS	Listen, Mum. Tony's going to be home any minute, right? Do you want him to walk in on a fight?
MEG	Oh God, no!
CHRIS	So shut up, Kerri, will you?
	(pause)
KERRI	Besides, at least when Dad was living here, it was interesting.
MEG	Interesting? What's so interesting about arguments and punch ups?
KERRI	Better than Tony.
CHRIS	At least he's cheerful.
KERRI	Cheerful? He's not cheerful. He's Duh . . . brain dead.
	(sound of a truck parking outside)
MEG	Well, if you're going to put shit on Tony you can do it to his face.
TONY	*(off)* Hello, hello? Anyone in? Better be someone, 'cause I'm home! *(he bounds in)* Howdy, Chris.
CHRIS	G'day, Tony.
TONY	G'day, Kerri, how's it going?
	(no reply from KERRI. TONY walks past CHRIS and KERRI, and throws an arm around MEG and kisses her)
	Hello, darling.

292

MEG	Hello, sweetheart. How was your trip?
TONY	You got my gear ready?
KERRI	You working tonight?
TONY	Yeah. Going to Rocky. Be back on Sunday. *(points his finger at* KERRI*)* And I want that garage cleaned up before I get back.
KERRI	I said I'd do it.
TONY	And if it's clean . . . and I mean spotless . . .
KERRI	Yeah?
TONY	I'll take you with me next trip I make.
KERRI	Dead set! Really?
TONY	Yeah. *(pause)* Well, gotta go.
MEG	Tony wait . . . before you go . . .
KERRI	Oh, Mum, don't.
MEG	There's something I got to tell you.
KERRI	Aw, Mum, leave it till Sunday.
TONY	Better make it snappy. Gotta get this show on the road. Gotta get the big rig rolling.
MEG	Two blokes came around this morning. They were from the Department of Family Services. They're investigating a complaint.
TONY	A complaint about what?
MEG	A complaint about her getting bashed up. Here. At home.
TONY	What? But Kerri, you and me, we've sorted all that out, haven't we?
KERRI	Yeah.
TONY	And who complained, anyway? It wasn't the neighbours. I know that for a fact. The house next door is empty.
MEG	It must have been someone at the school.
TONY	Nah, couldn't have been the school. You told them you had a punch up in the street with your mates, didn't you?
KERRI	I didn't . . . well, that bruise you gave me. That thumping. The teacher noticed the lump and so I got taken to the school nurse and she took me to the doctor's . . .
TONY	Yeah, yeah. We've heard all that.
MEG	And then what happened?
KERRI	Well, they made me go see that Guidance Officer . . .
TONY	What, that Mr Hasluck?
MEG	You never told us this . . .
TONY	No, you bloody well didn't. And then what happened?
KERRI	Well, then I had to . . . I had to tell him . . .
TONY	What? That I hit you? Or that I pushed you — pushed you by accident? *(pause)* Well?
KERRI	I just told him we had a fight.

TONY	Anyway, I didn't. I just gave her a hard push.
KERRI	Yeah! Some push. You grabbed me by the hair and banged my head against the wall.
TONY	*(calm. To* MEG*)* Yeah, I did. And that's the truth. And I'm not proud of it. But look at why. 'Cause her and her mates . . . they stole my bloody beer . . . they drank 'em and then, like filthy bloody animals, they pissed into the window of my truck. All over the new shag pile. So I lost my temper and hit her. Well, after that we made peace, didn't we?
KERRI	Yeah.
TONY	But it just doesn't work. We don't get on. Meg, I've tried to fit in, but it's no good. So I'm going to go away for a while.
KERRI	Ah, why don't you tell her the real story?
TONY	What?
KERRI	We're not idiots, y'know. It doesn't take four days to drive to Rockhampton and back. You've got another woman up there. *(she gets up and leaves the room)*
TONY	Look, Meg, I won't be back this Sunday. I won't be back for a while. I've got to wait 'til this thing blows over.
MEG	Why?
TONY	It's not any good. I don't want the government knowing anything about me. I've been in trouble. I don't want them knowing where I live.
MEG	It's not the police . . .?
TONY	And besides, this kid! I can't live with her. If she's not winding me up, she's dobbing me in. Her and her mouth. She's just so vicious.
MEG	But Tony . . .
TONY	Look, I don't know. I don't know. Don't ask me. All I know is I gotta get that truck started.
	(he walks out. Spotlight on KERRI *outside)*
KERRI	I hope your wheelnuts fall out. I hope the bull bar falls off. I hope your oil gets carbonated. I hope your ignition won't start. I hope your diff buggers up and your gears get stripped. I hope . . .

Curse music

*(*TONY *walks past* KERRI, *neither acknowledging the other. A truck is heard being turned over but failing to start)*

TONY	*(off)* Oh, Jesus bloody Christ!
	*(*KERRI *walks inside)*
KERRI	Mum, I'm really sorry. Look, if Tony doesn't want to come back, I'll move out. I really will. 'Cause I'm the one who starts it . . .
MEG	Ah, who'd take you? *(pause)* You're both right, y'know. He probably has got somebody up there. And he probably won't be back. And he's right, too. 'Cause Kerri, every time you open your mouth . . .

(blackout)

The Hasluck's home. BILL enters L, wearing a shirt and tie and carrying a jacket over his arm.

BILL	Jill? Jill? I'm off.
JILL	*(enters L, hurrying)* Wait, wait, wait.
BILL	What?
JILL	Here are your new pills. Two sets. *(hands him a bottle of pills)* Your pink pills. *(another bottle)* And your blue pills.
BILL	What do they do?
JILL	If you get a pain in your chest or if you have any difficulty breathing, you take two of the pink pills and . . .
BILL	And . . .?
JILL	And you lie down. You lie down immediately. You lie down that instant.
BILL	Christ! Is that what the doctor told you?
JILL	Yes.
BILL	But what happens if it's school assembly?
JILL	You lie down in the aisle.
BILL	But what happens if I've taken some kid to court?
JILL	Then you lie down on the magistrate's bench.
BILL	Oh yeah? And what about the blue pills?
JILL	If you feel a pain in your chest, you take the pink pills. You lie down. You wait fifteen minutes. If you don't feel any better . . . if you've still got the pain . . . then you take a blue pill, and you get someone to call an ambulance.
BILL	Oh, Jesus!
JILL	Look, Bill, you've got to be responsible. If something happened to you . . .
BILL	You'd miss me, wouldn't you?
JILL	Of course I would . . . I'd be heartbroken.
BILL	But you'd find somebody else. Somebody'd snap you up.
JILL	Don't you believe it. It's not that easy for a woman. Not when they reach their thirties. A lot of them never find another partner. So if you keeled over, I might be sleeping alone for the rest of my life. I wouldn't like that.
BILL	I'm sorry. I'll do every . . . I'll take the pills. I'll lie down.
JILL	And where are you going to put them?
BILL	I'll keep them in my jacket.
JILL	And what are you doing with your jacket? You don't want to put it on now, Bill. It's too warm.
BILL	No, I'm going to carry it like this. See? Over my arm.

Bill's office.

BILL   Alright, Lockie. you've failed to go to any English classes for the last week. now you know what was said . . .

LOCKIE   Ah, Mr Hasluck, have a heart.

         (KERRI comes in)

KERRI   Mr Hasluck. Gotta talk to you.

BILL   Kerri, look, I'm busy.

KERRI   Ah, fuck that! This is important.

         (pause)

BILL   Alright. Lockie, could you wait outside, please?

         (LOCKIE nods and leaves)

         So, what's this about?

KERRI   You told the government . . .

BILL   What?

KERRI   The Department of Parents . . .

BILL   The Department of Famly Services.

KERRI   Yeah. About me and Tony and Mum and stuff. It was you, wasn't it?

BILL   Yes.

KERRI   Well why, for fuck's sake?

BILL   Kerri, they're not there to hurt you. The Department of Family Services is there to give you and your family advice, support . . .

KERRI   Right. Well, we don't need that. So call them up, Mr Hasluck, will you? And tell them not to come round anymore.

BILL   Kerri, if that fracture had been on your head instead of on your cheek, you could have had brain damage.

KERRI   But it wasn't.

BILL   And what if it happens again?

KERRI   It won't. *(pause)* You're not going to do it, are you?

BILL   Look. All you have to do is get your mum and Tony to sit down with these people, talk things through. It might clear the air. Things might get better.

KERRI   Mr Hasluck, we can't even find Tony. Jesus, and things were going so well. But now . . . well, Tony thinks I dobbed him in, just to get him in trouble. And so he pissed off. Jesus, you're a bloody dog, Mr Hasluck. I hope you drop dead!

                               Curse music

BILL   *(grabs his shirt, in pain)* Oh, no!

Place To Stay

copyright 9.8.90
Jason Spires, Natalie Grisonti, Ann and Susan Milligan,
Melissa Burton, Belinda Farmer, David Johnstone,
Jamie Rogers and Peter Stewart (Street Arts)

heavy rock beat (120)

Intro: (guitar riff)

1 Start- ed off in Bruce Road: said good- bye to 'home sweet home' Got-ta find a better place: some-where I can call my own. Chorus: All I need is a place to stay, to sort my-self out and get a- way. All I need is some- one who cares, some-one who'll al- ways be there.

2 Midnight down at Wembley Road
   Nothing but an empty street
   Hunger gnawing at my toes
   Gotta find a place to sleep

3 Three o'clock and the wind is cold
   Gotta find a place to hide
   Rough and hard, shelter or the street
   Can't get to sleep anywhere I tried

KERRI	I know. It's terrible, isn't it? And Mum . . . she thinks I planned it all, so I could split them up. It's the worst bloody thing that could have happened.
BILL	Oh God!
KERRI	Well, at least you're sympathetic.
BILL	My pills . . . where did I put them? In my jacket . . . where's my jacket? . . . Oh Christ, I left it in the car. *(he picks up the phone but gets another pain across his chest)* Oh. *(he staggers, holding the phone out)*
KERRI	Look, Mr Hasluck, all you got to do is get on to these people. The phone . . . tell them you made a mistake. *(pause)* Well, I'll call them if you want me to. *(she takes the phone)* What number?

(BILL whispers something. KERRI leans forward to hear and dials)

Zero double zero. Who should I ask for? *(she leans forward to hear. BILL whispers again)*

Who? *(speaks into phone)* Hello, is this the Department of Family Services? I'd like to speak to a woman who works for you . . . Her name is Anne Bulance. Well, if you're not the Department of Family Services, who are you? . . . Department of Emergency Services? What? Do I want an ambulance?

(she finally notices BILL's condition)

Shit . . . . Yes! East Logan State School. Round the back! And hurry! I think he's dying!

(lights down. A siren. Spotlight on a NEWSPAPER BOY)

NEWSBOY	Extra, extra, read all about it in the Beenleigh and Logan Times. Local school counsellor critically ill.
KERRI	Did I do that?
LOCKIE	*(enters)* Hey mate! Hey you! Weren't you in the office with him?
KERRI	Yeah.
LOCKIE	I was outside. And I heard you say it. I heard you say, 'Drop dead'. And he did. You know what that's like? That's like our culture. Pointing the bone. Singing people to death. You must have a pretty powerful spirit.
MEG	*(off — a memory)* You've got a real voodoo mouth.
KERRI	Did I do it?

(all leave the stage)

SONG: PLACE TO STAY

Started off — in Bruce Road
Said goodbye to 'home sweet home'
Gotta find — a better place
Somewhere I can call my home

(chorus)	All I need is a place to stay
	To sort myself out and get away
	All I need is someone who cares
	Someone who'll always be there

Midnight — down at Wembley Road
Nothing but an empty street
Hunger — gnawing at my toes
Gotta find a place to sleep

(chorus)	Three o'clock —and the wind is cold
	Gotta find a place to hide
	Rough and hard — shelter or the street
	Can't get to sleep anywhere I tried

(BILL enters and addresses the audience. He is still dressed like a man but changes into the dog costume as he talks)

DOG   Now, ladies and gentlemen, we've got a big story to tell . . . a lot of ground to cover . . . so I'm going to just fill you in on what happens next. Kerri has to leave home, because Meg decides she doesn't want to lose Tony, and she won't keep Tony if Kerri stays in the house. And as for me, I get taken to the hospital but I die on the operating table. So both me and Kerri are homeless. Kerri's got to find a new home for her body. I've got to find a new body for my home. Kerri goes to a welfare organisation. They know a family on Diamond Street who'll take Kerri in. I go up to heaven. They send me back to Logan City where I get reborn in the body of a dog.

Meanwhile, Chris, Kerri's sister, she's moving into a flat in Ewing Road . . .

(DOG turns left and right. Barks)

Party Music: Marimbas

copyright 1990
Jamie Rogers and Peter Stewart
(Street Arts)

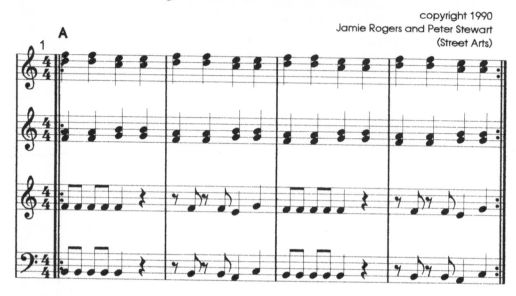

Arrangement: A B A B... Parts can be omitted or doubled up at an octave as required.

The share house. CHRIS *is looking at the television set.* PETER *comes in through rear door, a tape measure in his hand.*

PETER
Hey, Chris. Have you checked out the back room?

CHRIS
Well?

PETER
I've just measured it. Do you know how much space there'd be left if you put a mattress in? That much. *(indicates one inch)* That's not a bedroom, that's a closet with the shelves taken out.

CHRIS
So?

PETER
The ad said three bedrooms.

CHRIS
Ah, come on Peter, what do you expect? It's a real estate agent.

PETER
Yeah. And where is he, anyway?

(doorbell. FORSYTHE enters)

FORSYTHE
Good afternoon. Brian Forsythe.

CHRIS
I'm Christine Ryan.

FORSYTHE
Good. I'm sorry I'm late. But . . . you let yourselves in?

PETER
The lock's broken.

FORSYTHE
Oh dear, I'll send someone around to fix that. Now. Have you had a good look round? You have? What do you think?

PETER
Listen, that bedroom . . .

FORSYTHE
Bit small, you reckon?

PETER
It's just that the sign in your window said there were three bedrooms and . . .

FORSYTHE
Yes. That's a bit misleading. Well, the secretary typed that up and, to tell you the truth, I let it pass because I thought this place would get snapped up by a young couple.

CHRIS & PETER
We're not a couple!

FORSYTHE
A pity. I prefer to rent to couples. They're more stable.

CHRIS
Yeah, but . . . see, we were thinking that if this place had three bedrooms . . . I mean, three proper-sized bedrooms . . . well, then we could maybe rent the third bedroom to someone else . . .

FORSYTHE
Whoa! Now wait wait wait wait . . . you told me there were only two of you moving in.

PETER
Yeah.

FORSYTHE
Well, don't you think that's enough? I mean, any more it'll be a bit of a crowd, won't it?

PETER
Yeah, but we were thinking that . . . if we got behind with the bills . . . or found that the rent was too much . . . well, another person would make it cheaper.

FORSYTHE	Now wait . . . whoa whoa whoa! What do you mean, if the rent gets too much? What, don't you think you can pay for this place? I thought you said you were working.
CHRIS	I am working. I'm a checkout operator at K Mart.
FORSYTHE	And you?
PETER	I'm a —
CHRIS	He's a salesman.
PETER	Mechanic.
CHRIS	He sells tools to all the mechanics.
	(pause)
FORSYTHE	Right. Do you want to take the place or not?
CHRIS	Yeah, but if we take it . . . will you do something about the tiles?
PETER	What about the hole in my ceiling?
CHRIS	And the carpet stinks.
FORSYTHE	Really, take it or leave it. And come on. At a hundred and ten a week, it's a real cheapy.
	(pause)
PETER	I guess we'll take it.
FORSYTHE	Good. Now here's the lease. You'll both need to sign it. And the copy underneath is yours. I'll need two weeks' rent in advance, plus the bond. That's six hundred and sixty all up.

ACT II   Scene Two

One week later. CHRIS, PETER, STEVE *and* JOAN *are sitting on the floor in the share house. Kentucky Fried Chicken packets are scattered near each of them as well as a jar of tomato sauce, a tub of margarine and a loaf of sliced bread.*

STEVE	So anyway, we wind up at Beenleigh, and we rent this caravan, and it's not a bad size, say about ten metres long. And we're paying about ninety dollars a week for it. But suddenly we can't afford it anymore, 'cause I got kicked off the dole.
JOAN	They're always fucking hassling us, me and Steve.
PETER	So what did you do then?
STEVE	Spider and Janelle moved in with us.
CHRIS	What, you had four of you? Living in a caravan?
STEVE	Yeah.
CHRIS	For how long?
JOAN	'Bout a month.
PETER	Didn't you drive each other crazy?
STEVE	Nah . . . like I say, it was a big van . . .

JOAN	With an annexe.
STEVE	And a concrete floor,
JOAN	See, and with four of us . . . that was, what? Only forty-five bucks per couple.
STEVE	No, it was great! We were bopping along . . . raging! Then Janelle's little sister . . .
JOAN	Shelley . . .
STEVE	Turned up with Robbie, this bloke Robbie. She'd run away from home and *he* didn't have any place to go, so we had to take them in.
CHRIS	So there were six of you?
STEVE	Ah, mate, look. Since me and Joannie were . . . what? Fifteen?
JOAN	Yeah.
STEVE	We've been in so many situations . . .
JOAN	Foster homes, shelters . . .
STEVE	Short term accommodation programs, long term accommodation programs . . .
JILL	Refuges, on the street . . .
STEVE	And if you're under eighteen, the choices aren't all that good. I mean, on the one hand if you're in some sort of welfare situation, sure, you've got a place to sleep, but you haven't got your independence.
JOAN	You've always got somebody telling you what to do.
STEVE	But if you've got your independence . . .
JOAN	You probably don't have a place to sleep.
STEVE	Now that me and Joan are older, it's not so bad. But there's still a lot of younger kids out there without a place to sleep. So we've decided that anyone who wants to can come and stay with us. The more the merrier.
JOAN	And besides, the more people you've got to pay the rent and buy the food, the cheaper everything is.
STEVE	More money for alcohol. Hey Peter, you want to pass the chicken over?
PETER	None left.
STEVE	What about that packet of chips?
CHRIS	Empty.
STEVE	Christ, I'm hungry.
PETER	Shouldn't waste your money buying chicken, Steve. You should only buy chips. Then you can make chip sandwiches, and there's plenty for everyone.
STEVE	Are you that broke?
CHRIS	All our money went on bond.
JOAN	Yeah? Ah, you dopey pricks! Why don't you bloody well cook for yourselves?
CHRIS	We cant afford to get the gas put on.

STEVE	That's what's great about a caravan. The rent's about the same as a flat but there's no bond. And you get everything you need. Plates, cutlery, pots and pans, furniture, sheets, blankets . . .
PETER	All the things we don't have.
CHRIS	I reckon when we moved into this place . . . we must have been the most docile bunch of bastards . . . It's been a real disaster.
STEVE	Oh, I don't know. I reckon this place is pretty good.

(he stands up, puts out his arms and begins to sway from side to side)

PETER	What the fuck is he doing?
STEVE	Hey, Joan! Try this!

(JOAN stands up, puts out her arms and starts to sway also)

What do you reckon?

JOAN	It's wierd.
STEVE	Good, eh?
CHRIS	But what are you doing?
JOAN	You can't touch the walls. It's amazing.

(STEVE turns to CHRIS and PETER)

STEVE	Hey, how's this? Me and Joan rent the spare room, and you use the extra rent to get the gas on.
PETER	But that room's so small.
STEVE	Ah, mate, what are you talking about? Jesus, I reckon you could fit a **bed** in there!
CHRIS	Yeah, but what about the caravan?
STEVE	Yeah, well, we've been given notice. We've got to be out by Sunday.
JOAN	The owner reckons we've got too many people in it. And the neighbours have complained about the noise.

(lights down. All leave the stage)

ACT II   Scene Three

Lights up, but only to dim. Three figures move onto stage as though through the front door of the flat. We don't recognise them.

STEVE	Alright now, keep it quiet, 'cause everybody's asleep. No, don't turn the lights on, it might wake somebody. Got your sleeping bag? Alright, put it over there near the teev. Yeah, alright, we'll talk about it in the morning.

(the doorbell rings)

Oh, FOR CHRIST'S SAKE! Ssssh! Ssssh! Ssssh!

(he moves to the front door)

Who's that? Is that Robbie? Well, who else is there? Shelley. Okay, good. Thought we'd lost you there, matey. Janelle was real aggro but I told her you'd find the place. Alright, come on in, come on, I want to shut the door.

(lights up. CHRIS at rear of stage)

CHRIS
Steve, it's four in the morning.

STEVE
Oh, Christine, sorry about the doorbell. That was an accident.

CHRIS
Tomorrow's Monday. I've got to be at K Mart at eight o'clock. What're you doing? What's going on? Who are these people? Are you having a party or what?

STEVE
No, no party, Chris, this is Janelle and Shelley and Spider and Robbie. You know, the people who were staying with us at the caravan.

CHRIS
So?

STEVE
Well, today's Sunday. And today they got kicked out of the caravan.

CHRIS
So?

STEVE
Well, I said they could stay here. Well, where else can they go?

(lights down)

ACT II   Scene Four

Lights up on the boarding family. Morning. BRAD CADZOW and his wife JANET are getting dressed. JANET is putting on her makeup. BRAD, dressed in grey flannel trousers and a singlet is working out with a pair of dumbells.

JANET
I was out all morning, shopping for curtains for Kerri's room.

BRAD
Have you hung them yet?

JANET
I would have shown you. They're pink. With frills.

BRAD
Now, Janet. We've discussed this. Kerri's going to be quite different from Kim and her little friends. She's a toughie. And when you go and buy her pretty feminine things, you put your own values on her. And we can't do that.

JANET
Ah, tush. The social worker told us we shouldn't have any expectations. You're expecting her to be tough. Lots of little girls like frills and bows. Maybe Kerri does too, but hasn't had an opportunity to indulge in them. Maybe she's just never had a chance to be feminine. It's not wrong to give her the option.

BRAD
If she doesn't like them, will you take them down?

JANET
Oh, Brad! They were expensive. She's got to give them a fair try.

BRAD
Maybe you're right. But we've got to accept the fact that this won't be easy. We may have to change things to suit her.

JANET
What do you mean?

BRAD
We've been married sixteen years. We've got our lifestyle down pretty darn pat. And we raised our own girl on a fairly tight rein.

JANET	Kimbo? We haven't been strict with her.
BRAD	Taking Kerri on . . . a kid off the streets . . . we might have to compromise a bit. If we don't, we might never get to first base with her.
JANET	Compromise how?

ACT II   Scene Five

Boarding house. KERRY *and* KIM *washing up.*

KERRI	Ah, Jesus. I hate this place. Can't watch TV after eight o'clock. Have to be in bed by nine. Have to be in at six every night.
KIM	You can go out Thursday.
KERRI	Yeah, but only till eight-thirty. The shops aren't even shut.
KIM	Well, what do you want?
KERRI	I used to stay out till twelve. Sometimes later. Sux.
KIM	Well, you can't do that here. Mum and Dad don't like it.
KERRI	Yeah? They're stiffs.
KIM	You got to have rules.
KERRI	There are too many rules. Everything's too tidy. Everything's clean. Even the way you"re supposed to talk. How old are you?
KIM	Fifteen.
KERRI	Jesus. And it's always been like this? It's dull.
KIM	It was dull.
KERRI	What's that supposed to mean?
KIM	Ah, don't get me started.
KERRI	Go on!
KIM	Before you came, I wasn't allowed to watch TV in the afternoon. I wasn't allowed to go out on Thursday night. And every Sunday we went to church. The whole thing changed because of you. We're not even going to church tomorrow, 'cause they don't think you'd like it.
KERRI	You should thank me.
KIM	I'm not going to. I liked it how it was. I don't like it now you're here.
KERRI	Get stuffed!
KIM	And you can't even talk nicely about my mother and father. They've changed everything around for your sake, and you just put them down.
KERRI	I suppose if I thumped you, you'd go running to them for protection.
KIM	Yes, I would.
KERRI	Stiff!
KIM	You don't know much about how normal people live, do you? Of course I'd go running to my parents for protection. That's what parents are for.

Boarding family. BRAD, JANET, KIM *and* KERRI *at a picnic table or on a blanket, in front of set area.*

KIM	Mum. Dad. Can't we eat now?
JANET	Ask your father.
KIM	Dad?
BRAD	Well, I don't know. Let's find out what everyone wants to do. Kerri?
KERRI	Oh, I don't care, Mr Cadzow.
BRAD	Kerri, please don't keep on calling us Mr Cadzow and Mrs Cadzow.
JANET	Couldn't you call us Brad and Janet?
BRAD	We know we're not your real parents. But we are trying to provide you with some family life, so if you could . . . it might help us, don't you think?
KERRI	*(flat)* I-don't-care-when-we-eat-Brad.
BRAD	Rightio. Well, **Janet**, I guess it's up to you.
JANET	In that case, **Brad**, I think that these two should run off and get a bit of exercise.
BRAD	How's that sound, Kerri? You want to do that?

(KERRY shakes her head — sulks)

I think she might want to stay and help me unpack. I'm sure she'll go down in a while.

JANET	Alright. Come on, Kim. You and I will walk down to the creek.

(they walk off)

KERRI	I'm not going down. This place is stupid. I hate it.
BRAD	Ah, it's terrific. God's handiwork. Listen, do you know what you might see if you go down to the creek? Turtles! You like turtles, don't you? Ever seen one?
KERRI	Seen them on TV.
BRAD	Right. "Teenage Stupid Dingy Turtles". That's that cartoon you and Kim watch, isn't it? *(he sings)* "Teenage Stupid Dingy Turtles, Teenage Stupid Dingy Turtles". *(pause)* Wait a second. Wait a second. They live in the sewers, don't they? I work in the sewers.

(a conversational dead end)

I think what I'm trying to say, Kerri, is that we still don't know each other very well. And we may not like the same things. Cartoons. Forests. But if there's something you really do like or need, or that's important to you . . . well, we'd try and get it for you. I mean, we know that you're often very unhappy, and we don't want you to be.

KERRI	Yeah. *(she stands up)* I'm going to walk down to the creek.
BRAD	If you want to catch up to Janet and Kim . . .

KERRI	No, no. It's alright, I want to be on my own.
	(KERRI *leaves. JANET and* KIM *return*)
JANET	Where's she going?
BRAD	Ah, she's really upset about something. Better to leave her alone. Let's get this stuff unpacked.
	(KERRI *races back*)
KERRI	Mr . . .! Brad, Janet . . . Kim. *(pause)* Kim . . . Hey! You'll never guess what I found. On the other side of the embankment . . . it's not old or anything. I reckon you could house train it really quick . . . it was there, this dog, just licking the water, it's limping like anything, but eh, it jumped up on me and followed me just like that . . . Well, there it is. It's a dog.
	(the DOG *on edge of stage*)
	Well, what you were saying, Mr . . . Brad, about things that are important to me and might make me happy and that? Well, please, I'd look after it, feed it and walk it and everything.
BRAD	If you want it and nobody owns it . . . we'll take it home with us.
JANET	Now Brad, I don't think —
BRAD	That's what we're going to do.
	(they leave)

ACT II Scene Seven

Boarding home. Morning. JANET is putting on her makeup. BRAD is doing weights.

JANET	I'm really worried about Kerri.
BRAD	Is she unhappy?
JANET	Brad, I'm not so sure that that young lady's state of mind should be the be-all and end-all of my existence. Just at the moment, I'm more worried about my family's happiness. Me. You. Kim.
BRAD	Janet, she's trying.
JANET	She's trying my patience. Oh look, Brad. In one week she stayed out all night, she came home drunk, she stole from me and lied about it. And she and Kim had a punch up . . .
	(BRAD *stops using his weights*)
BRAD	They hit each other?
JANET	Yes.
BRAD	I'm not pleased about that.
JANET	Quite right! Poor Kimbo! She's scared in her own house.
BRAD	That's no good, Janet.
JANET	And she beats that dog, too. And neglects it. Despite all the fuss she made about having it.

BRAD	That'll have to be gone into.
JANET	Well, violence breeds violence.
BRAD	But not in our house. *(pause)* Look, she's been here three weeks. The social worker said they always misbehave around now. It's called testing the limit. It means that she's being deliberately naughty, to see if we still want her. She's trying to work out if she trusts us or not.
JANET	She's not very trusting, is she? She's suspicious. She won't take me into her confidence at all.
BRAD	Well, have a talk to her. Tell her that she can trust us.
JANET	Alright. I'll mention trust. But I'm going to talk mainly about discipline. She needs to wake up to herself.

ACT II   Scene Eight

KERRI *is lying on her bed. A knock on the door.*

KERRI	Yeah?
JANET	*(enters)* Kerri, I want to talk to you.
KERRI	You just want to rouse at me.
JANET	Now why do you say that? You know, one fine day you'll realise that family life doesn't have to be a whole lot of people grouching at each other all the time.
KERRI	So this isn't about me getting pissed or staying out all night, or anything like that?
JANET	No. *(sits)* But I guess with your background, it's natural for you to think I'd only want to see you when I'm mad. No. I haven't come in to rouse on you. I came in to tell you a bedtime story.
KERRI	A story? What about?
JANET	It's a story about a little boat. I've just this minute made it up. Would you like to hear it?
KERRI	Nope.
JANET	Why not?
KERRI	I don't like bedtime stories.
JANET	Kerri, being neglected is one thing. Being deliberately rude and uncooperative is another.
KERRI	Tell me the story.
JANET	Alright. There was a little boat. And this little boat, it went on a long voyage. But when it was miles from land, it ran into a big storm. And since the boat didn't really know how to sail properly, the storm tossed it and turned it and pitched it around. And it very nearly sank. And then the storm was over. The boat was all damaged and broken. And it didn't know what to do or which way to go.
KERRI	Why didn't it call the coatguard?
JANET	Umm . . . It couldn't. The radio got smashed.

309

KERRI	Then it should have turned around and gone home.
JANET	It couldn't do that either. Anyone could tell that it might sink if it couldn't get help . . . then all of a sudden the little boat saw three bigger boats, all sailing together . . . And do you know who they were?
KERRI	Pirates?
JANET	No, Kerri. They weren't pirates. They were a family of boats.
KERRI	A family?
JANET	Yes, a mother boat, a father boat and a teenage daughter boat. And they'd been sailing along for years . . . oh, they went through storms too, but they got through them, partly because they helped each other. Now they saw the little boat and they wanted to help it. But before they could do that, the broken down boat, it had to do two little things. Do you know what the little boat had to do?
KERRI	Yeah. It's got to ask the bigger boats to ring the coastguard.
JANET	No, Kerri, no one's going to ring the coastguard. Now, please . . . try harder. Think. If the little boat really wants to be helped, what has the little boat got to do first?
KERRI	I don't know.
JANET	It's got to agree to obey the rules that the other boats sail under. And it's got to learn to trust the bigger boats.
KERRI	Trust them? It can't trust **them**!
JANET	Why not?
KERRI	They won't even ring the coastguard.
	(pause. JANET lights a cigarette)
JANET	Kerri, I'm really not happy with the way we've been getting on.
KERRI	Ah, right. So you did come in to rouse at me.
JANET	Yes, but not about those incidents last week. You're not pulling your weight, Kerri.
KERRI	Now I know what this is about. I don't do my chores.
JANET	It's not even that. It's the fact that I have to ask you and ask you and ask you, and even so . . .
KERRI	Ah, now I gotcha. I'm disobedient.
JANET	I could even cope with disobedience. That's not as bad as the lying! I hate the way you lie to me. It means you either don't like me or don't trust me or both. And if you don't like me, why are you here?
KERRI	Ah, so now it's my attitude! Alright, Mrs Cadzow. (she turns on her side) I'll try to have a better one tomorrow.
JANET	(stands up) Well, that just sums it up, doesn't it. You call me Mrs Cadzow. And turn away.
KERRI	Well, I'm not calling you Mum. I've got a mum. And a dad.
JANET	We're supposed to be a family for you. You treat us like a hotel.

310

(KERRI gets out of bed. She is fully dressed. She reaches for her bag which is already packed)

KERRI   Yeah? Well in that case, I'm checking out. I've been thinking about it for a while. I'm not happy either. Don't worry, I'll find somewhere else to stay. Come on, dog.

JANET   I suppose you're going to leave your room like this.

(KERRI shrugs)

You're just a dirty little hooligan.

KERRI   Yeah? And you're a really clean person, Mrs Cadzow. And your husband's a sanitary engineer. And I hope one day one of his pipes backs up, bursts . . . or something, and this whole house gets flooded with filth.

Curse music *(KERRI feels it)*

MEG   *(off — a memory)* You've got a real voodoo mouth.

JANET   *(smug)* There aren't any pipes near here.

KERRI   Oh God. I think I did it again.

(lights change)

NEWSBOY: Toxic Waste Discovered in Diamond Street! Unlucky Kingston Residents Plagued by Black Goo! Read all about it in the Courier Mail!

ACT II   Scene Nine

The share house. The living room is now covered in bodies and sleeping gear. CHRIS is standing downstage dressed for work, a cup of coffee in her hand. PETER enters.

PETER   Morning.

CHRIS   Up early.

PETER   Yeah. I wish I could have slept in. But the cold woke me up. Did you hear the noise last night?

CHRIS   Yeah.

PETER   What time did it stop?

CHRIS   About four o'clock.

PETER   Jesus.

JOAN   *(enters)* Morning.

PETER   Morning.

CHRIS   Good morning.

(a whistle offstage)

Oh, there's the mail. *(to PETER)* So, what are you doing today?

PETER   I'm going round to see my mum. I'm going to see if I can have my old room back.

CHRIS   Ah, bullshit. You're not moving out?

PETER	Yeah. I'm thinking about it. Well, it's just not working, is it? There's never any food in the house. And if there is, somebody else always eats it. People we don't know coming through the place. And every night, all these people staying over. I moved out of home to have some space of my own. A bit of privacy.
	(some of the figures on the floor begin to wake up)
SLEEPER 1	Hey, shut up, will you? I'm trying to sleep.
CHRIS	Ah, get stuffed.
SLEEPER 2	What, you reckon you own the place, do you?
PETER	Fuck off.
SLEEPER 3	*(sits up)* Look, if people don't start shutting up, and letting me sleep, somebody's going to bet a real belting . . .
PETER	Ah, Betty, shut your trap! *(he pushes her back down. She bobs up)*
SLEEPER 3	What are you doing here, Peter?
PETER	This is my bloody house!
SLEEPER 3	Oh, sorry. Look, my mate here said this was her sister's. *(she shakes the nearest sleeping figure)* Hey, mate, mate! Open your eyes. Jesus, have you stuffed up! We're in the wrong house!
	(the figure sits up. It is KERRI)
KERRI	No we're not!
CHRIS	Kerri! What are you doing here? You're supposed to be at your Cadzows.
KERRI	I pissed them off, didn't I? *(she stands up)* I'm going to the toilet. Talk to you in a minute. *(exits)*
	(JOAN enters waving an opened letter)
STEVE	*(off)* Hey, watch out, mate! There's already one arsehole on this toilet!
JOAN	Oh bullshit, bullshit, bullshit. Here. Read this!
	(gives letter to CHRIS who then passes it to PETER. Meanwhile STEVE returns)
STEVE	Alright everybody! Rise and shine! Can't hang around here, too many of you. Don't tell me about your hangover, Brian, it's your own fault for skulling the wine. Now, who's making the coffee? Who's got some money? Who's going down to the shop? Who's pissing off?
CHRIS	But that's stupid. We paid the rent last week, didn't we?
PETER	Well, I gave you my money.
CHRIS	And I gave it to Steve and Joan. Steve?
STEVE	Yeah? Oh look Chris, sorry about all the people. But they'll all be gone in a tick.
PETER	Steve . . . last week . . . we gave you all our rent money, right?
STEVE	Yeah.
PETER	Well, did you take it down to the real estate agent's or what?
STEVE	Well, see . . .

CHRIS	Well, did you?
STEVE	Well, I meant to. But see, Joannie and I had spent all our last cheque, and I knew another one was coming this week, so I thought I'd hold it over and give them like a month's rent after the weekend. It'll be alright.
JOAN	It won't be bloody alright! Read this! *(gives letter to STEVE)*
STEVE	"To Peter Smith and Christine Ryan." I didn't know your name was Ryan.
JOAN	Ah, you dickhead. Further down.
STEVE	"Failure to pay rent on time means that you have breached your leasing agreement. We therefore serve notice for you to quit the property by August the 13th, when your current installment of rent has expired." What is this?
JOAN	It's an eviction notice.
STEVE	Ah, look I'll go down Monday. I'll give them the rent then.
CHRIS	August the 13th is Monday.
JOAN	And they're coming around this morning to "negotiate the return of our bond and inspect the premises".
CHRIS	What, they're coming round now?
PETER	Yeah. We're going to have to get this place . . .

(the doorbell rings)

JOAN	That'll be them.
CHRIS	I'll get it. *(exits)*
PETER	. . . clean. We're going to have to get it clean.

(CHRIS comes back with FORSYTHE)

FORSYTHE	Not a chance in the world. You can't stay. Look, we handle the houses next door. And your neighbours have complained five times about the noise that comes out of here at night. They pay the rent. And now they're talking about moving out. I'm not having them move out because of you. And besides. The place is disgusting. The yard's full of trash. The carpet's filthy.
CHRIS	The carpet was always filthy.
FORSYTHE	The carpet stinks!
CHRIS	The carpet smelt when we moved in.
FORSYTHE	There's a dog over there, a puppy dog. And what's that puppy dog been doing? It's been doing its business on my carpet. I've been in this game a long time. I know what the carpet smells of.
JOAN	That dog . . . we've never seen it before. It just wandered in last night.
FORSYTHE	Well, who owns it?
STEVE	It's a stray. Off the streets.

(KERRI comes back in and listens)

FORSYTHE	And it's not the only one. Where do these little kids come from? What, don't they have homes to go to?

PETER	No.
CHRIS	Some don't.
JOAN	That's why we let them stay here.
FORSYTHE	Ah, now don't try to make me feel guilty. I'm a real estate agent. If there are homeless kids in Logan City, it's not my problem. That's a job for the City Council. Alright?
CHRIS	What about our bond? Do we get it back?
FORSYTHE	Sure. If the place is decent on Monday. But first of all you've got to clean up the house, pick up the rubbish in the yard, mow the lawn, take all this broken down furniture away . . . TV, couch, mattresses. Get the carpet shampooed, fix the hole in the ceiling, stick the tiles down in the kitchen . . . and fix the door.
CHRIS	The door was always broken!
	(FORSYTHE checks his notebook)
FORSYTHE	Oh, yeah, so it was. Don't worry about the door. Do all those other things . . . by Sunday . . . and you can have your bond back. Otherwise . . .
KERRI	That's right. Steal their bond and kick them out!
FORSYTHE	Business is business.
KERRI	Well, I hope yours goes broke!

faint curse music

(FORSYTHE exits. KERRI and DOG exit)

(lights change)

NEWSBOY	Extra, extra. Hooker Pty Ltd Goes to the Wall! Read all about it in The Australian!

LISA *wanders across the stage, stops, buys a newspaper and, obviously glancing at the front page, moves to the hangout set. She sits down, crumples the newspaper, adds twigs, wood, lights it. The fire glows. LOCKIE and SMITTY step out of the shadows, holding out their hands. DOG and KERRI take centre stage. KERRI mimes breaking into a car.*

DOG   *(steps to front stage and addresses audience)* Me and Kerri, we spent the next three days on the streets. We slept on benches and she stole things in order to get food. It was a dangerous way to live but she didn't care what happened to her. Well, think about it. The world's full of happy families — but hers was unhappy. It was her fault. So she must be evil, wicked . . .

curse music

           . . . bad medicine.

KERRI   ˙Shut up, dog! I'm trying to break into this car.

DOG   And then she moves in with a family. Perfect strangers. After three weeks, they can't stand her. She must be . . . repulsive . . . despicable . . .

curse music

           . . . a monster.

KERRI   Stop barking! If you don't shut up, they'll see us!

DOG   Well, maybe in some neighbourhoods even monsters can find a home. But Kerri knows she'll never find a home round here. Not in a place where even decent kids like Christine and Peter and Steve get thrown out on the streets. So it's hopeless. Why take care of yourself? I began to think there might be something I could do . . . after all, I'd been a counsellor. I decided I just had to say something.

           (KERRI jumps up, hides the coat hanger and walks quickly towards DOG)

KERRI   You stupid mongrel . . .

DOG   Kerri, don't take it so hard . . .

KERRI   I could kill you!

DOG   Go and see your mum . . . talk to her . . .

KERRI   Stop barking! *(raises coat hanger as if to strike DOG)*

           (lights down. DOG howls)

The hangout.

SMITTY   Hey, who's that coming up the path?

LOCKIE   It's Kerri Ryan. You know, from school.

DOG   But if you've decided you've had enough of boarding families, you could try an independent living program . . .

KERRI   Shut up, dog! Stop moaning and howling.

DOG   You could get young homeless allowance . . .

KERRI   Be quiet! *(she kicks him)*

LOCKIE   Wo! Scary Kerri!

KERRI   G'day everyone.

LISA   What are you doing up here? Why aren't you hanging around with your gubba mates?

KERRI   I came to talk to you, didn't I.

SMITTY   That's alright, isn't it? If she wants to come and talk.

DOG   You could get AUSSTUDY. Go back to school!

LOCKIE   And what's that thing with her?

KERRI   That? That's just a dog. Go on, piss off! Piss off, you bloody animal, take your stupid face away!

             (she hits him. DOG howls, edges away)

LISA   So, what do you want to talk about?

KERRI   I want to talk about Aboriginal culture and stuff.

LISA   Yeah? Well, what about it? Anything in particular? How much time have you got? I hope you got more than fifteen minutes.

KERRI   Yeah. I wanted to know about magical stuff. About witchcraft and putting spells on people and pointing the bone. Y'know, Dreamtime?

SMITTY   Ah, don't do it, Lisa. Too creepy for night time.

KERRI   Well in that case I'm just going to sit here drinking until I'm drunk enough to go and lie down on the railway tracks.

LISA   You're really upset about something.

SMITTY   What is it? Problems with your family or something?

KERRI   Ah, no. Look, Lisa. You got to help me. It's really important. I reckon I've got this power . . . when I lose my temper? I really get angry sometimes . . . and then I say something bad . . . and then the bad thing . . . happens.

LISA   What, like a curse?

KERRI   It's not a joke. *(pause)* I think I killed somebody.

LISA   Who?

KERRI   The guidance officer at school, Mr Hasluck.

SMITTY   Ah, bullshit you killed him! We heard about that in assembly. He had a weak heart. He'd just got out of hospital. He had an attack and he didn't have his pills with him

KERRI   I told him to drop dead. And he did!

LOCKIE   No, that's true. I heard her.

LISA	You got mad at him just before he had a heart attack? That's just coincidence.
	(pause)
KERRI	Last week I told my boarding family that I hoped their house got covered in filth.
LISA	And what happened?
KERRI	The next day they found toxic waste in their garden. And this morning I told a crooked real estate agent that his business would go bung. Well, this afternoon . . . did you see the paper? That was his company.
LISA	So?
KERRI	So I've got this power. I can ruin things just by speaking about them. Even my mum says so.
LISA	Ah, bull. In the first place, that toxic waste . . . what? You reckon you put it there? That toxic waste was put in the ground twenty years before you were even born. And that real estate company. It went broke in Sydney. You think you did that? Jeez, you've got a high opinion of yourself.
KERRI	Yeah, look. You know a lot more about Murri stuff than me, you're the expert, right? But maybe you don't know everything.
LISA	Probably don't.
KERRI	Well, maybe I should speak to your mum or dad sometime? Somebody older? Might know more.
SMITTY	Why?
KERRI	'Cause dead set. I reckon it's gotta be some old dreamtime power or something . . . and I've inherited it through my dad.
LISA	What, 'cause your dad was black, you're the Kadaicha Man? Ah, don't give me a pain. One, you haven't done all these things and two, it's got nothing to do with being a Murri. Who put that in your head?
KERRI	Lockie.
LISA	Lockie?
SMITTY	What would he know? He's not a Murri. He's a Fijian.
KERRI	Ah, bullshit. You crap artist.
LOCKIE	Sucked in, eh? But hey, Kerri. You reckon when you say bad things to people it makes those things happen, right? So you should tell me to get fucked.
KERRI	Why?
LOCKIE	'Cause I haven't had a root in ages.
KERRI	Ah, go fuck that dog.
	(LOCKIE and DOG look at each other. DOG howls)
KERRI	Ah shut up, you dumb bastard. Get out of here!
	(she picks something up and throws it at him)
LOCKIE	Jesus, Kerri. You're not very nice to your dog.

SMITTY	So are you okay now? Got it sorted out? You're just plain Kerri.
KERRI	Yeah.
SMITTY	And you don't have the power to wreck people's lives.
KERRI	But I do! When Dad left, he said I was one of the reasons. And I broke up my mum's relationship. And even my boarding family ended up hating me. It only took three weeks.
LISA	*(kinder)* Ah, what do you reckon? She's still big noting her dot. She still fancies herself.
KERRI	What's that supposed to mean?
LISA	Ah, parents say lots of things when they're mad. But kids don't break up families. They're not responsible. And it's stupid if you think you are.
KERRI	I've heard that from the social workers. I reckon it's bullshit. I reckon kids often do break up families.
LOCKIE	Look. That dog. He's your dog, right? But you don't treat it very well.
	(pause)
KERRI	No.
LOCKIE	You kick it and you throw things at it and you curse it and you say 'bad dog'. Right?
KERRI	Yeah.

It's A Dog's Life

copyright 22.8.90
Jamie Rogers, Justin Victorson,
Hugh Watson and Peter Stewart (Street Arts)

they don't want you round. It's a dog's life,

shit-ting on grass, dig-ging up plants, get-ting hit on the arse.

Just when you've got-ten used to the street, they put you in the

pound. Chorus: You're a nui- sance to soc-

i- e- ty, You're a mon- grel or a bitch. They

try to make you shut your mouth, but when you get the itch,

___ it's (BARK BARK BARK) Raise the roof

(HOWL_____) Yelp and yell (BARK BARK BARK)

Bite the leash (GROWL_____) Let's raise hell!

LOCKIE	Well, if that dog can think, it's probably convinced by now that it is a bad dog.
DOG	*(to audience — or to himself)* I feel such an idiot. If only I could talk to her, tell her it's not her fault. God, if I could only make the right sounds. *(he tries)* Sow - rund! Sow . . . Row! Row, row row row row!
KERRI	Ah, shut up! It's always barking.
LOCKIE	And if it's smart, then it can hear from the sound of your voice that you're not happy, so then it thinks, 'Oh, Kerri's unhappy and it must be my fault, I must be responsible 'cause I'm such a bad dog'.
DOG	*(as before, to the audience or himself)* If only I wasn't a dog. If I was a human being . . . if I was still her school guidance counsellor, I'd know what to say. But I'm probably a dog because I did that job so badly. It's probably all my fault.
LOCKIE	And if you refused to feed it, and kicked it out and made it homeless, it'd probably say to itself, 'I deserved that'. And the thing is, it's not a bad dog. It's just got an arsehole for an owner. You see what I mean?
KERRI	Yeah.
LOCKIE	So maybe you're not responsible. Maybe your parents are at fault, too. *(pause)* What's so funny?
KERRI	Ah, just the idea of that dog thinking. I mean, it's the stupidest animal in the whole of Australia.

It's a Dog's Life

It's a dog's life,
Stealing bones, dodging cars, being alone,
Just when you think you've found a home,
They don't want you round.

It's a dog's life,
Shitting on grass, digging up plants, getting hit on the arse,
Just when you've gotten used to the street,
They put you in the pound.

(chorus) You're a nuisance to society,
You're a mongrel or a bitch,
They try to make you shut your mouth,
But when you get the itch, it's . . .
(Bark bark bark) . . Raise the roof,
(Howl) . . . . Yelp and yell,
(Bark bark bark) . . Bite the leash,
(Growl) . . . . Let's raise hell!

END OF PLAY

OUT OF THE BLUE
(A Jailbird's Story)
by
Therese Collie

OUT OF THE BLUE was first performed by Street Arts at The Paint Factory, West End, Brisbane on 27 February 1991 with the following cast:

Toey/Officer Jemmison	Ainsley Burdell
Delma Kite	Kathryn Fisher
Kris/Officer Shepherd	Bernadette Ryan
Nancy Fine	Kaye Stevenson
Correctional Custodian Officer	Mark Shortis
Rachael McLeod	Marguerite Wesselinoff

The production team was as follows:

Playwright	Therese Collie
Director/Dramaturg	Hilary Beaton
Musical Director/Sound design	Mark Shortis
Designer/Set Construction	Gavan Fenelon
Production Manager	Bernard Lewis
Costume	Kathryn Porrill
Stage Manager/Lighting	Bernard Lewis
Construction Assistant	Mark Hetherington
Lighting Assistant	Philip Robinson
Assistant to the Director	Lisa Smith*
Co-ordinator/Publicity	Kara Miller
Office Manager	Pauline Atkinson
Graphics	Gavan Fenelon
Photography	Fiora Sacco

* Seconded from QUT Kelvin Grove B.A. (Drama)

A women's prison. The recreation room in medium/minimum security. There is a television set in one corner, blue plastic armchairs, an institutional coffee table. It is 4 o'clock on a rainy Monday afternoon in summer.

DELMA, *a 35 year old Murri, sits beside the TV. NANCY, a 63 year old lady, is knitting. TOEY, a 19 year old street kid, sits with her feet on the table, smoking a rollie. RACHAEL, a 24 year old Murri, is writing a letter. SHEPHERD, a prison officer, is in the observation room behind the T.V. The women are bored.*

RACHAEL	Toey! Get your feet off the table! You don't want to attract her attention!
	(TOEY does as she's told slowly, looking towards the P.O. and ashing flamboyantly on the floor)
	Here! Put your ash in here!
	(RACHAEL makes a little ashtray out of one of her sheets of writing paper. TOEY takes it and puts it on her head. RACHAEL laughs. NANCY smiles nervously. TOEY bows her head, the ashtray drops on the table and she ashes in it. She pushes it aside and puts her feet back on the table)
	Toey!
TOEY	Rachael? *(pause)* What?
	(RACHAEL puts her feet on the table. TOEY understands and takes her feet off the table, as does RACHAEL)
	I'm bored stupid!
RACHAEL	In order to live freely, you must first of all sacrifice boredom.
TOEY	Give us a break!
NANCY	Why don't you do some knitting?
RACHAEL	Give me a poem, then.
TOEY	Rain, rain, go away, Come again another day, 'Cause me and Ray want to play. How's that?
RACHAEL	No, one of your hot love poems . . . for my soul mate in Borallon.
NANCY	I didn't know you had a boyfriend.
TOEY	Who's that?
RACHAEL	You know.
TOEY	I forget.
RACHAEL	Tony.
TOEY	Right. Okay. That's easy. Oh Tone, you make me groan 'Cause you've got a great big —
RACHAEL	No, come on, one of your romantic ones!
TOEY	Oh Tone, I'm all alone I need you by my side

	When I go to sleep at night There is no place to hide. No! Your love is like a tide.
RACHAEL	That's great, Toey! Can you say it again slowly?
TOEY	When I go to sleep at night . . . Your love is . . . like a tide.
RACHAEL	*(with difficulty)* Your love . . . is like . . . a tide. Yeah?
TOEY	I see your face in my dreams Your hair of brown, your eyes of blue I feel your hands upon —
RACHAEL	Brown. His eyes are brown. Like his hair.
TOEY	Fuck!
NANCY	*(starts, prudishly, making a sound)* Tut!
TOEY	I see your face in my dreams Your hair and eyes of brown I feel your hands upon my skin . . . brown . . . frown . . . drown . . . down They stroke me up and down.
RACHAEL	Up . . . and . . . down.
TOEY	And I am like a fire Burning in my slot —
NANCY	I wish you "ladies" wouldn't use such foul language!
TOEY	What do you fucking mean?
NANCY	It's an insult in the face of God, using words like that.
TOEY	Like what?
NANCY	Like . . . in your . . . poem . . . about burning in your . . . you know.
	(RACHAEL *and* TOEY *start laughing and even* DELMA *smiles*)
RACHAEL	Burning in my "you know"?
	(more giggles)
NANCY	Yes, well, it's not proper!
RACHAEL	What do you think a slot, I mean a "you-know" is. Nancy?
NANCY	*(unsure)* You know as well as I do, Rachael.
RACHAEL	No, I don't know. Do you know, Toey?
TOEY	No, I don't know. I used to know but.
RACHAEL	Did you? I don't think I ever did.
TOEY	Yeah, but I forgot, you know.
RACHAEL	Yeah, I know. They take your brains away when you come in here.
NANCY	That's obvious!
TOEY	You oughter know!
DELMA	Nancy, a slot is a cell.

(the phone in the observation room starts ringing)

NANCY	Thank you, Delma.
RACHAEL	*(getting up)* Do you want a cup of coffee, Delma?
DELMA	Yes, thank you. *(pause)* Ray? Can I have three sugar?
RACHAEL	Good go!
NANCY	*(to DELMA)* Shouldn't you use saccharine with your condition?

(RACHAEL and TOEY pull faces behind NANCY's back)

DELMA	I got a sweet tooth. I don't care what the doctor says.
NANCY	I just think you should look after yourself.
DELMA	*(together)* Well, you know what they say about diabetics, Nancy.
RACHAEL	*(together)* Why don't you mind your own business!

(NANCY starts to roll a cigarette — she is not practiced)

RACHAEL	You want a coffee, Toey?
TOEY	Why not? *(she hops up and looks out)* Is it time for medication?

(there is no response. She sits down)

NANCY	How come you give **them** your coffee?
RACHAEL	How come you think you're better than us?
NANCY	You owe me a coffee.
RACHAEL	I don't owe you anything, not even the time of day.

(RACHAEL leaves, taking NANCY's cup)

NANCY	*(disconcerted)* Why doesn't she answer the blasted phone?
TOEY	'Cause she's a dickhead, that's why!

(the phone finally stops ringing. RACHAEL comes back with plastic cups of coffee for everyone. DELMA and TOEY start rolling their own. NANCY is still having difficulty rolling hers and tries to hide it without success)

RACHAEL	Here! Have one of "Rachael's Tailor-Mades".

(RACHAEL offers NANCY a Winfield packet of rolled fags)

NANCY	Thank you, Rachael.

(NANCY lights hers and RACHAEL's fags. TOEY lights hers and DELMA's. TOEY hops up again and looks out)

TOEY	Is it time for medication, yet?

(there is no response. She sits down. While the women enjoy their fags and coffee the TV sound comes up and above it someone's rock box blares out —)

> *(Milli Vanilli)* 'Blame it on the rain
> Blame it on the rain that was falling, falling
> Blame it on the stars that shined at night
> Whatever you do, don't put the blame on you
> Blame it on the rain, yeah, yeah.'

DELMA	I heard Kris is coming up here. You know, that one from Max.
TOEY	*(together)* Shit!
NANCY	*(together)* Who's she?
RACHAEL	*(together)* Who told you that?
DELMA	Oh, you know, a certain little bird.
RACHAEL	It's a rumour, just another bloody rumour!
DELMA	Well, they reckon.
NANCY	*(together)* Who is she?
RACHAEL	*(together)* Aw shit! What're we gunna do?
TOEY	I'm gunna kill myself.
RACHAEL	What's the good of that? Where will that get you?
TOEY	Dead. That's where it'll get me. And that's better than here.
NANCY	*(together)* Who is Kris?
RACHAEL	*(together)* When's she coming?
DELMA	Maybe tomorrow.
NANCY	Who is this girl?
RACHAEL	Girl! She's not a girl! She's a monster, a top dog, a toughie, a heavy! We'll be like lambs to the slaughter!
TOEY	Lame ducks on the water.
RACHAEL	I can't stand it! They're bullies, rock apes! I've been through this before! They get at you and at you . . .
NANCY	Well, if we mind our own business, trust in —
RACHAEL	Crap! She's the sort that eats people like you for breakfast!
TOEY	With milk and sugar.
NANCY	We could always talk to one of the nice officers. Jemmy, maybe or the manager —
RACHAEL	*(together)* No way, Jose!
TOEY	*(together)* I'm not a crawling cunt!
DELMA	They put you on the dog?
NANCY	On the dog?
RACHAEL	On the maggot. Your life wouldn't be worth living. No one talks to you.
TOEY	They put rats' tails in your soup!
DELMA	Pour hot water on you. I seen that.
RACHAEL	The screws wouldn't do anything about it, anyway! They're just as scared as us.
NANCY	*(together)* Well, I'm not going to let her upset *me*!
TOEY	*(together)* When's fucking medication?
NANCY	Don't swear, Lily!
TOEY	Don't call me Lily!
RACHAEL	That's all right for you! You'll be out in a few weeks!

TOEY	*(together)* Praise the Lord!
NANCY	*(together)* If I get parole.
RACHAEL	And Toey can spit at them and do her thing, but I can't. I try to do the right thing, to be . . . Christian like you, Nancy . . . but I can't take it anymore! And I've got nine more bloody months.
SHEPHERD	Medication! Medication! Come on! It's already after 4.30. Time for medication!
	(TOEY is first out the door. NANCY starts picking up the cups as DELMA pats RACHAEL)
NANCY	How long have you got, Delma?
	(DELMA exits)
RACHAEL	Life.

ACT I   Scene Two

Monday night, 9 p.m. It is still raining. Silhouette of the women lining up to go into their cells. They are chatting, laughing and wrestling with each other before being locked in for the night.

SHEPHERD	Nine o'clock! Lock up! Come on, you girls! Let's go! Lock up time! Nine o'clock!
RACHAEL	I don't want to go to bed!
NANCY	I never imagined the food would be so bad.
TOEY	Tell me a story, Ray!
RACHAEL	"Carrie" scared the shit out of me!
DELMA	It's not that bad.
TOEY	*(chanting)* You promised me, You said you would.
NANCY	It's just like boarding school! Soggy sauces!
DELMA	I like 'em.
TOEY	*(chanting)* You gotta give in so I'll be good Tell me a story and then I'll go to bed!
RACHAEL	No way, Jose!
TOEY	I'll use my psycho-kinetic powers on you! *(she lets out a high pitched sound)*
RACHAEL	Look out!
NANCY	Don't be silly, Lily!
DELMA	She alright. Let her go!
RACHAEL	Okay! Okay! Once upon a time there was a girl who looked like a mouse.
	(TOEY starts making mouse sounds as she goes into her cell)
	Get out of here, Minnie!

DELMA	She an eggroll, that one!
NANCY	I'm going to write and complain. It's not good for my health.
SHEPHERD	Look, lay off the letters, Fine, and you might get what you want.
RACHAEL	Yeah, a sandwich short of a picnic —
DELMA	A stubby short of a six-pack —
RACHAEL	A brick short of a load. See yas!
	(RACHAEL *goes into her cell*)
NANCY	The manager promised me ice-cream, too!
DELMA	Yeah, I'm supposed to have ice-cream for me sugar levels, but —
NANCY	I'm going to write and complain. It's just not good enough!
	(NANCY *goes into her cell*)
DELMA	I'm glad when it's lock up time.
SHEPHERD	I know what you mean, Kite.

(DELMA's *door slams shut. SFX: Keys rattling. The key turns in the lock three times. This sequence happens four times.*

Lights up on the five cells side by side. In each cell is a bed with a blanket, a toilet and a shower. From r. to l. are TOEY, RACHAEL, an empty cell, NANCY, and DELMA. The lights are low.

What follows is a sequence of stylized movements that reflect the surreal nature of the lack of privacy in prison. The women look out through the small viewing window in the door. Satisfied no prison officers are around, they begin to undress)

TOEY	Officer approaching!
RACHAEL	Officer approaching!
NANCY	Officer approaching!
DELMA	Officer approaching!

(*the women jump into bed under the blanket. SHEPHERD walks past. Footsteps are heard echoing past the cells, keys rattling. The women undress, go to the shower and look out through the small viewing window in the shower wall. They turn on the showers; sound of gushing water)*

DELMA	Psst! Screw!
NANCY	Screw on landing!
TOEY	Officer on landing!
RACHAEL	Screw approaching!

(*the women sit in the corner of the showers. SHEPHERD walks past. Footsteps are heardechoing past the cells, keys rattling)*

TOEY	Bitch! She'll get hers!

(*the women turn off the showers. They put their pyjamas on. NANCY and RACHAEL get writing paper and pen. TOEY gets a sci-fi book and DELMA gets her harmonica. They sit on the toilet. DELMA plays softly)*

NANCY   (writing) Medium Security, Women's Correctional Centre. To the Manager, Women's Correctional Centre. Dear Sir, (Oh Lord, give me strength.) It has come to my attention (not to mention my bowels) that the food at the Women's Correctional Centre has deteriorated by 75% in the last week. ("Vengeance is mine" saith the Lord!) It is cooked badly and there is a distinct absence of potatoes, pumpkins and carrots. I am still waiting for my ice-cream once a week! (I'm still waiting for a letter, too.) Oh Brian, where is the love you said would ever be mine? I know you're spent and exhausted. (Must see the Chaplain tomorrow. See if she can arrange someone to visit him.) I do so miss our going to Church on Sundays. How is dear Mrs Marsh? (Oh dear, what am I doing?)

(she crosses out the sentences she wrote to Brian)

(she reads) "I am still waiting for my ice-cream once a week! (writes) If Christ could feed five thousand on five loaves and two fishes, can you not feed a hundred lost women? (If only I could hear from you. And Vera, Joan, Suzanne, Marjorie, Sam . . . I haven't felt this lonely since I was sent to boarding school when I was . . . seven and a half. Oh God, I hope this Kris doesn't terrorise me! I need something to calm me down . . . Rohypnol . . . Rohypnol . . . Oh Brian, I forgive you for not being the man I wanted you to be! Oh Brian, why have you forsaken me?)

DELMA   Are you alright in there, Mum?

NANCY   Huh? Yes, dear. (writing) Whilst I realise there are reasons . . . reasons why . . . you can't visit me. You say you can't handle it yet. You say you would break down. I know my house is . . . in a mess . . .

(she realises she has written to Brian again and screws up the letter)

It was your father's wish that you would marry a strong woman. I am not strong enough. I am broken down, too. (she weeps)

TOEY   Male on landing!

RACHAEL   Male on landing!

DELMA   Male on landing!

(TOEY, RACHAEL and DELMA grab toilet paper. It spills off the roll, they can't tear it properly in their haste)

TOEY   Oh shit!

RACHAEL   Oh shit!

DELMA   Oh goona!

(they get caught up in the toilet paper. Sounds of flushing, footsteps, keys. The women are a mess but they adopts seriously innocent expressions as the male officer passes. The footsteps die away.

Lights fade. A harmonica bridge. A gate slams. It is 3 a.m.)

TOEY   Wish they'd learn to shut the gate quietly, arseholes.

(a train whistle is heard)

RACHAEL   What was that?

TOEY   Just a train.

RACHAEL	I'm going mad. I thought I murdered someone.
TOEY	Just so long as it wasn't me.
RACHAEL	No, I mean it, Toey. I never felt like this before.
TOEY	The rain gets you down.
RACHAEL	Yeah, and this heavy coming on top.
TOEY	Just ignore her. Hey, you heard this one? "Spring is sprung! The grass is riz! I wonder where the boydies is? The little boyds is on the wing. Why, how absoyd! We always hoyd the little wings was on the boyd!"
RACHAEL	I guess I'm not the only bird who can't fly.
TOEY	We'll just ignore her, Ray.

ACT I   Scene Three

A bell rings, clanging doors.

SHEPHERD	Breakfast! Seven a.m. Breakfast! Let's go!
	(the women come out of their cells like horses out of the barrier. RACHAEL keeps up a racing commentary as they race to the dining area.
	Lights up on a table and six chairs in the dining area beside the rec. room. It is Tuesday, 7 a.m. The sun is shining. The women are sitting, TOEY and RACHAEL one side, DELMA the other. TOEY, whose plastic bowl — all the bowls, cups and plates are plastic — is piled high with Weet-Bix, is shovelling it in at a rate of knots. NANCY enters with an empty lunch box)
NANCY	Who took my fruit?
	(the women ignore her)
	Who took my fruit?
TOEY	You ate it. Don't you remember?
NANCY	No. I didn't. Did I?
DELMA	Sit down, luvey!
NANCY	It was in the fridge.
TOEY	How long was it in for?
NANCY	I want to know who stole my apple.
TOEY	You've been hanging on to it for a fucking week!
NANCY	I bought it!
DELMA	You can order some more today, Nancy.
NANCY	It cost me a dollar!
DELMA	Damn it, Nancy, some women got no money! Now, sit down!

NANCY	(sitting) That's not why they do it, Delma. I know why they do it. (she watches TOEY eat) Even Delma has better manners than you!
TOEY	(together) This isn't the fucking Hilton!
DELMA	(together) I beg your pardon.
NANCY	Oh, you know I didn't mean that!
DELMA	Yeah, I know what you mean.

(RACHAEL pours hot water into the cups — the same tea bag is used four times)

NANCY	Do you have any papers, Rachael?

(RACHAEL gets some cigarette papers from her tobacco pouch)

TOEY	We get our buy-ups today you know, Nancy!
DELMA	If they don't go walkabout.
NANCY	Thank you, Ray.
TOEY	She bought them you know, Nancy. They cost her 30 cents a packet.
NANCY	When I read about young people who throw their lives away on drugs, I think, what a waste!
TOEY	Shit, it must be hard being a fucking saint!
NANCY	(smiles) You always raise the tone of the place, Lily!
TOEY	Don't call me fucking —
RACHAEL	Hey, did I tell you about when we're locked in the other night? I hear this noise — SKRR! SKRR! SKRR! I'm lying there with me blanket up to me chin. And first I think it's a cockroach. Then me imagination takes over and it's a mouse, then it's a rat! I can't stand mice and rats! So I get out of bed and I see it. It's a cockroach, a big one, just about as big as a mouse. I think of calling the screw, but think that's stupid.

So I get the bathmat and give it a big thump! I don't like to hit them with me shoe, 'cause their guts go everywhere. So it's lying on its back with its legs in the air. Dead, I think . . . and while I'm sitting there watching it, it rolls over onto its feet and starts walking towards me. So I hit it with the bathmat again. WHAM!! And it's dead. I scoop it up with a bit of paper and chuck it in the bin.

I decide to make myself a cup of coffee then, 'cause I'm awake. I can't understand why I get so many cockroaches — I must be over a drain or something. Anyway, I'm sitting on me bed, drinking me coffee, when I hear the sound again — SKRR! SKRR! SKRR! — and there's the cockroach come back to life, peeping over the edge of the bin. I scream and drop me coffee all over meself and me bed! Coffee everywhere!!

(the women are laughing and interjecting during RACHAEL's storytelling. They forget their quarrels for the time being. KRIS, a broad strong woman with tatts enters behind RACHAEL. The others stop laughing and stare at her. RACHAEL's story peters out)

Then this Rambo . . . of a cockroach . . . crawls . . .

(she turns to stare at KRIS, too. KRIS holds their eyes, then slowly smiles. DELMA and TOEY look away. NANCY smiles nervously. RACHAEL turns back and finishes her story quickly)

Yeah, it crawls over the edge of the bin, down the side, takes six steps along the floor and dies.

(KRIS laughs. Silence)

KRIS   So . . . who shit in your cornflakes? Have you all got P.M.T.?

(she looks at her hand and licks her index finger)

Hmm. I'll just check my appointment book. Yes, here it is! Tuesday morning, up top, welcoming party for Kris. That's me. So, who are you? Cat's got your tongue?

RACHAEL   I'm Rachael. This is Toey and —

NANCY   I'm Nancy and I don't have P.M.T.

KRIS   You don't have Prison Mental Trauma? (RACHEL giggles) Hmm. Maybe up top **is** really different.

RACHAEL   Heard about you.

KRIS   What?

RACHAEL   Nothing.

KRIS   Do you believe everything you hear?

DELMA   Believe none of what you hear and half of what you see.

KRIS   You must be Delma.

DELMA   How're the Woosup girls?

KRIS   Stacy's out on three years parole.

DELMA   No! True?

KRIS   Yeah, it was a surprise to everyone. Maybe she dobbed someone in to the cops.

NANCY   I'd like that kind of surprise.

KRIS   What's your lag?

NANCY   Three months.

KRIS   What's your bottom?

NANCY   Six weeks, but I'm trying to get parole earlier. I've —

KRIS   You're laughing, lady.

RACHAEL   Yeah, I got no bottom.

DELMA   There some pretty big bottoms.

KRIS & TOEY   (together) You can say that again!

(TOEY is disturbed)

VOICE   (off) Cutlery girl! Cutlery girl! Table one!

(NANCY collects the cutlery)

NANCY	One—two—three—four.
TOEY	Life inside's a fucking bore.
RACHAEL	In order for one to live freely, you must first of all sacrifice boredom.
TOEY	Where did you get that? Off a toilet wall?
	(NANCY *leaves.* DELMA *and* TOEY *half-heartedly collect the other things.* TOEY *whispers to* RACHAEL. DELMA *leaves.* KRIS *stands in* TOEY's *way.* TOEY *is confused.* KRIS *steps aside and* TOEY *leaves)*
PRISON OFFICER	*(off)* Table two!
PRISONER	*(off)* One—two—three—four.
KRIS	I can't see my mates no more.
PRISON OFFICER	*(off)* Table three!
PRISONER	*(off)* One—two—three—four, *etc.*
RACHAEL	You can't do anything about that.
KRIS	Why not?
RACHAEL	You commit the crime, you do the time!
KRIS	So, what do you girls "up top" do for a good time?
RACHAEL	Nothin' much.
KRIS	Pieces of meat! Pieces of meat!
RACHAEL	What?
KRIS	You don't have to do dead time.
JEMMY	*(off)* Muster! Muster!
	(a bell rings)
	(off) Muster! Muster!
	*(*KRIS *and* RACHAEL *are joined by* NANCY *and* DELMA. *They line up in front of the rec. room)*
NANCY	That's why I can only do light duties. I wrote to the manager and told him in no uncertain terms that it's just not good enough. I'm not one to complain, Delma, as you know, but there are certain foods that I must have for my bad heart.
RACHAEL	Poo! It's not your heart that's bad, bad fart!
NANCY	All we ever get is cake, crumble and custard!
	(Prison Officer Base Grade JEMMISON — JEMMY *[played by* TOEY] — comes in with a clipboard and her arm in a sling. She trips. The women laugh good-humouredly. They all like* JEMMY)
RACHAEL	Lay off the floor, Jemmy! We gotta clean that!
JEMMY	It's not my fault!
	*(*KRIS *circles* JEMMY)
KRIS	Then whose fault is it?
RACHAEL	She musta had an unstable childhood!

334

KRIS	No, not Jemmy. Shepherd maybe, but not our Jemmy. She's never had to mistrust anyone . . . yet.
RACHAEL	Look! She's going red!
JEMMY	Alright! Alright! Give us a break!
DELMA	What, the other one?
	(the women laugh. JEMMY smiles uncomprehendingly)
JEMMY	When you hear your name, take one step over the line and answer your name correctly.
	(DELMA and RACHAEL repeat the last part of the sentence with JEMMY)
RACHAEL	And try not to fall over, please girls!
JEMMY	That's enough, McLeod!
RACHAEL	Didn't you get any last night, Jemmy?
JEMMY	Wouldn't you like to know!
DELMA	*(together)* Ooh . . .
NANCY	*(together)* Who's the poor fellow?
RACHAEL	*(together)* What's your boyfriend gunna say?
JEMMY	Okay Rachael.
RACHAEL	Sorry, Miss.
JEMMY	Fine!
NANCY	Here, Officer Jemmison!
JEMMY	Kite!
DELMA	Huh?
JEMMY	Kite!
DELMA	Yes, Miss.
JEMMY	McLeod!
RACHAEL	Present, Miss.
JEMMY	Mistle! Mistle! Where's Toey?
RACHAEL	*(worried)* She's on holiday.
KRIS	Yes, she said to start the excitement without her.
JEMMY	Shit!
KRIS	It's alright. The chief wanted to see her.
	(RACHAEL and NANCY look questioningly at each other)
JEMMY	Oh good. What're you doing here?
KRIS	I'm a dangerous criminal, but you can call me Kris.
JEMMY	I know who you are, Margaret. I mean, why are you here?
KRIS	Didn't they tell you?
JEMMY	Tell me what?
KRIS	Gee, that's not like Officer Shepherd.

JEMMY	Well, I've just come on.
KRIS	*(to the others)* They don't tell the new ones anything, do they? Except to do as they're told. And to forget everything they've learnt. So, what have you learnt?
JEMMY	Put a sock in it will you, Canto?
KRIS	What if I don't? Will you send me back to Max?
JEMMY	No, I'll growl at you!
KRIS	Yeah, after you bash me up!
JEMMY	That's right. Okay. There's a rule from the manager before you go to duties.
KRIS & RACHAEL	*(sarcastically)* Oh, goody!
JEMMY	I don't think you girls will be too happy when you hear what it is.
	(the women laugh. Sarcasm goes over JEMMY's head)
	Rule 8 A. To maintain the order and discipline of the prison, female prisoners shall not engage in behaviour that could be interpreted as having sexual overtones. 'Sexual overtones' is caressing and/or stimulating body contact between prisoners; prolonged hugging; holding hands; full mouth kissing; sitting more than one to a chair. Prisoners are to be reprimanded and/or breached for this behaviour.
RACHAEL	*(together)* What does he think he's fucking doing?
NANCY	*(together)* That's the most ridiculous thing I ever heard!
DELMA	*(together)* I'm sick of your rules! I'm going now.
JEMMY	Look, I know it sounds bad —
RACHAEL	Bad?
KRIS	It's a violation of our human rights!
DELMA	*(to JEMMY)* Another one.
KRIS	You'll have to breach all of us. And **then** you'll have to put all our mattresses in the corridor! It'll be against health regulations —
RACHAEL	Fire regulations —
DELMA	Hygiene —
JEMMY	I'm sure it won't come to that —
KRIS	You mean you're not going to enforce it?
	(JEMMY does not respond)
	You won't last long, sweetheart!
JEMMY	I think you'll find that a lot of us —
KRIS	You mean we can't do this.
	(KRIS links arms with DELMA)
RACHAEL	We can't do this.
	(RACHAEL flings her arm around NANCY's shoulders)

DELMA	Or this.
	(DELMA joins in)
NANCY	Or this.
	(NANCY joins in. The positions are getting more ridiculous)
KRIS	Or this.
	(KRIS culminates with the audacious act of kissing JEMMY. The women, including JEMMY, laugh)
JEMMY	Get out of here, you big galoot! Off to work now, girls! *(to KRIS)* You come with me.
	(JEMMY leaves. The women are laughing uncontrollably)
NANCY	Did you see the look on her face!
DELMA	I'd like to see her kiss Shepherd!
NANCY	I don't think she's into bestiality!
	(RACHAEL looks at KRIS who shrugs her shoulders with mock humility)
	(a bell rings)
VOICES	*(off)* Work duties! Tailor shop! Outside nursery! Inside garden! Kitchen! Laundry! Book-binding! Reception! To your work areas!
	(the women leave)
DELMA	Where's Toey?
RACHAEL	Playing tennis.

Prison Officer Conversation (1)

SHEPHERD *and* JEMMY *are looking at their work roster.*

SHEPHERD	I hear congratulations are in order.
JEMMY	What, did I do something right?
SHEPHERD	No, your engagement.
JEMMY	Oh, that.
SHEPHERD	Well, don't get too excited.
JEMMY	No, it's just, well . . . we had a date tonight, so I changed my shift to suit him and now he says he can't come!
SHEPHERD	*(lightly)* Men are bastards.
JEMMY	Hmm. Now I need to swap Saturday night.
SHEPHERD	I'll do it.
JEMMY	Thanks. I'll do Monday morning for you. Okay?
SHEPHERD	Monday morning . . . sure.
JEMMY	Turner's going on stress leave.
SHEPHERD	Can't handle the pace, hey?

JEMMY	They're looking for people to do her shifts. They should get someone in to replace her.
SHEPHERD	Fine by me. I'll get time and a half.
JEMMY	I don't know how you do it. I threw my alarm clock into the wall this morning.
SHEPHERD	And that's how you broke your arm?
JEMMY	It's just sprained.
SHEPHERD	You want to be careful about things like that.
JEMMY	What do you mean?
SHEPHERD	They'll take advantage of you.

ACT I   Scene Four

It is eleven o'clock. RACHAEL is working in the inside garden, downstage of the dining area. NANCY and DELMA are sitting on white plastic garden chairs on the other side of the garden, downstage of the rec. room. DELMA is asleep in the sun and NANCY is knitting. RACHAEL is digging the soil with a mattock. Her rhythmic movement echoes her enjoyment of working outside. The sound of crows is heard.

RACHAEL	Good. Great. The sun on me skin. The wooden handle in me hands. Like to feel me muscles. Smell the earth when I break it. Dig deep. Feel the swing up and down.
NANCY	She's good with her hands, Rachael.
DELMA	She in limbo, that girl.
RACHAEL	Feel close to Pop when I'm gardening. I suppose 'cause he was a groundsman. For three schools. Pop reckons my mother was beautiful, very black, almost purple. I'm the image of her, Pop says. Only saw her once when I was eleven. She was an alcoholic. She would've been nicer than my stepmother. **She** made me sit at the back of the church so people wouldn't say, 'Is she your child, too?' Pop didn't see what was happening. He didn't love me. So I left home at thirteen. Hung round the streets with the other kids. My mother would've taken me fishing. We'd sit on the wharf jagging for sardines. Hook 'em up. Catch big fish. Flashing in the sun —

(TOEY runs in. RACHAEL is startled)

TOEY	Look at that bloke on the wall next door! He's got no clothes on!

(RACHAEL, NANCY and DELMA look up)

RACHAEL	Where?
TOEY	Stand sideways! We can't see it!

(DELMA and NANCY whistle and shout)

RACHAEL	Bullshit! Stop carrying on and come and help me!
TOEY	I can't.
RACHAEL	Why can't you?

TOEY	'Cause I can't!
RACHAEL	What's that supposed to mean?
TOEY	It's supposed to mean I can't do what I want to do.
RACHAEL	So what do you want to do?
TOEY	I dunno.
RACHAEL	Good one, Toey.
	(RACHAEL *continues digging*)
NANCY	You should've seen Kris on muster, Lily. She was very good.
RACHAEL	She stuck up for you and everything.
TOEY	Yeah, I heard.
NANCY	Where were you?
TOEY	I was playing tennis, but me partner didn't show up.
RACHAEL	And then, when Jemmy read out that stupid rule —
TOEY	I heard alright!
RACHAEL	Alright! You don't have to bite me head off! Just 'cause you didn't score.
TOEY	Anyway, anyone can put one over Jemmy! She's an eggroll.
RACHAEL	Yeah, a snag short of a barbie.
TOEY	A drunk short of a party.
RACHAEL	A bikkie short of —
	(RACHAEL *sees* KRIS *enter near* DELMA *and* NANCY)
	Hi, Kris. How're you going?
TOEY	Don't suck!
KRIS	I'm going . . . I'm going . . . to sleep. Wherever I look, I see white walls.
RACHAEL	Yeah, I know the problem.
	(KRIS *lies down on her back on the grass*)
KRIS	I think I've got prison blindness. Wait a minute! *(with pleasure)* Aah!
RACHAEL	What is it?
KRIS	Blue. Beautiful blue. Come and have a look.
	(RACHAEL *lies down*)
RACHAEL	Yeah.
KRIS	Do you like the sea? When I was working on the boats, I used to do this. The sky and me staring at the sea.
RACHAEL	You don't know what you've got 'til it's gone.
TOEY	Jesus!
	(RACHAEL *touches* KRIS)
	Hey!
RACHAEL	What's eating you?

TOEY	Rule eight, ey?!
KRIS	Rules are made to be broken.
TOEY	Yeah, we've noticed.
RACHAEL	If you love someone, set them free.
TOEY	If they come back, check for V.D.
NANCY	I feel like a child in here. Nothing to do but do as you're told.
KRIS	Look at the birds.
	(everyone stops. Everyone looks up)
DELMA	Pelicans.
TOEY	What a curious bird is the pelican, His bill holds more than his belly can.
KRIS	You know, I think something wonderful is going to happen. I don't know what it is, but it's wonderful.
	(TOEY is not convinced)
	(sparrows chirping. A bell rings)
VOICE	*(off)* Lunch! 11.30. Come on, you girls! Lunchtime! Let's go!

ACT I Scene Five

The rec. room about 2 p.m. NANCY is knitting. DELMA is eating bread and jam and flicking through a women's magazine. RACHAEL is watching "Days of Our Lives" on TV, saying the lines before they happen.

NANCY	My husband doesn't know how I can watch Days of Our Lives. Did you watch it at home, Delma?
DELMA	No. At my sister's place.
NANCY	Did I tell you I received a letter from Brian today?
DELMA	How is he?
NANCY	It's his first one. He wants me to send a letter to the solicitors. It must be about my parole. I hope everything's alright. He didn't want to say too much because I told him the officers read your letters. He couldn't believe it, the poor —
RACHAEL	Shut up!
DELMA	It's only an ad, Ray.
NANCY	*(softly)* He couldn't believe that they stripsearch us after visitors either!
	(KRIS enters with pen and paper)
KRIS	I don't know how you can watch that show. It's chewing gum for the brain!
	(KRIS turns the TV off)
RACHAEL	Hey! I was watching that!
KRIS	Shouldn't you be in the garden?

340

RACHAEL	Mind your own business!
KRIS	You can practically say the lines before them!
RACHAEL	So?
KRIS	So don't be a deadhead, Ray!
RACHAEL	I'll be whatever I want!
KRIS	Systematic slave!
RACHAEL	What?
KRIS	"Your heads swing from side to side Your minds are blank and your eyes are wide What have you left but to be My Systematic Slaves."

(RACHAEL switches the TV back on — (closing music for "Days of Our Lives")

RACHAEL	Aw shit! Now I don't know what's happened to Calliope.
KRIS	Everyone's fucking everyone else! That's all you need to know!
RACHAEL	She just had a car accident.
KRIS	Want to read my poem, Delma?

(DELMA shakes her head at KRIS)

RACHAEL	The show could've snuffed her!
KRIS	No, it's okay. I don't mind. Here you are.

(KRIS tries to give her poem to DELMA)

NANCY	She can't.
KRIS	But you're reading that —
DELMA	I just look at the pictures.
KRIS	Oh, look how fat Ryan O'Neal's got!
RACHAEL	I reckon they're gunna cark her.
DELMA	He's spread right across the page!
NANCY	*(to DELMA)* You should be careful you don't put on too much weight, luvey. I know I have to watch myself in here, especially with my bad heart.
RACHAEL	Yous don't care if Calliope's dead!

(KRIS laughs, but stops when she sees RACHAEL is serious. RACHAEL sulks)

DELMA	Nancy, you know I went out on L.O.A., you know?
NANCY	Leave of absence, yes. When was it?
DELMA	I can't remember.
NANCY	Yes, Friday night. You went to see your family.
DELMA	It was really nice. My little sister was there. It was really, really good.

(DELMA is hugging herself, remembering how good it was)

NANCY	That must've been nice, dear.
DELMA	Yeah, it was really nice. And you know what she told me? She said, 'Don't you worry 'bout your kids 'cause we're looking after 'em'. She said, 'Don't you worry about Rodney, you just . . . you know . . .
NANCY	Yes, I know.
	(pause)
KRIS	Look, I know I'm losing my memory in here but weren't you gunna tell us something else, Delma?
DELMA	Huh?
KRIS	About your weight?
DELMA	*(laughing)* Oh yeah. When I went to go out, I found I was too big for my old clothes. I looked that funny, I bust out laughing! Shame! But a nice lady give me some other ones.
NANCY	I had a bit of trouble with my clothes fitting when I came in. I mean, what do you do with a 63 year old size twelve shoulders to waist and a size sixteen to eighteen bottom?
KRIS	They don't worry 'bout that! They give you some ugly clothes that are about six sizes too big for you and you walk in and everybody watches you and you feel like —
	(she caves her chest in)
	"Uhh! Where am I?"
NANCY	Be that as it may. I always wanted a denim jacket but I always thought I was too old to wear one. But I think I look rather good now with my denim hip jeans, green check blouse and denim jacket! Clothes maketh the woman!
KRIS	Give us a twirl, Nancy!
NANCY	Oh no, I couldn't!
	(KRIS gets up to act out the part)
KRIS	And now modelling the hottest fashions from inside the cold-hole — Nancy Fine, the Lady from Boggo Boutique!
	(RACHAEL laughs)
DELMA	Go on, Nancy!
NANCY	I feel stupid . . .
KRIS	Come on! Nancy is wearing a lovely ensemble, tailor-made to fit her every prison need from bowing to scraping. These versatile garments are long-lasting for lifers and up-to-date for girls who come and go.And come and go and come and go . . . We call it — the Recidivists' Range! Thanks to The Lady!
	(RACHAEL claps and turns to DELMA as JEMMY enters)
RACHAEL	And now . . .
DELMA	Oh no you don't. I too shame.
NANCY	I'll help you, dear.

(NANCY *drags* DELMA *up who is very shy but laughing*)

RACHAEL   And now in our winter stock we have red tracksuits, modelled by the woman who never sleeps —

KRIS   The owl of C Block . . . Delma!

RACHAEL   Doesn't she look like one of Santa's little helpers? Everyone who's anyone is wearing them on the slopes this year.

KRIS   Thank you, Owl!

(they clap)

So, if you feel like a downhill slide into crime and fashion, come to Boggo Boutique! Take no notice of those who sneer and call it the chooks' pen 'round the back of the men's! We have more fashion sense than Lindy Chamberlain and Leisha Harvey rolled into one!

RACHAEL   And don't forget to tell your visitors that all our fabrics are plain colours, not black or blue, and without any motifs!

KRIS   We don't want you escaping with our fashion secrets. do we?

(they are all laughing hysterically)

RACHAEL   That was great, Kris!

DELMA   You was really funny, Ray!

NANCY   I haven't laughed this much since I was a schoolgirl!

RACHAEL   We oughta have a fashion parade.

NANCY   Who for?

KRIS   For us! No, not a fashion parade! A fancy dress!

JEMMY   *(together)* What a great idea!

DELMA   *(together)* Yeah, I like them!

NANCY   *(together)* Lovely!

RACHAEL   C Block?

KRIS   All of us! In the gym!

RACHAEL   Up top?

KRIS   Yeah! And the Max!

NANCY &
  DELMA   They wouldn't let us!

RACHAEL   Would they?

KRIS   You gotta stand up for something or you fall down for nothing!

JEMMY   She's right.

RACHAEL   Yeah, we gotta stand up for something. Delma, you could get the music together, make tapes and that!

KRIS   And The Wild One's in the kitchen, so she could get the food!

RACHAEL   The Wild One?

KRIS   Toey.

DELMA   Yeah, that a good name for her.

NANCY	I could help with ideas for costumes. After all, I travelled the world.
KRIS	Now, what about you, Angel?
RACHAEL	Who, me?
KRIS	Yes . . . Angel.
RACHAEL	Well . . . I can decorate . . . with flowers and plants from my garden.
KRIS	Ah yes! The gardening angel!
DELMA	All this planning's made me hungry again.

(DELMA *gets up to leave*)

NANCY	Would you like a cup of coffee, Kris?
KRIS	Thanks, Lady.

(NANCY *starts to leave with* DELMA)

NANCY	Now, Delma, have you thought about who you might like to be? I have a few ideas. You see —
DELMA	I got an idea too.
NANCY	Oh well, that's good. I wonder what I should go as . . .
DELMA	A Christian martyr.

(*they leave*)

RACHAEL	I gotta tell Toey.
JEMMY	Back to the garden. Tell her later.
RACHAEL	Aw, come on, Miss!
JEMMY	The garden, McLeod!
RACHAEL	Bitch!
JEMMY	Good luck, Kris.

(JEMMY *exits to the observation room.* RACHAEL *leaves for the garden*)

KRIS	One—Two—Three—Four I'm gunna see me mates for sure. Five—Six—Seven—Eight—Nine Get those Max girls past the line! Okay Mouth, don't fail me now!

(KRIS *follows* RACHAEL)

Prison Officer Conversation (2)

SHEPHERD *and* JEMMY *are supervising mopping.*

SHEPHERD	Want a lolly?
JEMMY	Thanks. How's things?
SHEPHERD	Today was cancelled due to a lack of inspiration.
JEMMY	The women are inspired.
SHEPHERD	So I heard.

344

JEMMY	Don't you think it's a good idea?
SHEPHERD	Maybe.
JEMMY	It'll be fun.
SHEPHERD	They're not here to have a good time.
JEMMY	Yeah, but there's no need to make their lives more difficult.
SHEPHERD	Oh, you're one of these do-gooders.
JEMMY	No. I just —
SHEPHERD	Look, I know these girls.
JEMMY	Yes, but they —
SHEPHERD	Look, if you make friends with 'em, you're in trouble when you need to discipline them. Give 'em an inch and they'll take a mile.
JEMMY	Yes, I can see that.

(pause)

SHEPHERD	It was Canto's idea, wasn't it!
JEMMY	Yes.
SHEPHERD	She must be missing her mates in Max.
JEMMY	Why was she moved up top?
SHEPHERD	She was stirring up trouble. She was the gun and her mates were the bullets. You know what I mean?
JEMMY	Yes.
SHEPHERD	She's up to something, you can be sure of it!
JEMMY	There's nothing else to do. She's a smart cookie.
SHEPHERD	Not so smart to get herself in here.

(silence)

	You gunna have a honeymoon?
JEMMY	If I can get the time off. We were thinking of going to Bali.
SHEPHERD	Oh yeah, I can see you now, Jemmison, lolling 'round in those . . . what do you call 'em?
JEMMY	Sarongs. Naw, they make your boobs droop!
SHEPHERD	I've gotta supervise medication. See you at the march tomorrow!
JEMMY	Yes, maybe.
SHEPHERD	You're not a scab, are you?
JEMMY	No, I just heard the inmates are better off at the private prison . . .
SHEPHERD	Eight weeks' training and you new breed think you know everything! Look, these bleeding hearts that're in charge, they don't know what they're doing. They just walked in off the street. I've been doing the general run for five years now. You don't know what it's about till you've done it, dearie!

(SHEPHERD and JEMMY part ways)

Tuesday, 4.30 p.m. The rec. room without the coffee table and TV and with the armchairs rearranged — three on one side, two on the other.

SHEPHERD   *(off)* Medication! 4.30! Time for medication!

(lights up on NANCY *and* DELMA *standing in line waiting for medication)*

NANCY   And not too much high rock, Delma. I'm not one to complain but the only peace we have here is the three seconds when they change cassettes!

DELMA   I want a desk to set things up for the dance.

NANCY   How will you get a desk?

DELMA   Carry it.

NANCY   I can't even get ice-cream. How come you can get a desk?

DELMA   Welcome to my gunyah!

NANCY   You'll have to hide it, won't you?

DELMA   If I want a desk I'll just go and get it, not hide it. If you hide something, they look!

NANCY   Ah, that's how you do it!

DELMA   *(smiles)* Yeah.

(TOEY enters wearing a hand-dyed sweatshirt. She sits and begins filling out a form for a telephone call but her pen is not working. She keeps shaking it and trying to write. Her leg is also shaking. She is very agitated)

NANCY   Well, I'll help as much as I can but as you know I have a bad, nice sweatshirt, Lily —

DELMA   Foot.

NANCY   Heart. And I mustn't lift things that might cause me to have another angina attack —

(Prison Officer First Class SHEPHERD — played by KRIS — enters to supervise medication)

SHEPHERD   Medication! Medication!

NANCY   Excuse me, Officer Shepherd, but did my husband say anything about my parole?

(SHEPHERD ignores her. NANCY is hurt)

SHEPHERD   Where's Canto?

DELMA   Dunno, miss. Doncha know?

SHEPHERD   *(to DELMA)* What's in your hand?

(DELMA shows there is nothing)

Other hand!

(nothing again)

Okay, come with me.

	(SHEPHERD and DELMA exit)
NANCY	Why is she so hard today?
TOEY	Have you seen Ray and Kris?
NANCY	What are you doing, Lily?
TOEY	I'm filling out a fucking form for a phone call to my son, alright?
NANCY	Of course. Did you do that yourself?
TOEY	No, I got the screws to do it.
NANCY	No, I mean the dye. Maybe I could use it for my costume —
	(SHEPHERD and DELMA enter. DELMA has a dustpan and brush)
TOEY	Delma, have you seen Ray?
DELMA	No.
	(DELMA begins sweeping up butts. TOEY pulls out some photos)
SHEPHERD	What you got there?
TOEY	Nothing.
SHEPHERD	Come on.
	(TOEY shows SHEPHERD the photos)
SHEPHERD	Nice kid. How old's he? 'Bout four?
TOEY	Three.
SHEPHERD	Looks like you got a bikie on your hands. It's better than being on the streets. What're you gonna do when you get out? Gunna clean up your act?
TOEY	Gunna do Years Eleven and Twelve.
SHEPHERD	You tried Eleven in here, didn't you? Why didn't you finish? You could get yourself a decent job and look after your son.
TOEY	'Cause I don't want to work! I'm too used to stealing. When I pay for something, I feel like I'm getting ripped off!
	(RACHAEL bounces in and lies on the chairs beside TOEY)
SHEPHERD	Do you want medication, McLeod?
	(in the following exchange, SHEPHERD and RACHAEL overlap in their speech, trying to outjoke each other)
RACHAEL	No way, José! *(sings)* I don't need no medication!
SHEPHERD	Can you whistle?
RACHAEL	Ha! Ha! Miss. If you got some ganja I'll have it!
SHEPHERD	Talk to the doctor about it!
RACHAEL	Yeah, I'll make an appointment to see him in six months.
SHEPHERD	You do that, McLeod! Or when you come back next time!
RACHAEL	There won't be a next time.
SHEPHERD	That's what you said last time!
RACHAEL	Yeah, but last time I meant it!

FEMALE NURSE	*(off)* Fine!
	(NANCY takes her drugs through a window)
TOEY	Where's your mate?
RACHAEL	I like your sweatshirt, Toey. How'd you do that?
TOEY	Tell you later.
RACHAEL	Have you done something to your hair?
TOEY	Yeah. I didn't brush it!
RACHAEL	Did you hear about the fancy dress?
TOEY	Yeah, I heard about the stupid fancy dress.
	(RACHAEL and TOEY speak in code about drugs. RACHAEL pulls faces behind SHEPHERD's back)
RACHAEL	What's wrong with you? Don't you want a **taste** of the good life? It's a chance to have some **fun**, to be **up top** with the others! I got some good ideas.
TOEY	I'm not sharing nothing with her!
RACHAEL	Shut up! *(pause)* What's with you?
TOEY	What do you mean?
RACHAEL	Did I do something wrong?
TOEY	Yeah, you ask too many fucking questions.
	(SHEPHERD has been listening to this exchange with interest and fuels the argument)
SHEPHERD	Well, I think the fancy dress sounds like a great idea, McLeod. What're you going as?
RACHAEL	I don't know.
SHEPHERD	When's it going to be?
RACHAEL	Next Saturday, we think. Kris is talking to the manager about it.
TOEY	Kris is talking to the manager about it. Will you shut up about it?
SHEPHERD	You're a good influence on Kris.
RACHAEL	Why should I?
TOEY	If you don't know, don't ask!
RACHAEL	You don't want to help yourself!
TOEY	Who said that? Her?
SHEPHERD	What will I go as?
RACHAEL	Look, you are the sum total of your happiness, not your childhood, not the system!
TOEY	Don't give me that psych shit!
SHEPHERD	Maybe I could go as a gypsy?
RACHAEL	You decide how you're gunna feel!
TOEY	You didn't think that on Monday!
RACHAEL	What do you mean?

TOEY	You were shitting yourself about that big-noting bitch coming up top!
RACHAEL	That was before I met her.
TOEY	You're so easy, you just bend with the wind . . . **Angel**!
SHEPHERD	An angel! Yes, that's me!
NURSE	*(off)* Kite!

(DELMA *takes her drugs through the window*)

RACHAEL	It's my business who I talk to!
TOEY	*(sings, drowning out* RACHAEL*)* Jesus on the drug line Tell him what you want, Jesus on the drug line Tell him what you want.
SHEPHERD	You should go as Elvis, Mistle!
TOEY	You should go as a turd, 'cause you're a pain in the arse!
SHEPHERD	What did you say, Mistle?
TOEY	Best forgotten.
SHEPHERD	I asked you a question.
TOEY	I said if you had a poofter on your back, would you leave him there or pull him off? I said do you give our brains back when we leave here? I said what's a fuzzy duck?
SHEPHERD	Get off of there!
TOEY	Don't talk to me like that! I'm not a fucking dog! I'm a pussy cat, meeow!
SHEPHERD	I'll put you on a Section 39!
TOEY	*(explodes)* Screws! Blues! Kangaroos — Tk! Tk! Tk! Johns! Jacks! Bully boys! *(spits)* Bluebirds! Turnkeys! Section 39, jam it up your jack! Breaches! Badges! Whistles! Forms! You put your form in You put your form out You put your form in And they shake it all about! And you put your form in And you put your form in And you put your form in And I'll see about that I'll see about that When I get back I'll see about that! Feeling blue! Browned off! Feeling down! Slashing up! Sharp as a razor! Dangerous! Ground down! Cut off! Locked in!

(SHEPHERD *responds, in tandem with* TOEY)

SHEPHERD	Sticks and stones will break my bones But names will never hurt me.

Scumbag! Scum!
Not fit to be a mum!
Bitch! Witch!
Slut! Whore!
Walking dead! What a bore!
B and Ees! Armed robs!
Addicts! Pushers!
Murderers! Slobs!
Don't laugh! Don't cry!
Don't think! Don't sigh!
Don't touch! Don't kiss!
Don't forget to call me Miss!
Muster! Muster! Must we muster?
Yes, you must!
Slam shut! Lock! Double lock!
Lock down!!!

(SHEPHERD *throws* TOEY's *mattress out of her cell.* TOEY *goes in*)

TOEY   Out of the blue — into the white
Out of the day — into the night!

Prison Officer Conversation (3)

SHEPHERD   Hullo Allan. Susan Shepherd. Yeah, long time no see. How's your love life? Listen. Why don't you come over to my place tonight? Tuesday. That's okay, I don't knock off till ten. Good. Good. Look, can you bring some tallies? May as well get a carton. I'll give you the money when you get here. Yeah, Fourex. Aw, get fucked! Gees, you're a smooth-talking bastard! Yeah, same place. Yeah, me too. Okay, see you then. Bye.

ACT I   Scene Seven

Wednesday 8 a.m. KRIS *and* DELMA *are in the rec. room.* KRIS *is filling out forms.* DELMA *is mopping.* RACHAEL *and* NANCY *are in the garden.* RACHEL *is digging.* NANCY *is collecting feathers for costumes.* TOEY *is locked in her cell, asleep. Her mattress is outside in the corridor. A bell rings.*

VOICES   (*off*) Work duties! Tailor shop! Outside nursery! Inside garden! Kitchen! Laundry! Book-binding! Reception! To your work areas!

DELMA   Psst! Toey!

(DELMA *puts some tobacco under* TOEY's *door and hurries away.* TOEY *wakes up, goes over and picks it up*)

TOEY   (*laughs*) Alright!

(*she picks up the Bible, the only reading matter in her cell, opens it and reads slowly*)

TOEY   They say unto him, Master, this woman was taken in adultery, in the very act. (Poor bitch!) Now Moses in the law commanded us that such should be stoned. (Sounds alright to me!) But what sayest thou? But Jesus stooped down and with his finger wrote on the ground as though he heard them not. So when they continued asking him he lifted up himself and said unto them, 'He that is without sin among you, let him cast a stone at her'.

(TOEY *nods to herself, then tears out the page and rolls a smoke. Behind the toilet she finds a match and a bit of striking surface. She sits on her bed and lights up her durrie)*

ACT I   Scene Eight

Thursday afternoon. The women line up for medication. NANCY *is showing* DELMA *the feathers.* KRIS *is still filling out forms.* RACHAEL *is beside her, tearing a Minties wrapper to make a long continuous strip.*

VOICES   *(off)* Medication! Medication! 4.30! Time for medication!

              (TOEY *is on her toilet. She starts to cry and pulls the toilet roll to wipe her eyes when she notices writing on it)*

TOEY   *(reads)* Jokes by Ray. What is the definition of pathetic? A bloke whose hand falls asleep while he's wanking. What is the definition of vanity? Mooning? Oh, moaning your own name while you're masturbating. What is the definition of hope? A pregnant schoolgirl rubbing vanishing cream on her belly. What is the definition of agony? Going to heaven and finding out God's a cockroach!

              (TOEY's *tears turn to hysterical laughter)*

ACT I   Scene Nine

Friday night. The women sit around the table having tea. TOEY *is sitting on the end of her bed playing with a piece of sharp metal, about to slash up her arms.* DELMA *puts her trannie in the centre of the table.* 4ZZZ *Prisoners' Program is heard.*

FEMALE
ANNOUNCER   And now here's a request, dedicated to Toey who's been breached for three days on a Section 39, from Delma, Nancy and Kris and special love from Ray. Hope you're not doing it too hard. We need you.

              (song) Wild thing, you make my heart sing
              You make everything groovy
              Wild thing, I think I love you
              But I wanna know for sure . . .

              (train whistle — as TOEY *slashes up)*

BLACKOUT

Saturday afternoon. The rec. room. The TV is not on.

KRIS tears the month of May off the calendar. She is standing in front of the others with pen and papers. TOEY and RACHAEL are sitting side by side. TOEY has scars on the inside of both forearms. NANCY, DELMA, and RACHAEL are making paper chains. They talk nervously, trying to involve TOEY.

RACHAEL	I wish we had scissors.
	(NANCY brings some scissors out of her bag)
	How did you get them?
NANCY	What you don't know won't hurt you.
RACHAEL	What's Kiriakis' nephew's name?
KRIS	Jason.
NANCY	I've got a visitor today.
DELMA	You're lucky to have visitors.
RACHAEL	Anyway, what happened was . . . it was Happy New Years —
NANCY	Kris was reading my palm yesterday —
DELMA	She told me I was gunna win Lotto. I'm still waiting for the big one.
RACHAEL	*(acting it out)* And Neil Curtis said, 'Happy New Years —' Oh, what's her fucking name? Anyway, Mrs Johnson, Patch's mum.
KRIS	Jo.
RACHAEL	And she said, 'Happy New Years, Neil', and they go like this. *(she shows how they kiss)* I was waiting for the tongue to go in, but it never came.
NANCY	And she said I was going to meet a handsome man and I am! It's my husband, Brian! He's been to see the solicitor about my appeal. I'm pushing for a drop in sentence. Do I look alright? I used this lovely silver shampoo when they locked us in at lunchtime.
RACHAEL	And Kayla and Patch are getting back together.
DELMA	You look really nice, Nancy.
RACHAEL	They acknowledge their love. What's that mean? Anyway, they're all gooey. Patch says, 'Trust me, Kayla, trust me'. And she says, Okay Steve, darling'. You know how she only calls him Steve. And Melissa was the odd one —
KRIS	SHUT UP!
	(pause)
TOEY	I got a lot more poems for you, Ray.
	(silence. The women wait)
RACHAEL	What's happening with the fancy dress, Kris?

KRIS	The girls from Max can't come, thanks to Susan Shepherd of the S.S. running to the powers that fucking be, **but** they're gunna send up a special trolley of food for us.
TOEY	Look out for Meds and cottonwool balls!
	(KRIS *looks daggers at* TOEY)
	I was only joking.
	(RACHAEL *touches* TOEY's *hand*)
KRIS	Trust, that's the word, Kayla! Trust.
	(NANCY *and* DELMA *laugh*)
	Right! Now I've been doing a lot of work for this, filling out a rainforest of forms . The Greenies would hate me. So Owl, Keeper of the Dance, how's the music?
DELMA	Barb said she give us her player for the night, long as we make sure no one steal it! And I got tapes and —
RACHAEL	Have you got anything decent?
DELMA	I got the Warumpis, Joey Geia and I taped some reggae and rock 'n roll from Murri Hour on —
RACHAEL	What about Madonna?
KRIS	What about her, Angel?
NANCY	She can come, too.
	(TOEY *and* DELMA *laugh*)
RACHAEL	Shepherd's gunna make it hard for us. She's got it in for Toey.
KRIS	She's got it in for me. But she'll get hers!
TOEY	I'm gunna put a bag over my head and escape. Do you think she'll recognise me?
RACHAEL	No.
TOEY	Aw, go bag your head!
KRIS	Look, If we're not fucking satisfied with the sheep herder, her little flock of crooks can see the senior. We have that right and if we're not fucking satisfied with her, we can go to the Chief and I fucking know if we're not satisfied with him, we can go to the next boss!
NANCY & RACHAEL	Good on ya, Kris!
DELMA	Jemmy reckons she going as an exotic dancer.
RACHAEL	She can be entertainment!
TOEY	She is the entertainment!
	(RACHAEL *does a bit of a dance.* DELMA *hums.* NANCY *claps.* KRIS *and* TOEY *watch her closely*)
MALE VOICE	(*off*) Sit down, McLeod!
KRIS	(*sings quietly*) Hey, hey, you, you, get off of McLeod!

(all except TOEY *laugh)*

DELMA	What about prizes for the best costume and that?
NANCY	Yes, we must have prizes for first, second and third places.
RACHAEL	I know! First prize could be a man!
DELMA	No, first prize — an island cruise!
RACHAEL	Yeah!
NANCY	This is going to be lovely!
DELMA	I won first prize once.
NANCY	What did you get?
RACHAEL	Yeah, what?
DELMA	Some talc . . . shampoo and conditioner.
KRIS	Who's gunna pay for it?
NANCY	Not us!
RACHAEL	No way, Jose!
KRIS	*(sarcastically)* Oh well, that's sorted out!
NANCY	What are you going as, Rachael?
RACHAEL	Milli Vanilli.
NANCY	That's lovely. Who's she?

*(*TOEY *and* RACHAEL *laugh)*

MALE VOICE	*(off)* Keep it down in there!

(their voices drop to a whisper)

TOEY	That's if it happens.
NANCY	Are you sure it's alright, Kris?
DELMA	We don't want to be told the day before, sorry it's not on!
RACHAEL	Yeah.
NANCY	And I'm praying, pushing and penning for parole, so I hope it really **is** alright!
TOEY	If it fucks up, it's your fault.
DELMA	We don't want to be branded as troublemakers.
TOEY	The buckle that holds the belt will pull it tighter.
KRIS	That's why we've gotta stand together! Look, the men've been having things like this for years!
TOEY	There are more of them than us.
KRIS	Even if there's only one of us, we should fight to have the same things men do!
TOEY	Come on, get off your soapbox.
RACHAEL	It's alright for you! You're a lifer!
TOEY	Yeah, you got nothin' to lose.
KRIS	Oh yeah, Angel! What if you come back again?

RACHAEL	I'm not gunna come back! I'm gunna change me lifestyle! Get me act together!
KRIS	Pigs might fly!
TOEY	Get off her back, Mouth!
KRIS	*(losing it)* You toe raggers make me sick. You come in for a few months, do stupid fucking things like pinching scissors, so we get landed with more rules, and you tell **me** to lay off!
TOEY	You're living on the fame of the name of what you claim!
KRIS	We're the same. That's what I like about you. You're like me.
TOEY	Nobody loves me, everybody hates me Think I'll go eat worms.
NANCY	I don't know about the rest of you ladies, but I shouldn't even be in here!
TOEY	Big ones, small ones Fat ones, thin ones Worms that squiggle and squirm.
KRIS	You're a pack of pathetic fucking arseholes! You want change, but you don't want to do anything about it!
TOEY	Bite their heads off Suck their blood out Throw their skins away.
RACHAEL	Nothing's gunna change this place!
	(RACHAEL, NANCY and DELMA join TOEY in humming the rhyme under KRIS's outburst)
KRIS	What! You want to be 'droids for the rest of your lives? Happy little Vegemites, you switch your brains off. 'That's life! I'm fucked. They want clones like you. They don't want people who think. You might start a riot! If you don't shut off, you blow up! You know what it's like trying to get you lot to do anything? It's like moving the Statue of fucking Liberty! That's a joke. The joke of the fucking year. You're nothing but a bunch of whingers! If I rock the boat I'll be in for years. Let someone else do it.' Well, I'm not even in the fucking boat! I've had enough! I'm fucking gone! I'm out of here! And you know why? 'Cause there aren't any fucking lifebelts! You're gunna have to swim for yourselves! It's your turn, now! This is the Big Gig! Start thinking, start feeling, start being . . . something fucking different! You've got to rock the boat! We're a sinking ship — at least pick up the fucking paddle! We're gunna go under if you don't.
TOEY	Nobody knows how much I enjoy Eating worms three times a day!
	(KRIS picks up the scissors)
KRIS	SHUT THE FUCK UP, MISTLE!
	(the women are shocked into silence)
MALE VOICE	*(off)* Get off your arses, stop smoking and clean the louvres! McLeod and Kite! Do the toilets!
DELMA	Not again.

DELMA *and* RACHAEL *are cleaning the cell toilets.*

DELMA — Sit down a minute, bub. Some of our woman been talking. They reckon you're a bit stuck up.

RACHAEL — No way, Auntie! I just don't want to do shit jobs.

DELMA — You'll get shit jobs if you stick with Toey. You been playing with her and Kris.

RACHAEL — No, I haven't!

DELMA — It looks like that from here.

RACHAEL — I gotta be with Kris or she'll kick me head in.

DELMA — She's not so bad. *(pause)* Why don't you help your mob?

RACHAEL — I got whitefellas one way and blackfellas the other way. I'm not black, I'm not white. I'm **me**!

DELMA — Can't you see? You're acting like them now.

RACHAEL — You think I'm a bloody coconut, ey? Black on the outside, white on the inside! Fucking I don't know what I am!

DELMA — You can ask.

RACHAEL — It's hard to ask.

DELMA — If you want to know 'bout your family, ask the old woman.

RACHAEL — All I know is my mum came from Yarrabah.

DELMA — We all lost a little bit. *(pause)* Hey, you can help the other woman with the fancy dress. We'll do a big corroboree, ey? Clapsticks and didjeridu . . .

RACHAEL — Am I allowed to play didjeridu?

DELMA — No, it's not allowed for woman.

RACHAEL — Why not?

(DELMA whispers. RACHAEL laughs)

The dining area. JEMMY *is talking to* NANCY.

JEMMY — How's your husband?

NANCY — He didn't show up.

JEMMY — Oh, luvey.

NANCY — Do you think he could've been in an accident?

JEMMY — No, luvey, it doesn't mean anything.

NANCY — Maybe he got lost. It's his first time.

JEMMY — Yeah, that's probably it.

NANCY	Maybe it's my parole and he couldn't face me.
JEMMY	No, lovey.
NANCY	Maybe reception stopped him.
JEMMY	There's no reason why they —
NANCY	Maybe I shouldn't have taken those —
JEMMY	What, lovey?
NANCY	I hope he's alright.
JEMMY	*(joking)* All those stripsearches for nothing, hey!
NANCY	*(laughing weakly)* Yeah.

(JEMMY *puts her arm around her.*
KRIS *and* RACHAEL *are cleaning the louvres, not really talking to each other)*

KRIS   When I came in here, you know, I was ready for the concrete floors and bars. I was even ready for firehoses! That's what the cops reckoned. But I never thought it'd be like this. The boredom, the staring and the mind games . . . it gets to everybody. Da-de-da. It's like a cat falling out of a tree. You twist and you turn and you know you're gunna fall, but you just gotta land the best way you can. I got V 8 motivation, you know, but I'm getting worn down. It's not what they do, it's the way they treat you, talk to you. We're humiliated, stripped of our dignity, our pride, our mates. I've seen women with children, when they get outside they give their kids away because they don't think they're worthy to look after them. I've seen proud women walk in here, go out lost and confused with a broken spirit. You can't repair that. I'd rather be hit in the face, really have my face smashed in, than let them break me.

RACHAEL   My friend Dawn was shanghaied to Stuart Creek. We were friends in F troop here. She knew my mother's people. I went out and six weeks later I was back in Max. We couldn't see each other, but I could always feel her presence and that made me feel kinda peaceful. When Dawn left I went past the line in Max, ran past the screws and put my hand through the bars . . . because I wanted to touch Dawn. She wrote to me, 'Sister girl, my feet were heavy when I saw your hands through the bars. It haunted me all the way to Townsville. I'm happy here now. I could stay all my life. I can see mountains, waterfalls and trees'. I wrote her a poem with "ey" on the end, 'cause she comes from North Queensland . . . ey?

KRIS   You know this fancy dress? At first I did it to get me mates up from Max. I did it for you too, Angel. Then, when Shepherd put a spanner in the works, I thought, 'Payback time! She's gunna have a cunt of a weekend'. But now I reckon — have you seen The Owl? She's as high as a kite, getting the music together. And you, Angel, you're positively blooming. Even The Lady's stopped whingeing! Toey? Well, The Wild One's only in it for the drugs, but she's not an eggroll. She'll see. 'It's bigger than all of us, Baby!' 'Cause we're organising something for ourselves . . . we're getting our shit together . . . the walking dead have come alive. I can't live in a world watching my back. We do our time, we pay our debt. But there's gotta be respect for us and I guess for them in blue. But first, **we** gotta respect us. And then we'll take off. We'll be like that flock of pelicans **inside**.

RACHAEL	Are we still going to have it, Kris?
KRIS	If I've got anything to do with it . . . Angel.

(DELMA is leaning out joking with her mob in the corridor outside the rec. room)

(laughter from the other women during the following)

DELMA Hey, you fellas! I told this bloody sister 'bout my bleeding but all I got was two lousy Panadol. No, not two lousy banana! Panadol! You womba woman, need stress leave! True, ey? We have to cope 24 hour a day, seven day a week. Seen my cousin today. We met on Straddie he reckon. I don't remember him. Must've been pissed, ey? Hey, hear 'bout that Kerry? She escape from the screws at the hospital. They was running round that smoke stack like chooks with they heads cut off! Hey! Don't forget the fancy dress! We'll do a big corroboree, ey? Like that Wilson mob up north. Ooh! Watch 'em move!

(RACHAEL is telling a joke to the other women)

RACHAEL They're doing a big corroboree for the tourists, see. They're painted up. They got their lap laps on. Full bit. All the tourists are up top with their cameras watching the corroboree. They got the clapsticks going. *(the women make the SFX)*

The didje is playing. *(the women make the SFX)*

They all singing like one thing. *(the women make the SFX)*

The tourists are taking photos. *(the women make the SFX)*

Everything's great. They're painted up! They got their lap laps on. But one fella's boobles are hanging out!

(DELMA starts laughing)

So the fellas on the clapsticks they start going . . . *(RACHAEL shows how the fellas on the clapsticks try to get that fella's attention, using facial gestures)*

And the fella with his boobles hanging out, he's going . . . *(RACHAEL shows that fella happily singing and clapping, nodding back, oblivious of his exposure)*

So the fella on the didje starts going . . . *(as the didjeridu player)* 'Your boobles are hanging out. Your boobles are hanging out. Your boobles are hanging out'.

(DELMA is laughing harder)

And the fella with his boobles hanging out, he's going . . . *(RACHAEL shows that fella nodding and singing happily; as that fella)* We sound great, deadly, ey? Tourists taking photos!

(the music speeds up. DELMA is hysterical with laughter)

So the fellas on the clapsticks are going . . . *(more extreme facial gestures from RACHAEL)*

358

And the fella on the didje is going, 'Your boobles are hanging out! Your boobles are hanging out!' And they all singing like one thing, 'Your boobles are hanging out! Your boobles are hanging out!' And that fella, he's going, 'Deadly, ey? Ohh we're good! Good today!' And the tourists are taking photos. And the clapsticks are —

(a whistle blows authoritatively. The women stop making sounds and dancing. DELMA continues laughing)

MALE VOICE   *(off)* What're you laughing at?! What's so funny, Kite? You'll be laughing on the other side of your stupid black face in a minute!

(DELMA keeps laughing)

(off) Right! That's it!

(whispers of the news spreading)

KRIS   The Owl's been breached.

RACHAEL   For seven days. For laughing.

KRIS   Delma's on "39 Shit".

NANCY   Seven days.

TOEY   They put her on the cunt.

(DELMA keeps laughing)

ACT II   **Scene Thirteen**

KRIS is in the garden. She notices something in a garden bed, then moves out of sight to watch. TOEY enters and starts searching in the garden. She finds what she is looking for — a tennis ball, which she tosses up and down. KRIS comes out and catches the ball mid-flight. TOEY tries to get it back. The MALE OFFICER passes. KRIS and TOEY turn their struggle into a game. When the OFFICER leaves, there is a moment of hesitation, then KRIS chucks the ball to TOEY. It lands on the ground. It doesn't bounce. KRIS leaves. TOEY picks up the ball eagerly and leaves.

ACT II   **Scene Fourteen**

Sunday night. DELMA is in her cell. She is humming sadly to herself as she sews coloured thread onto a white nightie.

DELMA   Seven days alone . . .
Six days alone . . .
Five days alone . . .
Four days alone . . .
Three — wait! Who's that? Who's there?
My little sister!
What you doing here?

Come to help me?
Oh, I'm just making my costume for the fancy dress.
It's a surprise. No, I'm not gunna tell you. No.
You said you come to help me.
What colour do you think, little sister?
You like red now?
You always like red.
No, red's a good colour.
Yeah, red's the colour of our heart.
You know what I miss, little sister?
Yeah, I miss family, but . . . it's red . . .
It's a can of coke! With ice-cream! A spider!
You like spiders, too? Yeah, long as it's a money one, ey?

(she laughs)

Look out! Don't laugh too hard!
Boogieman's gunna get ya!
Like he got me.
You remember when things went wrong, little sister?
On Palm Island we was fighting from daybreak to nightfall.
I was so sad. He got angry and he bashed me up.
I feel shame in the dirt.
I wasn't drunk, not that time.
Every day I think of what I did.
I can't even begin to talk about it.

(she hums some more — maybe "Oh P.I."*)*

What colour you want now? Red again?
Are you angry now, little sister?
Don't be angry!
I was shitty with everyone the other day, ey?
My blood pressure was up. I had no sugar and I hadn't taken me pills.
I was shouting at everyone, ey?
They got a big shock. They reckon I'm a wild woman, ey?

(she laughs)

Suppose you want more red? A whole line of red, ey?
One for our brother Eric, next door.
One for my son, your nephew, Rodney, in Westbrook.
One for Lorraine's man in Wacol
and our cousin brother in Woodford.
One for Ray's friend in Borallon
and the boys at David Longlands.
They eyes gone sad.
What can you do, little sister?
Cry tears for nothing?
Or turn around the game and say,
'Stand tall, brothers,
Stand tall, sisters'
Me and my little sister say, 'Stand tall'.

(the bell rings)

VOICE   *(off)* Nine o'clock! Lock up! Let's go! Lock up time!

Sunday night late. TOEY and RACHAEL are in the garden, pilled out of their minds, dressed as Milli Vanilli but still in their nighties. RACHAEL is fossicking among the plants.

TOEY	*(singing)* Blame it on the rain that was falling, falling Blame it on the stars that shined at night.
RACHAEL	Is there any more of that stuff?
TOEY	Whatever you do, don't put the blame on you Whatever you do, don't put the blame on you Whatever you do, don't put the —
RACHAEL	Shut up, Wild One! You'll wake up Mouth!
TOEY	Blame on you . . . Sorry!
RACHAEL	Never say sorry to me.
TOEY	Oh yeah, I forgot. Sorry. Oops! Sorry. Oops! Sorry —
RACHAEL	Shhh.
TOEY	Shhh.

(they move across the garden)

SFX	*(coughing from DELMA's cell)*
	Just a minute! I've got to have a fag. Where's me fucking fags? What cunt took me fucking fags? Nancy? Fucking cunt! Wack up!
RACHAEL	Shhh. Have one of these.

(RACHAEL gives TOEY a smoke. TOEY sits down on her fags in her back pocket)

TOEY	Oh, here they are! No worries! *(shouting)* Only joking!! I was only joking!!
RACHAEL	Trust, that's the word, Kayla! Trust.
TOEY	Shhh. I was only joking, Patch Baby.
RACHAEL	Shhh!
TOEY	Shhh!

(they kiss)

I can't wait to flick a Bic.

(TOEY lights her fag)

RACHAEL	Yeah.
TOEY	And see me mates.
RACHAEL	Yeah. One—Two—Three—Four.
TOEY	I can't see me mates no more.
RACHAEL	Five—Six—Seven—Eight—Nine.
TOEY	You commit the crime, you do the time.
RACHAEL	Pieces of meat! Pieces of meat!

TOEY	I need a drink.
RACHAEL	I need a joint.
TOEY	I need a hit.
RACHAEL	I need . . . I need . . . I need a pee.
TOEY	Me too.
RACHAEL	Not on me flowers.

(they pee in the garden)

TOEY	We're happy little Vegemites As bright as bright can be We all enjoy our Vegemite For breakfast, lunch and tea! Because we — Look at the birds!
RACHAEL	Pelicans.
TOEY	I'm fucking scared of heights.
RACHAEL	Come on! We'll take off.

(they are drawn to the roof)

Wow! Blue. Beautiful blue.

TOEY	I can see the moon walking towards me.
RACHAEL	I can see the Storey Bridge.
TOEY	*(sings)* Tell me a story. Tell me a story.
RACHAEL	Hi, Mum! Hi Dad!
TOEY	Tell me a story and then I'll go to bed.
RACHAEL	I never thought it'd be like this! Da-de-da.
TOEY	It's bigger than all of us, Baby!

(telephone ringing)

RACHAEL	I wish I could fly.
TOEY	You're an angel, aren't you?
RACHAEL	No, I'm not an angel. Angels have long blonde hair.

(bells ringing. Shouting)

VOICE	*(off)* Get down!
TOEY	Get fucked!
RACHAEL	We can't! We're allergic to prison!
TOEY	Hey, look at 'em going round and round in circles!

(the other women are laughing now)

DELMA	Hey, Nancy! Look at those fellas!
NANCY	Have you lost your way, Ray?
DELMA	Naw! Yous are sleepwalking, ey?
KRIS	Don't jump!

VOICE	(off) You'll be sorry! You'll pay for this!
NANCY	'Like Sands through the Hourglass . . .
DELMA	. . . So are the Days of Our Lives.'
TOEY	Hey, Shepherd! If my dog was as ugly as you, I'd shave its arse and make it walk backwards!
KRIS	Don't do it! Please don't jump!

(more laughter. TOEY and RACHAEL really ham it up for everyone's benefit. A bright light spots them from the ground)

VOICE	(off) Come on, Mistle! Come on, McLeod! You've had your fun!
RACHAEL	We haven't started, Baby!
TOEY	We're over the moon and heading for the stars!
KRIS	Don't jump! **Please!** Please don't jump!
DELMA	Hey, Ray, Toey, they playing your theme song!

(DELMA puts her transistor radio to the window of her cell. A crackly but gradually becoming clearer and louder version of —)

> We gotta get outta this place
> If it's the last thing we ever do
> We gotta get outta this place
> Girl, there's a better life for me and you.

(RACHAEL and TOEY are dancing around. Everyone is singing. Suddenly there are coloured lights from above and the sound of a helicopter)

RACHAEL	Toey! Hey, Toey! We are saved, Sister! Hallelujah! We are free!
TOEY	Here we are! Here we are! Wings and power are what we need To take us from this place of greed!
RACHAEL	So long, girls! It's been good to know you! We're going to live on the streets of paradise! Goodbye hell on earth! Hello Dreamtime!
NANCY	Don't forget my parole!
DELMA	Say hullo to my little sister when you get there!
NANCY & DELMA	Goodbye!
TOEY	The sharks are circling, Angel.

(they hold on to each other and prepare to jump)

TV PRESENTER	Tonight, two jailbirds are perched on the roof of the Women's Correctional Centre. The bizarrely dressed criminals are considered to be armed and dangerous. The drama started when a fancy dress was planned at the prison. Illicit drugs are thought to have been smuggled in with costume materials during visiting hours this afternoon. 'Their ability to get the drugs past the guards is due to staff cuts and changes in routine surveillance', an unnamed officer said. Reliable sources indicate that the prisoners' escape was carefully planned since they had been closely studying the flight patterns of pelicans in the region in

recent days. Fierce electrical storms are forecast. More on tonight's news at six.

KRIS	*(screams)* **Don't jump!**

(a train whistle)

(the women are in their beds. KRIS and RACHAEL wake up. The others stir)

RACHAEL	Kris! Hey Kris! Kris! You alright?
KRIS	Angel, you and Toey're on the roof . . .
RACHAEL	Dream on, Kris!
KRIS	In your costumes . . .
TOEY	I'm fucking scared of heights!

(DELMA starts to play softly)

NANCY	Was I in the dream, Kris?
KRIS	There were screws running everywhere . . .
TOEY	You think we're gunna fuck it!
RACHAEL	Go easy, Toe!
TOEY	Trust, that's the word, Kayla. Trust!
RACHAEL	Yeah.
TOEY	I can't believe that bitch thought we was gunna fuck it!

(TOEY picks up the tennis ball, tossing it from hand to hand. KRIS gets up, goes to the shower and turns it full on. KRIS leans against the shower wall and cries)

RACHAEL	Shut up, Toey!
TOEY	She doesn't give a shit about you, Ray!
RACHAEL	You don't know the half of it!
TOEY	I can fucking guess.
NANCY	Some of us are trying to sleep here!
TOEY	I couldn't give a damn!
NANCY	It's your life, young lady.

(TOEY stops tossing the ball and looks at it, thinking about her life of drugs)

RACHAEL	Shhh.

(they hear KRIS crying above the noise of the shower. They all get tearful)

Hey Kris . . . Kris!

KRIS	Yeah.
RACHAEL	You alright?
KRIS	Yeah.
RACHAEL	Are you sure?
KRIS	Yeah.
NANCY	It'll be alright, dear. Don't worry.

RACHAEL	Yeah, we'll have a good time.
TOEY	That's right.
KRIS	I don't want your fucking pity.
	(they are all crying by now)
NANCY	*(to KRIS)* You be quiet, young lady.
TOEY	*(to KRIS)* Yeah, shut your mouth.

(the sound of DELMA's blues harp comes over the shower noise. RACHAEL starts to sing. TOEY and NANCY join in. There are no decipherable words to the song. It is a unified anthem of feeling for KRIS and each other)

Prison Officer Conversation (4)

KRIS *and* TOEY *put on track suit pants over their nighties to become* SHEPHERD *and* JEMMY *after a workout in the gym.*

SHEPHERD	Delma Kite'll be out today. Jesus! Seven days for laughing! Some of those male officers are scumbags.
JEMMY	Yeah.
SHEPHERD	Did you hear some scissors went missing? Now I wonder who's behind that!
JEMMY	You shouldn't always jump to conclusions. I heard she had a bad night.
SHEPHERD	Yeah, well . . . maybe you're right. Anyway they can kiss their fancy dress goodbye.
JEMMY	What? Oh no! When did this come down?
SHEPHERD	Just now. Just got word from the manager. And guess who's been elected to tell Canto and her mob?
JEMMY	Aw shit!
SHEPHERD	You think I'm behind all this, don't you!
JEMMY	Yes.
SHEPHERD	That's because you've never been in a situation where there are six of them and one of you.
JEMMY	Does it always have to be them and us?
SHEPHERD	Look, if you can't hack it, go somewhere else!
JEMMY	What about you!
SHEPHERD	There is nowhere else for people like me.
JEMMY	What? No remission for good behaviour? Sounds like a life sentence.
SHEPHERD	Alright, I'll do it. But just this once!
JEMMY	Thanks a lot, Susan, but . . . no, I think it'll sound better coming from me.
SHEPHERD	Okay. Gees! It's enough to make you wish you were in here with them!
	(they laugh ironically)

Saturday morning in the rec. room. The TV is on. TOEY has her feet up on the coffee table. She is smoking a rollie, staring at the ceiling and ashing on the floor. RACHAEL is sitting beside TOEY writing a letter. KRIS is smoking, staring at the TV. NANCY is rummaging through her knitting bag. They are all still in their nighties.

MALE OFFICER   Nine o'clock! Visitors! Any of you girls got visitors? Fine! You're to go to discharge!

NANCY   Thank you, sir.

(he leaves)

Well, I'm going now. I made you these. This one's for you, Lily.

(she gives them each a beanie with lots of ugly pompoms on them. They put them on)

RACHAEL   Hey! It's Huey, Dewey and Louie!

(RACHAEL and TOEY quack and muck around)

TOEY   How come in the cartoons when Donald Duck gets his head blown off, it comes back again?

NANCY   I didn't really expect gratitude —

TOEY   Oop! There goes my head!

NANCY   — but I did expect some common courtesy.

RACHAEL   Thank . . .

TOEY   You . . .

RACHAEL   Nan- . . .

TOEY   -cy!

RACHAEL   It's . . .

TOEY   Love- . . .

RACHAEL   -ly!

(RACHAEL and TOEY giggle)

TOEY   What're you going to do now?

NANCY   Well . . . my husband's coming to get me. I didn't think he would. He's bringing me a mishmash of clothes. He's got no idea, really, but the navy trousers'll be a winner if I can still fit —

TOEY   I meant, now that you've been inside.

NANCY   Well . . . I'd like to give some of the lessons I've learnt back.

TOEY   (hitting the palm of her hand) Yeah, me too!

NANCY   No, I meant in a good way!

(there is an air of disbelief)

'Your boobles are hanging out! Your boobles are hanging out!'

(the women laugh but peter out when they realise that KRIS is not responding)

And I guess I'll just pick up where I left off.

(no comment)

Where's Delma? Isn't she out yet? I wanted to give her my batteries for her trannie.

RACHAEL	I'll give 'em to her.
NANCY	Thanks, Ray. I'm sorry about the fancy dress. It was my fault.
RACHAEL	Naw! I think it was great you took those scissors. It took guts.
TOEY	Yeah. Anyway they woulda found something else to stop it. Fuck— Mongrels!
KRIS	They take everything.
NANCY	They can't take anything away from you, dear. That's something I've learnt in here.

(RACHAEL hugs NANCY goodbye, as does KRIS)

RACHAEL	Goodbye, Nancy.
KRIS	Thanks, Lady.
TOEY	See ya!
NANCY	Lily?
TOEY	What?
NANCY	Thanks for the . . . send off.
TOEY	*(surprised)* Yeah? See ya!

(NANCY leaves. They take off their beanies)

RACHAEL	Shit, I hope nothing goes wrong at discharge.
TOEY	Yeah. We don't want her back. Do you think we should pray to the Lord?

(RACHAEL and TOEY laugh)

RACHAEL	What about the coleslaw I put in her toilet bowl, ey?
TOEY	Yeah, and I wallpapered her room with surfboards.
RACHAEL	*(like an ad)* "To keep her dry and confident all day long!"

(desperate laughter from RACHAEL and TOEY)

TOEY	That must've spun her out for a sixer!
RACHAEL	I think she liked it.
TOEY	Yeah.
RACHAEL	She didn't complain or nothing.
TOEY	What's she got to complain about? She's got her freedom.

(silence — only the sound of the TV)

Well, what're we gunna do?

RACHAEL	Kris?
KRIS	Don't ask me, Angel.

(RACHAEL and TOEY continue looking at KRIS for direction)

	They've taken away my green lantern ring!
TOEY	Two little jailbirds sitting all the day One named Toey, one named Ray. Fly up high, Toey! Fly up high, Ray! Shit on Shepherd! Make Kris's day!

(RACHAEL *laughs.* KRIS *doesn't respond*)

(*silence*)

(DELMA *enters dressed as a Native American Indian in her white nightie with V-lines of coloured wool, moccasins, make-up and feathered earrings*)

	Look out, here comes Delma Kite! Out of the white, **Out of the white!**
RACHAEL	You look deadly, Auntie!
TOEY	Alright, Delma! Alright!
RACHAEL	Fucking cool! Look at you!
TOEY	Where did you get the textas?
RACHAEL	Grouse colours, Auntie!
TOEY	Knock me down with a feather!
RACHAEL	Auntie, the fancy dress isn't on.
DELMA	I know it.
TOEY	I can't believe what I see!
DELMA:	(*to* KRIS) We got no time for prison blindness, ey, you woman?
TOEY	That's right, Delma.
RACHAEL	True, Auntie!
KRIS	You are a vision, Owl. What a change.

(DELMA *puts* KRIS's *beanie on her*)

DELMA	Birds of a feather stick together, ey?

(*they laugh.* TOEY *puts on her beanie.* RACHAEL *puts on hers.* TOEY *picks up the forms from the table*)

RACHAEL	This is from Nancy, Auntie.
TOEY	(*holding up to* KRIS *a bunch of forms*) Hey! Let's see if we can get our families to come this time.
DELMA	My little sister. (*she takes a form*)
RACHAEL	My pop. (*she takes a form*)
TOEY	My son.

(*they all wait for* KRIS *to respond*)

One—Two—Three—Four. We ain't taking this shit no more.

(TOEY *offers* KRIS *a form*)

If they thought we were down, they're wrong. We're just taking flight.

(KRIS *takes it and the women gather round to commence the battle again*)

END OF PLAY

APPENDICES

APPENDICES

I. The Popular Theatre Troupe
Administrators

1975 - 76	Peter Sutherland
1976 - 77	Paul Richards
1977	Lorenzo Boccabella
1977 - 78	Roslyn Atkinson
1978 - 79	Jan Oates
1980	Kay Boulden
1981 - 82	Pat McNair

II. Street Arts
Committee Members
(1983 — 1994)

Janet Allison	Tony Hannon	Paul O'Shea
Jeannie Bell	Sally Herbert	Pauline Peel
Alex Black	Norm Hoare	Di Porrill
Helen Black	Sandy	Ian Reece
Les Browell	Horneman-Wren	Donna Richters
Richard Carew	Pauline Jones	Mark Shortis
Antonella Casella	Meg Kanowski	Vik Stark
Pat Castensen	Sue Koch	Geoff Street
Di Craig	Bill Kyle	Coralie Stringer
Phil Davison	Douglas Leonard	Dean Tuttle
Effie Detsimas	Bernie Lewis	Stephanie
Katrina Devery	Rebecca Lister	Walkem
Chantal Eastwell	Steve McCarthy	Hugh Watson
Gary Fenelon	Brent McGregor	Sharon Weston
Julie Geiser	Bill McPherson	Rick Woodyatt
Alison Hallahan	Errol O'Neill	Bill Yarrow

III. STREET ARTS COLLECTIVE MEMBERS [Employees] (1982 - 1994)
(not including those employed on a project basis)

YEAR	COORDINATORS	PERFORMERS	ADMINISTRATION	TRAINEES	TECHNICAL
1982	Pauline Peel (Andrea Lynch)	Steve Capelin (Denis Peel)			
1983	Pauline Peel	Steve Capelin Denis Peel			
1984	Pauline Peel	Steve Capelin Denis Peel Therese Collie	Del McClymont		
1985	Pauline Peel	Steve Capelin Denis Peel Therese Collie	Del McClymont		
1986	Pauline Peel	Steve Capelin Denis Peel Katrina Devery Jane Brown	Del McClymont Mandy Stevens (P/T)	Lachlan McDonald	
1987	Simon McDonald (March - May) Fiona Winning (from August)	Steve Capelin (to June) Denis Peel Katrina Devery Meg Kanowski	Del McClymont (to June) Genevieve Darch (June - December)	Derek Ives John Smout	Noel Ryan
1988	Fiona Winning	Katrina Devery Meg Kanowski Peter Stewart	Del McClymont Di Craig (P/T)	Ann Scanlon Bill McPherson (from May) Peter Barraclough (May - August)	
1989	Fiona Winning (to August) Kara Miller (from August)	Katrina Devery Meg Kanowski Peter Stewart Bill McPherson	Lel Black	Vik Stark (July - December)	
1990	Kara Miller	Peter Stewart Bill McPherson Ainsley Burdell	Pauline Atkinson		Bernie Lewis
1991	Kara Miller (to May) Cynthia Irvine (from May)	Ainsley Burdell Mark Shortis	Pauline Atkinson		Bernie Lewis
1992	Cynthia Irvine	Ainsley Burdell (to October) Mark Shortis (to July)	Pauline Atkinson (to February P/T) Marissa Byram (P/T Feb. to May) Kate Bradford (from June P/T)		
1993	Cynthia Irvine (to March) Loani Prior (February to April) Brent McGregor (from April)		Anna Fairley Panos Couros (from March)		
1994	Brent McGregor		Anna Fairley Panos Couros		

IV. STREET ARTS
GUEST ARTISTS
(1983 — 1994)

Mike Alderdice
Maria Allen
Chris Anderson
Doug Anderson
Richard Andrews
Ellen Appleby
Frankie Armstrong
Jenny Austin
Anthony Babicci
Angela Bailey
Peter Barraclough
Hilary Beaton
John Beck
Nichole Beechy
Jeannie Bell
Louise Bitcon
John Boardman
Anna Bourke
David Bourke
Anita Boyd
June Brown
Cheryl Buchanan
Ainsley Burdell
Ken Bushby
Bradley Byquar
John Campbell
Linda Carroli
Antonella Casella
Lafe Charlton
Rose Claiden
Greg Clarke
Maria Cleary
Nick Collie
Therese Collie
Peter Cossar
Gary Couchy
Di Craig
Pat Cranney
Mark Crocker
Michelle Crocker
Andrea Crouch
Desa Cvetkovic
Tony Darby
Genevieve Darch
Alison Davies
James Davies
Phil Davison
Amanda Daylight
Jenny De Hayr
Katrina Devery
Alison Dittman
Greg Drahm
Sheena Dunn
Paul Dunne
Mark Eades

Chantal Eastwell
Toni Edgar
Kate Eglitis
Maria Elisseos
Elizabeth Elworth
Catherine Fargher
Gavan Fenelon
Danny Fine
Kathryn Fisher
Vanessa Fisher
Elsie Forest
Jo Forsythe
Angelika Fremd
Nick Fury
Paul Gabbert
Marcia Gibbs
Vicki Gordon
David Gorton
Donna Graham
Steve Gration
Neil Greenaway
Joanna Greenwood
Kate Harrison
Sally Hart
Janine Hetherington
Mark Hetherington
Matthew Hill
Noelene Hill
Nick Hughes
Elspeth Hurse
Janelle Hurst
Joe Hurst
Derek Ives
John Jiggins
Hedley Johnson
Anne Jones
Teresa Jordan
Meg Kanowski
Terrie Kavanagh
Suzannah Kinivan
Tony Kishawi
Peter Knapman
Kris Kneen
Kieran Knox
Dushyant Kumar
Torie La Rosa
Robyn Laurie
Damien Ledwich
Douglas Leonard
Bernie Lewis
Rebecca Lister
Michael Long
Tim Low
Andrea Lynch
Steve McCarthy

James McCaughey
Ceri McCoy
Lachlan McDonald
Robyn McDonald
Gary McFeat
Bill McPherson
Raelee Marsden
Peter Marshall
Chris Maver
Matt Mawson
Eliza Mealey
Sean Mee
Sue Monroe
Sarah Moynihan
Colleen Mullin
Lawrie Mullins
Elizabeth Navratil
Art Nicholls
Anthony Noble
Mandy Nolan
Fiona Noone
Lawrence Noone
Julianne O'Brien
Errol O'Neill
Hector Orellana
Leonor Orellana
Nigel Orloff
Kerry O'Rourke
Robert Osmotherly
Phyllis Paterson
Rob Peagram
Andrew Pearson
Maria Philipow
Judy Pippen
Linsey Pollak
Kathryn Porrill
Vic Porrill
Maria Porter
Leah Purcell
Liz Ramsey
Richard Rankine
Andrew Raymond
Ruby Red
Michael Richards
Sue Rider
Phil Robinson
Debra Rodriguez
Alan Rogers
Michael Roper
Bill Rough
Mark Ross
Roger Rosser
Alexandra Ruiz
Carl Rush
Bernadette Ryan

Fiora Sacco
Libby Sara
Ann Scanlan
Matthew Scott
Gary Shambrook
Donna Shepherd
Mark Shortis
Mark Simmonds
George Simpson
Chris Sleight
Lisa Small
Lisa Smith
Nicky Smith
Peter Stewart
Phil Sumner
Shauna Smith
Tunde Solanke
Chris Stannard
Vik Stark
Kaye Stevenson
Peter Stewart
Lisa Jane Stockwell
Gavin Strawhan
Harley Stumm
Vic Szram
Florence Teillet
Marina Thacker
Danny Thompson
Carl Tinambacan
Luzminda
   Tinambacan
Peter Tissot
Nat Trimarchi
Barry Trotter
Helen Wallace
Peggy Wallach
Hugh Watson
Maureen Watson
Roslyn Watson
Trilby Webb
Guy Webster
Peter Weeks
Marguerite
   Wesselinoff
Simba Keefe West
Jacqui Willis
Jessica Wilson
Fiona Winning
Geoff Woollin
Peter Wykes
Hank Wymarra
Peter Young
Anna Zsoldos
Pat Zuber

V. STREET ARTS PROJECTS (1982 — 1994)

YEAR	DATE	PROJECT TITLE	WRITER	COMPOSER	DESCRIPTION
1982	Jul - Oct	Scrubby Creek Clown Troupe	Steve Capelin & Kingston High Students	—	Young People Logan City *Festival '82* Circus & Clowning
	Nov-Dec	*The Big Shot*	Steve Capelin & Sean Mee	—	TIE: Primary Clown Show
1983	March	West End Community Circus Festival	Arts workers & Participants	Denis Peel & Greg Howard	West End Community Musgrave Park Young People Crcus
	Apr-May	*The Big Shot* (Repeat Season)	Steve Capelin & Sean Mee	—	TIE: Primary Clown Show
	April	Inala West Primary School Workshops *Inala Sundae Circus*	—	—	Young People Inala Circus
	May-June	*Inala In Cabaret*	Steve Capelin & Participants	Trilby Webb	Inala Community
	Jun-Jul	Multicultural Fiesta Workshops	—	—	NESB Communities West End Circus
	July	Rockhampton Youth Theatre Workshops	—	—	Young People Regional Queensland Circus
	Jul-Aug	*The Manly Brothers*	Steve Capelin & Denis Peel	—	Touring Company Show Circus & Comedy
	Aug-Sep	*The Big Shot* (Second Repeat Season)	Steve Capelin & Sean Mee	—	TIE: Primary Clown Show
	Sep-Oct	Thrills'n'Spills Circus *At The Beach*	Arts workers & Participants	–	Circus West End *Warana* Festival
	Nov-Dec	Training at Albury-Wodonga with *Nanjing Circus*	—	—	Professional Development Circus
		Miscellaneous Workshops (7)	—	—	—
1984	Feb-Mar	Second West End Community Circus Festival	Arts workers & Participants	Mark Simmonds & Denis Peel	West End Community Musgrave Park Young People Circus
	Mar-Apr	*La Fa La Ful, La Fa Little, La Fa Lot*	Steve Capelin, Denis Peel, Therese Collie & Tony Kishawi	Denis Peel & Mark Simmonds	TIE: Primary Circus & Comedy

YEAR	DATE	PROJECT TITLE	WRITER	COMPOSER	DESCRIPTION
1984 (contd.)	April	Thrills'n'Spills Circus *An Evening At So-So's*	Arts workers & Participants	—	Circus West End
	May-Jun	*Logan City Story*	Pat Cranney & Woodridge and Kingston High Students	Danny Fine & Students	Young People Logan City Community
	Jun-Aug	Inala West Primary School Workshops	—	—	Young People Inala Circus
		Once Upon Inala	Nick Hughes & Participants	Vicki Gordon & Denis Peel	Inala Community
	Aug-Sep	Rockhampton Youth Theatre *Fantastic Flying Fish Family*	—	—	Young People Regional Queensland *Capricana* Festival Circus
	Sep-Oct	Thrills'n'Spills Circus *It's A Mall World*	Arts workers & Participants	—	Circus West End *Warana* Festival
	Oct-Nov	*Artesian Yarns* (Ayr / Home Hill)	Steve Capelin & Participants	Denis Peel	Regional Community Residency
	Dec	*Humpybong Happenings*	Arts workers & Participants	—	Redcliffe Community Young People Circus
1985	Jan	ASEA Conference Workshops	—	—	Teachers
	Mar-May	*Rites, Wrongs and Offbeat Thongs*	Phil Sumner St Thomas More College Students & Cast	Danny Fine	Young People TIE: Secondary
		Gravity Unlimited	Nick Fury & Participants	—	Circus
		Thrills'n'Spills Circus at *La Bamba*	Arts workers & Participants	Peter Stewart	Circus West End
	May-Jun	*Next Stop West End*	Ros Prosser & Participants	Ceri McCoy & Denis Peel	West End Community (inc. NESB Communities & Murri Community)
	Aug-Oct	*Busted Axles* (Townsville, Brisbane)	Cast	—	*Pacific* Festival *Warana* Festival Company Comedy Show
	Dec	*Kockroach Cabaret*	Arts workers & Participants	Libby Sara, Denis Peel & Vonny Clearskye	Inala Community Women
		Comedy Sweatshop	Arts workers & Participants	—	West End Community

YEAR	DATE	PROJECT TITLE	WRITER	COMPOSER	DESCRIPTION
1985 (contd.)		Miscellaneous Workshops	—	—	—
1986	Jan	McGregor Summer School Workshops (Toowoomba)	Arts workers & Participants	—	Young People Regional Queensland Circus
	Mar	*A Few Bobs Short Of A Quid*	Pat Cranney & Cast	Jane Brown	Cabaret West End Company Show
	Apr	Boundary Street Festival	—	—	West End & Murri Communities
	May-Jun	*Sweeping Statements*	Pat Cranney	Jane Brown	Art In Working Life Show (FMWU)
	Jul-Aug	*Rites, Wrongs and Offbeat Thongs* (Tour)	Phil Sumner St Thomas More Students & Cast	Danny Fine	Young People TIE: Secondary
	Aug-Sep	*Crocadillo Circus* (Innisfail)	Arts workers & Participants	—.	Regional Community Young People Circus
		Monsoon Madness (Innisfail)	Steve Capelin & Participants	Jane Brown	Regional Community (incl. Murri & Italian Communities
	Apr-Nov	*Rock'n'Roll Circus*	Participants	Peter Stewart Jane Brown & the band	Circus West End Community
	Oct-Dec	*Postcards*	Steve Capelin & Students	Jane Brown	Young People Rochedale State High School
	Dec	*Xmas at the Bougainville Bob Club* (Panguna)	Meg Kanowski & Cast	Jane Brown & Peter Stewart	Overseas Engagement Company Circus Show
		Miscellaneous Workshops	—	—	—
1987	Jan	McGregor Summer School Workshops 2 (Toowoomba)	Arts workers & Participants	—	Young People Regional Queensland Circus
	Apr-May	*Sparring Partners*	Cast	Jane Brown	Company Show West End
		Comedy Sweatshop 2	Arts workers & Participants	—	West End Community

YEAR	DATE	PROJECT TITLE	WRITER	COMPOSER	DESCRIPTION
1987 (contd.)	Jun-Jul	*Sweeping Statements* (Tour)	Pat Cranney	Jane Brown & Denis Peel	Regional Queensland Art In Working Life Show
	Sep	QPAT D'Arts Workshops	—	—	People With A Disability
	Sep-Oct	Second Boundary Street Festival	—	—	West End Community Murri Community
	Nov-Dec	*Happy Families*	Hugh Watson & Participants	Michael Roper & Participants	Peace Groups West End Community Murri Community
		Miscellaneous Workshops (incl. *The Very Very Hot Choir*)	—	—	West End Community
1988	Jan	McGregor Summer School Workshops 3 (Toowoomba)	Arts workers & Participants	—	Young People Regional Queensland Circus
	Feb-Mar	*High Rent Low Life*	Mandy Nolan & Cast	Peter Stewart	Company Show West End
	Apr-May	Glendon Workshops	Arts workers & Participants	—	Regional Queensland Young People Circus
	Apr	Youth Arts Festival Maroochydore	—	—	Young People Regional Queensland
	May-Jul	*Underwraps: City For Sale*	Kerry O'Rourke & Participants	Peter Stewart, Peter Barraclough & Participants	West End Community Murri Community
	Aug	Clermont Workshops	—	Peter Stewart & Participants	Regional Queensland Young People
		Boggo Road Workshops (Women's Prison)	Arts Workers & Participants	Arts workers & Participants	Prisoners Women
	Oct-Dec	*The Reunion Show*	Gavin Strawhan	Peter Stewart	Art In Working Life Show (TLC)
		Miscellaneous Workshops (incl. *The Very Very Hot Choir*)	—	—	—
1989	Jan	McGregor Summer School 3 (Toowoomba)	Arts workers & Participants		Young People Regional Queensland Circus

YEAR	DATE	PROJECT TITLE	WRITER	COMPOSER	DESCRIPTION
1989 (contd.)	Feb-Mar	*The Reunion Show* (Tour)	Gavin Strawhan	Peter Stewart	Regional Queensland Art In Working Life Show
	Apr-May	*The Ballad of Lois Ryan* (Melbourne Workers Theatre Script)	Andrew Bovell	Irene Vela	Company Show Art In Working Life
	Apr-Jul	*Charged Up*	Hugh Watson & Participants	Peter Stewart & Participants	Young People Logan City Community
	Aug	Workshops with James McCaughey	—	—	Professional Development
	Sep-Oct	Ipswich Workshops	Participants	Carl Rush & Participants	Ipswich Community Young People
	Sep-Dec	*Quick Quick Slow*	Julianne O'Brien	Peter Stewart & Carl Rush	Company Show Ipswich & Brisbane
		Miscellaneous Workshops & Events	—	—	—
1990	Jan	Workshops with Frankie Armstrong	—	—	Professional Development
	Feb-Mar	*Quick Quick Slow* (Tour and Workshops)	Julianne O'Brien & Cast	Peter Stewart & Carl Rush	Regional Queensland Company Show
	Feb-Apr	Boggo Road Workshops (Women's Prison)	Therese Collie & Participants	—	Prisoners Women
	Mar-May	*Trading Hours*	Hilary Beaton	Peter Stewart & Alexandra Ruiz	Art In Working Life Show (PSU, TLC) Women & NESB Workers
	Jun	Workshops with Linsey Pollak	—	Participants	Professional Development
	Jul-Sep	*Raise The Roof*	Hugh Watson & Participants	Peter Stewart & Participants	Young People Logan & Albert Communities incl. Murri Community
	Sep-Nov	*Jalalu Jalu: Land, Law and Lies*	Steve McCarthy, Cheryl Buchanan & Participants	Peter Stewart Chris Anderson & Participants	Murri Community Environment Groups West End Community Prisoners at Borallon Correctional Centre
	Dec	*Out Of The Blue* Creative Development	Therese Collie	—	Brisbane Women's Prison
		Miscellaneous Workshpos	—	—	—

YEAR	DATE	PROJECT TITLE	WRITER	COMPOSER	DESCRIPTION
1991	Feb-Mar	*Out Of The Blue* (Season and Prisons Tour)	Therese Collie	Mark Shortis	Prisoners and their Families Women Murri Community
	Apr-Jun	Duaringa/Woorabinda Residency (Central Queensland)	Maria Porter & Participants	Mark Shortis & Participants	Regional, Rural & Murri Communities
	Jul-Sep	*Cabaret d'Esperanza: Cabaret of Hope*	Therese Collie & Participants	Mark Shortis & Participants	NESB Communities West End Community
	Oct	*Stories from Musgrave Park* Creative Development	Maureen Watson	—	Murri Community West End Community
		Miscellaneous Workshops (incl, *This Is Your Lifer*)	Ainsley Burdell & Participants	Mark Shortis & Participants	Women in Prison
1992	Feb-Mar	Carole Park Festival	Arts workers & Participants	Mark Shortis & Participants	Carole Park Community Young People Circus
	Apr-Jun	*Liveable Streets* Project	Catherine Fargher & Participants	Mark Shortis & Participants	West End & New Farm Communities Town Planners Young Parents
	Aug-Oct	*Thru Murri Eyes* (formerly *Stories from Musgrave Park*) (Season and Tour)	Maureen Watson, Kathryn Fisher & Cast	HedleyJohnson, Gary Couchy & Greg Drahm	Murri Company Show Murri Communities Prisons
		Miscellaneous Workshops (incl. Kabalikat & Prisoners)	Arts workers & Participants	Arts workers & Participants	Filipino Young People Prisoners
1993	[Misc. Dates]	*Cityzen* (based on *Liveable Streets*)	Catherine Fargher & Cast	Mark Shortis	Company Touring Show Young People
	Sep-Oct	Kabalikat Young People's Workshops	—	—	Filipino Young People
	Oct	*GRASP!* Young People's Theatre	Arts workers & Participants	—	Young People
	Nov	*The Catchment Game* Touring Participation Game	—	—	Brisbane River Management Group
		Miscellaneous Workshops, Playreadings & Events	—	—	West End, Dysart Young People Circus
1994	Jan-Mar	*Busted* (Existing Script)	Pat Cranney	—	TIE: Secondary

YEAR	DATE	PROJECT TITLE	WRITER	COMPOSER	DESCRIPTION
1994 (contd.)	Apr-May	*Daily Grind* (Melbourne Workers Theatre Script)	Vicki Reynolds	—	Company Show Art In Working Life Women
	Jun	Carole Park Festival	Arts workers & Participants	Arts workers & Participants	Carole Park Community Young People
	Mar-May Nov-Dec	*Live Art* by *GRASP!* & *GRASP!* Workshops	Peggy Wallach & Participants	Panos Couros & Participants	Young People
	Aug-Sep	*My Identikit* (Four New Works)	Tereza Loizou Peggy Wallach Douglas Leonard Anthony Babicci	—	Company Season
	Sep	Serviceton State School Workshops	—	—	Young People Inala
	Sep-Oct	Deception Bay Community Festival	—	—	Deception Bay Community
	Sep-Dec	Kabalikat Projects: Women's Video & Young People's Magazine	Arts workers & Participants	—	Filipina Women Filipino Young People
		Miscellaneous Workshops & Events	—	—	Ipswich, People with Disabilities, Teachers

BIBLIOGRAPHY

Listed below is a selected list of articles and books which may be of further interest to readers.

Popular Theatre Troupe

Fotheringham, Richard
> The Popular Theatre Troupe, *Social Alternatives*, 1.2 (1978) pp.27-30
> Crook Shop, *Social Alternatives*, 8.3 (1989) pp.11-19.

Hughes, Nick
> *Report on Smaller Scale Theatre Companies in Australia,* (unpublished) Australia Council (CCDU), 1992.

O'Neill, Errol
> Staging a Revolution, *Social Alternatives*, 8.3 (1989) pp.8-9
> The Popular Theatre Troupe: Freedom of Expression and Community Theatre, *Meanjin*, 43.1 (1984) pp.86-95

Street Arts Community Theatre Company

Australia Council: Once Upon Inala, *Caper*, 24, (1985)

Queensland Community Arts Network, *Art Starters*. 1989, pp. 14-19

Queensland Community Theatre Committee, *Fourth National Community Theatre Conference Report*, Brisbane 1987

Stanwell, J. & Jones, A. The Logan City Story, in Fotheringham, R.(ed)(1987) *Community Theatre in Australia*, N.Ryde, NSW. Methuen.

Watt, David and Graham Pitts: Community Theatre as Political Activism: Some Thoughts and Practices in the Australian Context, in Binns,V. (Ed.) *Community and the Arts*, 1991, Leichhardt, NSW. Pluto Press.

General References

AUSTRALIA:

Binns, Vivienne, (Ed.) (1991) *Community and the Arts*, Leichhardt NSW. Pluto Press.

Fitzgerald, C. Afternoon Tea with Mrs I've Always Been Interested In The Arts, *Artwork Magazine*, Issue 9, December 1990.

Fotheringham, Richard (Ed.) (1987) *Community Theatre in Australia*, N.Ryde, NSW. Methuen.

Hawkins, Gay (1991) *From Nimbin to Mardi Gras, Constructing Community Arts*, St. Leonards, NSW. Allan & Unwin.

Horne, Donald (1986) *The Public Culture*, London, Pluto Press.

Mills, D. A Personal Journal, *Artwork Magazine*, Issue 9, December 1990.

INTERNATIONAL:

Boal, A. (1992) *Games for Actors and Non-actors*, London, Routledge.

Coult, T and Kershaw, B. (Eds.) 1983) *Engineers of the Imagination*, London, Methuen.

Friere, P. (1993) *Pedagogy of the Oppressed*, New York, Continuum.

Gooch, S. (1984) *All Together Now; An Alternative View of Theatre and the Community*, London, Methuen.

Itzen, C. (1980) *Stages in the Revolution; Political Theatre in Britain Since 1968*, London, Eyre Methuen.

Kelly, Owen (1984) *Community, Art and the State; Storming the Citadels*, London, Comedia.

Kershaw, B. (1992) *The Politics of Performance*, London, Routledge.

McGrath, John (1981) *A Good Night Out*, London, Methuen.

Morley, D. *et al* (1985) *What a Way to Run a Railroad*, London, Comedia.

CONTRIBUTORS

STEVE CAPELIN was born in Brisbane in 1950, Steve had the rich and at times terrifying experience of a Catholic education. After an Economics degree at the University of Queensland, a stint as a primary school teacher and then as a clown with WEST Community Theatre Company in Melbourne, Steve returned to Brisbane as a founding member of Street Arts Community Theatre Company. An actor, director, writer and organizer with Street Arts from 1982-1987, he then spent a twelve month period fulfilling his paternal responsibilities. Since 1988 he has worked as a freelance artist in schools, on special projects and in institutions. Much of the past five years has been spent teaching in the QUT Academy of the Arts Drama Program.

THERESE COLLIE toured with the Popular Theatre Troupe as an actor before studying for two years at Ecole Jacques Lecoq in Paris. Returning to Brisbane, she joined Street Arts where she began to direct and write. Therese wrote and directed *Long Way Round* for the SBS/Film Australia Drama Series; *Under the Skin* which won the 1994 ATOM Award for best TV series and received a commendation in the 1994 Human Rights Awards. She has directed for the Murray River Performing Group in Albury-Wodonga, Icy Tea and Rock'n'Roll Circus. Her writing credits also include *Murri Time* (with Cathie Craigie) for KITE Theatre and *I Yitha — The She-Goat* for Street Arts. She is currently writing a play entitled *Upsadaisy* which is based on her mother's family history.

PENNY GLASS is a graduate (BA Hons. in French) of the University of New South Wales and the Victorian College of the Arts Drama School. She has worked as a theatre worker, musician and administrator with the Popular Theatre Troupe, Death Defying Theatre, Order By Numbers and Teatro Unidad y Liberacion. She worked as musician and manager of the band "Nancahuazu". During 1990 and 1991 Penny lived in Chile and made contact with many workers in popular theatre with the assistance of an individual Professional Development Grant from the Australia Council. She has a long association with cultural development work in communities of non-English-speaking backgrounds, particularly the Latin American community.

ERROL O'NEILL has been working in theatre as an actor, writer and director since the early seventies. From 1977 to 1982 he worked in all three capacities with the Brisbane-based Popular Theatre Troupe, touring Australia with political satire and theatre of social comment. He wrote five plays for the Troupe. Since then he has written a trilogy of plays dealing with the history of the Queensland Labour movement which have been published by Playlab Press.

PETER STEWART was born in Rockhampton in 1957. After a happy childhood and a tortured adolescence he converted to socialism in 1973, Christianity in 1974 and was a beneficiary of Whitlam's free tertiary education policy in Brisbane. He became a convert to Community arts in 1982, married in 1985 and was a member of Street Arts Community Theatre Collective 1988-90. He describes himself as a pianist, songwriter, composer, teacher, musical director, clerk, writer, dilettante, househusband, actor and graphic designer.

HUGH WATSON was born in America in 1959. He has been a bookseller and a kitchen hand as well as a writer. He has worked for all the companies mentioned in this volume, writing or co-writing eight community and/or political plays. He has also written *"The Valley"*, a main-stage work about homeless youth, welfare workers, and political corruption, set in Fortitude Valley during the Fitzgerald Enquiry. A production of his most recent script *"Cabaret Erratica"* toured to New South Wales and Victoria and appeared at the National Theatre Festival in Canberra in 1994.

DAVID WATT is a Senior Lecturer in the Department of Drama at the University of Newcastle. He has published internationally on political and community theatre and made occasional forays into the field, most recently as co-director with Brent McGregor of *Aftershocks*, a play about the Newcastle earthquake.

GLOSSARY

AC	Australia Council — the Federal Government's Arts funding and advisory body
ATEA	Australian Telecommunications Employees Association
BEMAC	Brisbane Ethnic Music and Arts Centre
CAB	Community Arts Board of the Australia Council
CAG	Children's Activity Group
CART	Citizens Advocating Responsible Transportation
CAST	Cartoon Archetypal Slogan Theatre
CCDB	Community Cultural Development Board of the Australia Council
CCDU	Community Cultural Development Unit of the Australia Council
ESL	English as a Second Language
ETU	Electrical Trades Union
FMWU	Federated Miscellaneous Workers Union
ICT	Icy Tea — Inala Community Theatre
IPCHAC	Incarcerated People's Cultural Heritage Aboriginal Corporation
Murri	Preferred term for people of Aboriginal descent living in southern, central and northern Queensland
NESB	Non English Speaking Background
NIDA	National Institute of Dramatic Art
OBN	Order By Numbers
PAB	Performing Arts Board of the Australia Council
PSU	Public Sector Union
PTT	Popular Theatre Troupe
QCAN	Queensland Community Arts Network
QUT	Queensland University of Technology
QTC	Queensland Theatre Company
SBS	Special Broadcast Service (TV)
SEQEB	South East Queensland Electricity Board
TIE	Theatre-in-Education
TLC	Trades and Labour Council (Qld)
TSI	Torres Strait Islanders
YFS	Youth & Family Services

INDEX

In
CLASSICAL
mood

Solitude

Solitude

*S*olitude can be expressed in many ways: as loneliness, as much-needed peace, or as an opportunity for reflection. This volume of *In Classical Mood* brings together pieces to suit a broad range of solitary moods—from the calm contemplation of Mozart's *Flute and Harp Concerto* and Fauré's lyrical *Élégie*, to the passionate introspection of Rodrigo's famous *Concierto de Aranjuez* and little-known British composer Gerald Finzi's masterful *Clarinet Concerto*. So make the most of your quieter moments and let *Solitude* be your musical companion.

THE LISTENER'S GUIDE — WHAT THE SYMBOLS MEAN

THE COMPOSERS
Their lives... their loves.. their legacies...

THE MUSIC
Explanation... analysis... interpretation...

THE INSPIRATION
How works of genius came to be written

THE BACKGROUND
People, places, and events linked to the music

Contents

JOAQUÍN RODRIGO *b.1901*

Concierto de Aranjuez

SECOND MOVEMENT

This tender, yet passionate, musical evocation portrays the very soul of Spain. It was written while Joaquín Rodrigo was exiled from his homeland because of the Spanish Civil War. As the movement begins, solitary guitar chords support a tender melody played on the cor anglais to conjure up a warm, still, Spanish summer night. Then the temperature begins to rise, culminating in a powerful and passionate solo, before the guitar returns to its original theme—this time with richer orchestration—to bring the movement to a close.

CAREFUL SCORING

Despite the popularity of the classical guitar, there have been very few successful guitar concertos. This is most likely due in part to the careful scoring needed to stop the guitar's delicate, intimate sound from being drowned by the rest of the orchestra. Rodrigo's concerto is a fine example of how this can be achieved in the hands of a sensitive craftsman.

CONSTANT WIFE

Although Rodrigo lost his sight when he was only three years old, his talent and inner strength spurred him on to become the best-known Spanish composer of the late 20th century. In 1928, Rodrigo met a beautiful Turkish pianist, Victoria Kahmi, who had been told by a gypsy that she would marry a famous man whose name began with the letters "Jo." The prophecy came true, and they married in 1933. During their marriage, the couple had worked as a team, with Victoria acting as her husband's assistant—lending him her eyes and hands.

MAGICAL PALACE

Rodrigo and Victoria's courtship was conducted in the area surrounding the palace of Aranjuez *(below)*, located to the south of Madrid and once the summer residence of the 18th-century Bourbon kings of Spain. For Rodrigo, the palace evoked a magical time in Spain's history. He once referred to the period as being "subtly characterized by young

women and bullfighters, and by Spanish-American tunes." In this guitar concerto, Rodrigo pays homage to the age, to the region, and to his bride.

KEY NOTES

The idea of a concerto for the guitar was suggested to Rodrigo by his friend, the guitar virtuoso Regino Sainz de la Maza, who premiered the Concierto in 1940.

3

ERIK SATIE *1866–1925*

Gnossienne No.1

The brooding, mysterious nature of this piano piece suggests an atmosphere of quiet solitude—a peaceful retreat to escape to when the pace of life seems too hectic. The exotic harmonies suggest imaginary faraway lands. The cryptic title of the piece also holds an air of mystery. "Gnossienne" is a word that was actually invented by Satie and no one knows for certain what he intended it to mean.

THE RELUCTANT STUDENT

Erik Satie's music rebelled against the Romantic tradition of the late 19th century, with its emphasis on expressing deep, personal feelings. This may have been a reaction to his childhood experiences: Satie's Scottish mother died when he was six and his father married a Romantic composer and pianist, Eugénie Barnetsche. The young Erik soon developed a strong dislike for his stepmother and became rebellious. Satie's behavior got him into more trouble at the Paris Conservatoire de Musique where he was a student. Although he was clearly gifted, he rarely attended lessons and failed to meet the conservatory's requirements. A piano teacher's scathing report on his work read: "Nothing. Three months to learn a piece. Incapable of sight-reading."

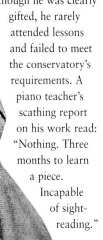

Satie's parents: The respectable Alfred and his first wife.

AN INDIVIDUAL

In later life, Satie's individuality won him the admiration of the group of 20th-century French composers known collectively as "Les Six." From his humble one-room flat in the suburbs of Paris, Satie *(right)* held court over this younger generation of musicians, who were eager to cast off the influence of Richard Wagner and were attracted to Satie's anti-Romanticism. Satie even turned against Impressionism, and especially Debussy. Although the two of them had once been good friends, it is thought that Satie became jealous of Debussy's success. Satie's years of poverty and drinking took their toll and led to his death from liver failure in 1925.

CULT COMPOSER

Satie's inquiring mind and independent nature brought him into contact with circles of people far beyond the mainstream of French society. These included members of the "Rose et Croix" movement, an esoteric order that took its name from the 15th-century mystical writer Christian Rosenkreutz *(right)*. Satie became a dedicated member of the Rosicrucian fraternity, which pursued psychic and spiritual enlightenment, as well as its official composer. The movement spread to America in the 19th century.

RECORD BREAKER

One of Satie's works broke the record for the longest piece of continuous music ever written. *Vexations*, composed in the early 1890s, appears to be a simple piano piece of 180 notes—until one reads Satie's instructions *(below)*, which state that it should be played non-stop 840 times! In 1963, a team of 10 pianists in New York worked in relays to play the extraordinary work in its entirety: It took them 18 hours to complete.

Vexations

ERIK SATIE

NOTE DE L'AUTEUR:
Pour se jouer 840 fois de suite ce motif, il sera bon de se préparer au préalable, et dans le plus grand silence, par des immobilités sérieuses

Très lent

KEY NOTES

Satie's eccentricities extended to the way he actually wrote music. In his 1886 composition Ogives, he first abandoned bar lines. In Gnossiennes, Satie began what was to become a habit of writing bizarre instructions for the pianist, such as "Light as an egg," "With astonishment," "Open your head," and "Work it out for yourself."

WOLFGANG AMADEUS MOZART
1756–1791

Concerto for Flute and Harp in C Major

K299: SECOND MOVEMENT

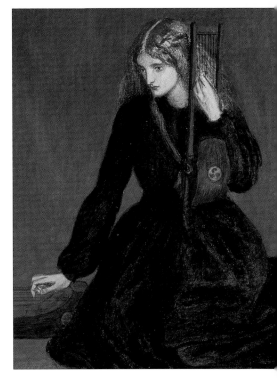

Although Mozart was reluctant to write this concerto, it is among his most popular works. The contrasting textures of the rippling harp and soaring flute in this contemplative piece of music complement each other with an exquisite classical simplicity that marks all of his finest work. However, by the end of the piece, it is the flute's liveliness and purity of tone that the listener fondly remembers.

SMALL REWARD

Mozart wrote this concerto on a visit to Paris in 1778 for the flute-playing Count de Guines and his harpist daughter. Despite the piece's beauty, de Guines only paid him half the agreed fee!

KEY NOTES

Mozart's reluctance to write this piece may have been because he disliked both the flute and the harp— perhaps because in his time, their lack of sophistication offered far less freedom of expression than today.

7

LUDWIG VAN BEETHOVEN
1770–1827

Piano Sonata in F Minor

OPUS 57, "APPASSIONATA": SECOND MOVEMENT

This noble musical contemplation from the *Appassionata* sonata takes the form of a number of variations, of which Beethoven was the acknowledged master. It begins with the solemn theme on which the variations are based. Then come the variations themselves, growing steadily more red-blooded and elaborate before the main theme returns. The last chord leaves an air of questioning and foreboding that indicates Beethoven's state of mind and introduces the next movement.

FATHER AND SON

Beethoven had a difficult childhood with a father who tried to exploit his musical talents. His father, Johann, was a small-time musician and teacher in Bonn who earned little and drank much. Although he was the one who introduced his son to both the piano and the violin, Beethoven senior was harsh in trying to cure young Ludwig's "bad habit" of improvising.

"What is all that silly nonsense you are scraping? Scrape from notes, or your scrapings will be of no use to you," he once screamed at his son *(left)*. But Johann van Beethoven was also extremely proud of his son's obvious talent and would boast prophetically: "My Ludwig! My Ludwig! In time he will be a great man. Those of you who see it come about, remember my words."

NEVER MARRIED

Beethoven's mother died when he was only sixteen, and he felt the loss greatly during the turbulent early years of his life. His mother's death may also help to explain why Beethoven, although frequently in love, never attained the perfect union that he craved. Although his upbringing left him short on social graces, numerous sophisticated women, such as Therese von Brunswick *(above)*, were attracted to his genius. But Beethoven died never having married.

KEY NOTES

Appassionata, *like many of Beethoven's sonatas, was nicknamed by his publisher. The sonata's passion is believed to have been inspired by Josephine Deym, the love of Beethoven's life at the time it was written.*

GERALD FINZI *1901–1956*

Clarinet Concerto in C Minor

OPUS 31: SECOND MOVEMENT

*O*f all the instruments in the orchestra, Gerald Finzi wisely chose the clarinet to evoke feelings of solitude. This sublime concerto by a little-known English composer uses the instrument against a background of strings to define the joyful peacefulness that was part of his rural lifestyle. The music owes much to Finzi's love of the English countryside. For instance, the subdued opening string chords, tinged with melancholy, immediately establish a pastoral theme. Then comes the clarinet, soaring, rising, and dipping before retiring to let the strings stir up a flurry. After the storm becomes calm again, the soloist returns to bring the piece to a touching, reflective close.

COUNTRY MAN

Gerald Finzi *(right)* was born in 1901. Although he enjoyed a comfortable middle-class upbringing in London, his heart remained in the more isolated countryside. He married the artist Joyce Black, and soon after their union they built a house in the English countryside. During his lifetime, Finzi was not prolific, but he composed steadily and built a solid rather than a glittering reputation. In 1951, at the age of fifty, Finzi learned that he had leukemia and only had ten years left. He chose to keep it a secret from all but his family. Tragically, he died only five years later from shingles he had contracted following an exposure to chickenpox.

NEWBURY DAYS

While Finzi often found his desired solitude at his English country home *(below)* near Newbury, he took an interest in the musical community. At the outbreak of World War II in 1939, he founded the Newbury String Players, a mainly amateur ensemble which

went on to gain a national reputation. The Players were set up to encourage gifted young musicians and provide a platform for contemporary composers. After Finzi's death, his son Christopher became the ensemble's conductor and continued his father's legacy. In addition to his devotion to the ensemble, Finzi also pioneered the revival of 18th-century English music and published new editions of Handel's English contemporaries, such as Boyce and Stanley.

LITERARY INFLUENCES

As well as composing, Finzi had a deep interest in literature. His enthusiasm for the work of English author Thomas Hardy *(below)* prompted him to set a number of Hardy's poems to music, and he later repeated the exercise with poets as varied as Wordsworth and Milton. Finzi's choice of English texts was always informed by his literary knowledge, and among his finest settings is a collection entitled *Let Us Garlands Bring* with words by Shakespeare. But although Finzi wrote mainly for choral and solo voice, it is for his fresh, original *Clarinet Concerto* that he is best known.

LET US
GARLANDS BRING

FIVE
SHAKESPEARE SONGS

Set to Music
by

GERALD FINZI

BOOSEY & HAWKES

Thomas Hardy (right), whose poems inspired Finzi.

TRAGIC LOSSES

Finzi's life was filled with tragedy: His father died when he was eight, he later lost three brothers, and he was deeply affected when his music teacher, Ernest Farrar, was killed in World War I. These tragedies made Finzi introspective, which led to his devoted interest in music and literature. His awareness of the transience of human life was clearly reflected in his choice of reading, such as Wordsworth's, "Intimations of Immortality."

In Memoriam
GERALD FINZI
1901-1956

Above: *Finzi died in 1956. He and his wife Joyce are buried together.*

KEY NOTES

Finzi's Clarinet Concerto was an immediate success when it was first performed in Hereford Cathedral in September 1949, at the Three Choirs Festival, with Frederick Thurston as soloist.

ARAM KHACHATURIAN *1903–1978*

Masquerade

NOCTURNE

This haunting and mysterious nocturne begins with a long, beautiful melody on solo violin that hints at the onset of loneliness as darkness falls. Thereafter the violin line grows in richness and refinement, at times tinged with a more exotic coloring. The lower strings provide a warm accompaniment, while a plaintive solo clarinet adds delicate finishing touches to the melody.

THE FULL SUITE

This work dates back to the year 1940 when Khachaturian was invited to write music to accompany the 19th-century play *Masquerade*. He later reworked his incidental music into an orchestral suite with five movements, the other four being *Waltz*, *Mazurka*, *Romance*, and *Galop*.

RUSSIAN ROMANTIC

The play *Masquerade (right)*, for which Khachaturian composed his *Nocturne*, was written by the Russian poet Mikhail Lermontov. Born in 1814 into an aristocratic family of Scottish descent, whose name was originally Learmont, Mikhail was destined to became a major force in 19th-century Russian literature. As a student, his revolutionary ideas offended his professors. After being forced to leave the university, he joined the Life Guards where he began

Masquerade, a light satire about the lower-middle classes. When the Russian poet Alexander Pushkin was killed in a duel, Lermontov achieved overnight fame with a poem in which he accused the Tsar and the Russian nobility of hounding Pushkin. And his desire for an end to the feudal system in Russia was so well expressed in his poem "Borodino"—a Russian first in that the hero was a common man—that it inspired novelist Leo Tolstoy's epic *War and Peace*. Lermontov's life echoed that of Pushkin in many ways. Both went into exile and, like Pushkin, Lermontov died young, killed in a duel that was fought over a woman.

Mikhail Lermontov (left) *made a lasting contribution to Russian literature in spite of his tragically short life.*

SOVIET QUARTET

With Prokofiev, Shostakovich, and Kabalevsky, Khachaturian was one of the four composers who dominated Russian music after the Bolshevik revolution of 1917. It was not until the 1930s that they began to make their mark as composers—and there was a price to pay: Their output was strictly monitored by the state, and they were restricted to producing accessible, patriotic works that reflected Soviet culture in a positive light. In 1948, Stalin's Zhdanov Decree condemned all four men for their so-called "modernity." But after Stalin's death, in 1953, Khachaturian took the lead in pleading for greater artistic freedom, which resulted with more relaxed rules.

The Soviet "Big Four": Prokofiev, Shostakovich, Khachaturian, and Kabalevsky.

TRAGIC NATION

Khachaturian was Armenian by birth. During a brief period in the 1st century B.C., Armenia was a great nation, stretching from the Mediterranean to the Caucasia, and in 300 A.D., it was the first country to adopt Christianity. For the next 1,600 years it was Armenia's destiny to be conquered by its neighbors, and in 1915, while fighting for freedom from the Ottoman Empire, nearly 1.75 million Armenians were either killed *(above)* or deported. The following year Armenia was occupied by Russia. The nation finally achieved its independence in 1991.

KEY NOTES

Khachaturian had at least five Top 20 hits in the West since 1948, including the lively Sabre Dance from his ballet Gayaneh.

15

GABRIEL FAURÉ *1845–1924*

Élégie

OPUS 24

This unmistakably personal and melancholy *Élégie* is an expression of Fauré's emotional state during a time he was suffering from severe bouts of depression. Yet as the cello sings its noble lament over supportive piano chords, there is an underlying tone that speaks of renewed determination and strength of spirit. Later, the main theme is contrasted with another theme, which is equally mournful in character but not wholly dejected. Then the stately first theme returns in quiet contemplation. As in his later and more famous *Requiem*, Fauré never abandons the elegance and restraint that were to become his hallmarks.

PART-TIME COMPOSER

As a boy in southwest France, Fauré spent many hours playing the harmonium, a small portable reed organ, in a local chapel. Later he recalled that it was an elderly blind woman, who often listened to him, who first spotted his talent and pointed it out to his father. The boy was sent to a music school, École Niedermeyer, in Paris, where the composer Saint-Saëns introduced him to the works of Schumann, Liszt, Wagner, and other contemporary composers. Fauré's youthful efforts at composing clearly showed his musical promise, but he was unable to earn a living from writing music alone. Instead, he supported himself as an organist and a music teacher. In fact, almost all his works were composed during the brief periods of time that he could snatch away from his "day job."

Left: *Fauré caricatured as a "musical scientist."*

FAMILY AFFAIRS

In 1883, at the age of thirty-eight, Fauré *(above, right)* married Marie Fremiet, the daughter of a sculptor. They had two sons, Emmanuel *(above, left)* and Philippe *(above, center)*. Despite Marie's difficult and withdrawn nature—and her husband's roving eye that led him into more than one affair—she and her husband had a close relationship.

KEY NOTES

Fauré's Élégie, which he wrote in 1880, was originally for cello and piano. But sixteen years later the composer made another equally successful arrangement of it for cello and full orchestra.

17

ANTONIO VIVALDI
1678–1741

Concerto for Recorder and Orchestra

SECOND MOVEMENT

Like many woodwinds, the recorder has the ability to paint a peaceful musical picture as it does so elegantly in this concerto. In Vivaldi's time the recorder was a popular solo instrument and many of the composer's five hundred or so concertos were written for it. This graceful piece played in C major is also an example of the *ritornello* form, where the music returns to its starting point and repeats with subtle changes. The graver pulse of the music is held mainly by the organ and bass.

REDISCOVERING VIVALDI

Within decades of his death, Vivaldi's music fell into obscurity. It remained largely unknown until the 20th century, when renewed interest in J.S. Bach led music scholars back to Vivaldi. In 1926, Alberto Gentili, an expert on Vivaldi, discovered fourteen volumes of unpublished music in a monastery in Borgo San Martino, northern Italy. The volumes had been given to the monastery by the family of Conte Giacomo Durazzo, a contemporary of Vivaldi who acquired them after the composer's death. Further study led Gentili to believe that the volumes were only half of Vivaldi's personal collection, and the hunt began for the rest. Gentili eventually traced them through the Marchese Giuseppe Maria Durazzo, who had inherited the Vivaldi family library. In 1930, the entire collection was brought to the Biblioteca Nazionale in Turin.

Above: *The Istituto Salesiano S. Carlo in Italy, where the manuscripts were found.*

THE LITTLE FLUTE

The solo recorder heard in this concerto is a *sopranino* recorder *(left)*. One of the smallest and highest-pitched members of the recorder family, it was used regularly in orchestras until about 1725. Its clear tone enabled it to ride comfortably above even quite large ensembles. The recorder family consists of the sopranino, descant, treble, tenor, bass, and great bass recorders.

KEY NOTES

King Henry VIII of England was an accomplished recorder player. At one time he possessed no fewer than seventy-six recorders and seventy-eight flutes.

FRANCIS POULENC *1899–1963*

Sonata for Oboe and Piano

SECOND MOVEMENT

few instruments of the orchestra speak so profoundly of solitude as the oboe. Its sound can evoke a still landscape with particular poignancy. Yet in the whimsical hands of Poulenc, the instrument's familiar mournful tones take on an altogether fresher and more sprightly character. Four high, piercing notes on the oboe open the movement, after which a blend of melodic textures and seamless piano chords sets the prevailing mood. Later, the piano takes the lead, while the oboe protests and cajoles. There is a brief moment of silence, then the pattern is repeated. Calm is eventually restored as the oboe returns with the original melody, reminding the listener of the music's essentially reflective quality.

BEHIND THE SMILES

Poulenc *(above)* enjoyed an advantage over many composers in that his father owned a large pharmaceutical company and he never had to worry about money. This gave him the freedom to follow his own distinct style of composing without having to conform to traditional forms and styles in order to make a living. Poulenc revealed his irreverent side from the start, with his first published work, *Rapsodie nègre*, dedicated to the eccentric composer Erik Satie. And although Poulenc reveled in his playful image as the rascal of French music, the underlying melancholy of much of his works hints at the rather solitary and serious man behind the humorous façade.

ACT OF FAITH

Poulenc restored his Roman Catholic faith in his mid thirties. In 1936, prompted by the death of a close friend in a car accident, he visited the shrine of Notre Dame de Rocamadour *(below)* in southwest France. Poulenc was deeply moved by the experience, and from then on began composing music to sacred settings. The first such work was *Litanies à la vierge noire* ("Litanies to the Black Madonna"), written a week after his visit to the shrine. Ironically, the lighthearted Poulenc went on to become one of France's most noted composers of religious music.

A MUSICAL PARTNERSHIP

 Francis Poulenc wrote many songs in the course of his long career. A major influence in his life and on his musical works was his longtime friend Pierre Bernac *(right)*, the celebrated French baritone. From 1935 onward, Poulenc and Bernac formed a strong working partnership. For many years they gave recitals both in France and abroad, with the composer accompanying the singer on the piano. They also made a large number of gramophone records together. Bernac is generally regarded as the finest interpreter of Poulenc's songs, or *mélodies,* as he called them.

LAST DAYS

 During the postwar years of the 1940s and 1950s, Poulenc divided his time between touring with Bernac and composing in Paris and relaxing at his large country house in Touraine in western France. He continued to work up to his death with the *Sonata for Oboe and Piano,* completed in 1962, in memory of the Russian composer Prokofiev, being his last work. The piece has come to be regarded as one of the finest of its kind by a 20th-century composer, proving that Poulenc's powers remained strong to the end.

Above: *Poulenc's final resting place in Paris.*

KEY NOTES

The year 1963 was a sad one for the world of music and the arts: It not only marked the death of Poulenc himself, but also that of his frequent collaborator, playwright Jean Cocteau. The composer Paul Hindemith and the renowned Hungarian-born conductor Fritz Reiner also died in the same year.

MAURICE RAVEL *1875–1937*

Piano Concerto in G Major

SECOND MOVEMENT

*F*eelings of solitude abound in this magical movement, which opens to the gentle, measured strains of the piano. A flute joins in, soaring high above the orchestra, followed by an oboe, and there is deep passion in the often changing phrases. Ravel's piece continues on with curious note sequences on the keyboard weaving their way through the constantly discordant orchestral passages, creating an exotic tapestry of sound. As the movement rolls on effortlessly to a close, a beautiful harmony emerges. This is some of the most original and inventive music ever written.

SINGLE-HANDED SUCCESS

While he was writing this concerto, in 1930, Ravel simultaneously worked on a commission from the pianist Paul Wittgenstein that was for a concerto for the left hand only. Wittgenstein lost an arm in World War I.

KEY NOTES

The two piano concertos came at the end of Ravel's composing career, and the effort of writing them both at once took its toll. He declared: "It nearly killed me!"

GREGORIAN MONKS

Gregorian Chant: Tenebrae factae sunt

Gregorian chants, a type of music that has been connected with the Roman Catholic Church since early Christian times, have the ability to paint a musical picture of solitude. The sparse and regimented nature of the chant, which is generally sung by a monastic choir with little or no accompaniment, is intended to foster a mood of reverence and deep contemplation. The music is stripped bare of frivolity, encouraging the listener to look inward. Yet in spite of this chant's somber overtones, *Tenebrae factae sunt* remains uplifting and instills a sense of hope.

ALONE ON THE CROSS

Tenebrae factae sunt ("And then there was darkness") refers to Christ's crucifixion when darkness descended at midday. After three dark hours, Jesus exclaimed "My God, my God, why have you forsaken me?" as his last words.

CHANTS OF THE WORLD

Chanting is common to many religions throughout the world. It was adopted in ancient times as a means of reciting sacred texts with respect, without veering into the more sensuous realms of secular music. In some of the more orthodox branches of the Jewish and Muslim faiths, for example, it is considered highly blasphemous to recite the holy scriptures in anything other than chant form. The sacred book of Islam, the Koran, is written in verse form and lends itself well to daily chanting in the mosque. The same is true of Judaism, in which the psalms of the Bible are easily transcribed into flowing chants. In the Far East, monks in Buddhist monasteries have been chanting since the 3rd century B.C. Buddhist monks chant as a form of meditation and spend much of their day intoning sacred verses, some of which the Buddha (563–483 B.C.) is said to have written himself.

JEWISH LEGACY

The Gregorian chant is thought to have evolved from ancient Jewish traditions of prayer that were carried over into the early Christian church. As Christianity spread, different musical traditions became associated with the chant. But in the 6th century, the Vatican, fearing that lack of uniformity might breed dissent, codified the various forms and called the results Gregorian chants after Pope Gregory the Great (540–604).

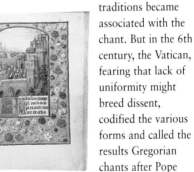

Above: *A 16th-century illustration of Pope Gregory on his way to Rome.*

KEY NOTES

The term "Gregorian chant" first appeared in writing in a letter from Pope Leo IV (847–855) to a certain Abbot Honoratus, threatening that failure to use the official Roman chant would result in excommunication (exclusion from the protection of the Church).

Credits & Acknowledgments

PICTURE CREDITS

Cover /Title and Contents Pages/ IBC:

Getty Images AKG London: (Carl Spitzweg: Self Portrait in the Garden): 4; (Hans Thoma: Blick ins Tal): 8, 9(r); (P.A. Fedotow: The Young Widow): 13, 15(tr); Bridgeman Art Library, London/Index/Museo Sorolla, Madrid (Joaquin y Bastida Sorolla: The Gardens of the Sorolla Family): 2; The Maas Gallery, London (D.G. Rossetti: The Harp Player): 7; (Marie Spartali Stillman: Girl With Peacock Feathers): 18; Boosey & Hawkes: 12(tl); Britstock-IFA/Bernd Ducke: 3(bl);

Corbis/Bettmann/UPI: 21(tl); Reproduced bypermission of Editions Max Eschig, Paris/United Music Publishers Ltd.: 6(b); E.T. Archive: 23, 24, 25; Mary Evans Picture Library: 9(l), 12(b), 17(bl); Graham Flack: 19(bl); Robert Harding Picture Library/Nigel Francis: 16; Images Colour Library: 10, 21(br); Peter Kent: 11(bl), 12(r); Lebrecht Collection: 5(r, bl & cl), 11(tr), 14(tr), 15(bl), 17(tr), 11(t); Joanne Harris: 22(t); MC Picture Library: 3(tr); Novosti (London): 14(bl), 15(bl); Rosicrucian Order/AMORC: 6(tr); The Stock Market: 20.

All illustrations and symbols: John See